ADOBE® PHOTOSHOP® 7.0
DESIGN PROFESSIONAL

By Elizabeth Eisner Reding

Adobe® Photoshop® 7.0—Design Professional

by Elizabeth Eisner Reding

Managing Editor:
Nicole Jones Pinard

Senior Product Manager:
Rebecca Berardy

Contributing Author:
Michael Reding

Associate Product Manager:
Christina Kling Garrett

Editorial Assistant:
Elizabeth Harris

Production Editor:
Melissa Panagos

Development Editor:
Holly Lancaster

Composition House:
GEX Publishing Services

QA Manuscript Reviewers:
Jeffrey Schwartz, Ashlee Welz

Text Designer:
Ann Small

Illustrator:
Philip Brooker

Cover Design:
Philip Brooker

Credits

Some of the images used in this book are royalty-free and the property of Getty Images, Inc. The Getty images include artwork from the following royalty-free CD-ROM collections: Education Elements, Just Flowers, Portraits of Diversity, Sports and Recreation, Texture and Light, Tools of the Trade, Travel Souvenirs, Travel & Vacation Icons, and Working Bodies.

Disclaimer

Course Technology reserves the right to revise this publication and make changes from time to time in its content without notice.

ISBN 0-619-11017-1

BRIEF CONTENTS

iv

UNIT C   MAKING SELECTIONS

CONTENTS

UNIT D   INCORPORATING COLOR TECHNIQUES

UNIT E   PLACING TYPE IN AN IMAGE

UNIT F   USING PAINTING TOOLS

UNIT G   WORKING WITH SPECIAL LAYER FUNCTIONS

UNIT J   ADJUSTING COLORS

UNIT M — LIQUIFYING AN IMAGE

UNIT N — PERFORMING DOCUMENT SURGERY

Design Professional Series Vision

The Design Professional Series is your guide to today's hottest multimedia applications. These comprehensive books teach the skills behind the application, showing you how to apply smart design principles to multimedia products, such as dynamic graphics, animation, Web sites, and video.

A team of design professionals including multimedia instructors, students, authors, and editors worked together to create this series. We recognized the unique learning environment of the digital media or multimedia classroom and have created a series that:

- Gives you comprehensive step-by-step instructions
- Offers in-depth explanation of the "why" behind a skill
- Includes creative projects for additional practice
- Explains concepts clearly using full-color visuals

It was our goal to create a book that speaks directly to the multimedia and design community—one of the most rapidly growing computer fields today.

This series was designed to appeal to the creative spirit. We would like to thank Philip Brooker for developing the inspirational artwork found on each unit opener and book cover. We would also like to give special thanks to Ann Small of A Small Design Studio for developing a sophisticated and instructive book design.
—The Design Professional Series

Author's Vision

Each book represents a collaborative effort and this particular project is no exception. This is the first revision of a Design Professional book. This book was the first in the Design Professional series, and because Photoshop is so much fun to use, the revision was also quite enjoyable.

What is different about this particular revision is that it marks the first time I worked directly with my husband, Michael. It was fun—and stressful—to work on such a tight schedule. My sincere thanks go to him for taking on such a difficult project and making it so successful.

Others involved with this revision are:

- Rebecca Berardy, Senior Product Manager. Rebecca and I have worked together often. Each new project we undertake together becomes that much easier because we have become such a great team.
- Nicole Pinard, Managing Editor. Let's face it, without support from the top, a project doesn't get off the ground. Nicole has been very supportive in making this book a success.
- Holly Lancaster, Development Editor. Holly was instrumental in making the words of two authors blend into a single voice. The pace was ridiculous; the outcome is great.
- Ashlee Welz and Jeff Schwartz, QA Manuscript Reviewers. If it weren't for Ashlee and Jeff, well, I just don't know how this book would have turned out. QA is the quality control that catches all sorts of nasty errors and inconsistencies.
- Melissa Panagos, Production Editor. Melissa made it possible for a series of manuscripts and graphics files to become a book. I don't know how she does it, but without her, the final book would never exist.
- Christina Garrett, Associate Product Manager. Christina created a fun atmosphere in which the instructor's resources could be created. She was somehow able to inspire me to write these extra materials.

So you can see that it takes many people to create a book. All of them are important to the process. And also, I would like to thank my mother, Mary Eisner, for all her support and enthusiasm while this project went from beginning to end.
—Elizabeth Eisner Reding

Introduction to Adobe Photoshop 7.0

Welcome to *Adobe® Photoshop® 7.0—Design Professional*. This book offers creative projects, concise instructions, and complete coverage of basic to advanced Photoshop skills, helping you to create dynamic Photoshop art! Use this book both in the classroom and as your own reference guide.

This text is organized into 16 units. In these units, you will learn many skills including how to work with layers, make selections, adjust color techniques, use paint tools, work with filters, transform type, liquify an image, annotate and automate a Photoshop document, and create Photoshop images for the Web!

LESSON 1

WORK WITH COLOR TO TRANSFORM A DOCUMENT

What You'll Do

In this lesson, you'll use the Color palette, the Paint Bucket Tool, and the Eyedropper Tool to add a new color to the background.

Learning About Color Models

Photoshop reproduces colors using models of color modes. The range of displayed colors, or **gamut**, for each model, is shown in Figure D-1. The shape of each color gamut indicates the range of colors it can display. If a color is out of gamut, it is beyond the color space that your monitor can display or that your printer can print. You select the color mode from the Mode command on the Image menu.

QUICK TIP

A color mode is used to determine which color model will be used to display and print an image.

Understanding the psychology of color

Have you ever wondered why some colors make you react a certain way? You might have noticed that some colors affect you differently than others. Color is such an important part of our lives, and in Photoshop, it's key. Specific colors are used in print and Web pages to evoke the following responses:
- Blue tends to instill a feeling of safety and stability and is commonly used by financial services.
- Certain shades of green can generate a soft, calming feeling, while others suggest youthfulness and growth.
- Red commands attention and can be used as a call to action; it can also distract a reader's attention from other content.
- White evokes the feeling of purity and innocence, looks cool and fresh, and is often used to suggest luxury.
- Black conveys feelings of power and strength, but can suggest darkness and negativity.

ADOBE PHOTOSHOP D-4

Incorporating Color Techniques

What You'll Do

A What You'll Do figure begins every lesson. This figure gives you an at-a-glance look at the skills covered in the unit and shows you the completed project file of the lesson. Before you start the lesson, you will know—both on a technical and artistic level—what you will be creating.

Comprehensive Conceptual Lessons

Before jumping into instructions, in-depth conceptual information tells you "why" skills are applied. This book provides the "how" and "why" through the use of professional examples. Also included in the text are helpful tips and sidebars to help you work more efficiently and creatively.

Step-by-Step Instructions

This book combines in-depth conceptual information with concise steps to help you learn Photoshop. Each set of steps guides you through a lesson where you will apply Photoshop tasks to a dynamic and professional project file. Step references to large colorful images and quick step summaries round out the lessons.

At the back of Unit O, you will find a Steps Summary. The Steps Summary is a listing by Unit of all the tasks performed in the lessons.

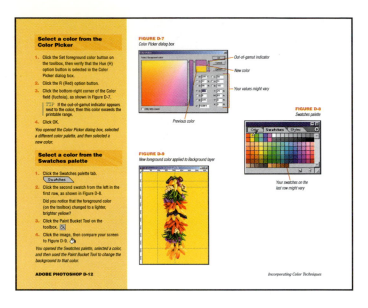

Projects

This book contains a variety of end-of-unit material for additional practice and reinforcement. The Skills Reference is a table of keyboard shortcut keys and quick references, showing you the most efficient way to complete a task. The Skills Review contains hands-on practice exercises that mirror the progressive nature of the lesson material. The unit concludes with four projects: two Project Builders, one Design Project, and one Group Project. The Project Builder cases require you to apply the skills you've learned in the unit to create one document. Design Projects examine design principles and send students to the Web to research desktop publishing issues. Group Projects encourage group activity as students use the resources of a team to create a project.

What Instructor Resources are Available with this Book?

The Instructor's Resource CD-ROM is Course Technology's way of putting the resources and information needed to teach and learn effectively into your hands. All the resources are available for both Macintosh and Windows operating systems, and many of the resources can be downloaded from *www.course.com*.

Instructor's Manual

Available as an electronic file, the Instructor's Manual is quality-assurance tested and includes unit overviews and detailed lecture topics for each unit with teaching tips. The Instructor's Manual is available on the Instructor's Resource CD-ROM, or you can download it from *www.course.com*.

Syllabus

Prepare and customize your course easily using this sample course outline (available on the Instructor's Resource CD-ROM).

PowerPoint Presentations

Each unit has a corresponding PowerPoint presentation that you can use in lecture, distribute to your students, or customize to suit your course.

Figure Files

Figure Files contain all the figures from the book in bitmap format. Use the figure files to create transparency masters or in a PowerPoint presentation.

Solutions to Exercises

Solution Files are Data Files completed with comprehensive sample answers. Use these files to evaluate your students' work. Or, distribute them electronically or in hard copy so students can verify their work. Sample solutions to all lessons and end-of-unit material are also provided.

ExamView Test Bank and Test Engine

ExamView is a powerful testing software package that allows instructors to create and administer printed, computer (LAN-based), and Internet exams. ExamView includes hundreds of questions that correspond to the topics covered in this text, enabling students to generate detailed study guides that include page references for further review. The computer-based and Internet testing components allow students to take exams at their computers, and also save the instructor time by grading each exam automatically.

Data Files for Students

To complete most of the units in this book, your students will need Data Files. Put them on a file server for students to copy. The Data Files are available on the Instructor's Resource CD-ROM, the Review Pack, and can also be downloaded from *www.course.com*. Instruct students to use the Data Files List at the end of this book. This list gives instructions on copying and organizing files.

Additional Activities for Students

The Instructor's Manual includes two additional projects for each unit, giving the instructor even more content for additional exercises.

Intended Audience

This text is designed for the beginner or intermediate student who wants to learn how to use Adobe Photoshop 7.0. The book is designed to provide basic and in-depth material that not only educates, but encourages the student to explore the nuances of this exciting program.

File Identification

Instead of printing a file, the owner of a Photoshop document can be identified by reading the File Info dialog box. Use the following instructions to add your name to a document.

1. Click File on the menu bar, then click File Info.
2. Click the Section list arrow, then click General, if necessary.
3. Click the Caption text box.
4. Type your name, course number, or other identifying information.
5. Click OK.

There are no instructions with this text to use the File Info feature other than when it is introduced in Unit A. It is up to each user to use this feature so that their work can be identified.

Measurements

When measurements are shown, needed, or discussed, they are given in pixels. Use the following instructions to change the units of measurement to pixels.

1. Click Edit on the menu bar, point to Preferences, then click Units & Rulers.
2. Click the Rulers list arrow, then click pixels.
3. Click OK.

You can display rulers by clicking View on the menu bar, then clicking Rulers, or by pressing [Ctrl][R] (Win) or [command][R] (Mac). A check mark to the right of the Rulers command indicates that the Rulers are displayed. You can hide visible rulers by clicking View on the menu bar, then clicking Rulers, or by pressing [Ctrl][R] (Win) or [command][R] (Mac).

Icons, Buttons, and Pointers

Symbols for icons, buttons, and pointers are shown each time they are used.

Fonts

Data and solution files contain a variety of fonts, and there is no guarantee that all of these fonts will be available on your computer. (Nearly all computers have the Arial and Times New Roman fonts, but if these were the only fonts used, it would make for a boring, ugly book.) The fonts are identified in cases where less common fonts are used in the files. Every effort has been made to use commonly available fonts in the lessons. If any of the fonts in use are not available on your computer, please make a substitution.

Menu Commands in Tables

In tables, menu commands are abbreviated using the following format: Edit ➤ Preferences ➤ Units & Rulers. This command translates as follows: Click Edit on the menu bar, point to Preferences, then click Units & Rulers.

Skills Reference

As a bonus, a Power User Shortcuts table is included at the end of every Photoshop unit. This table contains the quickest method of completing tasks covered in the unit. It is meant for the more experienced user, or for the user who wants to become more experienced. Tools are shown, not named.

Grading Tips

Many students have Web-ready accounts where they can post their completed assignments. The instructor can access the student accounts using a browser and view the images online. Using this method, it is not necessary for the student to include his/her name on a type layer, because all of their assignments are in an individual password-protected account.

Creating a Portfolio

One method for students to submit and keep a copy of all of their work is to create a portfolio of their projects that is linked to a simple Web page that can be saved on a CD-ROM. If it is necessary for students to print completed projects, work can be printed and mounted at a local copy shop; a student's name can be printed on the back of the image.

UNIT A

GETTING STARTED WITH ADOBE PHOTOSHOP 7.0

1. Start Adobe Photoshop 7.0.

2. Learn how to open and save a document.

3. Examine the Photoshop window.

4. Use the Layers and History palettes.

5. Learn about Photoshop by using Help.

6. View and print a document.

7. Close a document and exit Photoshop.

UNIT A
GETTING STARTED WITH
ADOBE PHOTOSHOP 7.0

Using PhotoShop

Adobe Photoshop is an image-editing program that lets you create and modify digital images. A **digital image** is a picture in electronic form. Using Photoshop, you can create original artwork, manipulate color images, and retouch photographs. In addition to being a robust application popular with graphics professionals, it is practical for anyone who wants to enhance existing artwork or create new masterpieces. For example, you can repair and restore damaged areas within an image, combine images, and create graphics and special effects for the Web.

Understanding Platform Interfaces

Photoshop is available in both Windows and Macintosh platforms. Regardless of which type of computer you use, the features and commands are very similar. Some of the Windows and Macintosh keyboard commands differ in name, but they have equivalent functions. For example, the [Ctrl] and [Alt] keys are used in Windows, and the [command] and [option] keys are used on Macintosh computers. There is a dramatic visual difference between the two platforms from the moment the program is started. These differences are due to the user-interface found in each type of computer.

Understanding Sources

Photoshop allows you to work with images from a variety of sources. You can create your own original artwork in Photoshop, use images downloaded from the Web, or use images that have been scanned or created using a digital camera. Whether you create Photoshop images to print in high resolution or optimize them for multimedia presentations, Web-based functions, or animation projects, Photoshop is a powerful tool for communicating your ideas visually.

Tools You'll Use

File

New...	Ctrl+N
Open...	Ctrl+O
Browse...	Shft+Ctrl+O
Open As...	Alt+Ctrl+O
Open Recent	▶
Close	Ctrl+W
Save	Ctrl+S
Save As...	Shft+Ctrl+S
Save for Web...	Alt+Shft+Ctrl+S
Revert	
Place...	
Import	▶
Export	▶
Workgroup	▶
Automate	▶
File Info...	
Page Setup...	Shft+Ctrl+P
Print with Preview...	Ctrl+P
Print...	Alt+Ctrl+P
Print One Copy	Alt+Shft+Ctrl+P
Jump To	▶
Exit	Ctrl+Q

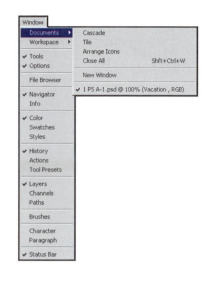

Window

Documents	▶
Workspace	▶
✔ Tools	
✔ Options	
File Browser	
✔ Navigator	
Info	
✔ Color	
Swatches	
Styles	
✔ History	
Actions	
Tool Presets	
✔ Layers	
Channels	
Paths	
Brushes	
Character	
Paragraph	
✔ Status Bar	

Documents submenu:
Cascade	
Tile	
Arrange Icons	
Close All	Shft+Ctrl+W
New Window	
✔ 1 PS A-1.psd @ 100% (Vacation , RGB)	

Toolbox

Lasso tools
- Lasso Tool — L
- Polygonal Lasso Tool — L
- Magnetic Lasso Tool — L

Zoom Tool

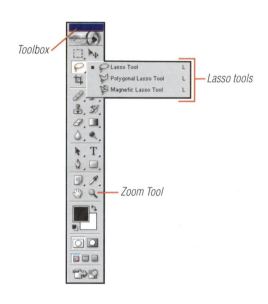

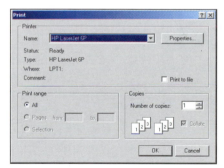

Tool options bar

Palette well

START ADOBE PHOTOSHOP 7.0

What You'll Do

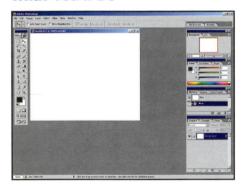

In this lesson, you'll start Photoshop for Windows or Macintosh (depending on the platform you are using), then create a file.

Defining Image-Editing Software

Photoshop is an image-editing program. An **image-editing** program allows you to manipulate graphic images so that they can be reproduced by professional printers using full-color processes. Using a toolbar, windows, various tools, menus, and a variety of techniques, you can modify a Photoshop image by rotating it, resizing it, changing its colors, or adding text to it. You can also use Photoshop to create and open different kinds of file formats, which enables you to create your own images, import them from a digital camera or scanner, or use files (in other formats) purchased from outside sources. Table A-1 lists the file formats that Photoshop can open and create.

Understanding Images

Every image is made up of dots, which are called **pixels**, and each pixel represents a color or shade. Pixels within an image can be added, deleted, or modified.

QUICKTIP

Photoshop files can become quite large. After a file is complete, it can be **flattened**, an irreversible process that combines all layers and reduces the file size.

Using Photoshop Features

Photoshop includes many tools that you can use to manipulate images and text. Within an image, you can add new items and modify existing elements, change colors, and draw shapes. For example, using the Lasso Tool, you can outline a section of an image and drag the section onto another area of the image. You can also isolate a foreground or background image. You can extract all or part of a complex image from nearly any background and use it elsewhere.

QUICKTIP

You can create a logo in Photoshop. A **logo** is a distinctive image that you can create by combining symbols, shapes, colors, and text. Logos give graphic identity to organizations, such as corporations, universities, and retail stores.

You can also create and format text, called **type**, in Photoshop. You can apply a variety of special effects to type; for example, you can change the appearance of text and the distance between characters. You can also edit type after it has been created and formatted.

Adobe ImageReady 7.0, a Web production software program included with Photoshop, allows you to optimize, preview, and animate images. Because ImageReady is fully integrated with Photoshop, you can jump seamlessly between the two programs.

You can also quickly turn any graphics image into a GIF animation. Photoshop and ImageReady let you compress file size (while optimizing image quality) to ensure that your files download quickly from a Web page. Using optimization features, you can view multiple versions of an image and select the one that best suits your needs.

Starting Photoshop and Creating a File

The way that you start Photoshop depends on the computer platform you are using. However, when you start Photoshop in either platform, the computer displays a **splash screen**, a window that displays information about the software, and then the Photoshop window opens.

After you start Photoshop, you can create a file from scratch. You use the New dialog box to create a file. You can also use the New dialog box to set the size of the image you're about to create by typing dimensions in the Width and Height text boxes.

TABLE A-1: Graphic File Formats Supported in Photoshop

file format	filename extension	file format	filename extension
Photoshop	.PSD	Filmstrip	.VLM
Bitmap	.BMP	Kodak PhotoCD	.PCD
PC Paintbrush	.PCX	Pixar	.PXR
Graphics Interchange Format	.GIF	Scitex CT	.SCT
Photoshop PostScript	.EPS	Photoshop PDF	.PDF
Tagged Image Format	.TIF or .TIFF	Targa	.TGA or .VDA
JPEG Picture Format	.JPG, .JPE, or .JPEG	PICT file	.PCT, .PIC, or .PICT
CorelDraw	.CDR	Raw	.RAW

Start Photoshop (Windows)

1. Click the Start button on the taskbar.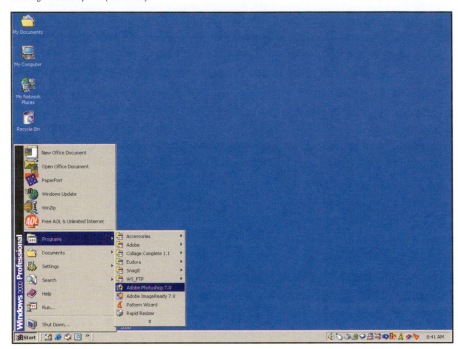

2. Point to Programs, then click Adobe Photoshop 7.0, as shown in Figure A-1.

   > **TIP** The Adobe Photoshop 7.0 program might be found in the Adobe folder, which is in the Program Files folder on the hard drive.

3. Click File on the menu bar, then click New.

4. Double-click the number in the Width text box, type **500**, click the Width list arrow, then click pixels, if necessary.

5. Double-click the number in the Height text box, type **400**, click the Height list arrow, then click pixels, if necessary.

6. Click OK.

You started Photoshop for Windows, then created a file with custom dimensions.

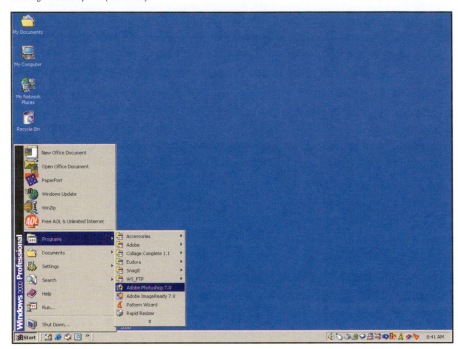

Understanding hardware requirements (Windows)

Adobe Photoshop 7.0 has the following minimum system requirements:
- Processor: Intel Pentium class III or 4
- Operating System: Microsoft® Windows® 98, Windows 98 Second Edition, Windows Millennium Edition, Windows NT with Service Pack 6a, Windows 2000 with Service Pack 2, or Windows XP
- Memory: 128 MB of RAM (192 MB recommended)
- Storage space: 280 MB of available hard-disk space
- Monitor: 800x600 color monitor with 16-bit color or greater video card

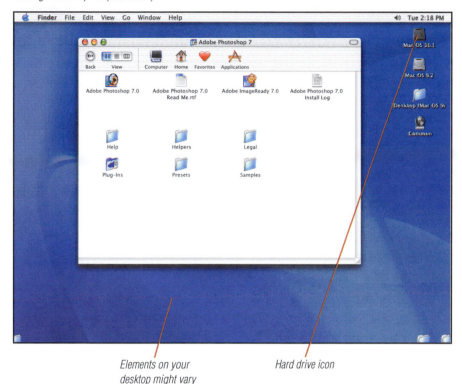

*Elements on your
desktop might vary*

Hard drive icon

Start Photoshop (Macintosh)

1. Double-click the hard drive icon, then double-click the Adobe Photoshop 7.0 folder.

2. Double-click the Adobe Photoshop 7.0 program icon. Compare your screen to Figure A-2.

3. Click File on the menu bar, then click New.

4. Double-click the number in the Width text box, type **500**, click the Width list arrow, then click pixels, if necessary.

5. Double-click the number in the Height text box, type **400**, click the Height list arrow, then click pixels, if necessary.

6. Click OK.

You started Photoshop for the Macintosh, then created a file with custom dimensions.

Understanding hardware requirements (Macintosh)

Adobe Photoshop 7.0 has the following minimum system requirements:

- Processor: PowerPC® processor (G3, G4, or G4 dual)
- Operating System: Mac OS software version 9.1, 9.2, or Mac OS X version 10.1.3
- Memory: 128 MB of RAM (192 MB recommended)
- Storage space: 320 MB of available hard-disk space
- Monitor: 800x600 color monitor with 16-bit color or greater video card

LEARN HOW TO OPEN AND SAVE A DOCUMENT

What You'll Do

In this lesson, you'll locate and open files using the File menu and the File Browser, then save a file with a new name.

Opening and Saving Files

Photoshop provides several options for opening and saving a file. Often, the project you're working on determines the techniques you use for opening and saving files. For example, you might want to preserve the original version of a file while you modify a copy. You can open a file, then immediately save it with a different filename, as well as open and save files in many different file formats. For example, you can open a Photoshop file that has been saved as a bitmap (.bmp) file, then save it as a JPEG (.jpg) file to use on a Web page.

Customizing How You Open Files

You can customize how you open your files by setting preferences. **Preferences** are options you can set that are based on your

Using the File Info dialog box

You can use the File Info dialog box to identify a file, add a caption or other text, or add a copyright notice. The Caption section allows you to enter printable text, as shown in Figure A-4. For example, to add your name to a document, click File on the menu bar, click File Info, then click in the Caption text box. (You can move from field to field by pressing [Tab] or by clicking in individual text boxes.) Type your name, course number, or other identifying information in the Caption text box. You can enter additional information in the other text boxes, then save all the File Info data as a separate file that has an .XMP extension. To select the caption for printing, click File on the menu bar, click Print with Preview. Verify that the Show More Options check box is selected, then select the Caption check box. To print the filename, select the Labels check box. You can also print crop marks and registration marks. If you choose, you can even add a background color or border to your image. After you select the items you want to print, click Print.

work habits. For example, you can use the Open Recent command on the File menu to instantly locate and open the files that you recently worked on, or you can allow others to preview your files as thumbnails. Figure A-3 shows the Preferences dialog box options for handling your files.

Browsing Through Files

You can easily find the file you're looking for by using the File Browser feature. You can open the File Browser by clicking the File Browser tab in the **palette** well (which is an area that is located near the top-right corner of the screen where you can assemble windows used to modify documents). You can also open the File Browser from the File

menu. When you open the File Browser, a hierarchical tree for your computer's hard drive is displayed. You can use this tree to find the file you are searching for. When you locate a file, you can click its thumbnail to see information about its size, format, and creation and modification dates. You can open a file using the File Browser by double-clicking its thumbnail. If the File Browser is docked in the palette well, you can close it by pressing [Esc].

Using Save As Versus Save

Sometimes it's more efficient to create a new image by modifying an existing one, especially if it contains elements and special effects that you want to use again. The

Save As command on the File menu creates a copy of the file, prompts you to give the duplicate file a new name, and then displays the new filename in the document's title bar. You use the Save As command to name an unnamed document or to save an existing document with a new name. For example, throughout this book, you will be instructed to open your project files and use the Save As command. Saving your project files with new names keeps them intact in case you have to start the lesson over again or you want to repeat an exercise. When you use the Save command, you save the changes you made to the open document.

FIGURE A-3
Preferences dialog box

FIGURE A-4
File Info dialog box

Select option for thumbnail preview

Enter number of files to appear in Open Recent list

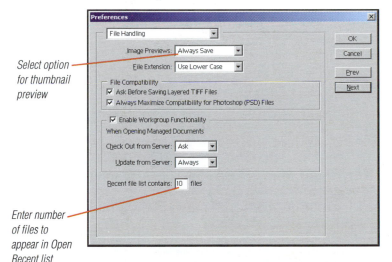

Type information that you want to be printed

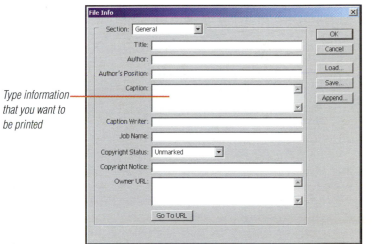

Open a file using the File menu

1. Click File on the menu bar, then click Open.

2. Click the Look in list arrow (Win) or the From list arrow (Mac), as shown in Figure A-5, navigate to the location where your Unit A project files are stored, then click Open.

3. Click PS A-1.psd, then click Open.

   TIP If you receive a message stating that some text layers need to be updated before they can be used for vector-based output, click Update (Mac).

You used the Open command on the File menu to locate and open a file.

Open a file using the File Browser

1. Click the File Browser tab in the palette well. `File Browser`

   TIP If the File Browser is not visible in the palette well, set your monitor resolution to greater than 800 × 600 pixels and click File on the menu bar, then click Browse. You can add the File Browser to the palette well by clicking the list arrow in the upper-right corner, then by clicking Dock to Palette Well.

2. Navigate through the hierarchical tree to the location where your Unit A project files are stored. Compare your File Browser palette to Figure A-6.

   (continued)

FIGURE A-5
Open dialog box for Windows and Macintosh

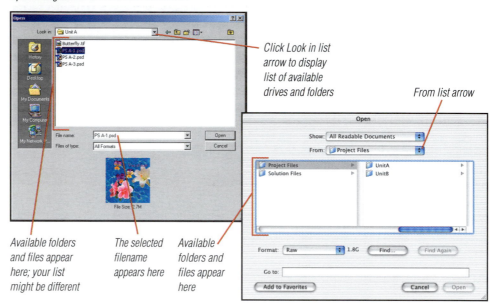

Click Look in list arrow to display list of available drives and folders

From list arrow

Available folders and files appear here; your list might be different

The selected filename appears here

Available folders and files appear here

FIGURE A-6
Docked File Browser palette

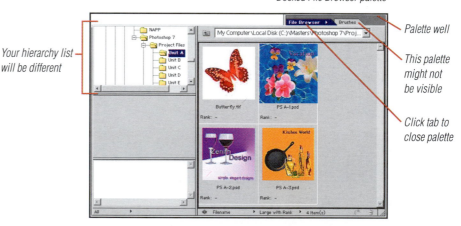

Your hierarchy list will be different

Palette well

This palette might not be visible

Click tab to close palette

FIGURE A-7

Save As dialog box

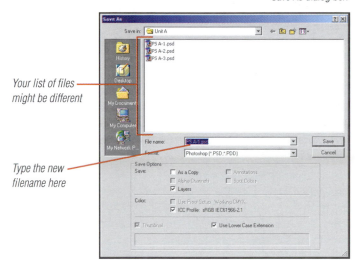

Your list of files might be different

Type the new filename here

FIGURE A-8

Vacation document

Duplicate file with new name

Lesson 2   Learn How to Open and Save a Document

3. Double-click Butterfly.tif.

> TIP   If you receive a message stating that some text layers need to be updated before they can be used for vector-based output, click Update (Mac).

The File Browser palette automatically closed when the Butterfly file opened.

You used the File Browser to locate and open a file.

Use the Save As command

1. Click the PS A-1.psd window to activate it.

2. Click File on the menu bar, click Save As, then compare your Save As dialog box to Figure A-7.

3. If the drive containing your project files is not displayed, click the Save in list arrow (Win) or the Where list arrow (Mac), then navigate to the location where your Unit A data files are stored.

4. Select the current filename in the File name text box, if necessary; type **Vacation**, then click Save. Compare your image to Figure A-8.

You used the Save As command on the File menu to save the file with a new name.

EXAMINE THE PHOTOSHOP WINDOW

What You'll Do

 In this lesson, you'll select a tool on the toolbox, use a shortcut key to cycle through the hidden tools, select and add a tool to the Tool Preset picker, use the Window menu to show and hide palettes in the workspace, and then create a customized workspace.

Learning About the Workspace

The **workspace** is the area within the program window that includes the entire window, from the command menus at the top of your screen to the status bar (Win) at the bottom. Desktop items are visible in this area (Mac). The workspace is shown in Figure A-9.

The **title bar** displays the program name (Adobe Photoshop) and the filename of the open document (for a new document, **Untitled-1**, because the file has not been named). The title bar also contains a Close button, and Minimize, Maximize, and Restore buttons (Win).

The **menu bar** contains menus from which you can choose Photoshop commands. You can choose a menu command by clicking it or by pressing [Alt] plus the underlined letter in the menu name (Win). Some commands display shortcut keys on the right side of the menu. Shortcut keys provide an alternative way to activate menu commands. Some commands might appear dimmed, which means they are not currently available. An ellipsis after a command indicates additional choices.

Finding Tools Everywhere

The **toolbox** contains tools associated with frequently used Photoshop commands.

Overcoming information overload

One of the most common experiences shared by first-time Photoshop users is information overload. There are just too many places and things to look at! When you feel your brain overheating, take a moment and step back. Remind yourself that the document window is the central area where you can see a composite of your work. All the tools and palettes are there to help you, not to add to the confusion.

The face of a tool contains a graphical representation of its function; for example, the Zoom Tool shows a magnifying glass. You can place the pointer over each tool to display a ScreenTip, which tells you the name or function of that tool. Some tools have additional hidden tools, indicated by a small black triangle in the lower-right corner of the tool.

The **tool options bar**, located directly under the menu bar, displays the current settings for each tool. For example, when you click

the Type Tool, the default font and font size appear on the tool options bar, which can be changed if desired. You can move the tool options bar anywhere in the workspace for easier access. The tool options bar also contains the Tool Preset picker. This is the left-most tool on the tool options bar and displays the active tool. You can click the list arrow on this tool to select another tool without having to use the toolbox. The tool options bar also contains the palette well, an area where you can assemble palettes for quick access.

QUICKTIP
The palette well is only available when your monitor resolution is greater than 800 pixels × 600 pixels.

Palettes are small windows used to verify settings and modify documents. By default, palettes appear in stacked groups at the right side of the window. You can display a palette by simply clicking the palette's name tab, which makes it the active palette. Palettes can be separated and moved

FIGURE A-9
Workspace

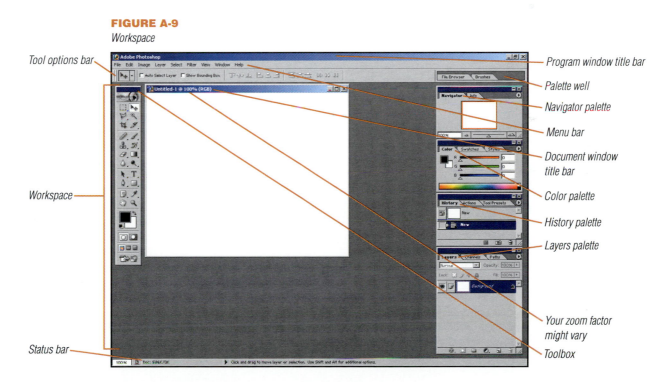

Tool options bar

Workspace

Status bar

Program window title bar

Palette well

Navigator palette

Menu bar

Document window title bar

Color palette

History palette

Layers palette

Your zoom factor might vary

Toolbox

anywhere in the workspace by dragging their name tabs to new locations. Each palette contains a menu that you can view by clicking the list arrow in its upper-right corner.

The **status bar** is located at the bottom of the program window (Win) or the document window (Mac). It displays information, such as the file size of the active window and a description of the active tool. You can display other information on the status bar, such as the current tool, by clicking the black triangle to view a pull-down menu with more options.

Rulers can help you precisely measure and position an object in the workspace. The rulers do not appear the first time you use Photoshop, but you can display them by clicking Rulers on the View menu.

Using Tool Shortcut Keys

Each tool has a corresponding shortcut key. For example, the shortcut key for the Type Tool is T. After you know a tool's shortcut key, you can select the tool on the toolbox by pressing its shortcut key. To select and cycle through a tool's hidden tools, you press and hold [Shift] then press the tool's shortcut key until the desired tool appears. See the Power User Shortcuts table at the end of each unit for a description of tool shortcut keys.

Customizing Your Environment

Photoshop makes it easy for you to position elements you work with just where you want them. If you move elements around to make your environment more convenient, you can always return your workspace to its original appearance by resetting the default palette locations. You can create a customized workspace by clicking Window on the menu bar, pointing to Workspace, then clicking Save Workspace. A named workspace appears in the Window menu under Workspace. So, if you want to open a named workspace, click Window on the menu bar, point to Workspace, then click the workspace you want to use.

Select a tool

1. Click the Lasso Tool on the toolbox, then press and hold the mouse button until a list of hidden tools appears, as shown in Figure A-10.

2. Click the Polygonal Lasso Tool, then note the shortcut key, L, next to the tool name.

3. Press and hold [Shift], press [L] three times to cycle through the list of tools, then release [Shift].

   TIP You can return the tools to their default setting by clicking the Click to open the Tool Preset picker list arrow on the tool options bar, clicking the list arrow, then clicking Reset All Tools.

You selected the Lasso Tool on the toolbox and used its shortcut key to cycle through the Lasso tools.

FIGURE A-10
Hidden tools

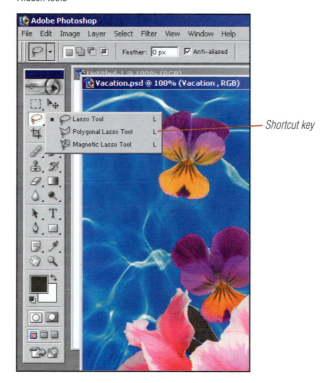

Shortcut key

Select a tool from the Tool Preset picker

1. Click the Click to open the Tool Preset picker list arrow on the tool options bar. See Figure A-11. ▽ ▪

   A button gets its name from its ScreenTip (descriptive text that appears when you place the pointer over the button).

2. Deselect the Current Tool Only check box, if necessary.

3. Double-click the Magnetic Lasso 24 pixels tool.

You selected the Magnetic Lasso Tool using the Tool Preset picker.

FIGURE A-11

Using the Tool Preset picker

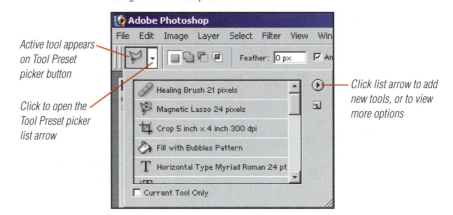

Active tool appears on Tool Preset picker button

Click to open the Tool Preset picker list arrow

Click list arrow to add new tools, or to view more options

1. Click the Move Tool on the toolbox.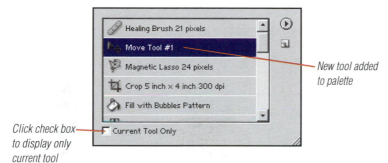
2. Click the Click to open the Tool Preset picker list arrow on the tool options bar.
3. Click the list arrow on the Tool Preset picker.
4. Click New Tool Preset, then click OK to accept the default name (Move Tool #1). Compare your list to Figure A-12.

   TIP You can display the currently selected tool alone by selecting the Current Tool Only check box.

You added the Move Tool to the Tool Preset picker.

FIGURE A-12
Move Tool added to Tool Preset picker

New tool added to palette

Click check box to display only current tool

Show and hide palettes

1. Click Window on the menu bar, then verify that Color has a check mark next to it.

2. Click the Swatches tab next to the Color tab to make the Swatches palette active, as shown in Figure A-13.

3. Click Window on the menu bar, then click Swatches to deselect it.

   TIP You can hide all open palettes by pressing [Shift], then [Tab], then show them by pressing [Shift], then [Tab] again. To hide all open palettes, the tool options bar, and the toolbox, press [Tab], then show them by pressing [Tab] again.

4. Click Window on the menu bar, then click Swatches to redisplay the Swatches palette.

You used the Window menu to show and hide the Swatches palette.

FIGURE A-13
Active Swatches palette

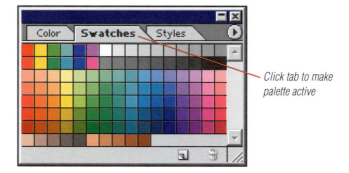

Click tab to make palette active

FIGURE A-14

Save Workspace dialog box

1. Click and drag the toolbox title bar so it appears to the right of the document.

2. Click Window on the menu bar, point to Workspace, then click Save Workspace.

3. Type **Sample Workspace** in the Name text box, as shown in Figure A-14.

4. Click Save.

5. Click Window on the menu bar, then point to Workspace.

   The name of the new workspace appears on the Window menu.

6. Click Reset Palette Locations.

You created a customized workspace, then reset the palette locations.

USE THE LAYERS AND HISTORY PALETTES

What You'll Do

 In this lesson, you'll hide and display a layer, move a layer on the Layers palette, and then undo the move by deleting the Layer Order state on the History palette.

Learning About Layers

A **layer** is a section within an image that can be manipulated independently. Layers allow you to control individual elements within a document and create great dramatic effects and variations of the same document. Each Photoshop document can consist of one layer, many individual layers, or groups of layers.

You can think of layers in a Photoshop image as individual sheets of clear plastic that are in a stack. It's possible for your document to quickly accumulate dozens of layers. Layers enable you to easily manipulate individual characteristics within an image. The **Layers palette** displays all the layers in an open document. You can use the Layers palette to create, copy, delete, display, hide, merge, lock, or reposition layers.

QUICKTIP

In Photoshop, using and understanding layers is the key to success.

Setting preferences

The Preferences dialog box contains several topics, each with its own settings: General, File Handling, Display and Cursors, Transparency and Gamut, Units and Rulers, Guides, Grids and Slices, Plug-ins and Scratch Disks, and Memory and Image Cache. To open the Preferences dialog box, click Edit on the menu bar, point to Preferences, then click a topic that represents the settings you want to change. If you move palettes around the workspace, or make other changes to them, you can choose to retain those changes the next time you start the program. To always start a new session with default palettes, click General on the Preferences menu, deselect the Save Palette Locations check box, then click OK. Each time you start Photoshop, the palettes will be reset to their default locations and values.

Understanding the Layers Palette

The order in which the layers appear in the Layers palette matches the order in which they appear in the document; the topmost layer in the Layers palette is the topmost layer in the image. You can make a layer active by clicking its name in the Layers palette. When a layer is active, it is highlighted in the Layers palette, a paintbrush icon appears next to the thumbnail, indicating that you can edit the layer, and the name of the layer appears in parentheses in the document title bar. Only one layer can be active at a time. Figure A-15 shows a document with its Layers palette. Did you notice that this image contains 5 layers? Each layer can be moved or modified individually within the palette to give a different effect to the overall document. If you look at the Layers palette, you'll see that the Finger Painting layer is dark, indicating that it is currently active.

QUICKTIP

Get in the habit of shifting your eye from the document to the Layers palette. Knowing which layer is active will save you time and help you troubleshoot an image.

Displaying and Hiding Layers

You can use the Layers palette to control which layers are visible in a document. You can show or hide a layer by clicking the Indicates layer visibility button next to the layer thumbnail. When a layer is hidden, you are not able to merge it with another, select it, or print it. Hiding some layers can make it easier to focus on particular areas of an image.

Using the History Palette

Photoshop records each task you complete in a document in the **History palette**. This record of events, called states, makes it easy to see what changes occurred and the tools or commands that you used to make the modifications. The History palette, also shown in Figure A-15, displays up to 20 states and automatically updates the list to display the most recently performed tasks. The list contains the name of the tool or command used to change the image. You can delete a state in the History palette by selecting it and dragging it to the Delete current state button. Deleting a state is equivalent to using the Undo command. You can also use the History palette to create a new document from any state.

QUICKTIP

When you delete a History state, you undo all the events that occurred after that state.

FIGURE A-15
Layers and History palettes

History states

Click a layer name to make the layer active

Hide and display a layer

1. Click the Azaleas layer on the Layers palette. 🖑

   TIP Depending on the size of the window, you might only be able to see the initial characters of the layer name.

2. Click the Indicates layer visibility button on the Azaleas layer to hide the image, as shown in Figure A-16. 👁

   TIP By default, transparent areas of an image have a checkerboard display on the Layers palette.

3. Click the Indicates layer visibility button on the Azaleas layer to reveal the image. ☐

You made the Azaleas layer active on the Layers palette, then clicked the Indicates layer visibility button to hide and display a layer.

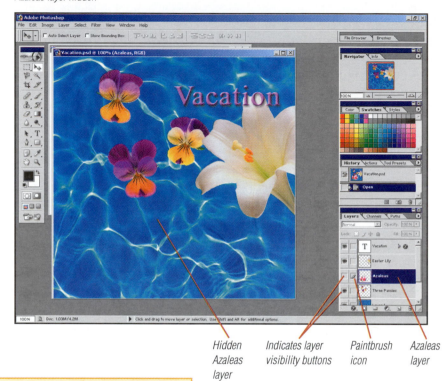

FIGURE A-16
Azaleas layer hidden

Hidden Azaleas layer

Indicates layer visibility buttons

Paintbrush icon

Azaleas layer

Considering ethical implications

Because Photoshop enables you to make so many incredible changes to images, you should consider the ethical ramifications and implications of altering images. Is it proper or appropriate to alter an image just because you have the technical expertise to do so? Are there any legal responsibilities or liabilities involved in making these alterations? Because the topic of **intellectual property** (an image or idea that is owned and retained by legal control) has become more pronounced with the increased availability of information and content, you should make sure you have the legal right to alter an image, especially if you plan on displaying or distributing the image to others. Know who retains the rights to an image, and if necessary, make sure you have written permission for its use, alteration, and/or distribution. Not taking these precautions could be costly.

FIGURE A-17

Layer moved in Layers palette

Pointer's appearance when dragging layer

Layer being moved

FIGURE A-18

Result of moved layer

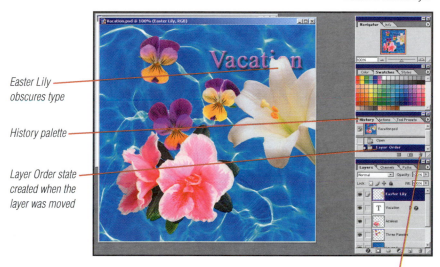

Easter Lily obscures type

History palette

Layer Order state created when the layer was moved

Delete current state button

FIGURE A-19

Deleting a History state

Selected state

Pointer when dragging a state to the Delete current state button

Move a layer on the Layers palette and delete a state on the History palette

1. Click the Easter Lily layer on the Layers palette, then drag it to the top position in the palette, as shown in Figure A-17.

   The object in the Easter Lily layer obscures part of the type. See Figure A-18.

2. Click Layer Order on the History palette, then drag it to the Delete current state button on the History palette, as shown in Figure A-19.

   TIP Each time you close and reopen a document, the History palette is cleared.

   The text is no longer obscured.

3. Click File on the menu bar, then click Save.

You moved the Easter Lily layer to the top of the Layers palette, then returned it to its original position by dragging the Layer Order state to the Delete current state button on the History palette.

LEARN ABOUT PHOTOSHOP
BY USING HELP

What You'll Do

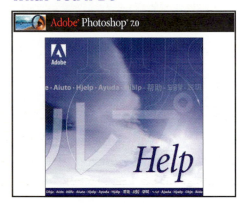

 In this lesson, you'll open Help, then view and find information from the following Help links: Contents, Index, Site Map, and Search.

Understanding the Power of Help

Photoshop features an extensive Help system that you can use to access definitions, explanations, and useful tips. Help information is displayed in a browser window, so you must have Web browser software installed on your computer to view the information; however, you do not need an Internet connection to use Photoshop Help.

Using Help Topics

The Help window has five links that you can use to retrieve information about Photoshop commands and features: Using Help, Contents, Index, Site Map, and Search, as shown in Figure A-20. The Using Help link displays information about the Help system. The Contents link allows you to browse topics by category; the Index link provides the letters of the alphabet, which you can click to view keywords and topics alphabetically. Each entry in the Index section is followed by a number, which represents the number of articles about the particular subject. The Site Map link displays a variety of links that take you directly to specific topics. The Search link allows you to enter keywords as your search criteria. When you choose a topic using any of the five methods, information about that topic appears in the right pane of the browser window.

Links in the Help window

Click a link for the
method you want to use

Using Help link

FIGURE A-21

Contents section of the Help window

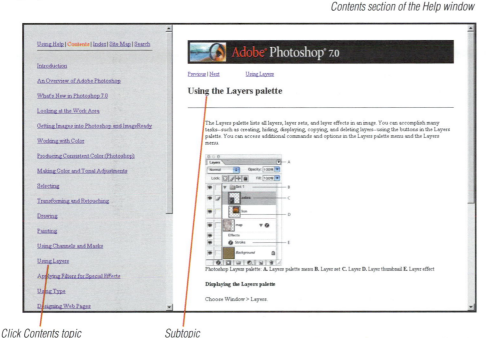

Click Contents topic   Subtopic

Find information in Contents

1. Click Help on the menu bar, then click Photoshop Help.

> **TIP** You can also open the Help window by pressing [F1] (Win) or [command] [?] (Mac).

2. If it's not already selected, click the Contents link, scroll down the left pane, then click the Using Layers link.

3. Click the Using the Layers palette link in the right pane. See Figure A-21.

You used the Photoshop Help command on the Help menu to open the Help window and viewed a topic in Contents.

Understanding the Help links

Many Help topics contain links at the bottom of the right pane that indicate the hierarchy of the current entry in Help and link to related topics. If you want to see a list of related topics, click the link to go up a level. Browsing the hierarchy of Help topics can help you understand Photoshop functionality. To ensure that the Help window is displayed properly, use Netscape 4.75 and later or Internet Explorer 5.0 and later, or contact your instructor or systems administrator for assistance.

Find information in the Index

1. Open Help, if necessary, then click the Index link in the Help window.

2. Click the L link, scroll down the left pane to layers, then click the 1 link next to about. Compare your Help window to Figure A-22.

You clicked an alphabetical listing and viewed an entry in the Index.

Find information in the Site Map

1. Open Help, if necessary, then click the Site Map link in the Help window.

2. Scroll down the left pane, then click the If you are new to Photoshop link. Compare your Help window to Figure A-23.

You clicked a link in the site map to find information on Photoshop.

FIGURE A-22
Topics in the Index window

Click number to
open topic

FIGURE A-23
Topics in the Site Map window

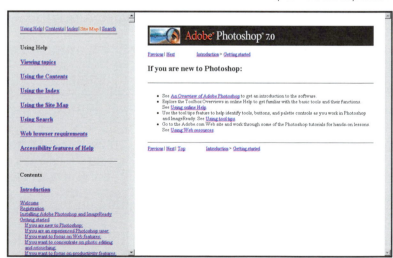

Getting Started with Adobe Photoshop 7.0

FIGURE A-24
Search topic in Help

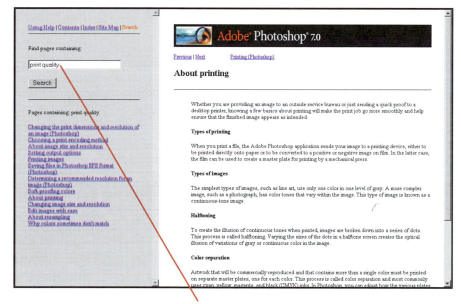

*Type search
term here*

1. Open Help, if necessary, then click the Search link in the Help window.

2. Type **print quality**, then click Search.

> TIP   You can search for multiple words by inserting a space; do not use punctuation in the text box.

3. Scroll down the left pane, if necessary, click the About printing link, then compare your Help screen to Figure A-24.

4. Click File on the menu bar, then click Close (Win) or Quit (Mac) when you are finished reading the topic.

You entered a search term, viewed search results, and exited the Help window.

VIEW AND PRINT A DOCUMENT

What You'll Do

 In this lesson, you'll use the Zoom Tool on the toolbox to increase and decrease your views of the image. You'll also change the page orientation settings in the Page Setup dialog box, and print the document.

Getting a Closer Look

When you edit an image in Photoshop, it is important that you have a good view of the area that you are focusing on. Photoshop has a variety of methods that allow you to enlarge or reduce your current view. You can use the Zoom Tool by clicking the image to zoom in on (magnify the view) or zoom out of (reduce the view) areas of your document. Zooming in or out enlarges or reduces your *view*, not the actual image. The maximum zoom factor is 1600%. The current zoom percentage appears in the document's title bar, in the Navigator palette, and on the status bar. When the Zoom Tool is selected, the tool options bar provides additional choices for changing your view as shown in Figure A-25. For example, the Resize Windows To Fit check box automatically resizes the window whenever you magnify or reduce the view. You can also change the zoom percentage using the Navigator palette and the status bar by typing a new value in the zoom text box.

Printing Your Document

In many cases, a professional print shop might be the best option for printing a Photoshop document to get the highest quality. You can, however, print a Photoshop document using a standard black-and-white or color printer. Regardless of the number of layers in an image, your printed image will be a composite of all visible layers. Of course, the quality of your printer and paper will affect the appearance of your output. The Page Setup dialog box displays options for printing, such as paper orientation. **Orientation** is the direction in which an image appears on the page. In **portrait orientation**, a document is printed with the short edges of the paper at the top and bottom. In **landscape orientation**, a document is printed with the long edges of the paper at the top and bottom.

Viewing a Document in Multiple Views

You can use the New Window command on the Window ➤ Documents menu to open multiple views of the same document. You can change the zoom percentage in each view so you can spotlight the areas you want to modify, and then modify the specific area of the image in each view. Because you are working on the same document in multiple views, not in multiple versions, Photoshop automatically applies the changes you make in one view to all views. Although you can close the views you no longer need at any time, Photoshop will not save any changes until you save the document.

FIGURE A-25
Zoom Tool choices on the tool options bar

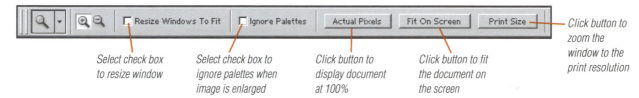

Select check box to resize window

Select check box to ignore palettes when image is enlarged

Click button to display document at 100%

Click button to fit the document on the screen

Click button to zoom the window to the print resolution

Using a scanner and a digital camera

If you have a scanner, you can use print images, such as those taken from photographs, magazines, or line drawings, in Photoshop. Make sure you remember that images taken from magazines are owned by others, and that you need permission to distribute them. Scanners are relatively inexpensive and easy to use. They come in many types, including flatbed or single-sheet feed. After you scan an image and save it as an electronic file, you can open and use it in Photoshop. See your instructor to learn how to use the scanner in your facility. You can also use a digital camera to create your own images. Although it operates much like a film camera, a digital camera captures images on some form of electronic medium, such as a floppy disk or SmartMedia card. After you upload the images from your camera to your computer, you can use the images in Photoshop.

So how can you use that scanned image or digital picture in Photoshop? Well, you can open the image (which usually has a .JPG extension or another file format) by clicking File on the menu bar, then by clicking Open. (Since All Formats is the default file type, you should be able to see all available image files.) After the Open dialog box opens, locate the folder containing your scanned or digital images, click the file you want to open, then click Open. A scanned or digital image will contain all its imagery in a single layer. You can add layers to the image, but you can only save these new layers if you save the image as a Photoshop document (with the extension .PSD).

Use the Zoom Tool

1. Click the Zoom Tool on the toolbox. 🔍

2. Select the Resize Windows To Fit check box on the tool options bar. ☐ Resize Windows To Fit

3. Position the pointer over the center of the image, then click the image. 🔍

   TIP Position the pointer over the part of the image you want to keep in view.

4. Press [Alt] (Win) or [option] (Mac), then click the center of the image twice. 🔍

5. Release [Alt] (Win) or [option] (Mac), then compare your image to Figure A-26.

   The zoom factor for the document is 66.7%.

You selected the Zoom Tool on the toolbox and used it to zoom in to and out of the image.

Zoom Tool options

Zoom Tool

Zoom percentage changed

Using the Navigator palette

You can change the magnification factor of an image using the Navigator palette or the Zoom Tool on the toolbox. By double-clicking the Zoom box on the Navigator palette, you can enter a new magnification factor, then press [Enter] (Win) or [return] (Mac). The magnification factor—shown as a percentage—is displayed in the lower-left corner of the Navigator palette. The red border in the palette, called the Proxy Preview Area, defines the area of the image that is magnified. You can drag the Proxy Preview Area inside the Navigator palette to view other areas of the image at the current magnification factor.

Page Setup dialog box

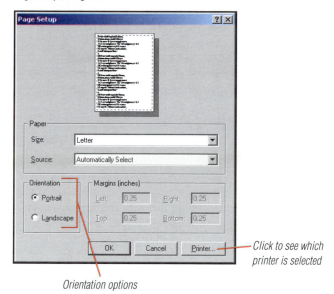

Orientation options

Click to see which printer is selected

FIGURE A-28
Print dialog box

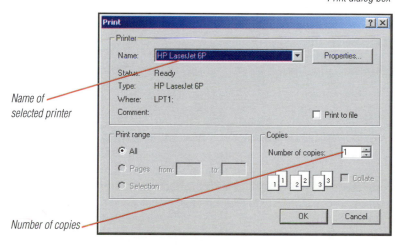

Name of selected printer

Number of copies

Modify print settings

1. Click File on the menu bar, then click Page Setup to open the Page Setup dialog box, as shown in Figure A-27.

   TIP If you have not selected a printer using the Chooser, a warning box might appear (Mac).

   Page setup and print settings vary slightly in Macintosh.

2. Click the Landscape option button, then click OK.

   | TIP Choose either Landscape option (Mac).

3. Click File on the menu bar, click Print, then click Proceed.

4. Make sure that the All option button is selected in the Print range section, and that 1 appears in the Number of copies text box (Win), or the From option button is selected in the Copies & Pages section (Mac), then click OK (Win) or Print (Mac), as shown in Figure A-28.

You used the Page Setup command on the File menu to open the Page Setup dialog box, changed the page orientation, then printed the document.

CLOSE A DOCUMENT
AND EXIT PHOTOSHOP

What You'll Do

In this lesson, you'll use the Close and Exit (Win) or Quit (Mac) commands to close documents and exit Photoshop.

Concluding Your Work Session

At the end of your work session, you might have opened several documents; you now need to decide which ones you want to save.

QUICKTIP

If you share a computer with other people, it's a good idea to reset Photoshop's preferences back to their default settings. You can do so when you start Photoshop by pressing and holding [Shift][Alt][Ctrl] (Win) or [Shift][option][command] (Mac).

Closing Versus Exiting

When you are finished working on a document, you need to save and close it. You can close one document at a time, or close all open documents at the same time by exiting the program. Closing a file leaves Photoshop open, which allows you to open or create another file. Exiting Photoshop closes the file, closes Photoshop, and returns you to the desktop, where you can choose to open another program or shut down the computer. Photoshop will prompt you to save any changes before it closes the files. If you do not modify a new or existing document, Photoshop will close it automatically when you exit.

QUICKTIP

To close all open documents, click Window on the menu bar, point to Documents, then click Close All.

Using Adobe online

Periodically, when you start Photoshop, an Update dialog box might appear, prompting you to search for updates or new information on the Adobe Web site. If you click Yes, Photoshop will automatically notify you that a download is available; however, you do not have to select it. You can also obtain information about Photoshop from the Adobe Photoshop Web site (www.adobe.products/photoshop/main.html), where you can link to downloads, tips, training, galleries, examples, and other support topics.

FIGURE A-29

Closing a document using the File menu

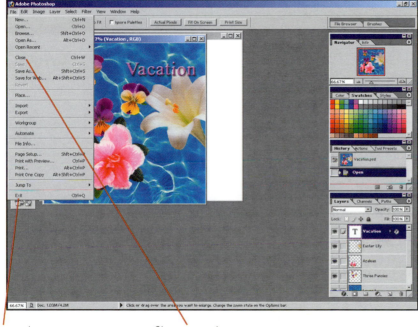

Exit command   Close command

1. Click File on the menu bar, then compare your screen to Figure A-29.

2. Click Close.

   TIP You can close an open file (without closing Photoshop) by clicking the Close button in the document window. Photoshop will prompt you to save any unsaved changes before closing the document.

3. If asked to save your work, click Yes (Win) or Save (Mac).

4. Click File on the menu bar, then click Exit (Win) or click Photoshop on the menu bar, then click Quit (Mac).

   TIP To exit Photoshop and close an open file, click the Close button in the program window. Photoshop will prompt you to save any unsaved changes before closing.

5. If asked to save your work, click No.

You closed the current document and exited the program by using the Close and Exit (Win) or Quit (Mac) commands.

Power User Shortcuts

Key: Menu items are indicated by ➤ between the menu name and its command. Blue bold letters are shortcuts for selecting tools on the toolbox.

to do this:	use this method:
Close a file	[Ctrl][W] (Win) ⌘[W] (Mac)
Create a new file	[Ctrl][N] (Win) ⌘[N] (Mac)
Create a workspace	Window ➤ Workspace ➤ Save Workspace
Drag a layer	🖑
Exit Photoshop	[Ctrl][Q] (Win), ⌘[Q] (Mac)
Hide a layer	👁
Lasso Tool	🔗 or **L**
Open a file	[Ctrl][O] (Win), ⌘[O] (Mac)
Open Help	[F1] (Win)
Open Preferences dialog box	[Ctrl][K] (Win) ⌘[K] (Mac)
Page Setup	[Shift][Ctrl][P] (Win) [Shift] option [P] (Mac)
Print File	File ➤ Print [Alt][Ctrl][P] (Win) option ⌘[P] (Mac)

to do this:	use this method:
Reset preferences to default settings	[Shift][Alt][Ctrl] (Win) [Shift] option ⌘ (Mac)
Save a file	[Ctrl][S] (Win) ⌘[S] (Mac)
Show a layer	☐
Show hidden lasso tools	[Shift] **L**
Show or hide all open palettes	[Shift][Tab]
Show or hide all open palettes, the tool options bar, and the toolbox	[Tab]
Show or hide Swatches palette	Window ➤ Swatches
Use Save As	[Shift][Ctrl][S] (Win) [Shift] ⌘[S] (Mac)
Zoom in using Zoom Tool	🔍
Zoom out using Zoom Tool	[Alt] 🔍 (Win) option 🔍 (Mac)
Zoom Tool	🔍 or **Z**

Start Adobe Photoshop 7.0.

1. Start Photoshop.
2. Create a new document that is 500 × 500 pixels, then name it **Review**.

Learn how to open and save a document.

1. Open PS A-2.psd.
2. Save it as **Zenith Design Logo**.

Examine the Photoshop window.

1. Locate the title bar and the current zoom percentage.
2. Locate the menu that is used to open a new document.
3. View the toolbox, the tool options bar, and the palettes that are showing.
4. Click the Move Tool, then view the Move Tool options on the tool options bar.

Use the Layers and History palettes.

1. Drag the Wine Glasses layer so it is above the Zenith layer, then use the History palette to undo the state.
2. Drag the Wine Glasses layer above the Zenith layer again.
3. Use the Indicates layer visibility button to hide the Wine Glasses layer.
4. Make the Wine Glasses layer visible again.
5. Hide the Zenith layer.
6. Show the Zenith layer.
7. Click the Tag Line layer. Notice that the Tag Line is now the active layer.
8. Save your work.

Learn about Photoshop by using Help.

1. Open the Adobe Photoshop 7.0 Help window.
2. Using the Contents tab, find information about resetting all tools.
3. Print the information you find.
4. Close the Help window.

View and print a document.

1. Make sure that all the layers are visible in the Layers palette.
2. Click the Zoom Tool, then make sure the setting is selected to resize the window to fit.
3. Zoom in on the wine glasses twice.
4. Zoom out to the original perspective.
5. Print one copy of the document.

Close a document and exit Photoshop.

1. Close the Zenith Design Logo file.
2. Close the Review file.
3. Compare your printed document to Figure A-30, then Exit (Win) or Quit (Mac) Photoshop.

FIGURE A-30
Completed Skills Review

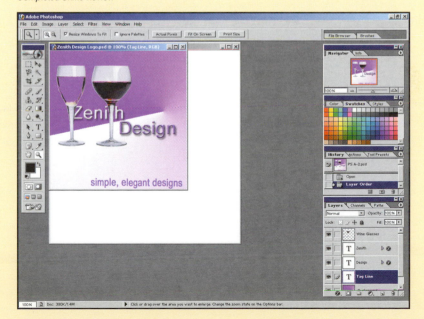

As a new Photoshop user, you are comforted knowing that Photoshop's Help system provides definitions, explanations, procedures, and other helpful information. It also includes examples and demonstrations to show how Photoshop features work. You use the Help system to learn about managing the color in your images.

1. Open the Photoshop Help window.
2. Click the Producing Consistent Color (Photoshop) link in the Contents pane.
3. Click the Why colors sometimes don't match link.
4. After you read this topic, use the Previous link to return to the previous screen.
5. Click the About color management link.
6. Print out the About color management topic, then compare your results to the sample shown in Figure A-31.

FIGURE A-31

Completed Project Builder 1

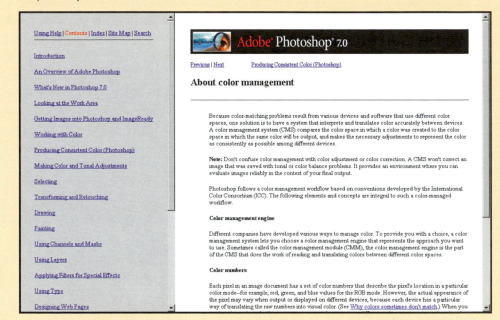

PROJECT BUILDER 2

Kitchen World, your local specialty cooking shop, has just added herb-infused oils to its product line. They have hired you to draft a flyer that features their new products. You use Photoshop to create a flyer.

1. Open PS A-3.psd, then save it as **Kitchen World**.
2. Make the Measuring Spoons layer visible.
3. Drag the Oils layer behind the Skillet layer.
4. Drag the Measuring Spoons layer in front of the Skillet layer.
5. Save the document, then compare your document to the sample shown in Figure A-32.

FIGURE A-32
Completed Project Builder 2

DESIGN PROJECT

As an avid, albeit novice Photoshop user, you have grasped the importance of how layers affect your document. Now, you're ready to examine the images created by Photoshop experts and critique them on their use of layers.

1. Connect to the Internet, and go to *www.course.com*, navigate to the page for this book, click the Student Online Companion link, then click Link 1 and Link 2 for this unit.
2. Review the categories, then download a complex image from each Web site.
3. Start Photoshop, then open the down-loaded images.
4. Save one document as **Critique-1** and the other as **Critique-2** in the Photoshop format (use the .psd extension.).
5. Analyze each image for its potential use of layers.
6. Open the File Info dialog box, then type in the Caption section the number of layers you observe in the image, their possible order in the Layers palette, and how moving the layers would affect the image.
7. Compare your documents to the sample shown in Figure A-33, then close the documents.

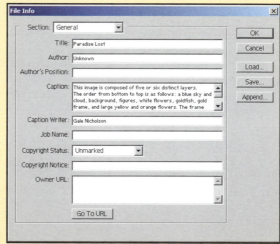

Depending on the size of your group, you can assign individual elements of the project to group members, or work collectively to create the finished product.

Now that you are somewhat familiar with Photoshop and its Help system, you decide to see what kind of information is available on the Adobe Photoshop Web site. This Web site has important product information, including user tips and feedback that can make you more skillful at using this program. As a Photoshop user, you want to become familiar with this Web site.

1. Connect to the Internet and go to the Adobe Web site at *www.adobe.com*.
2. Click the All link under the Products section, then click the Photoshop 7.0 link.
3. Use the links on the Web page to search for information about adjusting the monitor display. (*Hint*: Try User forums under support, or Tutorials under training & events.)
4. Print the relevant page(s).
5. Start Photoshop and open the Photoshop Help window.
6. Search for Adjusting the Monitor Display, then print the relevant page(s), as shown in the sample in Figure A-34.
7. Evaluate the information in the documents, compare any significant differences, then be prepared to discuss your findings.

FIGURE A-34
Completed Group Project

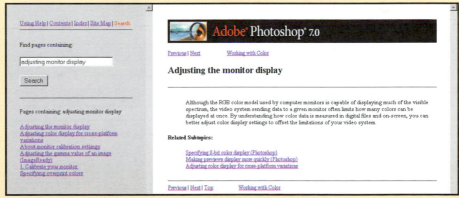

UNIT B

WORKING WITH LAYERS

1. Examine and convert layers.

2. Add and delete layers.

3. Add a selection from one document to another.

4. Organize layers with layer sets and colors.

UNIT B
WORKING WITH LAYERS

Layers Are Everything

You can use Photoshop to create sophisticated images because you can create multiple layers. Each object created in Photoshop exists on its own individual layer, making it easy to control the position and quality of each layer in the stack. Depending on your computer's resources, you can have a maximum of 8000 layers in each Photoshop document with each layer containing as much or as little detail as necessary. Adding layers to an image increases its file size, so after your document is finished, you can dramatically reduce its file size by combining all the layers.

> **QUICKTIP**
> The transparent areas in a layer do not increase file size.

Understanding the Importance of Layers

Layers make it possible to manipulate the tiniest detail within your document, which gives you tremendous flexibility when you make changes. By placing images, effects,

styles, and type on separate layers, you can modify them individually *without* affecting other layers. The advantage to using multiple layers is that you can isolate effects and images on one layer without affecting the others. The disadvantage of using multiple layers is that your file size might become very large.

Using Layers to Modify a Document

You can add, delete, and move layers in your document. You can also drag a portion of an image, called a **selection**, from one Photoshop document to another. When you do this, a new layer is automatically created. Copying layers from one document to another makes it easy to transfer a complicated effect, a simple image, or a piece of type. You can also hide and display each layer, or change its opacity. **Opacity** is the ability to see through a layer so that layers beneath it are visible. You can continuously change your document's overall appearance by changing the order of your layers, until you achieve just the look you want.

Tools You'll Use

Delete current state button

Opacity list arrow

Color list arrow

EXAMINE AND CONVERT LAYERS

What You'll Do

In this lesson, you'll use the Layers palette to delete a Background layer and the Layer menu to create a Background layer from an image layer.

Learning About the Layers Palette

The **Layers palette** lists all the layer names within a Photoshop file and enables you to manipulate one or more layers at a time. By default, this palette is located in the lower-right corner of the screen, but it can be moved to a new location by dragging the palette's tab. In some cases, the entire name of the layer might not appear in the palette. If a layer name is too long, an ellipsis appears, indicating that part of the name is hidden from view. You can view a layer's entire name, by holding the pointer over the name until the full name appears. The **layer thumbnail** appears to the left of the layer name and contains a miniature picture of the layer's content, as shown in Figure B-1. To the left of the layer thumbnail, you can add color, which allows you to easily identify layers. The Layers palette also contains common buttons, such as the Delete layer button and the Create new layer button.

QUICKTIP

You can hide or resize Layers palette thumbnails to improve your computer's performance. To remove or change the size of layer thumbnails, click the Layers palette list arrow, then click Palette Options to open the Layers Palette option dialog box. Click the option button next to the desired thumbnail size, or click the None option button to remove thumbnails, then click OK. A paintbrush icon appears in place of a thumbnail.

Recognizing Layer Types

The Layers palette includes several types of layers: Background, type, and image (non-type). The Background layer—whose name appears in italics—is always at the bottom of the stack. Type layers—layers that contain text—contain the type layer icon in the layer thumbnail, and image layers display a thumbnail of their contents, as shown in Figure B-1. In addition to dragging selections from one Photoshop document to another, you can also drag objects created in other applications, such as Adobe Illustrator, InDesign, or Macromedia Flash, onto a Photoshop document, which creates a layer containing objects created in another program.

QUICKTIP

It is not necessary for a Photoshop document to have a Background layer.

Organizing Layers

One of the benefits of using layers is that you can create different design effects by rearranging their order. Figure B-2 contains the same layers as Figure B-1, but they are arranged differently. Did you notice that the wreath is partially obscured by the gourds and the title text? This reorganization was created by dragging the Wreath layer below the Gourds layer on the Layers palette.

QUICKTIP

Did you notice the lines in the figures? These are moveable guides that you can use to help you place objects.

FIGURE B-1
Image with multiple layers

Position mouse over layer text to display full title

Delete layer button

Type layer thumbnail *Image layer thumbnail* *Create a new layer button*

FIGURE B-2
Layers rearranged

New layer order

Wreath obscured

Converting Layers

When you open an image created with a digital camera, you'll notice that the entire image appears in the Background layer. The Background layer of any document is the initial layer and is always located at the bottom of the stack. You cannot change its position in the stack, nor can you change its opacity or lighten or darken its colors. You can convert a Background layer into an image layer (nontype layer), and you can convert an image layer into a Background layer. You need to modify the image layer *before* converting it to a Background layer. You might want to convert a Background layer into an image layer so that you can use the full range of editing tools on the layer content. You might want to convert an image layer into a Background layer after you have made all your changes and want it to be the bottommost layer in the stack.

QUICKTIP

When converting an image layer to a Background layer, you must delete the existing Background layer. You can delete a Background layer by clicking it on the Layers palette, then dragging it to the Delete layer button on the Layers palette.

FIGURE B-3

Preferences dialog box

Rulers list arrow

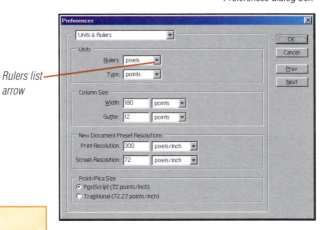

Using rulers and changing units of measurement

You can display horizontal and vertical rulers to help you better position elements. To display or hide rulers, you click View on the menu bar, then click Rulers. (A check mark to the right of the Rulers command indicates that the Rulers are displayed.) In addition to displaying or hiding rulers, you can also choose from various units of measurement. Your choices include pixels, inches, centimeters, micrometers, points, picas, and percentages. Pixels, for example, display more tick marks and can make it easier to make tiny adjustments. You can change the units of measurement by clicking Edit [Win] or Photoshop [Mac] on the menu bar, pointing to Preferences, then clicking Units & Rulers [Win]. In the Preferences dialog box, as shown in Figure B-3, click the Rulers list arrow, click the units you want to use, then click OK.

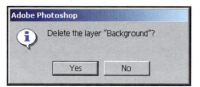

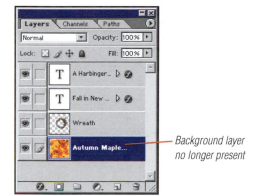

*Background layer
no longer present*

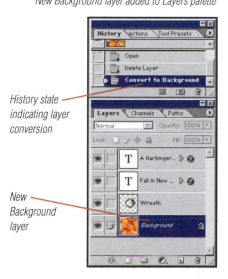

*History state
indicating layer
conversion*

*New
Background
layer*

Convert an image layer into a Background layer

1. Open PS B-1.psd, then save it as **New England Fall**.

   TIP If you receive a message stating that some of the text layers need to be updated before they can be used for vector-based output, click Update (Mac).

2. Click View on the menu bar, click Rulers if your rulers are not visible, then verify that your rulers are displayed in pixels.

   TIP If you are unsure which units of measurement are used, click Edit (Win) or Photoshop (Mac) on the menu bar, point to Preferences, then click Units & Rulers (Win). Click the Rulers list arrow, click Pixels, then click OK.

3. On the Layers palette, scroll down, click the Background layer, then click the Delete layer button.

4. Click Yes in the warning box, as shown in Figure B-4, then compare your Layers palette to Figure B-5.

5. Click Layer on the menu bar, point to New, then click Background From Layer.

   The Autumn Maple Leaves layer has been converted into the Background layer. Did you notice that in addition to the image layer being converted to the Background layer that a state now appears in the History palette that says Convert to Background? See Figure B-6.

6. Save your work.

You displayed the rulers, deleted the Background layer, then converted an image layer into the Background layer.

ADD AND DELETE LAYERS

What You'll Do

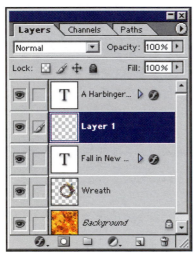

In this lesson, you'll create a new layer using the New command on the Layer menu, delete a layer, and create a layer using buttons on the Layers palette.

Adding Layers to a Document

Because it's so important to make use of multiple layers, Photoshop makes it easy to add and delete layers. You can create layers in three ways:

- Use the New command on the Layer menu.
- Use the New Layer command on the Layers palette menu.
- Click the Create a new layer button on the Layers palette.

Objects on new layers have a default opacity setting of 100%, which means that objects on lower layers are not visible. Each layer has the Normal (default) blending mode applied to it. (A **blending mode** is a feature that affects a layer's underlying pixels, and is used to lighten or darken colors.)

Merging layers

You can combine multiple image layers into a single layer using the merging process. Merging layers is useful when you want to make specific edits permanent. In order for layers to be merged, they must be visible and next to each other on the Layers palette. You can merge all visible layers within an image, or just the ones you select. Type layers cannot be merged until they are rasterized (turned into a bitmapped image layer), or converted into uneditable text. To merge two layers, make sure that they are next to each other and that the Indicates layer visibility button is visible on each layer, then click the layer in the higher position on the Layers palette. Click Layer on the menu bar, then click Merge Layers. The active layer and the layer immediately beneath it will be combined into a single layer. To merge all visible layers, click the Layers palette list arrow, then click Merge Visible. Most layer commands that are available on the Layers menu, such as Merge Layers, are also available using the Layers palette list arrow.

Naming a Layer

Photoshop automatically assigns a sequential number to each new layer name, but you can rename a layer at any time. After all, calling a layer "Layer 12" is fine, but you might want to use a more descriptive name so it is easier to distinguish one layer from another. If you use the New command on the Layers menu, you can name the layer when you create it. You can rename a layer at any time by using any of these methods:

- Click the Layers palette list arrow, click Layer Properties, type the name in the Name text box, then click OK.
- Double-click the name on the Layers palette, type the new name, then press [Enter] (Win) or [return] (Mac).

Deleting Layers From a Document

You might want to delete an unused or unnecessary layer. You can use four methods to delete a layer:

- Click the name on the Layers palette, click the Layers palette list arrow, then click Delete Layer as shown in Figure B-7.
- Click the name on the Layers palette, click the Delete layer button on the Layers palette, then click Yes in the warning box.
- Drag the layer name on the Layers palette to the Delete layer button on the Layers palette.

- Click the name on the Layers palette, press and hold [Alt] (Win) or [option] (Mac), then click the Delete layer button on the Layers palette.

You should be certain that you no longer need a layer before you delete it. If you delete a layer by accident, you can restore it during the current editing session by deleting the Delete Layer state on the History palette.

QUICKTIP

Photoshop always numbers layers sequentially, no matter how many layers you add or delete.

FIGURE B-7
Layers palette menu

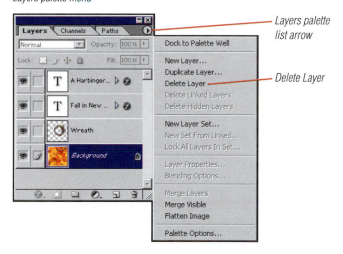

Layers palette list arrow

Delete Layer

Add a layer using the Layer menu

1. Click the Fall in New England layer on the Layers palette.

   A new layer will be added above the active layer.

2. Click Layer on the menu bar, point to New, then click Layer to open the New Layer dialog box, as shown in Figure B-8.

   > TIP   By default, Photoshop names new layers consecutively, starting with Layer 1. You can change the layer name in the New Layer dialog box before it appears on the Layers palette.

3. Click OK.

   The New Layer dialog box closes and the new layer appears above the Fall in New England layer on the Layers palette. The New Layer state is added to the History palette. See Figure B-9.

   You created a new layer above the Fall in New England layer, using the New command on the Layer menu.

FIGURE B-8
New Layer dialog box

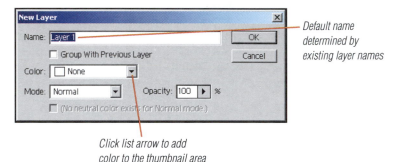

Default name determined by existing layer names

Click list arrow to add color to the thumbnail area

FIGURE B-9
New layer on Layers palette

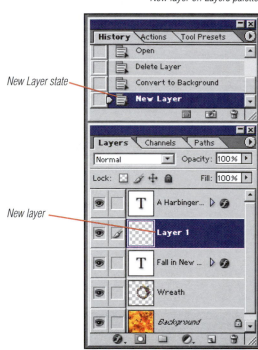

New Layer state

New layer

Delete a layer

1. Position the pointer over Layer 1 in the Layers palette. 🖑

2. Drag Layer 1 to the Delete layer button on the Layers palette. 🗑

   TIP   You can also delete the layer by dragging the New Layer state in the History palette to the Delete current state button.

You used the Delete layer button on the Layers palette to delete a layer.

Add a layer using the Layers palette

1. Click the Fall in New England layer on the Layers palette.

2. Click the Create a new layer button on the Layers palette, then compare your Layers palette to Figure B-10. 🔲

   TIP   You can rename a layer by clicking the Layers palette list arrow, clicking Layer Properties, typing a new name in the Name text box, then clicking OK.

3. Save your work.

You used the Create a new layer button on the Layers palette to add a new layer.

FIGURE B-10

New layer with default settings

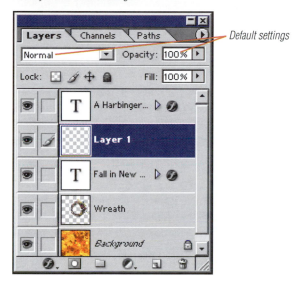

Default settings

ADD A SELECTION FROM ONE
DOCUMENT TO ANOTHER

What You'll Do

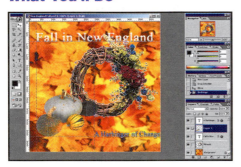

In this lesson, you'll use the Invert check box in the Color Range dialog box to make a selection, drag the selection to another document, and remove the fringe from a selection.

Understanding Selections

Often the Photoshop document you want to create involves using an image or part of an image from another file. To use an image or part of an image, you must first select it. Photoshop refers to this as "making a selection." A selection is an area of an image surrounded by a **marquee**, a dashed line that surrounds the area you want to edit or move to another document, as shown in Figure B-11. You can drag a marquee around a selection using four marquee tools: Rectangular Marquee, Elliptical Marquee, Single Row Marquee, and Single Column Marquee. Table B-1 displays the four marquee tools and other selection tools. You can set options for

each tool on the tool options bar when the tool you want to use is active.

Understanding the Extract and Color Range Commands

In addition to using selection tools, Photoshop provides other methods for incorporating imagery from other documents. The **Extract command**, located on the Filter menu, separates an image from a background or surrounding imagery. You can use the **Color Range** command, located on the Select menu, to select a particular color contained in an existing image. Depending on the area you want, you can use the Color Range dialog box to extract a portion of an image. For

Cropping an image

You might find an image that you really like, except that it contains a particular portion that you don't need. You can exclude, or **crop**, certain parts of an image by using the Crop Tool on the toolbox. Cropping hides areas of an image from view *without* losing resolution quality. To crop an image, click the Crop Tool on the toolbox, drag the pointer around the area you *want to keep*, then press [Enter] (Win) or [return] (Mac).

example, you can select the Invert check box to choose one color and then select the portion of the image that is every color *except* that one. After you select all the imagery you want from another document, you can drag it into your open document.

Making a Selection and Moving a Selection

You can use a variety of methods and tools to make a selection, which can be used as a specific part of a layer or the entire layer.

You use selections to isolate an area you want to alter. For example, you can use the Magnetic Lasso Tool to select complex shapes by clicking the starting point, tracing an approximate outline, then clicking the ending point. Later, you can use the Crop Tool to trim areas from a selection. When you use the Move Tool to drag a selection to the destination document, Photoshop places the selection in a new layer above the previously active layer.

Defringing Layer Contents

Sometimes when you make a selection, then move it into another document, the newly selected image can contain unwanted pixels that give the appearance of a fringe, or halo. You can remove this effect using a Matting command called Defringe. This command is available in the Layers menu and allows you to replace fringe pixels with the colors of other nearby pixels. You can determine a width for replacement pixels between 1 and 200. It's magic!

FIGURE B-11
Marquee selections

Area selected using the Rectangular Marquee Tool

Specific element selected using the Magnetic Lasso Tool

TABLE B-1: Selection Tools

tool	tool name	tool	tool name
▢	Rectangular Marquee Tool	◯	Lasso Tool
◯	Elliptical Marquee Tool	▽	Polygonal Lasso Tool
▭	Single Row Marquee Tool	▷	Magnetic Lasso Tool
▯	Single Column Marquee Tool	▱	Eraser Tool
⊅	Crop Tool	▱	Background Eraser Tool
✕	Magic Wand Tool	▱	Magic Eraser Tool

Make a color range selection

1. Open Gourds.psd, click the title bar, then drag it to an empty portion of the workspace so that you can see both documents.

2. Click Select on the menu bar, then click Color Range.

   TIP   If the background color is solid, you can select the Invert check box to pick only the pixels in the image area.

3. Click the Image option button, then type **0** in the Fuzziness text box (or drag the slider all the way to the left until you see 0).

   TIP   When more than one document is open, each has its own set of rulers.

4. Position the pointer in the white background of the image in the Color Range dialog box, and click the background.

5. Select the Invert check box. Compare your dialog box to Figure B-12.

6. Click OK, then compare your Gourds.psd document to Figure B-13.

You opened a document and used the Color Range dialog box to select the image pixels by selecting the image's inverted colors.

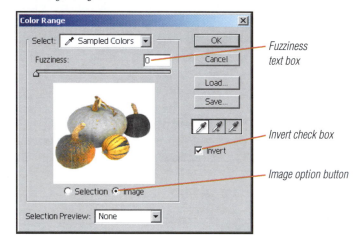

FIGURE B-12
Color Range dialog box

Fuzziness text box

Invert check box

Image option button

FIGURE B-13
Marquee surrounding selection

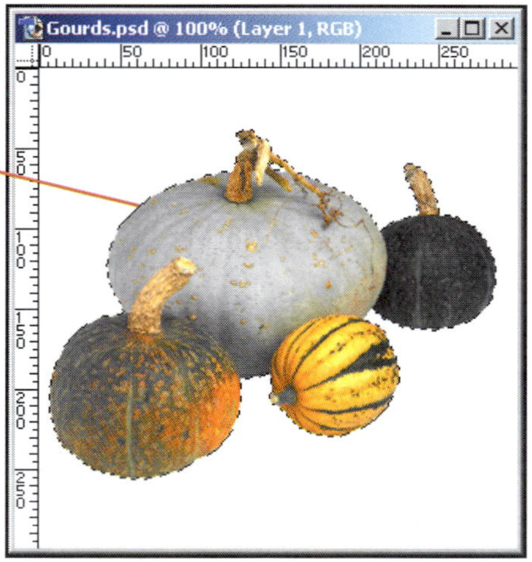

Marquee surrounds everything that is the inverse of the white background

Gourds image dragged to New England Fall document

White fringe
surrounds image

FIGURE B-15
Gourds layer defringed

Gourds image
in document

Gourds moved to active
layer in document

Move a selection to another document

1. Click the Move Tool on the toolbox.
2. Position the pointer anywhere over the selection in the Gourds document.
3. Drag the selection to the New England Fall document, then release the mouse button.

   The gourds image moves to the New England Fall document appearing on Layer 1.
4. If necessary, drag the gourds to the precise location shown in Figure B-14.

You dragged a selection from one document to another.

Defringe the selection

1. Click Layer on the menu bar, point to Matting, then click Defringe.
2. Type **2** in the Width text box, then click OK.
3. Save your work.
4. Close Gourds.psd, then compare your open document to Figure B-15.

You removed the fringe from a selection.

ORGANIZE LAYERS WITH LAYER SETS AND COLORS

What You'll Do

In this lesson, you'll use the Layers palette menu to create, name, and color a layer set, and then add layers to it. You'll add finishing touches to the document, save it as a copy, then flatten it.

Understanding Layer Sets

A **layer set** is a Photoshop feature that allows you to organize your layers on the Layers palette. In the same way that a folder on your hard drive can contain individual computer files, a layer set contains individual layers. For example, you can create a layer set that contains all the type layers in your document. To create a layer set, you click the Layers palette list arrow, then click New Layer Set. As with layers, it is helpful to choose a descriptive name for a layer set.

Organizing Layer Sets

After you create a layer set, you simply drag layers on the Layers palette directly on top of the layer set. You can remove layers from a layer set by dragging them out of the layer set to a new location on the Layers palette or by deleting them. Some changes made to a layer set, such as blending mode or opacity changes, affect every layer in the layer set. You can choose to expand or collapse layer sets, depending on the amount of information you need to see. Expanding a layer set

Duplicating a layer

When you add a new layer by clicking the Create a new layer button on the Layers palette, the new layer contains default settings. However, you might want to create a new layer that has the same settings as an existing layer. You can do so by duplicating an existing layer to create a copy of that layer and its settings. Duplicating a layer is also a good way to preserve your modifications, because you can modify the duplicate layer and not worry about losing your original work. To create a duplicate layer, select the layer you want to copy, click the Layers palette list arrow, click Duplicate Layer, then click OK. The new layer will appear above the original.

shows all of the layers in the layer set, and collapsing a layer set hides all of the layers in a layer set. You can expand or collapse a layer set by clicking the triangle to the left of the layer set icon. Figure B-16 shows one expanded layer set and one collapsed layer set.

Adding Color to a Layer

If your document has relatively few layers, it's easy to locate the layers. However, if your document contains several layers, you might need some help in organizing them. You can organize layers by color-coding them, which makes it easy to find the group you want, regardless of its location on the Layers palette. For example, you can put all type layers in red or put the layers associated with a particular portion of an image in blue. To color a layer, click the Layers palette list arrow, click Layer Properties, click the Color list arrow, click a color, then click OK. To color the Background layer, you must first convert it to a regular layer.

QUICKTIP

You can also color-code a layer set without losing the color-coding you applied to individual layers.

Flattening an Image

After you make all the necessary modifications to your document, you can greatly reduce the file size by flattening the image. **Flattening** merges all visible layers into a single Background layer and discards all hidden layers. Make sure that all layers that you want to display are visible before you flatten the document. Because flattening removes a document's individual layers, it's a good idea to make a copy of the original document *before* it is flattened. The status bar displays the document's current size and the size it will be when flattened. If you work on a Macintosh, you'll find this information in the lower-left corner of the document window.

FIGURE B-16
Layer sets

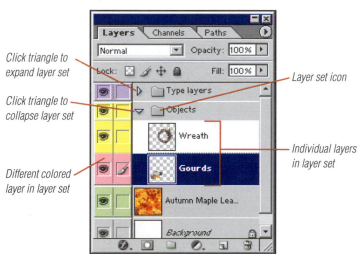

Click triangle to expand layer set

Click triangle to collapse layer set

Different colored layer in layer set

Layer set icon

Individual layers in layer set

Create a layer set

1. Verify that Layer 1 is active, click the Layers palette list arrow, then click New Layer Set.

   The New Layer Set dialog box opens, as shown in Figure B-17.

   > **TIP** Photoshop automatically places a new layer set above the active layer.

2. Type **All Type** in the Name text box.

3. Click the Color list arrow, click Red, then click OK.

   The New Layer Set dialog box closes. Compare your Layers palette to Figure B-18.

You used the Layers palette menu to create a layer set, then named and applied a color to it.

Move layers to the layer set

1. Click the Fall in New England type layer on the Layers palette, then drag it to the All Type layer set.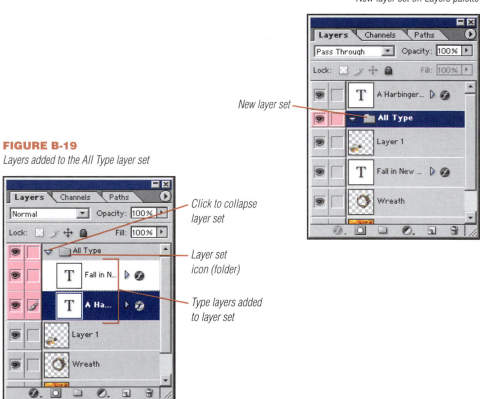

2. Click the A Harbinger of Change type layer, drag it to the All Type layer set, then compare your Layers palette to Figure B-19.

3. Click the triangle to the left of the layer set icon (folder) to collapse the layer set.

4. Click the Wreath layer.

5. Click Layer on the menu bar, point to Matting, then click Defringe.

6. Type 2 in the Width text box, then click OK.

You moved two layers into a layer set, then defringed a layer.

FIGURE B-17
New Layer Set dialog box

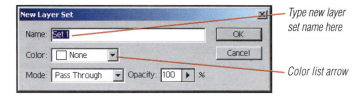

Type new layer set name here

Color list arrow

FIGURE B-18
New layer set on Layers palette

New layer set

FIGURE B-19
Layers added to the All Type layer set

Click to collapse layer set

Layer set icon (folder)

Type layers added to layer set

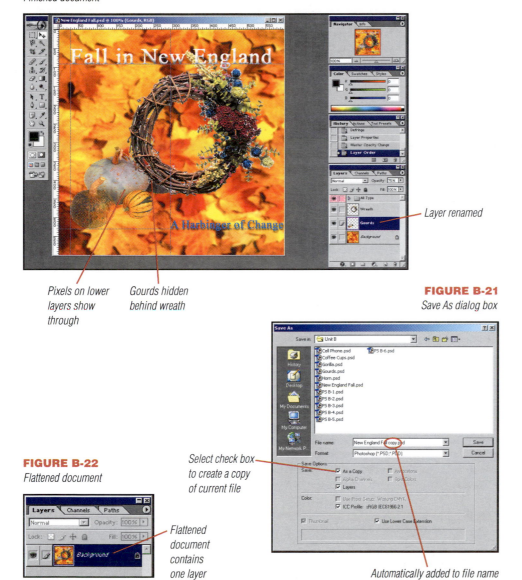

Pixels on lower
layers show
through

Gourds hidden
behind wreath

Layer renamed

Flattened
document
contains
one layer

Select check box
to create a copy
of current file

Automatically added to file name

Rename a layer and adjust opacity

1. Double-click Layer 1, type **Gourds**, then press [Enter] (Win) or [return} (Mac).

2. Double-click the Opacity text box on the Layers palette, type **75**, then press [Enter] (Win) or [return] (Mac).

3. Drag the Gourds layer on top of the Wreath layer, then compare your image to Figure B-20.

4. Save your work.

You renamed the new layer, adjusted opacity, and rearranged layers.

Flatten an image

1. Click File on the menu bar, then click Save As.

2. Select the As a Copy check box, then compare your dialog box to Figure B-21.

3. Click Save.

   Photoshop saves and closes a copy of the document containing all the layers and effects.

4. Click Layer on the menu bar, then click Flatten Image. Compare your Layers palette to Figure B-22.

5. Save your work.

You saved the document as a copy, and then flattened the document.

Lesson 4   Organize Layers with Layer Sets and Colors

Power User Shortcuts

to do this:	use this method:	to do this:	use this method:
Adjust layer opacity	Click Opacity list arrow on Layers palette, drag opacity slider or Double-click Opacity text box, type a percentage	Move Tool	⬆ or **V**
		New Background layer from existing layer	Layer ➤ New ➤ Background From Layer
Color a layer	Layers palette list arrow, Layer Properties, Color list arrow	New layer	Layer ➤ New ➤ Layer or
Create a layer set	Layers palette list arrow, New Layer Set or	Rename a layer	Layers palette list arrow, Layer Properties, Name text box
Delete a layer	🗑	Select color range	Select ➤ Color Range
Defringe a selection	Layer ➤ Matting ➤ Defringe	Show/Hide Rulers	View ➤ Rulers [Ctrl][R] (Win) ⌘ [R] (Mac)
Flatten an image	Layer ➤ Flatten Image		

Key: Menu items are indicated by ➤ between the menu name and its command. Blue bold letters are shortcuts for selecting tools on the toolbox.

Examine and convert layers.

1. Start Photoshop.
2. Open PS B-2.psd, then save it as **Music World**.
3. Make sure the rulers appear with pixels.
4. Delete the Background layer.
5. Verify that the Rainbow blend layer is active, then convert the image layer to a Background layer.
6. Save your work.

Add and delete layers.

1. Make Layer 2 active.
2. Create a layer using the Layer menu.
3. Accept the default name (Layer 4), and change the color of the layer to Orange.
4. Delete Layer 4.
5. Make Layer 2 active, then create a layer using the button on the Layers palette.
6. Save your work.

Add a selection from one document to another.

1. Open Horn.psd.
2. Reposition this image by dragging it to the right of the Music World document.
3. Open the Color Range dialog box. (*Hint*: Use the Select menu.)
4. Verify that the Image option button is selected, the Invert check box is selected, and that Fuzziness is set to 0.
5. Sample the white background in the dialog box.

6. Use the Move Tool to drag the selection into the Music World document.
7. Position the selection so that the upper-left edge of the instrument matches the sample.
8. Defringe the horn selection (in the Music World image) using a 3 pixel width.
9. Close Horn.psd.
10. Drag Layer 4 above Layer 3.
11. Rename Layer 4 to **Horn**, if necessary.
12. Change the opacity for the Horn layer to 55%.
13. Drag the Horn layer so it is beneath Layer 2.
14. Hide Layer 1.
15. Hide the rulers.
16. Save your work.

FIGURE B-23
Completed Skills Review

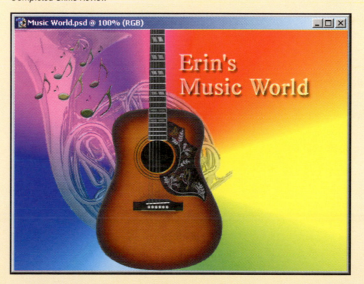

Organize layers with layer sets and colors.

1. Create a yellow Layer Set called Type Layers.
2. Drag the following layers into the Type Layers folder: Erin, Music World, Layer 2.
3. Collapse the Layer Set folder.
4. Save a copy of the Music World document using the default naming scheme.
5. Flatten the image. (*Hint*: Be sure to discard hidden layers.)
6. Save your work, then compare your document to Figure B-23.

A credit union is developing a hotline for members to use to help abate credit card fraud as soon as it occurs. They're going to distribute 10,000 refrigerator magnets over the next three weeks. As part of their effort to build community awareness of the project, they've sponsored a contest for the magnet design. You decide to enter the contest.

1. Open PS B-3.psd, then save it as **Fraud Magnet**.
2. Open Cell Phone.psd, use the Color Range dialog box or any selection tool on the toolbox to select the image, then drag it to the Fraud Magnet document.
3. Rename the newly created layer **Cell Phone**, if necessary, then apply a color to the layer on the Layers palette.
4. Convert the Background layer to an image layer, then rename it **Banner**.
5. Change the opacity of the Banner layer to any setting you like.
6. Defringe the Cell Phone layer using the pixel width of your choice.
7. Save your work, then compare your document to Figure B-24.

FIGURE B-24
Completed Project Builder 1

One of the gorillas in your local zoo is pregnant. The zoo hires you to create a promotional billboard commemorating this event for the upcoming season. The Board of Directors decides that the billboard should be humorous.

1. Open PS B-4.psd, then save it as **Zoo Billboard**.
2. Open Gorilla.psd, use the Color Range dialog box or any selection tool on the toolbox to create a marquee around the gorilla, then drag the selection to the Zoo Billboard document.
3. Name the new layer **Great Ape**.
4. Change the opacity of the Great Ape layer to 88%.
5. Save your work, then compare your document to Figure B-25.

FIGURE B-25
Completed Project Builder 2

DESIGN PROJECT

A friend of yours has designed a new heat-absorbing coffee cup for take-out orders. She is going to present the prototype to a prospective vendor, but first needs to print a brochure. She's asked you to design an eye-catching cover.

1. Open PS B-5.psd, then save it as **Coffee Cover**.
2. Open Coffee Cups.psd, then drag the entire image to Coffee Cover. (*Hint*: Use the All command on the Select menu to select the image.)
3. Close Coffee Cups.psd.
4. Rename Layer 1 with the name **Mocha**.
5. Delete the Background layer and convert the Mocha layer into a new Background layer.
6. Reposition the layer objects so they look like the sample. (*Hint*: You might have to reorganize the layers in the stack so all layers are visible.)
7. Create a layer set above the Coffee layer, name it **Java Text**, apply a color to the layer set, then drag the type layers to it.
8. Save your work, then compare your document to Figure B-26.

FIGURE B-26
Completed Design Project

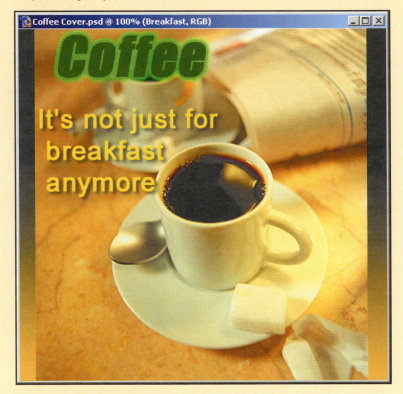

Depending on the size of your group, you can assign individual elements of the project to group members, or work collectively to create the finished product.

Harvest Market, a line of natural food stores, and the trucking associations in your state have formed a coalition to deliver fresh fruit and vegetables to food banks and other food distribution programs. The truckers want to promote the project by displaying a sign on their trucks. The only design requirement is that you use the Harvest Market vegetable logo as the background, keeping in mind that it needs to be seen from a distance.

1. Open PS B-6.psd, then save it as **Harvest Market**.
2. Obtain at least two images of different-sized produce. You can obtain images by using what is available on your computer, scanning print media, or connecting to the Internet and downloading images.
3. Open one of the produce files, select it, then drag or copy it to the Harvest Market document. (*Hint*: Experiment with some of the other selection tools found in Table B-1. Note that some tools require you to copy and paste the image after you select it.)
4. Repeat Step 3 then close the files.
5. Set the opacity of the Veggies layer to 50%.

6. Delete the Background layer, then convert the Veggies layer into a Background layer.
7. Arrange the layers so that smaller images appear on top of the larger ones.
8. Create a layer set for the type layers, and apply a color to it.
9. Save your work, then compare your document to Figure B-27.

10. Be prepared to discuss the advantages and disadvantages of using multiple images. How would you assess the ease and efficiency of the selection techniques you've learned? Which styles did you apply to the type layers, and why?

FIGURE B-27
Completed Group Project

UNIT C

MAKING SELECTIONS

1. Make a selection using shapes.

2. Modify a marquee.

3. Select using color and modify a selection.

4. Add a vignette effect to a selection.

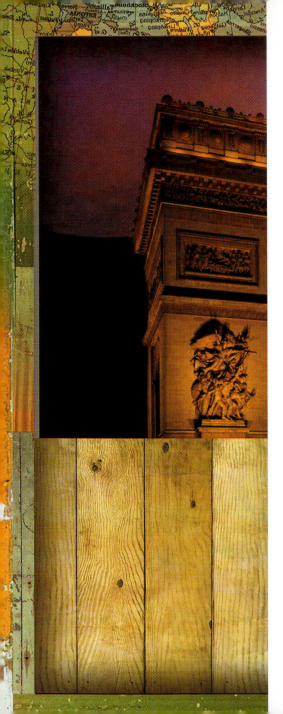

UNIT C
MAKING SELECTIONS

Combining Images

Most Photoshop documents are created using a technique called **compositing**—combining images from different sources. These sources include other Photoshop documents, royalty-free images, pictures taken from digital cameras, and scanned artwork. How you get that extraneous imagery into your Photoshop documents is an art unto itself. You can include additional images by using tools on the toolbox and menu commands.

Understanding Selection Tools

You can use two basic methods to make selections: using a tool or using color. You can use three freeform tools to create your own unique selections, four fixed area tools to create circular or rectangular selections, and a wand tool to make selections using colors. In addition, you can use menu commands to increase or decrease selections that you made with these tools, or you can make selections based on color.

Understanding Which Selection Tool to Use

With so many tools available, how do you know which one to use? After you know the different selection options, you'll learn how to look at images and evaluate selection opportunities. With experience, you'll learn how to identify edges that can be used to isolate imagery, and how to spot colors that can be used to isolate a specific object.

Combining Imagery

After you decide on an object that you want to place in a Photoshop document, you can add the object by cutting, copying, and pasting, dragging and dropping objects using the Move Tool, and using the **Clipboard**, the temporary storage area provided by your operating system.

Tools You'll Use

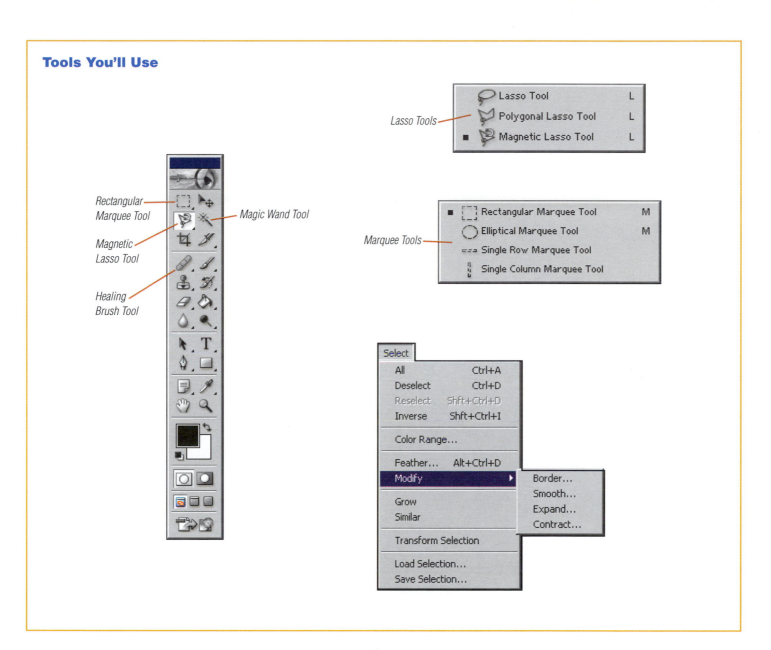

Lasso Tools
- Lasso Tool — L
- Polygonal Lasso Tool — L
- ■ Magnetic Lasso Tool — L

Rectangular Marquee Tool

Magic Wand Tool

Magnetic Lasso Tool

Healing Brush Tool

Marquee Tools
- ■ Rectangular Marquee Tool — M
- Elliptical Marquee Tool — M
- Single Row Marquee Tool
- Single Column Marquee Tool

Select
- All — Ctrl+A
- Deselect — Ctrl+D
- Reselect — Shft+Ctrl+D
- Inverse — Shft+Ctrl+I
- Color Range...
- Feather... — Alt+Ctrl+D
- Modify ▶
  - Border...
  - Smooth...
  - Expand...
  - Contract...
- Grow
- Similar
- Transform Selection
- Load Selection...
- Save Selection...

MAKE A SELECTION USING SHAPES

What You'll Do

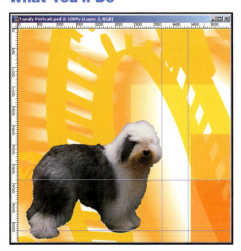

In this lesson, you'll make selections using a marquee tool and a lasso tool, position a selection with the Move Tool, deselect a selection, and drag a complex selection into another document.

Selecting by Shape

The Photoshop selection tools make it easy to select objects that are rectangular or elliptical in nature. Wouldn't it be a lovely world if every image we wanted fell into one of those categories? Well, unfortunately, they don't. While some objects are round or square, most are unusual in shape. Making selections can sometimes be a painstaking process because many objects don't have clearly defined edges. To select an object by shape, you need to click the appropriate tool on the toolbox, then drag the pointer around the object. The selected area is defined by a **marquee**, or series of dotted lines, as shown in Figure C-1.

Creating a Selection

Drawing a rectangular marquee is easier than drawing an elliptical marquee, but with practice, you'll be able to create both marquees easily. Table C-1 lists the tools you can use to make selections using

shapes. Figure C-2 shows a marquee surrounding an irregular shape.

QUICK**TIP**

A marquee is sometimes referred to as *marching ants* because the dots within the marquee appear to be moving.

Using Fastening Points

Each time you click one of the marquee tools, a fastening point is added to the image. A **fastening point** is an anchor within the marquee. When the marquee pointer reaches the initial fastening point (after making its way around the image), a very small circle appears on the pointer, indicating that you have reached the starting point. Clicking the pointer when this circle appears closes the marquee. Some fastening points, such as those in a circular marquee, are not visible, while others, such as those created by the Polygonal or Magnetic Lasso Tools, are visible.

Selecting, Deselecting, and Reselecting

After a selection is made, you can move, copy, transform, or make adjustments to it. A selection stays selected until you unselect, or **deselect**, it. You can deselect a selection by clicking Select on the menu bar, then clicking Deselect. You can also reselect a deselected object by clicking Select on the menu bar, then clicking Reselect.

QUICKTIP

You can select an entire image by clicking Select on the menu bar, then clicking All.

FIGURE C-1

Elliptical Marquee Tool used to create marquee

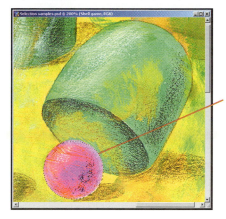

Elliptical marquee surrounding object

FIGURE C-2

Marquee surrounding irregular shape

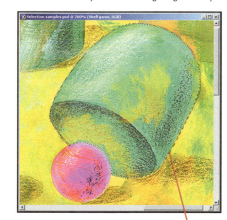

Marquee surrounding irregular shape

TABLE C-1: Selection Tools by Shape

tool	button	effect
Rectangular Marquee Tool		Creates a rectangular selection. Press [Shift] while dragging to create a square.
Elliptical Marquee Tool		Creates an elliptical selection. Press [Shift] while dragging to create a circle.
Single Row Marquee Tool		Creates a 1-pixel-wide row selection.
Single Column Marquee Tool		Creates a 1-pixel-wide column selection.
Lasso Tool		Creates a freehand selection.
Polygonal Lasso Tool		Creates straight line selections. Press [Alt] (Win) or [option] (Mac) to create freehand segments.
Magnetic Lasso Tool		Creates selections that snap to an edge of an object. Press [Alt] (Win) or [option] (Mac) to alternate between freehand and straight line segments.

Placing a Selection

You can place a selection into a Photoshop document in many ways. You can copy or cut a selection, then paste it to a different location in the same document or to a different document. You can also use the Move Tool to drag a selection to a new location.

Using Guides

Guides are non-printable horizontal and vertical lines that you can add to a document to help you position a selection. You can create an unlimited number of horizontal and vertical guides. You can create a guide by positioning the pointer on either ruler, then clicking and dragging the guide into position. You can delete a guide by selecting the Move Tool on the toolbox, positioning the pointer over the guide, then clicking and dragging it back to its ruler. If the Snap feature is enabled, as you drag an object toward a guide, the object will be pulled toward the guide. To turn on the Snap feature, click View on the menu bar, then click Snap. A check mark appears to the left of the command if the feature is enabled.

QUICKTIP

You can temporarily change *any selected tool* into the Move Tool by pressing and holding [Ctrl] (Win) or [command] (Mac). When you're finished dragging the selection, release [Ctrl] (Win) or [command] (Mac), and the functionality of the originally selected tool returns.

FIGURE C-3

Rectangular Marquee Tool selection

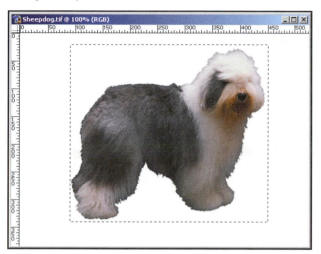

TABLE C-2: Working with a Selection

if you want to	then do this
Move a selection (within a document, or between documents) by positioning ⊹ over the selection, then dragging the marquee and its contents	Move Tool ⊹
Copy a selection to the Clipboard	Activate document containing the selection, click Edit ➤ Copy
Cut a selection to the Clipboard	Activate document containing the selection, click Edit ➤ Cut
Paste a selection from the Clipboard	Activate document where you want the selection, click Edit ➤ Paste
Delete a selection	Make selection, then press [Delete] (Win) or [delete] (Mac)

Create a selection with the Rectangular Marquee Tool

1. Start Photoshop, open PS C-1.psd, then save it as **Family Portrait**.

2. Click View on the menu bar, then click Rulers to select it, if necessary.

   TIP You can quickly change the unit of measurement by right-clicking a ruler and selecting the desired measurement.

3. Change the current unit of measurement to pixels, if necessary.

4. Open Sheepdog.tif, then display the rulers, if necessary.

5. Click the Rectangular Marquee Tool on the toolbox. ▢

6. Make sure the value in the Feather text box on the tool options bar is 0 px.

   Feathering determines the amount of blur between the selection and the pixels surrounding it.

7. Drag the pointer from 90 H/20 V to 450 H/340 V. See Figure C-3. ┼

   The first measurement refers to the horizontal ruler (H); the second measurement refers to the vertical ruler (V).

8. Click the Move Tool, then drag the selection to the Family Portrait document.

   The selection now appears in the Family Portrait document on a new layer (Layer 1).

   TIP Table C-2 describes methods you can use to move selections in a document.

Using the Rectangular Marquee Tool, you created a selection in an image, then you dragged the object into another document.

Position a selection with the Move Tool

1. Verify that the Move Tool is selected on the toolbox. ⊹

2. If you do not see guides, click View on the menu bar, point to Show, then click Guides.

3. Drag the object so that the bottom-right corner snaps to the ruler guides at 440 H/520 V. Compare your image to Figure C-4. ⊹

   Did you feel the snap to effect as you positioned the selection within the guides? This feature makes is easy to properly position objects within a document.

You used the Move Toola to reposition the selection in an existing document.

FIGURE C-4
Rectangular selection in document

Family Portrait.psd @ 100% (Layer 1, RGB)

White background
included in selection

FIGURE C-5

Deselect command

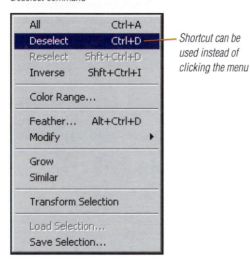

All	Ctrl+A
Deselect	Ctrl+D
Reselect	Shft+Ctrl+D
Inverse	Shft+Ctrl+I
Color Range...	
Feather...	Alt+Ctrl+D
Modify	▶
Grow	
Similar	
Transform Selection	
Load Selection...	
Save Selection...	

Shortcut can be used instead of clicking the menu

1. Click the Indicates layer visibility button on Layer 1 on the Layers palette. 👁
   Layer 1 is now hidden.

2. Click Window on the menu bar, point to Documents, then click Sheepdog.tif.

3. Click Select on the menu bar, then click Deselect, as shown in Figure C-5.

You hid the active layer, then eliminated the marquee from the source document using the Deselect command on the Select menu.

Create a selection with the Magnetic Lasso Tool

1. Click the Magnetic Lasso Tool on the toolbox.

2. Change the settings on the tool options bar so that they are the same as those shown in Figure C-6. Table C-3 describes Magnetic Lasso Tool settings.

3. Click the Magnetic Lasso Tool pointer once anywhere on the edge of the dog, to create your first fastening point.

4. Drag the pointer slowly around the dog until the dog is almost entirely selected, as shown in Figure C-7, then click directly over the initial fastening point.

   Don't worry about all the nooks and crannies surrounding the dog: the Magnetic Lasso Tool will take care of them for you. You will see a small circle next to the pointer when it is directly over the initial fastening point, indicating that you are closing the selection. The individual segments turn into a marquee. In Figure C-7, the selection was started at approximately 320 H/85 V.

   TIP   You can insert additional fastening points by clicking the pointer while dragging. For example, click the mouse button at a location where you want to change the selection shape.

You created a selection with the Magnetic Lasso Tool.

FIGURE C-6
Options for the Magnetic Lasso Tool

FIGURE C-7
Creating a selection with the Magnetic Lasso Tool

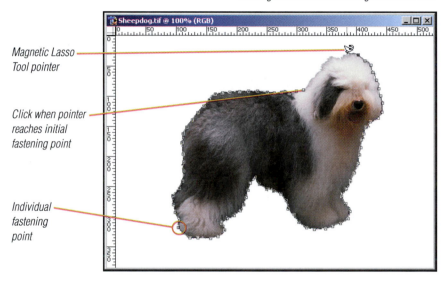

Magnetic Lasso Tool pointer

Click when pointer reaches initial fastening point

Individual fastening point

Mastering the art of selections

You might feel like a total goof when you first start making selections. Making selections is a skill, and like most skills, it takes a lot of practice to become proficient. In addition to practice, make sure that you're comfortable in your work area, that your hands are steady, and that your mouse is working well. A non-optical mouse that is dirty will make selecting an onerous task, so make sure your mouse is well cared for and is functioning correctly.

FIGURE C-8
Selection moved into document

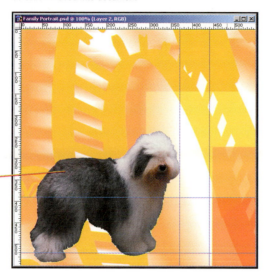

Complex selection includes only object, no background

TABLE C-3: Magnetic Lasso Tool settings

setting	description
Feather	Determines the amount of blur between the selection and the pixels surrounding it. This setting is measured in pixels and can be a value between 0 and 250.
Anti-aliased	Determines the smoothness of the selection by softening the color transition between edge and background pixels.
Width	Determines the width within by detecting an edge from the pointer. This setting is measured in pixels and can have a value from 1 to 40.
Edge Contrast	Determines the tool's sensitivity. This setting can be a value between 1% and 100%: high values detect high-contrast edges.
Frequency	Determines the rate at which fastening points are applied. This setting can be a value between 0 and 100: high values insert more fastening points.

Move a complex selection to an existing document

1. Click the Move Tool on the toolbox.

    TIP   You can also click the Click to open the Tool Preset picker list arrow on the tool options bar, then double-click the Move Tool.

2. Drag the selection to the Family Portrait document.

    The selection appears on a new layer (Layer 2).

3. Drag the object so that the right edge of the dog's cheek snaps to the guide at 370 H and the bottom of the dog's front paw snaps to the guide at 520 V.

4. Drag Layer 1 to the Delete layer button on the Layers palette.

5. Save your work, then compare your image to Figure C-8.

6. Click Window on the menu bar, point to Documents, then click Sheepdog.tif.

7. Close the Sheepdog.tif document without saving your changes.

You dragged a complex selection into an existing Photoshop document. You positioned the object using ruler guides and deleted an unnecessary layer.

MODIFY A MARQUEE

What You'll Do

 In this lesson, you'll move and enlarge a marquee, drag a selection into a Photoshop document, then position a selection using ruler guides.

Changing the Size of a Marquee

Not all objects are easy to select. Sometimes, when you make a selection, you might need to change the size of the marquee.

The tool options bar contains selection buttons that help you add to and subtract from a marquee, or intersect with a selection. The marquee in Figure C-9 was modified into the one shown in Figure C-10 by clicking the Add to selection button. After the Add to selection button is active, you can draw an additional marquee (directly adjacent to the selection), and it will be added to the current marquee.

One method you can use to increase the size of a marquee is the Grow command. After you make a selection, you can increase the marquee size by clicking Select on the menu bar, then by clicking

Grow. The Grow command selects pixels adjacent to the marquee.

QUICKTIP

Sometimes all that is needed to enlarge a marquee is to create a small selection then use the Grow command on the Select menu.

Modifying a Marquee

While a selection is active, you can modify the marquee by expanding or contracting it, smoothing out its edges, or enlarging it to add a border around the selection. These four commands: Border, Smooth, Expand, and Contract are sub-menus of the Modify command, which is found on the Select menu. For example, you might want to enlarge your selection. Using the Expand command, you can increase the size of the selection, as shown in Figure C-11.

Moving a Marquee

After you create a marquee, you can move the marquee to another location in the same document or to another document entirely. To do this, position the pointer in the center of the selection, then drag the marquee to the new location.

QUICKTIP

You can always hide and display layers as necessary to facilitate making a selection.

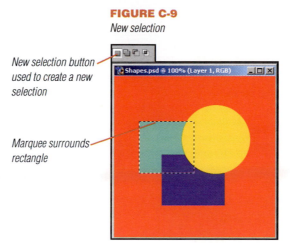

FIGURE C-9
New selection

New selection button used to create a new selection

Marquee surrounds rectangle

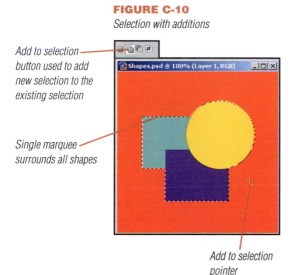

FIGURE C-10
Selection with additions

Add to selection button used to add new selection to the existing selection

Single marquee surrounds all shapes

Add to selection pointer

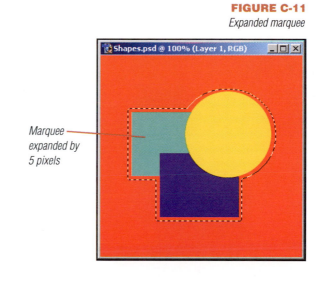

FIGURE C-11
Expanded marquee

Marquee expanded by 5 pixels

Move a marquee

1. Open Butterfly.tif.

2. Click the Elliptical Marquee Tool on the toolbox. ⬭

3. Click the New selection button on the tool options bar, if necessary. ▢

4. Drag the pointer from 50 H/50 V to 80 H/70 V. Compare your document to Figure C-12. ✛

5. Position the pointer in the center of the selection. ▷⋮⋮

6. Drag the pointer to 140 H/70 V, as shown in Figure C-13. ▸

   TIP You can also nudge a selection using the arrow keys. Each time you press an arrow key, the selection moves one pixel in the direction of the key.

You created a marquee, then dragged the marquee to reposition it.

FIGURE C-12
Marquee in document

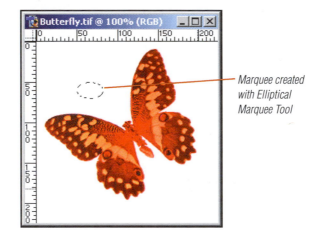

Marquee created
with Elliptical
Marquee Tool

FIGURE C-13
Moved marquee

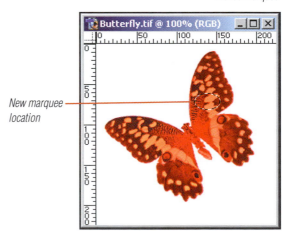

New marquee
location

FIGURE C-14

Expand Selection dialog box

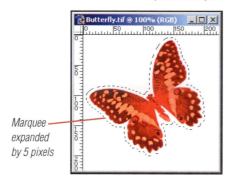

FIGURE C-15

Expanded marquee

Marquee
expanded
by 5 pixels

FIGURE C-16

Expanded selection moved to the Family Portrait document

Border formed
by expanding
the marquee

1. Click Select on the menu bar, then click Grow.

2. Click Select on the menu bar, then click Similar.

3. Click Select on the menu bar, point to Modify, then click Expand.

4. Type **5** in the Expand By text box of the Expand Selection dialog box, as shown in Figure C-14.

5. Click OK, then compare your selection to Figure C-15.

6. Click the Move Tool on the toolbox.

7. Position the pointer over the selection, then drag the selection to the Family Portrait document. ▶

8. Drag the butterfly so that the top-left wing is at 30 H/100 V.

9. Save your work, then compare your image to Figure C-16.

10. Make Butterfly.tif active.

11. Close Butterfly.tif without saving your changes.

You enlarged a selection marquee by using the Grow, Similar, and Expand commands, then you dragged the selection into an open document.

SELECT USING COLOR AND MODIFY A SELECTION

What You'll Do

 In this lesson, you'll make selections using both the Color Range command and the Magic Wand Tool. You'll also flip a selection, then fix an image using the Healing Brush Tool.

Selecting with Color

Selections based on color can be easy to make, especially when the background of an image is different from the image itself. High contrast between colors is an ideal condition for making selections based on color. You can make selections using color with the Color Range command on the Select menu, or you can use the Magic Wand Tool on the toolbox.

Using the Magic Wand Tool

When you select the Magic Wand Tool, the following options are available on the tool options bar:

- The four selection buttons.

- The Tolerance setting, which allows you to specify whether similar pixels will be selected. This setting has a value from 0 to 255, and the lower the value, the closer in color the selected pixels will be.
- The Anti-aliased check box, which softens the selection's appearance.
- The Contiguous check box, which lets you select pixels that are next to one another.
- The Use All Layers check box, which lets you select pixels from all layers.

Knowing which selection tool to use

The hardest part of making a selection might be determining which selection tool to use. How are you supposed to know if you should use a marquee tool or a lasso tool? The first question you need to ask yourself is, "What do I want to select?" Becoming proficient in making selections means that you need to assess the qualities of the object you want to select, and then decide which method to use. Ask yourself: Does the object have a definable shape? Does it have an identifiable edge? Are there common colors that can be used to create a selection?

See Figure C-17 to view the tool options bar when the Magic Wand Tool is selected.

Using the Color Range Command

You can use the Color Range command to make the same selections as with the Magic Wand Tool. When you use the Color Range command, the Color Range dialog box opens. This dialog box lets you use the pointer to identify which colors you want to use to make a selection. You can also select the Invert check box to *exclude* the chosen color from the selection. The **fuzziness** setting is similar to tolerance, in that the lower the value, the closer in color pixels must be to be selected.

QUICKTIP

The Color Range command does not give you the option of excluding contiguous pixels as does the Magic Wand Tool.

Transforming a Selection

After you place a selection in a Photoshop document, you can change its size and other qualities by clicking Edit on the menu bar, pointing to Transform, then clicking any of the commands on the sub-menu. After you select certain commands, small squares called **handles** surround the selection. To complete the command, you drag a handle until the image has the look you want, then press [Enter] (Win) or [return] (Mac). You can also use the Transfer submenu to flip a selection horizontally or vertically.

Using the Healing Brush Tool

If you place a selection then notice that the image has a few imperfections, you can fix the image. You can fix many imperfections (such as dirt, scratches, bulging veins on skin, or wrinkles on a face) using the Healing Brush Tool on the toolbox. This tool lets you sample an area that you want to duplicate, then paint over the imperfections. What is the result? The less-than-desirable pixels seem to disappear into the surrounding image. In addition to matching the sampled pixels, the Healing Brush Tool also matches the texture, lighting, and shading of the sample. This is why the painted pixels blend so effortlessly into the existing image.

QUICKTIP

A sample is taken by pressing and holding [Alt] (Win) or [option] (Mac) while dragging the pointer over the area you want to duplicate.

FIGURE C-17
Options for the Magic Wand Tool

Select using color range

1. Open Photographer.tif.

2. Click Select on the menu bar, then click Color Range.

3. Click the Image option button, if necessary.

4. Select the Invert check box.

5. Click anywhere in the white area surrounding the sample image.

6. Verify that your settings match those shown in Figure C-18, then click OK.

   The Color Range dialog box closes and the man in the image is selected.

7. Click the Move Tool on the toolbox.

8. Drag the selection into Family Portrait.psd, then position the selection as shown in Figure C-19.

You made a selection within an image using the Color Range command on the Select menu, and dragged the selection to an existing document.

FIGURE C-18
Completed Color Range dialog box

Modifies tolerance

Image sample appears here

Select check box to exclude selected color

FIGURE C-19
Selection in document

FIGURE C-20

Magic Wand Tool settings

FIGURE C-21

Selected area

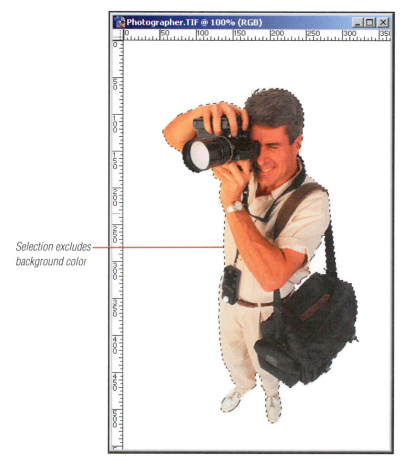

Selection excludes background color

Select using the Magic Wand Tool

1. Click the Indicates layer visibility button on Layer 4 of the Layers palette to hide it.

2. Make Photographer.tif active.

3. Click Select on the menu bar, then click Deselect.

4. Click the Magic Wand Tool on the toolbox.

5. Change the settings on the tool options bar to match those in Figure C-20.

6. Click anywhere in the white area of the image (such as 50 H/50 V).

7. Click Select on the menu bar, then click Inverse. Compare your selection to Figure C-21.

8. Click the Move Tool on the toolbox, then drag the selection into Family Portrait.psd.

You made a selection using the Magic Wand Tool, then dragged it into an existing document.

Flip a selection

1. Click Edit on the menu bar, point to Transform, then click Flip Horizontal.

2. Drag Layer 4 to the Delete layer button on the Layers palette, because it is no longer necessary.

3. Click Layer on the menu bar, point to Matting, then click Defringe.

4. Type **2** in the Width text box.

5. Click OK.

6. Drag the flipped selection so it is positioned as shown in Figure C-22.

7. Make Photographer.tif the active document, then close Photographer.tif without saving your changes.

You flipped and repositioned a selection.

FIGURE C-22
Flipped and positioned selection

Family Portrait.psd @ 100% (Layer 5, RGB)

Flipped selection
defringed

FIGURE C-23

Healing Brush Tool options

FIGURE C-24

Healed area

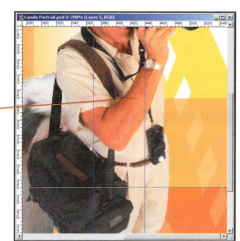

Veins removed
from image

FIGURE C-25

Image with fixed imperfections

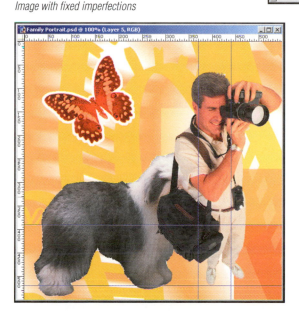

Fix imperfections with the Healing Brush Tool

1. Click the Zoom Tool on the toolbox. 🔍

2. Click the image at 400 H/300 V. 🔍

3. Click the Healing Brush Tool on the toolbox. Change the setting on your tool options bar to match those shown in Figure C-23. 🖊️

   TIP If you need to change the Brush settings, you can click the Click to open the Brush picker list arrow, then drag the sliders so the settings are 10 px diameter, 100% hardness, 25% spacing, 0° angle, 100% roundness, and pen pressure size.

4. Press and hold [Alt] (Win) or [option] (Mac), click the image at 400 H/300 V, then release [Alt] (Win) or [option] (Mac).

   You sampled an area so that you can use the Healing Brush Tool to paint a damaged area with the sample.

5. Click and drag the pointer over the photographer's vein (from approximately 435 H/250 V to 430 H/270 V).

6. Click and drag the pointer over the vein (from approximately 430 H/270 V to 410 H/285 V). Compare the repaired area to Figure C-24.

7. Click the Zoom Tool on the toolbox. 🔍

8. Press and hold [Alt] (Win) or [alt] (Mac), click the center of the image, then release [Alt] (Win) or [alt] (Mac). 🔍

9. Save your work, then compare your image to Figure C-25.

You used the Healing Brush Tool to fix imperfections in an image.

ADD A VIGNETTE EFFECT
TO A SELECTION

What You'll Do

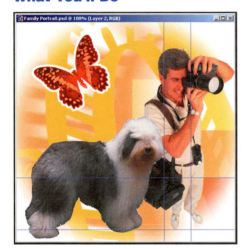

In this lesson, you'll create a vignette effect, using a layer mask and feathering.

Understanding Vignettes

Traditionally, a **vignette** is a picture or portrait whose border fades into the surrounding color at its edges. You can use a vignette effect to give an image an old-world appearance. You can also use a vignette effect to tone down an overwhelming background. You can create a vignette effect in Photoshop by creating a mask with a blurred edge. A **mask** lets you protect or modify a particular area and is created using a marquee.

Creating a Vignette

A **vignette effect** uses feathering to fade a marquee shape. The **feather** setting blurs the area between the selection and the surrounding pixels, which creates a distinctive fade at the edge of the selection. You can create a vignette effect by using a marquee or lasso tool to create a marquee in an image layer. After the selection is created, you can modify the feather setting (a 10- or 20-pixel setting creates a nice fade) to increase the blur effect on the outside edge of the selection. Click Layer on the menu bar, point to Add Layer Mask, then click Reveal Selection; the mask forms a frame resulting in a vignette.

FIGURE C-26
Marquee in document

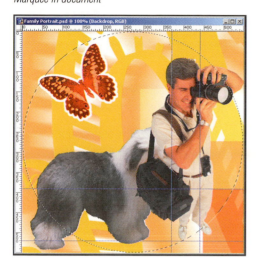

FIGURE C-28
Vignette effect in document

Vignette effect fades border

FIGURE C-27
Layers palette

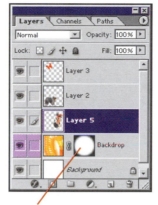

Feathered mask creates vignette effect

Create a vignette

1. Click the Backdrop layer on the Layers palette.

2. Click the Elliptical Marquee Tool on the toolbox.

3. Change the Feather setting on the tool options bar to 20.

4. Create a selection from 0 H/0 V to 550 H/550 V, as shown in Figure C-26.

5. Click Layer on the menu bar, point to Add Layer Mask, then click Reveal Selection.

   The vignette effect is added to the layer.

6. Click Layer 5 on the Layers palette, then drag it beneath Layer 2 to move the dog in front of the photographer. Compare your Layers palette to Figure C-27.

7. Click Layer 2, click Layer on the menu bar, point to Matting, then click Defringe.

8. Type **2** in the Width text box, then click OK.

9. Click View on the menu bar, then click Rulers to hide them.

10. Save your work, then compare your document to Figure C-28.

You created a vignette effect by adding a feathered layer mask. You also rearranged layers and defringed a selection.

Lesson 4   Add a Vignette Effect to a Selection

ADOBE PHOTOSHOP C-23

Power User Shortcuts

to do this:	use this method:
Copy selection	Click Edit ➤ Copy or [Ctrl][C] (Win) or ⌘ [C] (Mac)
Create vignette effect	Marquee or Lasso Tool, create selection, click Layer ➤ Add Layer Mask ➤ Reveal Selection
Cut selection	Click Edit ➤ Cut or [Ctrl][X] (Win) or ⌘ [X] (Mac)
Deselect object	Select ➤ Deselect or [Ctrl][D] (Win) or ⌘ [D] (Mac)
Elliptical Marquee Tool	⬭ or **Shift M**
Flip image	Edit ➤ Transform ➤ Flip Horizontal
Grow selection	Select ➤ Grow
Increase selection	Select ➤ Similar
Lasso Tool	⬭ or **Shift L**
Magnetic Lasso Tool	⬭ or **Shift L**
Move selection	⬭ or **V**

to do this:	use this method:
Move selection marquee	Position pointer in selection, drag to new location
Paste selection	Edit ➤ Paste or [Ctrl][V] (Win) or ⌘ [V] (Mac)
Polygonal Lasso Tool	⬭ or **Shift L**
Rectangular Marquee Tool	⬭ or **Shift M**
Reselect a deselected object	Select ➤ Reselect, or [Shift][Ctrl][D] (Win) or [Shift] ⌘ [D] (Mac)
Select all objects	Select ➤ All, or [Ctrl][A] (Win) or ⌘ [A] (Mac)
Select using color range	Select ➤ Color Range, click in sample area
Select using Magic Wand	⬭ or **W**, then click image with ⬭
Single Column Marquee Tool	⬭
Single Row Marquee Tool	⬭

Key: Menu items are indicated by ➤ between the menu name and its command.

Make a selection using shapes.

1. Open PS C-2.psd, then save it as **Everything Feline**.
2. Open Block cat.tif.
3. Display the rulers in each document, if necessary.
4. Use the Rectangular Marquee Tool to select the entire image in Block cat.tif. (*Hint*: Reset the Feather setting to O pixels, if necessary.)
5. Deselect the selection.
6. Use the Magnetic Lasso Tool to create a selection surrounding the Block cat. (*Hint*: You can use the Zoom Tool to make the image larger.)
7. Drag the selection into Everything Feline, positioning it so the right side of the cat is at 490 H, and the bottom of the right paw is at 450 V.
8. Save your work.
9. Close Block cat.tif without saving any changes.

Modify a marquee.

1. Open Calico cat.tif.
2. Create an elliptical marquee from 100 H/50 V to 200 H/100 V.
3. Use the Grow command on the Select menu.
4. Use the Inverse command on the Select menu.
5. Drag the selection into Everything Feline, positioning it so the upper-left corner is near 0 H/0 V.
6. Defringe the cat using a width of 2 pixels.

7. Save your work.
8. Close Calico cat.tif without saving any changes.

Select using color and modify a selection.

1. Open Kitten.tif.
2. Use the Color Range dialog box to select only the kitten.
3. Drag the selection into Everything Feline.
4. Flip the kitten image (in Everything Feline) horizontally.
5. Position the kitten image so the bottom right snaps to the ruler guides at 230 H/450 V.

FIGURE C-29
Completed Skills Review

6. Defringe the kitten using a width of 2 pixels.
7. Save your work.
8. Close Kitten.tif without saving any changes.

Add a vignette effect to a selection.

1. Use a 15-pixel feather setting and the Backdrop layer to create an elliptical selection surrounding the contents of Everything Feline.
2. Add a layer mask that reveals the selection.
3. Display the Everything Feline layer.
4. Turn off the rulers display, if necessary.
5. Save your work.
6. Compare your document to Figure C-29.

The FBI has hired you to create a new image for its personal investigation division. You have created the background artwork, but need to find other images to complete the assignment. Your employers want to stay with the theme of surveillance, and request that you use legal sources of artwork.

1. Open PS C-3.psd, then save it as **FBI**. (*Hint*: Click Update to close the warning box regarding missing fonts, if necessary.)
2. Open Plug.tif, then use the Magnetic Lasso Tool to select the plug and the wire.
3. Position the selection within FBI. (*Hint*: You can scale a selection, using the Transform command on the Edit menu, if you want it to be larger or smaller.)
4. Close Plug.tif without saving any changes.
5. Open Satellite.tif, then use the Color Range dialog box or the Magnetic Lasso Tool to isolate the antennae and satellites within the image. (*Hint*: You might have to use a combination of several methods to isolate the image.)
6. Position the selection within FBI.
7. Close Satellite.tif without saving any changes.
8. Open Headphones.tif, then use any selection method to select the Headphones.
9. Position the selection within FBI.

10. Close Headphones.tif without saving any changes.
11. Display the Type layer, then move the type to the top of the document.

FIGURE C-30
Completed Project Builder 1

12. Defringe any layers, as necessary.
13. Save your work, then compare your document to the sample in Figure C-30.

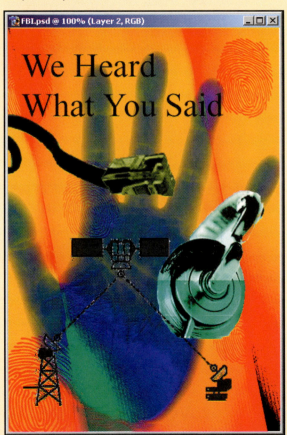

FBI.psd @ 100% (Layer 2, RGB)

We Heard
What You Said

The Boston Athletic Association, which sponsors the Boston Marathon, is holding a contest for artwork to announce the upcoming marathon. Submissions can be created on paper or computer-generated. You feel you have a good chance at winning this contest, using Photoshop as your tool.

1. Open PS C-4.psd, then save it as **Marathon Contest**.
2. Locate at least two pieces of appropriate artwork—either on your hard disk, in a royalty-free collection, or from scanned images—that you can use in this document.
3. Use any appropriate methods to select imagery from the artwork.
4. After the selections have been made, copy each selection into Marathon Contest.
5. Arrange the imagery in a professional design that is sure to win the contest.
6. Deselect the selections in the files you are no longer using, and close them without saving the changes.
7. Add a vignette effect to the Backdrop layer.
8. Display the type layers.
9. Defringe any layers, as necessary.
10. Save your work, then compare your document to the sample in Figure C-31.

FIGURE C-31
Completed Project Builder 2

Making Selections

DESIGN PROJECT

You are aware that there will be an opening in your firm's design department. Before you can be considered for the job, you need to increase your Photoshop compositing knowledge and experience. You have decided to teach yourself, using informational sources on the Internet and images that can be scanned or purchased.

1. Connect to the Internet and use your browser and favorite search engine to find information on image compositing. One possible site is located in the Student Online Companion. Go to *www.course.com*, navigate to the page for this book, click the Student Online Companion link, then click the link for this unit.
2. Create a new Photoshop document, using the dimensions of your choice, then save it as **Sample Compositing**.
3. Locate at least two pieces of artwork—either on your hard disk, in a royalty-free collection, or from scanned images—that you can use.
4. Use any appropriate methods to select imagery from the artwork.
5. Select the images in the artwork, then copy each into Sample Compositing, using the method of your choice.
6. Rename each of the layers using meaningful names.
7. Apply a color to each new layer.

8. Arrange the imagery in a pleasing design. (*Hint*: You can flip any image, if necessary.)
9. Deselect the selections in the artwork, then close the files without saving the changes.
10. If necessary, add a vignette effect to a layer.
11. Defringe any images, if necessary.

FIGURE C-32
Completed Design Project

12. Save your work, then compare your document to the sample in Figure C-32.
13. Make notes as you work regarding the information you find, print out at least one of the Web sites you visited, and be prepared to discuss your findings.

Depending on the size of your group, you can assign individual elements of the project to group members, or work collectively to create the finished product.

An anonymous Fortune 500 client plans to start a 24-hour cable sports network called Totally Sports that will cover any nonprofessional sporting events. You have been asked to create some preliminary designs for the network, using images from multiple sources.

1. Open PS C-5.psd, then save this file as **Totally Sports**. (*Hint*: Click Update to close the warning box regarding missing fonts, if necessary.)
2. Locate several pieces of sports-related artwork—either on your hard disk, in a royalty-free collection, or from scanned images. Remember that the images should not show professional sports figures, if possible.
3. Select imagery from the artwork and move it into Totally Sports.
4. Arrange the images in an interesting design. (*Hint*: You can flip any image, if necessary.)
5. Change each layer name to describe the sport in the layer image.
6. Deselect the selections in the files that you used, then close the files without saving the changes.

7. If necessary, add a vignette effect to a layer and/or adjust opacity. (In the sample, the opacity of the Backdrop layer was adjusted to 100%.)

8. Defringe any images if necessary.
9. Save your work, then compare your document to the sample in Figure C-33.

FIGURE C-33
Completed Group Project

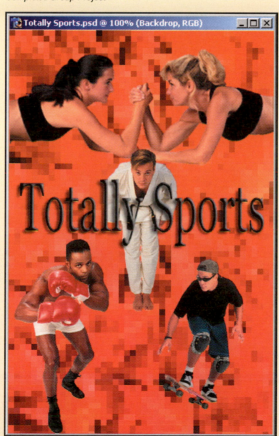

UNIT D

INCORPORATING COLOR TECHNIQUES

1. Work with color to transform a document.

2. Use the Color Picker and the Swatches palette.

3. Place a border around an image.

4. Blend colors using the Gradient Tool.

5. Add color to a grayscale image.

6. Use filters, opacity, and blending modes.

INCORPORATING COLOR TECHNIQUES

Using Color

Color can make or break an image. Sometimes colors can draw us into an image; other times they can repel us. We all know what colors we like, but when it comes to creating an image, it is helpful to have some knowledge of color theory and be familiar with color terminology.

Understanding how Photoshop measures, displays, and prints color can be valuable when you create new images or modify existing images. Some colors you choose might be difficult for a professional printer to reproduce or might look muddy when printed. As you become more experienced using colors, you will learn which colors can be reproduced well and which ones cannot.

Understanding Color Modes and Color Models

Photoshop displays and prints images using specific color modes. A **mode** is the amount of color data that can be stored in a given file format, based on an established model. A **model** determines how pigments combine to produce resulting colors. This is the way your computer or printer associates a name or numbers with colors. Photoshop uses standard color models as the basis for its color modes.

Displaying and Printing Images

An image shown on your monitor, such as an icon on your desktop, is a **bitmap**, a geometric arrangement of different color dots on a rectangular grid. Each dot, called a **pixel**, represents a color or shade. Bitmapped images are *resolution-dependent* and can lose detail—often demonstrated by a jagged appearance—when highly magnified. When printed, images with high resolutions tend to show more detail and subtler color transitions than low-resolution images.

Tools You'll Use

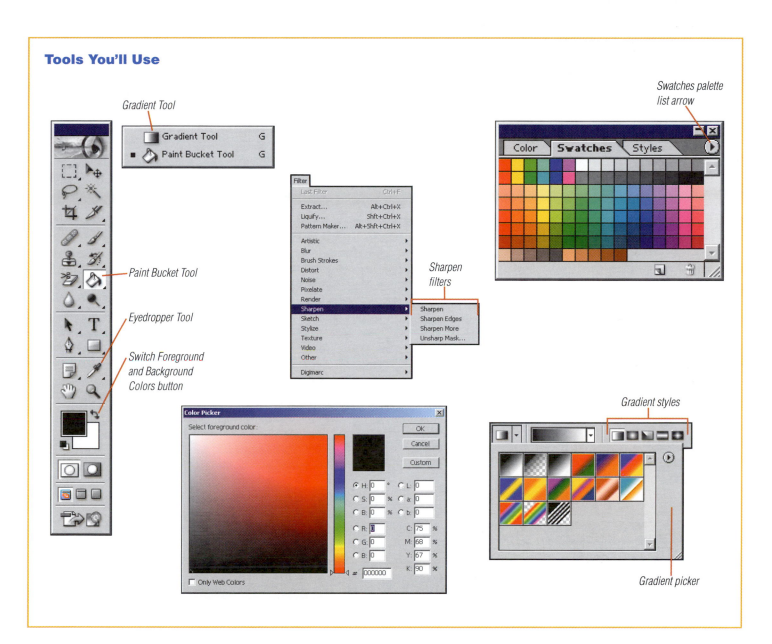

Gradient Tool

Gradient Tool   G

Paint Bucket Tool   G

Paint Bucket Tool

Eyedropper Tool

Switch Foreground
and Background
Colors button

Swatches palette
list arrow

Sharpen
filters

Gradient styles

Gradient picker

WORK WITH COLOR TO TRANSFORM A DOCUMENT

What You'll Do

In this lesson, you'll use the Color palette, the Paint Bucket Tool, and the Eyedropper Tool to add a new color to the background.

Learning About Color Models

Photoshop reproduces colors using models of color modes. The range of displayed colors, or **gamut**, for each model, is shown in Figure D-1. The shape of each color gamut indicates the range of colors it can display. If a color is out of gamut, it is beyond the color space that your monitor can display or that your printer can print. You select the color mode from the Mode command on the Image menu.

QUICKTIP

A color mode is used to determine which color model will be used to display and print an image.

Understanding the psychology of color

Have you ever wondered why some colors make you react a certain way? You might have noticed that some colors affect you differently than others. Color is such an important part of our lives, and in Photoshop, it's key. Specific colors are used in print and Web pages to evoke the following responses:

- Blue tends to instill a feeling of safety and stability and is commonly used by financial services.
- Certain shades of green can generate a soft, calming feeling, while others suggest youthfulness and growth.
- Red commands attention and can be used as a call to action; it can also distract a reader's attention from other content.
- White evokes the feeling of purity and innocence, looks cool and fresh, and is often used to suggest luxury.
- Black conveys feelings of power and strength, but can suggest darkness and negativity.

L*a*b Model

The L*a*b model is based on one luminance (lightness) component and two chromatic components (from green to red, and from blue to yellow). Using the L*a*b model has distinct advantages: you have the largest number of colors available to you and the greatest precision with which to create them. You can also create all the colors contained by other color models, which are limited in their respective color ranges. The L*a*b model is device-independent—the colors will not vary, regardless of the hardware. Use this model when working with photo CD images so that you can independently edit the luminance and color values.

HSB Model

Based on the human perception of color, the HSB (Hue, Saturation, Brightness) model has three fundamental characteristics: hue, saturation, and brightness. The color reflected from or transmitted through an object is called **hue**. Expressed as a degree (between 0° and 360°), each hue is identified by a color name (such as red or green). **Saturation** (or *chroma*) is the strength or purity of the color, representing the amount of gray in proportion to hue. Saturation is measured as a percentage from 0% (gray) to 100% (fully saturated). **Brightness** is the measurement of relative lightness or darkness of a color and is measured as a percentage from 0% (black) to 100% (white). Although you can use the HSB model to define a color on the Color palette or in the Color Picker dialog box, Photoshop does not offer HSB mode as a choice for creating or editing images.

RGB Mode

Photoshop uses color modes to determine how to display and print an image. Each mode is based on established models used in color reproduction. Most colors in the visible spectrum can be represented by mixing various proportions and intensities of red, green, and blue (RGB) colored light. RGB colors are additive colors. **Additive colors** are used for lighting, video, and computer monitors; color is created by light passing through red, green, and blue phosphors. When the values of red, green, and blue are zero, the result is black; when the values are all 255, the result is white. Photoshop assigns each component of the RGB mode an intensity value. Your colors can vary from monitor to monitor even if you are using the exact RGB values on different computers.

FIGURE D-1
Photoshop color gamuts

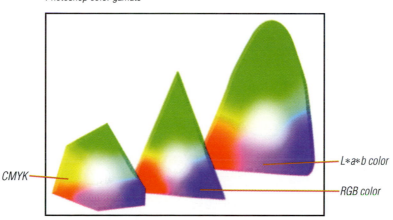

CMYK

L*a*b color

RGB color

CMYK Mode

The light-absorbing quality of ink printed on paper is the basis of the CMYK (Cyan, Magenta, Yellow, Black) mode. Unlike the RGB mode—in which components are *combined* to create new colors—the CMYK mode is based on colors being partially *absorbed* as the ink hits the paper and being partially *reflected* back to your eyes. CMYK colors are **subtractive colors**—the *absence* of cyan, magenta, yellow, and black creates white. Subtractive (CMYK) and additive (RGB) colors are complementary colors; a pair from one model creates a color in the other. When combined, cyan, magenta, and yellow absorb all color and produce black. The CMYK mode—in which the lightest colors are assigned the highest percentages of ink colors—is used in four-color process printing. Converting an RGB image into a CMYK image produces a **color separation** (the commercial printing process

of separating colors for use with different inks). Note, however, that because your monitor uses RGB mode, you will not see the exact colors until you print the image, and even then the colors can vary depending on the printer and offset press.

Understanding the Bitmap and Grayscale Modes

In addition to the RGB and CMYK modes, Photoshop provides two specialized color modes: bitmap and grayscale. The **bitmap mode** uses black or white color values to represent image pixels, and is a good choice for images with subtle color gradations, such as photographs or painted images. The **grayscale mode** uses up to 256 shades of gray, assigning a brightness value from 0 (black) to 255 (white) to each pixel. Displayed colors can vary from monitor to monitor even if you use identical color settings on different computers.

Using Foreground and Background Colors

In Photoshop, the **foreground color** is black by default and is used to paint, fill, and apply a border to a selection. The **background color** is white by default and is used

to make **gradient fills** (gradual blends of multiple colors) and fill in areas of an image that have been erased. You can change the foreground and background colors using the Color palette, the Swatches palette, the Color Picker, or the Eyedropper Tool. You can restore the default colors by clicking the Default Foreground and Background Colors button on the toolbox, shown in Figure D-2. You can apply a color to the background of a layer using the Paint Bucket Tool. When you click an image with the Paint Bucket Tool, the current foreground color on the toolbox fills the background of the active layer.

FIGURE D-2
Foreground and background color buttons

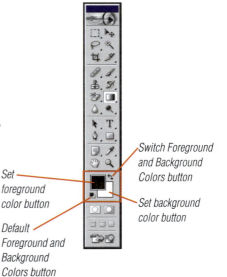

Switch Foreground and Background Colors button

Set foreground color button

Set background color button

Default Foreground and Background Colors button

FIGURE D-3

Document with rulers displayed

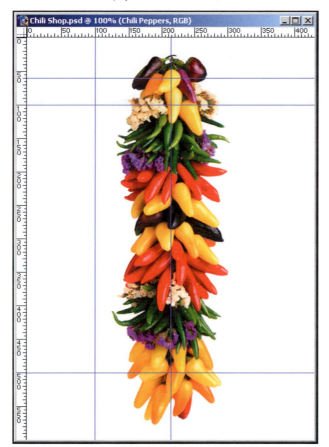

1. Start Photoshop, open PS D-1.psd, then save it as **Chili Shop**.

2. Click the Default Foreground and Background Colors button on the toolbox. ◼

3. Display the rulers in pixels if necessary, then compare your screen to Figure D-3.

    TIP   You can right-click (Win) or [control] click (Mac) one of the rulers to choose Pixels, Inches, Centimeters, Millimeters, Points, Picas, or Percent as a unit of measurement, instead of using the Rulers and Units Preferences dialog box.

You set the default foreground and background colors and displayed rulers in pixels.

Change the background color using the Color palette

1. Click the Background layer on the Layers palette. 👆

2. Click the Color palette tab. `Color`

3. Drag each color slider on the Color palette to the right until you reach the values shown in Figure D-4.

   The active color changes to the new color. Did you notice that this document is using the RGB mode?

   > **TIP** You can also double-click each component's text box on the Color palette and type the color values.

4. Click the Paint Bucket Tool on the toolbox. 🪣

   > **TIP** If the Paint Bucket Tool is not visible on the toolbox, click the Gradient Tool on the toolbox, press and hold the mouse button until the list of hidden tools appears, then click the Paint Bucket Tool.

5. Click the image. 🪣

6. Drag the Paint Bucket state on the History palette onto the Delete current state button. 🗑

   > **TIP** You can also undo the last action by clicking Edit on the menu bar, then clicking Undo Paint Bucket.

You set new values in the Color palette, used the Paint Bucket Tool to change the background to that color, then undid the change.

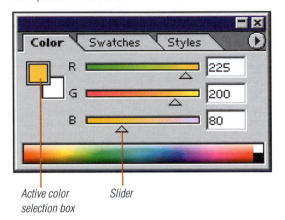

Active color
selection box   Slider

Using ruler coordinates

Photoshop rulers run along the top and left-hand sides of the document window. Each point on an image has a horizontal and vertical location. These two numbers, called x and y coordinates, appear in the Info palette (which is located behind the Navigator palette). The x coordinate refers to the horizontal location, and the y coordinate refers to the vertical location. You can use the guides to identify coordinates of a location, such as a color you want to sample. If you have difficulty seeing the ruler markings, you can increase the size of the image; the greater the zoom factor, the more detailed the measurement hashes.

FIGURE D-5

New foreground color applied to Background layer

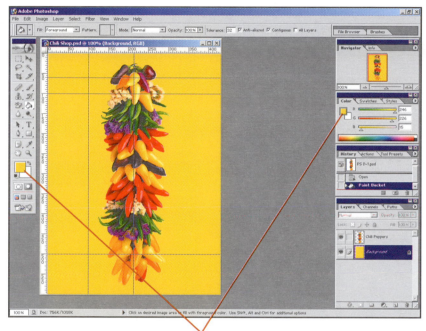

New foreground color

1. Click the Background layer on the Layers palette to make it active.

2. Click the Eyedropper Tool on the toolbox.

3. Click the image at 215 H/60 V, using the blue guides to help ensure accuracy.

   The Set foreground color button displays the color that you clicked (or sampled).

4. Click the Paint Bucket Tool on the toolbox.

5. Click the image, then compare your document to Figure D-5.

   TIP Your color values on the Color palette might vary from the sample.

6. Save your work.

You used the Eyedropper Tool to sample a color as the foreground color, then used the Paint Bucket Tool to change the background color to the color you sampled.

USE THE COLOR PICKER AND THE SWATCHES PALETTE

What You'll Do

 In this lesson, you'll use the Color Picker and the Swatches palette to select new colors, then you'll add a new color to the background and the swatches palette.

Making Selections from the Color Picker

Depending on the color model you are using, you can select colors using the **Color Picker**, a feature that lets you choose a color from a color spectrum or lets you numerically define a custom color. You can change colors in the Color Picker dialog box by using the following methods:

■ Drag the sliders along the vertical color bar.

■ Click inside the vertical color bar.

■ Click inside the Color field.

■ Enter a value in any of the text boxes.

A circular marker indicates the active color. The color slider displays the range of color levels available for the active color component. The adjustments you make by dragging or clicking on a new color are reflected in the text boxes; when you choose a new color, the previous color appears beneath it.

Using the Swatches Palette

You can also change colors using the Swatches palette. The **Swatches palette** is a visual display of colors you can choose from. You can add your own colors to the palette by sampling a color from an image, and you can also delete colors. When you add a swatch to the Swatches palette, Photoshop assigns a default name that has a sequential number, or you can name the swatch whatever you like. Photoshop places new swatches in the first available space at the end of the palette. You can view swatch names by clicking the Swatches palette list arrow, then clicking Small List. You can restore the default Swatches palette by clicking the Swatches palette list arrow, clicking Reset Swatches, then clicking OK. Figure D-6 shows a color in the Color Picker dialog box and on the Swatches palette.

FIGURE D-6

Color Picker dialog box and Swatches palette

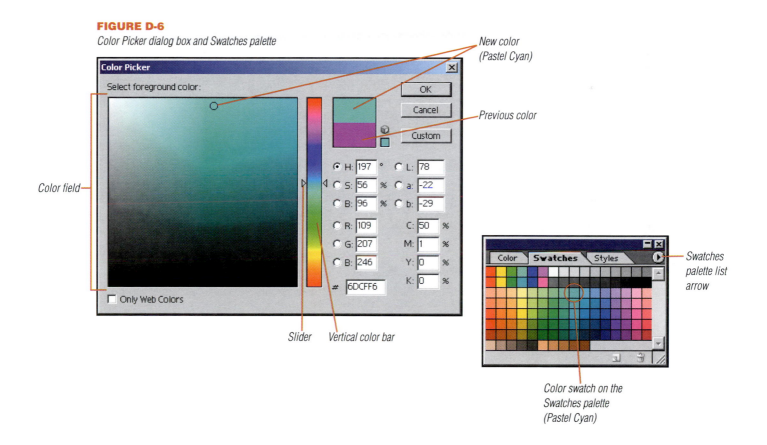

New color
(Pastel Cyan)

Previous color

Color field

Swatches palette list arrow

Slider   Vertical color bar

Color swatch on the
Swatches palette
(Pastel Cyan)

Select a color from the Color Picker

1. Click the Set foreground color button on the toolbox, then verify that the Hue (H) option button is selected in the Color Picker dialog box.

2. Click the R (Red) option button.

3. Click the bottom-right corner of the Color field (fuchsia), as shown in Figure D-7.

   TIP If the out-of-gamut indicator appears next to the color, then this color exceeds the printable range.

4. Click OK.

You opened the Color Picker dialog box, selected a different color palette, and then selected a new color.

Select a color from the Swatches palette

1. Click the Swatches palette tab.

   Swatches

2. Click the second swatch from the left in the first row, as shown in Figure D-8.

   Did you notice that the foreground color (on the toolbox) changed to a lighter, brighter yellow?

3. Click the Paint Bucket Tool on the toolbox.

4. Click the image, then compare your screen to Figure D-9.

You opened the Swatches palette, selected a color, and then used the Paint Bucket Tool to change the background to that color.

FIGURE D-7

Color Picker dialog box

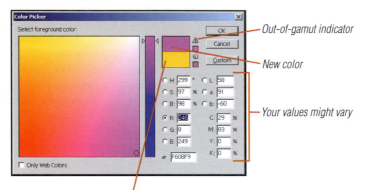

Out-of-gamut indicator

New color

Your values might vary

Previous color

FIGURE D-8

Swatches palette

Your swatches on the last row might vary

FIGURE D-9

New foreground color applied to Background layer

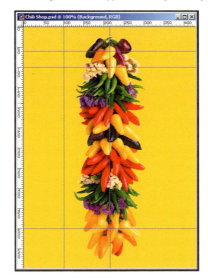

FIGURE D-10

Swatch added to Swatches palette

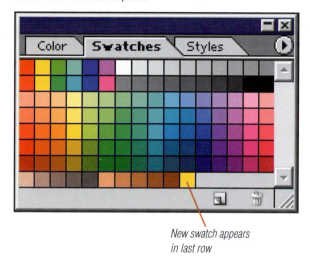

New swatch appears
in last row

1. Click the Eyedropper Tool on the
   toolbox.
2. Click one of the light yellow peppers.
3. Click an empty position in the last row of the
   Swatches palette.
4. Click OK to accept the default swatch name
   in the Color Swatch Name dialog box.

   TIP To delete a color from the Swatches
   palette, press [Alt] (Win) or [command]
   (Mac), position the pointer over a swatch,
   then click the swatch.

5. Save your work, then compare the
   new swatch in your Swatches palette to
   Figure D-10.

*You used the Eyedropper Tool to sample a color,
and then added the color to the Swatches palette.*

PLACE A BORDER AROUND AN IMAGE

What You'll Do

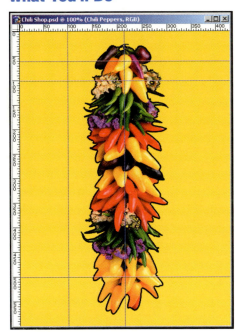

In this lesson, you'll add a border to an image.

Emphasizing an Image

You can emphasize an image by placing a border along its edges. This process is called **stroking the edges**. The default color of the border is the current foreground color on the toolbox. You can change the width, color, location, and blending mode of a border using the Stroke dialog box. The default stroke width is the setting last applied; you can apply a width from 1 to 16 pixels. The location option buttons determine where the border will be placed. If you want to change the location of the stroke, you must first delete the previously applied stroke, or Photoshop will apply the new border over the existing one.

Locking Transparent Pixels

As you modify layers, you can lock some properties to protect their contents. The ability to lock—or protect—elements within a layer is controlled from within the Layers palette, as shown in Figure D-11. It's a good idea to lock transparent pixels when you add borders so that stray marks

will not be included in the stroke. You can lock the following layer properties:

- Transparency: Limits editing capabilities to areas in a layer that are opaque.
- Image: Makes it impossible to modify layer pixels using painting tools.
- Position: Prevents pixels within a layer from being moved.

QUICKTIP

You can only lock transparency or image pixels in a layer containing an image, not type.

FIGURE D-11
Layers palette locking options

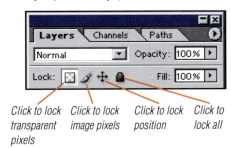

Click to lock transparent pixels   Click to lock image pixels   Click to lock position   Click to lock all

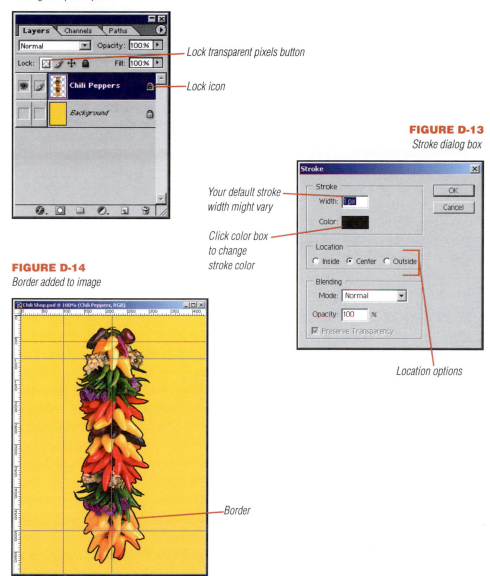

FIGURE D-12
Locking transparent pixels

Lock transparent pixels button

Lock icon

FIGURE D-13
Stroke dialog box

Your default stroke width might vary

Click color box to change stroke color

Location options

FIGURE D-14
Border added to image

Border

Create a border

1. Click the Indicates layer visibility button on the Background layer on the Layers palette.

   TIP You can click the Indicates layer visibility button to hide distracting layers.

2. Click the Default Foreground and Background Colors button on the toolbox to change the Foreground Color button to black.

   The foreground color will become the default border color.

3. Click the Chili Peppers layer on the Layers palette.

4. Click the Lock transparent pixels button on the Layers palette. See Figure D-12.

   The border will only be applied to the pixels on the edge of the chili peppers.

5. Click Edit on the menu bar, then click Stroke to open the Stroke dialog box. See Figure D-13.

6. Type **3** in the Width text box, click the Inside option button, then click OK.

   TIP Determining the correct border location can be confusing. Try different settings until you achieve the look you want.

7. Click the Indicates layer visibility button on the Background layer on the Layers palette.

8. Save your work, then compare your image to Figure D-14.

You hid a layer, changed the foreground color to black, locked transparent pixels, then used the Stroke dialog box to apply a border to the image.

BLEND COLORS USING THE GRADIENT TOOL

What You'll Do

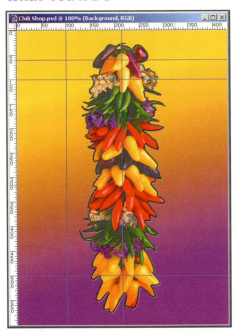

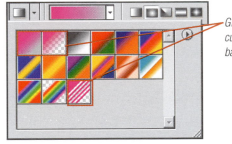

In this lesson, you'll create a gradient fill from a sampled color and a swatch, then apply it to the background.

Understanding Gradients

A **gradient fill**, or simply **gradient**, is a blend of colors used to fill a selection of a layer or an entire layer. A gradient's appearance is determined by its beginning and ending points, and its length, direction, and angle. Gradients allow you to create dramatic effects, using existing color combinations or your own colors. The Gradient picker, as shown in Figure D-15, offers multicolor gradient fills and a few that use the current foreground or background colors on the toolbox.

FIGURE D-15
Gradient picker

Gradient fills that use current foreground or background colors

Using the Gradient Tool

You use the Gradient Tool to create gradients in Photoshop. When you choose the Gradient Tool, five gradient styles become available on the tool options bar. The five gradient styles—Linear, Radial, Angle, Reflected, and Diamond—are shown in Figure D-16. In each example, the gradient was drawn from 50 H/50 V to 100 H/100 V.

Customizing Gradients

Using the **gradient presets**—predesigned gradient fills that are displayed in the Gradient picker—is a great way to learn how to use gradients. But as you become more familiar with Photoshop, you might want to venture into the world of the unknown and create your own gradient designs. You can create your own designs by modifying an existing gradient using the Gradient Editor. You can open the Gradient Editor, shown in Figure D-17, by clicking the selected gradient pattern that appears on the tool options bar. After it's open, you can use it to make the following modifications:

■ Create a new gradient from an existing gradient.
■ Modify an existing gradient.
■ Add intermediate colors to a gradient.
■ Create a blend between more than two colors.
■ Adjust the opacity values.
■ Determine the placement of the midpoint.

FIGURE D-16
Sample gradients

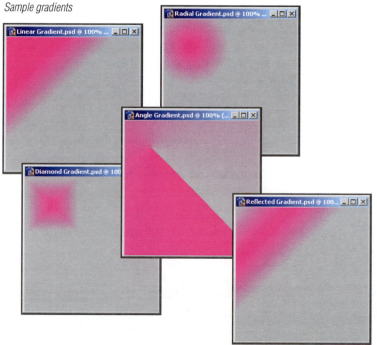

FIGURE D-17
Gradient Editor dialog box

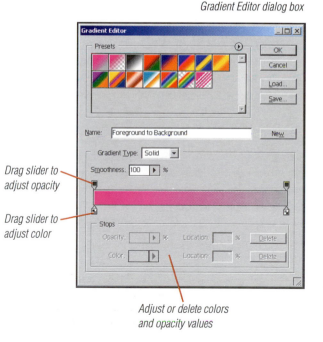

Drag slider to adjust opacity

Drag slider to adjust color

Adjust or delete colors and opacity values

Create a gradient from a sample color

1. Verify that the Eyedropper Tool is selected.

2. Click the image at 245 H/450 V.

   TIP To accurately select the coordinates, adjust the zoom factor as necessary.

3. Click the Switch Foreground and Background Colors button on the toolbox.

4. Click Swatch 1 on the Swatches palette (the new swatch you previously added to the Swatches palette).

5. Click the Indicates layer visibility button on the Chili Peppers layer.

6. Click the Background layer on the Layers palette to make it active, as shown in Figure D-18.

7. Click the Paint Bucket Tool on the toolbox, then press and hold the mouse button until the list of hidden tools appears.

8. Click the Gradient Tool, then click the Linear Gradient button on the tool options bar, if necessary.

9. Click the Click to open Gradient picker list arrow on the tool options bar, then click Foreground to Background (the first gradient fill in the first row), as shown in Figure D-19.

You sampled a color on the image to set the background color, changed the foreground color using an existing swatch, selected the Gradient Tool, and then chose a gradient fill and style.

FIGURE D-18
Chili Peppers layer hidden

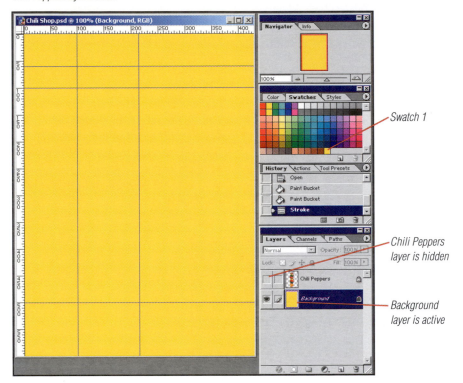

Swatch 1

Chili Peppers layer is hidden

Background layer is active

FIGURE D-19
Gradient picker

Click to open Gradient picker list arrow

Gradient styles

Foreground to Background (current foreground and background colors)

Gradient picker

FIGURE D-20
Gradient fill applied to Background layer

1. Click the Click to open Gradient picker list arrow to close the Gradient picker.

> **TIP** You can also close the Gradient picker by pressing [Esc](Win) or [esc](Mac).

2. Drag the pointer from 100 H/60 V to 215 H/500 V in the document window.

3. Click the Indicates layer visibility button on the Chili Peppers layer.

The chili peppers layer appears against the new background, as shown in Figure D-20.

> **TIP** It is a good idea to save your work early and often in the creation process, especially before making significant changes or printing.

4. Save your work.

You applied the gradient fill to the background.

ADD COLOR TO A GRAYSCALE IMAGE

What You'll Do

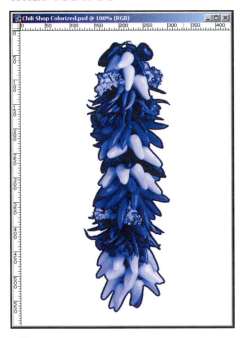

In this lesson, you'll convert an image to grayscale, change the color mode, then colorize a grayscale image using the Hue/Saturation dialog box.

Colorizing Options

Grayscale images can contain up to 256 shades of gray, assigning a brightness value from 0 (black) to 255 (white) to each pixel. Since the earliest days of photography, people have been tinting grayscale images with color to create a certain mood or emphasize an image in a way that brightly colored photographs could not. To capture this effect in Photoshop, you convert an image to the Grayscale mode, then choose the color mode you want to work in before you continue. When you apply a color to a grayscale image, each pixel becomes a shade of that particular color instead of gray.

Converting Grayscale and Color Modes

When you convert a color image to grayscale, the light and dark values—called the **luminosity**—remain, while the color information is deleted. When you change from grayscale to a color mode, the foreground and background colors on the toolbox change from black and white to the previously selected colors.

Colorizing a Grayscale Image

In order for a grayscale image to be colorized, you must change the color mode to one that accommodates color. After you change the color mode, and then adjust settings in the Hue/Saturation dialog box, Photoshop will determine the colorization range based on the hue of the currently selected foreground color. If you want a different colorization range, you need to change the foreground color.

FIGURE D-21
Gradient Map dialog box

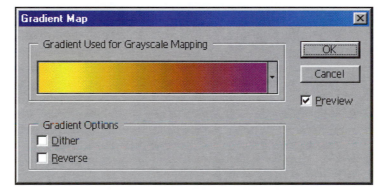

Applying a gradient effect

You can also use the Gradient Map to apply a colored gradient effect to a grayscale image. The Gradient Map uses gradient fills (the same ones displayed in the Gradient picker) to colorize the image, which can produce some stunning effects. You use the Gradient Map dialog box, shown in Figure D-21, to apply a gradient effect to a grayscale image. You can access the Gradient Map dialog box using the Adjustments command on the Image menu.

Change the color mode

1. Open PS D-2.psd, then save it as **Chili Shop Colorized**.

2. Click Image on the menu bar, point to Mode, then click Grayscale.

3. Click Flatten to close the warning box.

   The color mode of the document is changed to grayscale, and the image is flattened so there is only a single layer. All the color information in the image has been discarded.

4. Click Image on the menu bar, point to Mode, then click RGB Color.

   The color mode is changed back to RGB color, although there is still no color in the image.

5. Click Image on the menu bar, point to Adjustments, then click Hue/Saturation to open the Hue/Saturation dialog box, as shown in Figure D-22.

6. Select the Colorize check box in the Hue/Saturation dialog box.

You converted the image to Grayscale, then you changed the color mode to RGB color.

FIGURE D-22
Hue/Saturation dialog box

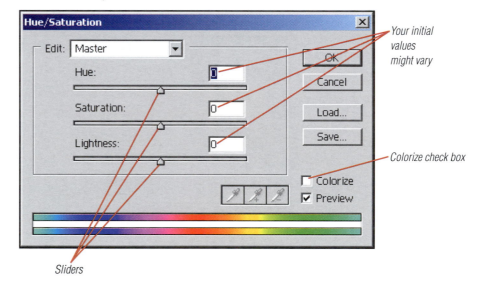

FIGURE D-23

Colorized image

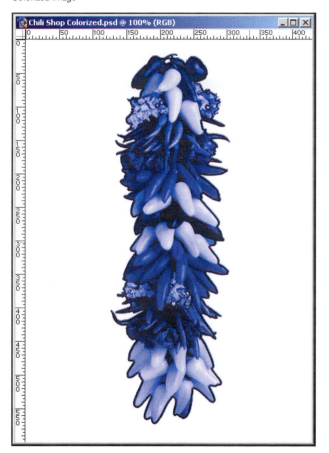

1. Drag the Hue slider until the text box displays 240.

    TIP You can also type values in the text boxes in the Hue/Saturation dialog box. Negative numbers must be preceded by a minus symbol or a hyphen. Positive numbers can be preceded by a plus sign (+), but it is optional.

2. Drag the Saturation slider until the text box displays 45.

3. Drag the Lightness slider until the text box displays +10.

4. Click OK.

5. Save your work, then compare your document to Figure D-23.

You colorized a grayscale image by adjusting settings in the Hue/Saturation dialog box.

USE FILTERS, OPACITY
AND BLENDING MODES

What You'll Do

In this lesson, you'll adjust the brightness and contrast, apply a Sharpen filter, and adjust the opacity of the lines applied by the filter. You'll also adjust the color balance of the Chili Shop document.

Manipulating an Image

As you work in Photoshop, you might realize that some images have fundamental problems that need correcting, while others just need to be further enhanced. For example, you might need to adjust an image's contrast and sharpness, or you might want to colorize an otherwise dull image. You can use a variety of techniques to change the way an image looks. For example, you can use the Adjustments command on the Image menu to modify hue and saturation, as well as brightness and contrast.

Understanding Filters

Filters are Photoshop commands that can significantly alter an image's appearance. Experimenting with Photoshop's filters is a fun way to add a different effect to your image. For example, the Watercolor filter gives the illusion that your image was

Fixing blurry scanned images

An unfortunate result of scanning a picture is that the image can become blurry. You can fix this, however, using the Unsharp Mask filter. This filter both sharpens and smoothes the image by increasing the contrast along element edges. Here's how it works: the smoothing effect removes stray marks, and the sharpening effect emphasizes contrasting neighboring pixels. Most scanners come with their own Unsharp Masks built into the TWAIN driver, but using Photoshop, you have access to a more powerful version of this filter. You can use Photoshop's Unsharp Mask to control the sharpening process by adjusting key settings. In most cases, your scanner's Unsharp Mask might not give you this flexibility. Regardless of the technical aspects, the result is a sharper image. You can apply the Unsharp Mark by clicking Filter on the menu bar, pointing to Sharpen, then click Unsharp Mask.

painted using traditional watercolors. Sharpen filters can appear to add definition to the entire image, or just the edges. Compare the different Sharpen filters applied in Figure D-24. The **Sharpen More filter** increases the contrast of adjacent pixels and can focus a blurry image. Be careful not to overuse sharpening tools (or any filter), because you can create high-contrast lines or add graininess in color or brightness.

Choosing Blending Modes

A **blending mode** controls how pixels are either made darker or lighter based on underlying colors. Photoshop provides a variety of blending modes, listed in Table D-1, to combine the color of the pixels in the current layer with those in layer(s) beneath it. You can see a list of blending modes by clicking the Add a layer style button on the Layers palette.

Understanding Blending Mode Components

You should consider the following underlying colors when planning a blending mode: **base color**, which is the original color of the image; **blend color**, which is the color you apply with a paint or edit tool; and **resulting color**, which is the color that is created as a result of applying the blend color.

Softening Filter Effects

Opacity can soften the line that the filter creates, but it doesn't affect the opacity of the entire layer. After a filter has been applied, you can modify the opacity and apply a blending mode using the Layers palette or the Fade dialog box. You can open the Fade dialog box by clicking Edit on the menu bar, then clicking the Fade command.

Balancing Colors

As you adjust settings, such as hue and saturation, you might create imbalances in your document. You can adjust colors to correct or improve a document's appearance. For example, you can decrease a color by increasing the amount of its opposite color. You use the Color Balance dialog box to balance the color in an image.

FIGURE D-24
Sharpen filters

Original image

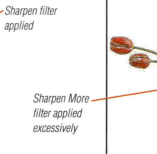

Sharpen filter applied

Sharpen More filter applied excessively

TABLE D-1: Blending Modes

blending mode	description
Dissolve, Behind, and Clear modes	Dissolve mode creates a grainy, mottled appearance. The Behind mode paints on the transparent part of the layer—the lower the opacity, the grainier the image. The Clear mode paints individual pixels. All modes are available only when the Lock transparent pixels check box is *not* selected.
Multiply and Screen modes	Multiply mode creates semitransparent shadow effects. This mode assesses the information in each channel, then multiplies the value of the base color by the blend color. The resulting color is always *darker* than the base color. The Screen mode multiplies the value of the inverse of the blend and base colors. After it is applied, the resulting color is always *lighter* than the base color.
Overlay mode	Dark and light values (luminosity) are preserved, dark base colors are multiplied (darkened), and light areas are screened (lightened).
Soft Light and Hard Light modes	Soft Light lightens a light base color and darkens a dark base color. The Hard Light blending mode creates a similar effect, but provides greater contrast between the base and layer colors.
Color Dodge and Color Burn modes	Color Dodge mode brightens the base color to reflect the blend color. The Color Burn mode darkens the base color to reflect the blend color.
Darken and Lighten modes	Darken mode selects a new resulting color based on whichever color is darker—the base color or the blend color. The Lighten mode selects a new resulting color based on the lighter of the two colors.
Difference and Exclusion modes	The Difference mode subtracts the value of the blend color from the value of the base color, or vice versa, depending on which color has the greater brightness value. The Exclusion mode creates an effect similar to that of the Difference mode, but with less contrast between the blend and base colors.
Color and Luminosity modes	The Color mode creates a resulting color with the luminance of the base color, and the hue and saturation of the blend color. The Luminosity mode creates a resulting color with the hue and saturation of the base color, and the luminance of the blend color.
Hue and Saturation modes	The Hue mode creates a resulting color with the luminance of the base color and the hue of the blend color. The Saturation mode creates a resulting color with the luminance of the base color and the saturation of the blend color.

FIGURE D-25

Brightness/Contrast dialog box

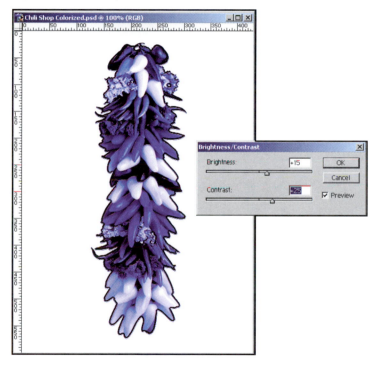

1. Click Image on the menu bar, point to Adjustments, then click Brightness/Contrast to open the Brightness/Contrast dialog box.

2. Drag the Brightness slider until +15 appears in the Brightness text box.

3. Drag the Contrast slider until +25 appears in the Contrast text box. Compare your screen to Figure D-25.

4. Click OK.

You adjusted settings in the Brightness/Contrast dialog box.

Work with a filter, blending mode, and an opacity setting

1. Click Filter on the menu bar, point to Sharpen, then click Sharpen More.

   The border and other features of the image are intensified.

2. Click Edit on the menu bar, then click Fade Sharpen More to open the Fade dialog box, as shown in Figure D-26.

3. Drag the Opacity slider until 55 appears in the Opacity text box.

   The opacity setting softened the lines applied by the Sharpen More filter.

4. Click the Mode list arrow, then click Dissolve to blend the surrounding pixels.

5. Click OK.

6. Save your work, then compare your document to Figure D-27.

You applied the Sharpen More filter, then adjusted the opacity and changed the color mode in the Fade dialog box.

FIGURE D-26
Fade dialog box

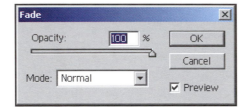

FIGURE D-27
Image settings adjusted

Incorporating Color Techniques

Color Balance dialog box

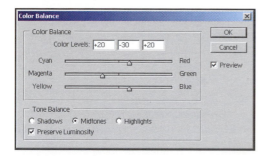

FIGURE D-29

Finished project

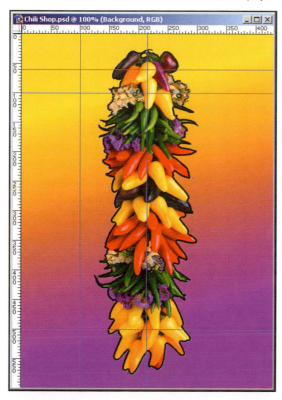

Adjust color balance

1. Click Window on the menu bar, point to Documents, then click Chili Shop.psd (Win) or Chili Shop (Mac).

   The original (color) document becomes active.

2. Click Image on the menu bar, point to Adjustments, then click Color Balance.

3. Drag the Cyan-Red slider until +20 appears in the first text box.

4. Drag the Magenta-Green slider until –30 appears in the middle text box.

5. Drag the Yellow-Blue slider until +20 appears in the last text box, as shown in Figure D-28.

   Subtle changes were made in the color balance in the image.

6. Click OK.

7. Save your work, then compare your document to Figure D-29.

You switched to the Chili Shop document, and then adjusted settings in the Color Balance dialog box.

SKILLS REFERENCE

Power User Shortcuts

Key: Menu items are indicated by ➤ between the menu name and its command. Blue bold letters are shortcuts for selecting tools on the toolbox.

to do this:	use this method:
Apply a sharpen filter	Filter ➤ Sharpen
Balance colors	Image ➤ Adjustments ➤ Color Balance
Change color mode	Image ➤ Mode
Choose a background color from the Swatches palette	[Ctrl]Color swatch (Win) ⌘ Color swatch (Mac)
Default Foreground and Background Colors button	◨
Delete a swatch from the Swatches palette	[Alt], click swatch (Win) ⌘, click swatch (Mac)
Eyedropper Tool	✐ or **I**
Fill with background color	[Shift][Backspace] (Win) ⌘ [delete] (Mac)
Fill with foreground color	[Alt][Backspace] (Win) option [delete] (Mac)
Gradient fill pointer	⊹
Gradient Tool	▭
Guide pointer	┿ or ╪
Hide a layer	👁

to do this:	use this method:
Hide or show rulers	[Ctrl][R] (Win) ⌘ [R] (Mac)
Hide or show the Color Palette	[F6] (Win)
Lock transparent pixels check box on/off	/
Make Swatches palette active	Swatches
Paint Bucket pointer	◊
Paint Bucket Tool	◊
Return background and foreground colors to default	**D**
Reverse background and foreground colors	**X**
Show a layer	▢
Show hidden Paint Bucket/ Gradient Tools	**Shift G**
Switch between open documents	[Ctrl][Tab] (Win) ⌘ [tab] (Mac)
Switch Foreground and Background Colors button	↰

Work with color to transform a document.

1. Start Photoshop.
2. Open PS D-3.psd, then save it as **Firetruck**.
3. Make sure the rulers appear (using pixels as the unit of measurement), and that the foreground and background colors are set to the default setting.
4. Use the Eyedropper Tool to sample the color at 90 H/165 V.
5. Use the Paint Bucket Tool to apply the new foreground color to the Background layer.
6. Undo your last step using the Edit menu or the History palette.
7. Switch the foreground and background colors.

Use the Color Picker and the Swatches palette.

1. Use the Set foreground color button to open the Color Picker dialog box.
2. Click the R, G, and B option buttons, one at a time. Note how the color palette changes.
3. With the B option button selected, click the palette in the upper-left corner.
4. Click OK.
5. Switch the foreground and background colors.
6. Add the foreground color (red) to the Swatches palette using the default name.

Place a border around an image.

1. Make Layer 1 active.
2. Revert to the default foreground and background colors.
3. Apply a 2-pixel outside stroke to the firetruck.
4. Save your work.

Blend colors using the Gradient Tool.

1. Change the foreground color to the eighth swatch from the left in the top row of the Swatches palette.
2. Switch foreground and background colors.
3. Use the new red swatch that you added previously as the foreground color.
4. Make the Background layer active.
5. Use the Gradient Tool, apply the Angle Gradient, then drag the pointer from 35 H/70 V to 145 H/325 V.
6. Save your work.

Add color to a grayscale image.

1. Open PS D-4.psd, then save it as **Firetruck Colorized**.
2. Change the color mode to RGB Color.
3. Open the Hue/Saturation dialog box, then select the Colorize check box.
4. Drag the sliders so the text boxes show the following values: 25, 75, and +15, then click OK.
5. Save your work.

Use filters, opacity, and blending modes.

1. Use the Sharpen filter to sharpen the image.
2. Open the Fade dialog box (Edit menu), change the opacity to 40%, then change the mode to Hard Light.
3. Use the Window menu to activate the Firetruck.psd image.
4. Open the Color Balance dialog box.
5. Change the color level settings so the text boxes show the following values: +61, −15, and +40.
6. Turn off the rulers display.
7. Compare your image to Figure D-30.
8. Save your work.

FIGURE D-30
Completed Skills Review

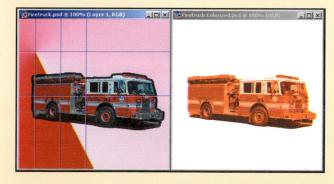

You are finally able to leave your current job and pursue your lifelong dream of opening a furniture repair and restoration business. While you're waiting for the laser stripper and refinisher to arrive, you start work on a sign design.

1. Open PS D-5.psd, then save it as **Restoration**.
2. Move the objects to any location.
3. Take a sample of the blue pliers (in the tool belt), then switch the foreground and background colors.
4. Take a sample of the red tape measure (in the tool belt).
5. Use any Gradient Tool to create an interesting effect on the Background layer.
6. Save the document, then compare your document to the sample shown in Figure D-31.

FIGURE D-31
Completed Project Builder 1

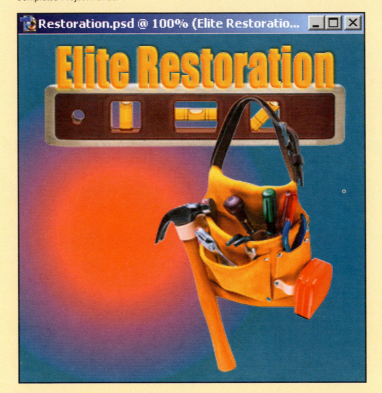

You're painting the swing set at the Artful Dodgers Preschool, when you notice a staff member struggling to create a flyer for the school. Although the basic flyer is complete, it doesn't convey the high energy of the school. You offer to help, and soon find yourself in charge of creating an exciting background for the image.

1. Open PS D-6.psd, then save it as **Preschool**.
2. Select a foreground color and apply it to the Background layer.
3. Add a new layer (Layer 3), then select a background color and apply a gradient you have not used before to the layer. (*Hint*: Immediately undo a gradient that you don't want.)
4. Add the foreground and background colors to the Swatches palette.
5. Apply a Sharpen filter to Layer 2 and adjust the opacity of the filter.
6. Save your work.
7. Compare your document to the sample shown in Figure D-32.

FIGURE D-32
Completed Project Builder 2

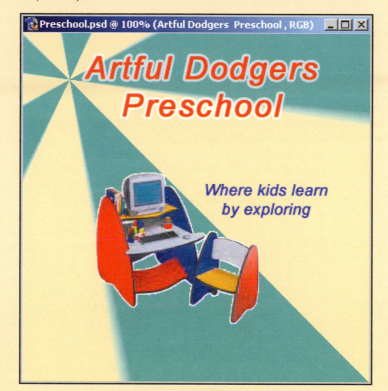

DESIGN PROJECT

A local Top 40 morning radio show recently conducted a survey about fruits and vegetables, and discovered that only 1 in 7 people knew what a gourd was. Now everyone is talking about gourds. An interior designer wants to incorporate gourds into her fall decorating theme, and has asked you to create a poster. You decide to highlight as many varieties as possible.

1. Open PS D-7.psd, then save it as **Cornucopia**.
2. If you choose, you can add any appropriate images from a scanner or digital camera.
3. Activate the Background layer, then sample colors from the image for foreground and background colors. (*Hint*: Try to sample less common colors.)
4. Add the sampled colors to the Swatches palette.
5. Display rulers, then move the existing guide to indicate the coordinates of the colors you sampled.
6. Create a gradient fill by using both foreground and background colors and the gradient style of your choice.
7. Defringe the cornucopia layer, if necessary.
8. Save your work, then compare your document to the sample shown in Figure D-33.

FIGURE D-33
Completed Design Project

Cornucopia.psd @ 100% (Cornucopia, RGB)

GROUP PROJECT

Depending on the size of your group, you can assign individual elements of the project to group members, or work collectively to create the finished product.

An educational toy and game store has hired you to design a poster announcing this year's Most Unusual Hobby contest. After reviewing the photos from last year's awards ceremony, you decide to build a poster using the winner of the Handicrafts Award. You'll use your knowledge of Photoshop color modes to convert the color mode, adjust color in the document, and add an interesting background.

1. Open PS D-8.psd, then save it as **Rubberband**.
2. Convert the document to Grayscale mode. (*Hint*: If Photoshop prompts you to flatten the layers, click Don't Flatten.)
3. Convert the document to RGB Color mode. (*Hint*: If Photoshop prompts you to flatten the layers, click Don't Flatten.)
4. Colorize the image and adjust the Hue, Saturation, and Lightness settings as desired.
5. Adjust Brightness/Contrast settings as desired.
6. Adjust Color Balance settings as desired.
7. Sample the image to create a new foreground color, then add a color of your choice as the background color.
8. Apply any two Sharpen filters and adjust the opacity for one of them.
9. Add a reflected gradient to the Background layer that follows the path of one of the main bands on the ball.
10. Save your work, then compare your document to the sample shown in Figure D-34.
11. Be prepared to discuss the color-correcting methods you used and why you chose them.

FIGURE D-34
Completed Group Project

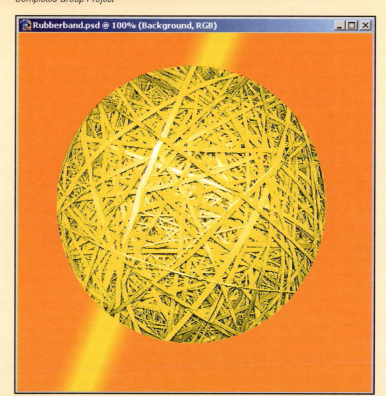

UNIT E

PLACING TYPE IN AN IMAGE

1. Learn about type and how it is created.

2. Change spacing and adjust baseline shift.

3. Use the Drop Shadow style.

4. Apply anti-aliasing to type.

5. Modify type with the Bevel and Emboss style.

6. Apply special effects to type using filters.

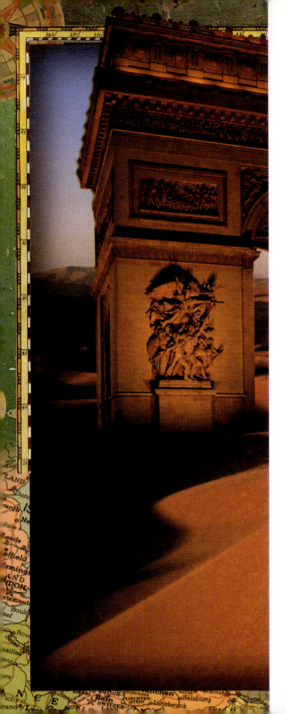

PLACING TYPE IN AN IMAGE

Learning About Type

Text can play an important role when used along with images, such as in magazine and newspaper advertisements. In Photoshop, text is referred to as **type**. You can use type to express the ideas displayed in a document's imagery or to deliver an additional message. You can manipulate type in many ways to convey or reinforce the meaning behind an image. As in other programs, type has its own unique characteristics in Photoshop. For example, you can change its appearance by using different typefaces and colors.

Understanding the Purpose of Type

Type is typically used along with imagery to deliver a message quickly and with flare. Because type is used sparingly (typically there's not a lot of room for it), its appearance is very important; color and imagery are often used to *complement* or *reinforce* the message within the text. Type should be short in length, but direct and to the point. It should be large enough for easy reading, but should not overwhelm or distract from the central image. For example, a vibrant and daring advertisement should contain just enough type to interest the reader, without demanding too much reading.

Getting the Most Out of Type

Type expresses ideas, but the appearance of the type can drive the point home. After you decide on the content you want to use and create the type, you can experiment with its appearance by changing its **font** (characters with a similar appearance), size, and color. You can also apply special effects that make it stand out, or appear to pop off the page.

Tools You'll Use

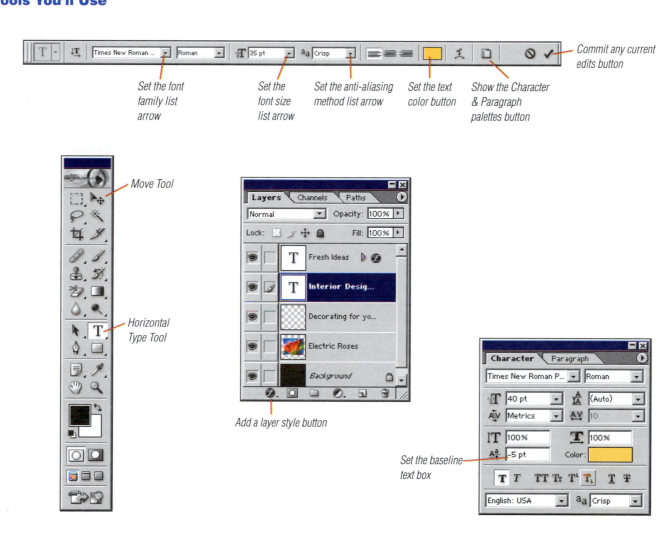

Set the font family list arrow

Set the font size list arrow

Set the anti-aliasing method list arrow

Set the text color button

Show the Character & Paragraph palettes button

Commit any current edits button

Move Tool

Horizontal Type Tool

Add a layer style button

Set the baseline text box

LEARN ABOUT TYPE AND HOW IT IS CREATED

What You'll Do

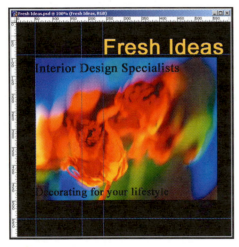

In this lesson, you'll create a type layer, then change the alignment, font family, size, and color of the type.

Introducing Type Types

Outline type is mathematically defined, which means that it can be scaled to any size without losing its sharp, smooth edges. Some programs, such as Adobe Illustrator, create outline type. **Bitmap type** is composed of pixels, and, like images, can develop jagged edges when enlarged. The type you create in Photoshop is initially outline type, but it is converted into bitmap type when you apply special filters. Using the type tools and the tool options bar, you can create horizontal or vertical type and modify its font size and alignment. You use the Color Picker dialog box to change type color. When you create type in Photoshop, it is automatically placed on a new type layer on the Layers palette.

Getting to Know Font Families

Each **font family** represents a complete set of characters, letters, and symbols for a particular typeface. Font families are generally divided into three categories: serif, sans serif, and symbol. Characters in **serif fonts** have a tail, or stroke, at the end of some characters. These tails make it easier for the eye to recognize words. For this reason, serif fonts are generally used in text passages. **Sans serif fonts** do not have tails and are commonly used in headlines. **Symbol fonts** are used to display unique characters (such as $, ÷, or ™). Table E-1 lists commonly used serif and sans serif fonts. After you select the Horizontal Type Tool, you can change font families using the tool options bar.

Measuring Type Size

The size of each character within a font is measured in **points**. **PostScript**, a programming language that optimizes printed text and graphics, was introduced by Adobe in 1985. In PostScript measurement, 1 inch is equivalent to 72 points or 6 picas. Therefore, 1 pica is equivalent to 12 points. In traditional measurement, 1 inch is equivalent to 72.27 points. The default Photoshop type size is 12 points. In Photoshop, you have the option of using PostScript or traditional character measurement.

Acquiring Fonts

Your computer probably has many fonts installed on it, but no matter how many fonts you have, you probably can use more. Fonts can be purchased from private companies, individual designers, computer stores, catalog companies, or from the Internet. Using your browser and your favorite search engine, you can locate Web sites that let you purchase or download fonts. Many Web sites offer specialty fonts, such as the Web site shown in Figure E-1. Other Web sites offer these fonts free of charge or for a nominal fee.

TABLE E-1: Commonly Used Serif and Sans Serif Fonts

serif fonts	sample	sans serif fonts	sample
Lucida Handwriting	*Adobe Photoshop*	Arial	Adobe Photoshop
Rockwell	**Adobe Photoshop**	Bauhaus	Adobe Photoshop
Times New Roman	Adobe Photoshop	Century Gothic	Adobe Photoshop

Create and modify type

1. Start Photoshop, open PS E-1.psd, then save the file as **Fresh Ideas**.

2. If necessary, display the rulers in pixels.

   TIP You can quickly display the rulers by pressing [Ctrl][R] (Win) or [command][R] (Mac).

3. Click the Default Foreground and Background Colors button.

4. Click the Horizontal Type Tool on the toolbox.

5. Click the Set the font family list arrow on the tool options bar, click Times New Roman (or a similar substitute), if necessary, then verify that Roman appears in the text box next to the Set the font family list arrow.

6. Click the Left align text button on the tool options bar, if necessary.

7. Click the Set the font size list arrow on the tool options bar, then click 60 pt, if necessary.

8. Click the document at 240 H/250 V, then type **Fresh Ideas**, as shown in Figure E-2.

   TIP Type should be short enough to be read in a glance. Thinking during the reading process means there's too much type.

You created a type layer by using the Horizontal Type Tool on the toolbox, then modified the font family, alignment, and font size.

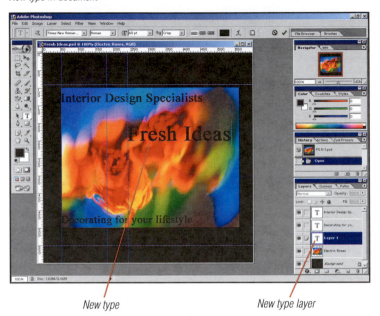

New type   New type layer

Using the active layer palette background (Macintosh)

Icons used in Macintosh to identify type layers are similar to those found in Windows. In Macintosh, the active layer has the same Type and Layer style buttons. The active layer's background color is the same color as the Highlight Color chosen in the Appearance control panel menu item. (In Windows, the active layer's background color is navy blue.)

Placing Type in an Image

FIGURE E-3
Type with new color

Type with —
new color

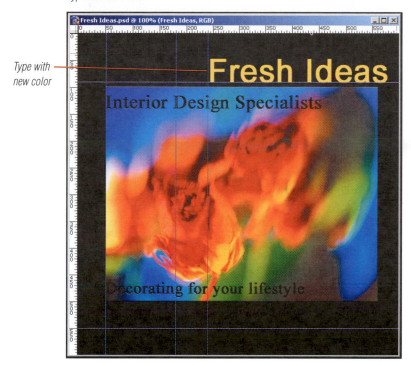

 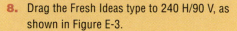
Using the Swatches palette to change type color

You can also use the Swatches palette to change type color. Select the type, then click a color on the Swatches palette. The new color that you click will appear in the Set foreground color button on the toolbox and will be applied to type that is currently selected.

CHANGE SPACING AND ADJUST BASELINE SHIFT

What You'll Do

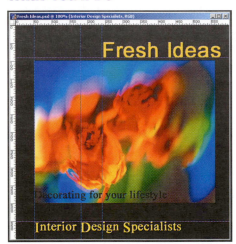

 In this lesson, you'll adjust the spacing between characters and change the base-line of type.

Spacing Between Lines and Type Characters

Competition for readers on the visual land-scape is fierce. To get and maintain an edge over other designers, Photoshop provides tools that make finite adjustments to your type, thereby making your type more dis-tinctive. These adjustments might not be very dramatic, but they can influence read-ers in subtle ways. For example, type that is too small and difficult to read might make the reader angry (at the very least), and he or she might not even look at the docu-ment (at the very worst). You can make finite adjustments, called **type spacing**, to the space between characters and between lines of type. Adjusting type spacing affects the ease with which words are read.

Understanding Character and Line Spacing

Fonts in desktop publishing and word pro-cessing programs use proportional spacing, whereas typewriters use monotype spacing. In **monotype spacing**, each character occupies the same amount of space. This means that characters such as "o" and "w" take up the same area as "i" and "l". In **proportional spacing**, each character can take up a different amount of space, depending on its width. **Kerning** controls the amount of space between characters and can affect several characters, a word, or an entire paragraph. **Tracking** inserts a *uniform* amount of space between selected characters. Figure E-4 shows an example of type before and after it has been kerned.

The second line of text takes up less room and has less space between its characters, making it easier to read. You can also change the amount of space between lines of type, or **leading**, to add or decrease the distance between lines of text.

Using the Character Palette

The **Character palette**, shown in Figure E-5, helps you manually or automatically control type properties such as kerning, tracking, and leading. You open the Character palette from the tool options bar.

Adjusting the Baseline Shift

Type rests on an invisible line called a **baseline**. Using the Character palette, you can adjust the **baseline shift**, the vertical distance that type moves from its baseline.

You can add interest to type by changing the baseline shift.

QUICKTIP

Clicking the Set the text color button on either the tool options bar or the Character palette opens the Color Picker dialog box.

FIGURE E-4
Kerned characters

FIGURE E-5
Character palette

Kern characters

1. Click the Fresh Ideas type layer on the Layers palette, if necessary.

2. Click the Horizontal Type Tool on the toolbox. T.

3. Click the Toggle the Character and Paragraph palettes button on the tool options bar.

   TIP You can close the Character palette by clicking the Close button in the upper-right corner of its title bar or by clicking the Toggle the Character and Paragraph palettes button.

4. Click between "I" and "d" in the word "Ideas."

   TIP You can drag the Character palette out of the way if it blocks your view.

5. Click the Set the kerning between two characters list arrow on the Character palette, then click –25. Metrics

   The spacing between the two characters decreases.

6. Click between "r" and "e" in the word "Fresh."

7. Click the Set the kerning between two characters list arrow, then click –10, as shown in Figure E-6. Metrics

8. Click the Commit any current edits button on the tool options bar. ✓

You modified the kerning between characters by using the Character palette.

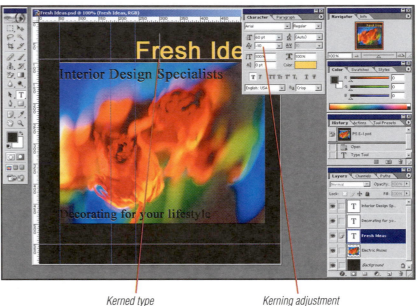

Kerned type   Kerning adjustment

Correcting spelling errors

Are you concerned that your gorgeous image will be ruined by misspelled words? Photoshop understands your pain and has included a spelling checker to make sure you are never plagued by incorrect spellings. If you want, the spelling checker will check the type on the current layer, or all the layers in the document. First, make sure the correct dictionary for your language is selected. English: USA is the default, but you can choose another language by clicking the Set the language on selected characters for hyphenation and spelling list arrow at the bottom of the Character palette. To check spelling, click Edit on the menu bar, then click Check Spelling. The spelling checker will automatically stop at each word not already appearing in the dictionary. One or more suggestions might be offered, which you can either accept or reject.

Color Picker dialog box

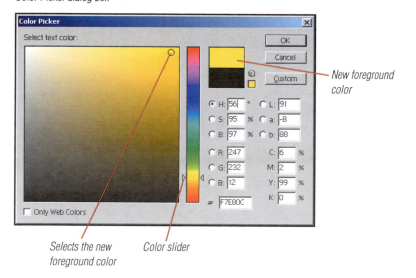

Selects the new foreground color

Color slider

FIGURE E-8

Type with baseline shifted

New foreground color

Shift the baseline

1. Double-click the layer thumbnail on the Interior Design Specialists type layer.

2. Click the Set the text color button on the tool options bar.

3. If necessary, click the H (Hue) option button in the Color Picker dialog box, click yellow in the color slider, click in the upper-right corner of the color field, as shown in Figure E-7, then click OK.

4. Select the capital "I" in "Interior," double-click 35 in the Set the font size text box on the Character palette, type 40, double-click 0 in the Set the baseline shift text box on the Character palette, then type **–5**.

5. Select "D" in "Design," double-click 35 in the Set the font size text box, type **40**, double-click 0 in the Set the baseline shift text box, then type **–5**.

6. Select "S" in "Specialists," double-click 35 in the Set the font size text box, type **40**, double-click 0 in the Set the baseline shift text box, then type **–5**.

7. Click the Commit any current edits button on the tool options bar.

8. Click the Toggle the Character and Paragraph palettes button on the tool options bar.

9. Click the Move Tool on the toolbox, then drag the Interior Design Specialists type to 50 H/550 V, as shown in Figure E-8.

10. Save your work.

You changed the type color, then adjusted the baseline of the first character in each word.

USE THE DROP SHADOW STYLE

What You'll Do

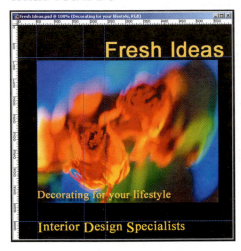

 In this lesson, you'll apply the drop shadow style to a type layer, then modify drop shadow settings.

Adding Effects to Type

Layer styles (effects which can be applied to a type or image layer) can greatly enhance the appearance of type and improve its effectiveness. A type layer is indicated by the appearance of the T icon in the layer's thumbnail box. When a layer style is applied to any layer, the Indicates layer effects icon (*f*) appears in that layer when it is active. The Layers palette is a great source of information. You can see which effects have been applied to a layer by clicking the arrow to the left of the Indicates layer effects icon on the Layers palette if the layer is active or inactive. Figure E-9 shows a layer that has two type layer styles applied to it. Layer styles are linked to the contents of a layer, which means that if a type layer is moved or modified, the layer's style will still be applied to the type.

QUICKTIP

Type layer icons used in the Macintosh version of Photoshop are similar to those found in the Windows version of Photoshop.

Using the Drop Shadow

One method of placing emphasis on type is to add a drop shadow to it. A **drop shadow** creates an illusion that another colored layer of identical text is behind the selected type. The drop shadow default color is black, but can be changed to another color using the Color Picker dialog box, or any of the other methods for changing color.

Applying a Style

You can apply a style, such as a drop shadow, to the active layer, by clicking Layer on the menu bar, pointing to Layer Style, then clicking a style. (The settings in the Layer Style dialog box are "sticky," meaning that they display the settings that you last used.) An alternative method to using the menu bar is to select the layer that you want to apply the style to, click the Add a layer style button on the Layers palette, then click a style. Regardless of which method you use, the Layer Style dialog box opens. You use this dialog box to add all kinds of effects to type. Depending on which style you've chosen, the Layer Style dialog box displays options appropriate to that style.

QUICKTIP

You can apply styles to objects as well as type.

Controlling a Drop Shadow

You can control many aspects of a drop shadow's appearance, including its angle, its distance behind the type, and the amount of blur it contains. The **angle** determines where the shadow falls relative to the text, and the **distance** determines how far the shadow falls from the text. The **spread** determines the width of the shadow

text, and the **size** determines the clarity of the shadow. Figure E-10 contains two samples of drop shadow effects. The first line of type uses the default background color (black), has an angle of 160 degrees, distance of 10 pixels, a spread of 0%, and a size of 5 pixels. The second line of type uses a blue background color, has an angle of 120 degrees, distance of 20 pixels, a spread of 10%, and a size of 5 pixels. As you modify the drop shadow, the preview window displays the changes.

FIGURE E-9
Effects in an inactive type layer

FIGURE E-10
Sample drop shadows

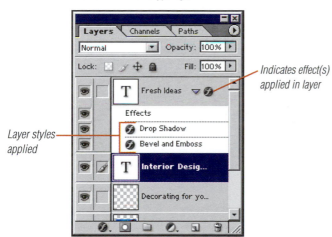

Layer styles applied

Indicates effect(s) applied in layer

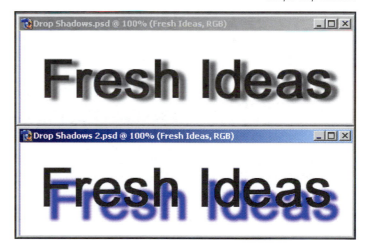

Add a drop shadow

1. Double-click the layer thumbnail on the Decorating for your lifestyle type layer.

2. Click the Set the text color button on the tool options bar. ▮

3. Click the "F" in "Fresh." ⌶

4. Click OK in the Color Picker dialog box.

5. Click the Commit any current edits button on the tool options bar. ✔

6. Click the Add a layer style button on the Layers palette. ⊘.

7. Click Drop Shadow.

   The default drop shadow settings are applied to the type as shown in Figure E-11. Table E-2 explains drop shadow settings.

   TIP You can also open the Layer Style dialog box by double-clicking a layer on the Layers palette.

You changed the color of the type and created a drop shadow by using the Add a layer style button on the Layers palette.

Type color changed

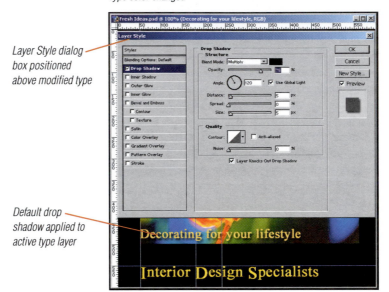

Layer Style dialog box positioned above modified type

Default drop shadow applied to active type layer

TABLE E-2: Drop Shadow Settings

setting	scale	explanation
Angle	0–360 degrees	At 0 degrees, the shadow appears on the baseline of the original text. At 90 degrees, the shadow appears directly below the original text.
Distance	0–30,000 pixels	A larger pixel size increases the distance from which the shadow text falls relative to the original text.
Spread	0–100%	A larger pixel size increases the width of the shadow text.
Size	0–250 pixels	A larger pixel size increases the blur of the shadow text.

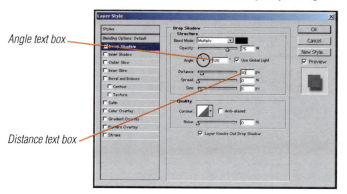

Angle text box

Distance text box

Drop shadow
appears behind text

Displays effect(s)
applied in layer

Modify drop shadow settings

1. Double-click the number in the Angle text box, then type **120**, if necessary.

    TIP   You can also set the angle by dragging the dial slider in the Layer Style dialog box.

2. Double-click the number in the Distance text box, then type **10**, if necessary. See Figure E-12.

3. Click OK.

4. Click the triangle to the left of the Indicates layer effects icon on the Decorating for your lifestyle layer, as shown in Figure E-13. ▷

5. Click the triangle to the left of the Indicates layer effects icon on the Decorating for your lifestyle layer to close the list. ▽

6. Save your work.

You used the Layer Style dialog box to modify the default settings for the drop shadow.

APPLY ANTI-ALIASING TO TYPE

What You'll Do

 In this lesson, you'll view the effects of the anti-aliasing feature, then use the History palette to return the type to its original state.

Eliminating the "Jaggies"

In the good old days of dot-matrix printers, jagged edges were obvious in many print ads. You can still see these jagged edges in designs produced on less sophisticated printers. To prevent the jagged edges (sometimes called "jaggies") that often accompany bitmap type, Photoshop offers an anti-aliasing feature. **Anti-aliasing** partially fills in pixel edges with additional colors, resulting in smooth-edge type and an increased number of colors in the document. Anti-aliasing is useful for improving the display of large type in print media; however, this can cause a file to become large.

Knowing When to Apply Anti-Aliasing

As a rule, type that has a point size greater than 12 should have some anti-aliasing method applied. Sometimes, smaller type sizes can become blurry or muddy when anti-aliasing is used. As part of the process, anti-aliasing adds intermediate colors to your image in an effort to reduce the jagged edges. As a designer, you need to weigh the following factors when determining if you should apply anti-aliasing: type size versus file size and image quality.

Understanding Anti-Aliasing

Anti-aliasing improves the display of type against the background. You can use five anti-aliasing methods: None, Sharp, Crisp, Strong, and Smooth. An example of each method is shown in Figure E-14. The **None** setting applies no anti-aliasing, and can result in type that has jagged edges. The **Sharp** setting displays type with the best possible resolution. The **Crisp** setting gives type more definition and makes type appear sharper. The **Strong** setting makes type appear heavier, much like the bold attribute. The **Smooth** setting gives type more rounded edges.

FIGURE E-14
Anti-aliasing effects

Anti-aliasing method: None

Anti-aliasing method: Sharp

Anti-aliasing method: Crisp

Anti-aliasing method: Strong

Anti-aliasing method: Smooth

Apply anti-aliasing

1. Double-click the layer thumbnail on the Interior Design Specialists layer.

2. Click the Set the font family list arrow, scroll up, then click Arial MT or Arial.

3. Click the Set the anti-aliasing method list arrow on the tool options bar. `Crisp ▾`

4. Click None, then compare your work to Figure E-15.

5. Click the Commit any current edits button on the tool options bar. ✔

You applied the None anti-aliasing setting to see how the setting affected the appearance of type.

Effect of None anti-aliasing

Jagged appearance
to type

Placing Type in an Image

FIGURE E-16

Deleting a state from the History palette

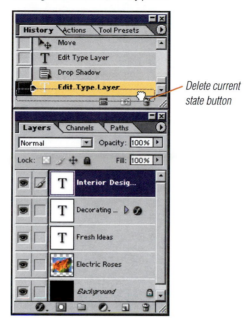

Delete current
state button

1. Click the Edit Type Layer state in the History palette, then drag it to the Delete current state button, as shown in Figure E-16.

   TIP   Various methods of undoing actions are reviewed in Table E-3.

2. Save your work.

You deleted a state in the History palette to return the type to its original appearance.

TABLE E-3: Undoing Actions

method	description	keyboard shortcut
Undo	Edit ➢ Undo	[Ctrl][Z] (Win) [command][Z] (Mac)
Step Backward	Click Edit on the menu bar, then click Step Backward	[Alt][Ctrl][Z] (Win) [alt][command][Z] (Mac)
History palette	Drag state to the Delete current state button on the History palette	[Alt] 🗑 (Win) [option] 🗑 (Mac)

MODIFY TYPE WITH THE
BEVEL AND EMBOSS STYLE

What You'll Do

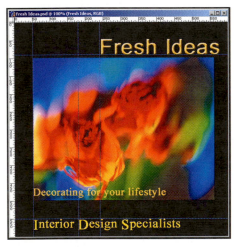

▶ In this lesson, you'll apply the Bevel and Emboss style, then modify the Bevel and Emboss settings.

Using the Bevel and Emboss Style

You use the Bevel and Emboss style to add combinations of shadows and highlights to a layer and make type appear to have dimension and shine. You can use the Layer menu or the Layers palette to apply the Bevel and Emboss style to the active layer. Like all Layer styles, the Bevel and Emboss style is linked to the type layer that it is applied to.

Understanding Bevel and Emboss Settings

You can use two categories of Bevel and Emboss settings: structure and shading. **Structure** determines the size and physical properties of the object, and **shading** determines the lighting effects. Figure E-17 contains several variations of Bevel and Emboss structure settings. The shading used in the Bevel and Emboss style determines how and where light is projected on

Filling type with imagery

You can use the imagery from a layer in one file as the fill pattern for another image's type layer. To create this effect, open a multi-layer file that contains the imagery you want to use (the source), then open the file that contains the type you want to fill (the target). In the source file, activate the layer containing the imagery you want to use, use the Select menu to select all, then use the Edit menu to copy the selection. In the target file, press [Ctrl] (Win) or [command] (Mac) while clicking the type layer to which the imagery will be applied, then click Paste Into on the Edit menu. The imagery will appear within the type.

the type. You can control a variety of settings, including the angle, altitude, and gloss contour, to create a unique appearance. The **Angle** setting determines where the shadow falls relative to the text, and the **Altitude** setting affects the amount of visible dimension. For example, an altitude of 0 degrees looks flat, while a setting of 90 degrees has a more three-dimensional appearance. The **Gloss Contour** setting determines the pattern with which light is reflected, and the **Highlight Mode** and **Shadow Mode** settings determine how pigments are combined. When the Use Global Light check box is selected, *all the type* in the document will be affected by your changes.

FIGURE E-17
Bevel and Emboss style samples

Add the Bevel and Emboss style and modify settings

1. Click the Fresh Ideas layer on the Layers palette.

2. Click Layer on the menu bar, point to Layer Style, then click Bevel and Emboss.

3. If necessary, move the Layer Style dialog box, shown in Figure E-18, so you can see the Fresh Ideas type.

4. Double-click number in the Angle text box, then type **120**, if necessary.

   Some of the Bevel and Emboss settings are listed in Table E-4. You can use the Layer Style dialog box to change the structure by adjusting style, technique, direction, size, and soften settings.

   (continued)

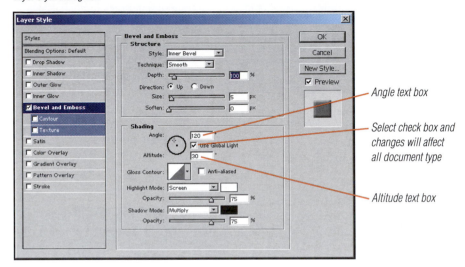

Angle text box

Select check box and changes will affect all document type

Altitude text box

TABLE E-4: Bevel and Emboss Structure Settings

sample	style	technique	direction	size	soften
1	Inner Bevel	Smooth	Up	5	1
2	Outer Bevel	Chisel Hard	Up	5	8
3	Emboss	Smooth	Down	10	3
4	Pillow Emboss	Chisel Soft	Up	10	3

Placing Type in an Image

FIGURE E-19
Bevel and Emboss style applied to type

*Bevel and Emboss
style applied to layer*

Bevel and Emboss style

5. Double-click the Altitude text box, then type **30**, if necessary.

6. Click OK, then compare your type to Figure E-19.

7. Save your work.

You applied the Bevel and Emboss style by using the Layer menu, then modified the default settings.

Warping type

You can add dimension and style to your type by using the Warp Text feature. After you select the type layer you want to warp, click the Horizontal Type Tool on the toolbox. Click the Create warped text button on the tool options bar to open the Warp Text dialog box. (If a warning box opens telling you that your request cannot be completed because the type layer uses a faux bold style, click the Toggle the Character and Paragraph palettes button on the tool options bar, click the Character palette list arrow, click Faux Bold to deselect it, then click the Create warped text button again.) You can click the Style list arrow to select from 15 available styles. After you select a style, you can modify its appearance by dragging the Bend, Horizontal Distortion, and Vertical Distortion sliders.

APPLY SPECIAL EFFECTS TO TYPE USING FILTERS

What You'll Do

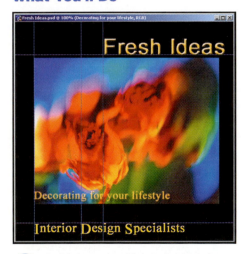

 In this lesson, you'll rasterize a type layer, then apply a filter to it to change its appearance.

Understanding Filters

Like an image layer, a type layer can have one or more filters applied to it to achieve special effects and make your text look unique. Some filter dialog boxes have preview windows that let you see the results of the particular filter before it is applied to the layer. Other filters must be applied to the layer before you can see the results. Before a filter can be applied to a type layer, the type layer must first be **rasterized**, or converted to an image layer. After it is rasterized, the type characters *can no longer be edited* because it is composed of pixels, just like artwork. When a type layer is rasterized, the T icon in the layer thumbnail becomes an image thumbnail while the Effects icons remain on the type layer.

Creating Special Effects

Filters enable you to apply a variety of special effects to type, as shown in Figure E-20. Notice that none of the original type layers on the Layers palette displays the T icon in the layer thumbnail because the layers have all been rasterized.

QUICKTIP

Because you cannot edit type after it has been rasterized, you should save your original type by making a copy of the layer *before* you rasterize it, then hide it from view.

Producing Distortions

Distort filters let you create waves or curves in type. Some of the types of distortions you can produce include Glass, Pinch, Ripple, Shear, Spherize, Twirl, Wave, and Zigzag. These effects are sometimes used as the basis of a corporate logo. The Twirl dialog box, shown in Figure E-21, lets you determine the amount of twirl effect you want to apply. By dragging the Angle slider, you control how much twirl effect is added to a layer. Most filter dialog boxes have zoom in and zoom out buttons that make it easy to see the effects of the filter.

Using Textures and Relief

Many filters let you create the appearance of textures and **relief** (the height of ridges within an object). One of the Stylize filters, Wind, applies lines throughout the type, making it appear shredded. The Wind dialog box, shown in Figure E-22, lets you determine the kind of wind and its direction. The Texture filter lets you choose the type of texture you want to apply to a layer: Brick, Burlap, Canvas, or Sandstone.

Blurring Imagery

The Gaussian Blur filter softens the appearance of type by blurring its edge pixels. You can control the amount of blur applied to the type by entering high or low values in the Gaussian Blur dialog box. The higher the blur value, the blurrier the effect.

QUICKTIP
Be careful: too much blur applied to type can make it unreadable or cause it to disappear entirely.

FIGURE E-20
Sample filters applied to type

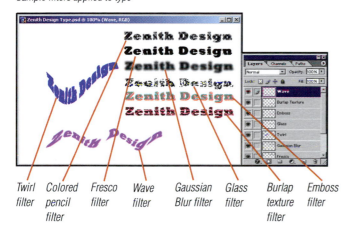

Twirl filter | Colored pencil filter | Fresco filter | Wave filter | Gaussian Blur filter | Glass filter | Burlap texture filter | Emboss filter

FIGURE E-21
Twirl dialog box

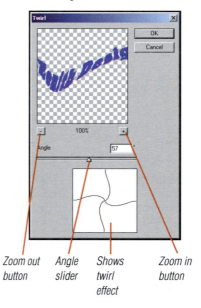

Zoom out button | Angle slider | Shows twirl effect | Zoom in button

FIGURE E-22
Wind dialog box

Rasterize a type layer

1. Click the Decorating for your lifestyle layer on the Layers palette.

2. Click Filter on the menu bar, point to Blur, then click Gaussian Blur.

3. Click OK to rasterize the type and close the warning box shown in Figure E-23.

   TIP   You can also rasterize a type layer by clicking Layer on the menu bar, pointing to Rasterize, then clicking Type.

   The Gaussian Blur dialog box opens.

You rasterized a type layer in preparation for filter application.

FIGURE E-23
Warning box

Using multiple filters
Sometimes, adding one filter doesn't achieve the effect you might have had in mind. You can use multiple filters to create a unique effect. Before you try your hand at filters, though, it's a good idea to make a copy of the original layer. That way, if things don't turn out as you planned, you can always start over. You don't even have to write down which filters you used, because you can always look at the History palette to see which filters you applied.

Modify filter settings

1. Drag the slider in the Gaussian Blur dialog box until 0.8 appears in the Radius text box, as shown in Figure E-24.

2. Click OK.

3. Hide the rulers.

4. Save your work. Compare your blurred type to Figure E-25.

You modified the Gaussian Blur filter settings to change the blur effect.

FIGURE E-25
Type with Gaussian Blur filter

Slider

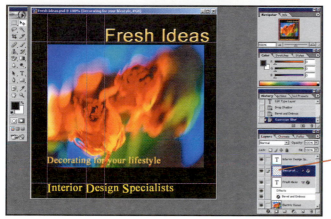

No longer a type layer

Creating a neon glow

Want to create a really cool effect that takes absolutely no time at all, is super-easy, and works on both type and objects? You can create a neon glow that appears to surround an object. You can apply the Neon Glow filter (one of the Artistic filters) to any flattened image. This effect works best by starting with any imagery—either type or objects—that has a solid color background. Flatten the image so there's only a Background layer. Click the Magic Wand Tool on the toolbox, then click the solid color (in the background). Click Filter on the menu bar, point to Artistic, then click Neon Glow. Adjust the glow size, the glow brightness, and color, if you wish, then click OK. (An example of this technique is used in the Design Project at the end of this unit.)

Power User Shortcuts

to do this:	use this method:
Apply anti-alias method	Crisp
Apply Bevel and Emboss style	, Bevel and Emboss
Apply blur filter to type	Filter ➤ Blur ➤ Gaussian Blur
Apply Drop Shadow style	, Drop Shadow
Change font family	Times New Roman ...
Change font size	T 60 pt

to do this:	use this method:
Change magnification factor	Double-click 100%, type value, press [Enter] (Win) or [return] (Mac)
Change type color	
Close type effects	
Commit current edits	
Display/hide rulers	[Ctrl][R] (Win) or ⌘ [R] (Mac)

Key: Menu items are indicated by ➤ between the menu name and its command. Blue bold letters are shortcuts for selecting tools on the toolbox.

Power User Shortcuts

to do this:	use this method:
Erase a History state	Select state, drag to 🗑
Horizontal Type Tool	T. or **T**
Kern characters	Metrics ▾
Move Tool	⊹ or **V**
Open Character palette	▤
Save document changes	[Ctrl][S] (Win) or ⌘ [S] (Mac)

to do this:	use this method:
See type effects (active layer)	▷
See type effects (inactive layer)	▷
Select all text	[Ctrl][A] (Win) or ⌘ [A] (Mac)
Shift baseline of type	A᷎ᵗ

Key: Menu items are indicated by ➤ between the menu name and its command. Blue bold letters are shortcuts for selecting tools on the toolbox.

Learn about type and how it is created.

1. Open PS E-2.psd, then save it as **ZD-Logo**.
2. Make sure the rulers appear.
3. Use the Horizontal Type Tool to create a type layer at 45 H/95 V.
4. Use a 35 pt Myriad font. (If necessary, substitute another font.)
5. Type **Zenith**.
6. Use the Horizontal Type Tool (and a smaller type size) to create a type layer at 70 H/180 V, then type **uncompromising excellence**.
7. Save your work.

Change spacing and adjust baseline shift.

1. Use the Horizontal Type Tool to create a new type layer at 205 H/95 V.
2. Use a 35 pt Myriad font. (If necessary, substitute another font.)
3. Type **Design**.
4. Select the Design type.
5. Change the type color to the color used in the lower-left background. (*Hint*: Use the Eyedropper pointer.)
6. Change the type size of the Z and D to 50 pts.
7. Adjust the baseline shift of the Z and D to –5.
8. Save your work.

Use the Drop Shadow style.

1. Activate the Zenith type layer.
2. Apply the Drop Shadow style.
3. If necessary, in the Layer Style dialog box, set the angle to 150°.
4. Close the Layer Style dialog box.
5. Save your work.

Apply anti-aliasing to type.

1. Activate the Zenith type layer.
2. Change the Anti-Alias setting to Smooth.
3. Save your work.

Modify type with the Bevel and Emboss style.

1. Activate the Design type layer.
2. Apply the Bevel and Emboss style.
3. In the Layer Style dialog box, set the style to Inner Bevel, if necessary.

4. Set the angle to 150° and the altitude to 30°, if necessary.
5. Close the Layer Style dialog box.
6. Activate the Zenith type layer.
7. Apply the Bevel and Emboss style.
8. In the Layer Style dialog box, set the style to Inner Bevel, if necessary.
9. Set the angle to 150° and the altitude to 30°, if necessary.
10. Close the Layer Style dialog box.
11. Save your work.

Apply special effects to type using filters.

1. Apply a 1.0 pixel Gaussian Blur effect to the "uncompromising excellence" layer, rasterizing the layer when necessary.
2. Turn off the ruler display.
3. Save the document, then compare your work to the sample in Figure E-26.

FIGURE E-26
Completed Skills Review

A local flower shop, Beautiful Blooms, asks you to design its color advertisement for the trade magazine, *Florists United*. You have already started on the image, and need to add some type.

1. Open PS E-3.psd, then save it as **Beautiful Blooms Ad.**
2. Click the Horizontal Type Tool, then type **Beautiful Blooms** using a 48 pt Impact font in black.
3. Create a catchy phrase using an 18 pt Verdana font.
4. Apply a drop shadow style to the name of the flower shop using the following settings: Multiply blend mode, 75% Opacity, 120° angle, 5 pixel distance, 0° spread, and 5 pixel size.
5. Apply a bevel and emboss style to the catch phrase using the following settings: Inner Bevel style, Smooth technique, 100% depth, Up direction, 5 pixel size, 0 pixel soften, 120° angle, 30° altitude, and using global light.
6. Compare your document to the sample in Figure E-27.
7. Save your work.

FIGURE E-27

Completed Project Builder 1

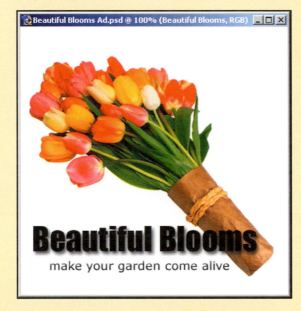

Beautiful Blooms Ad.psd @ 100% (Beautiful Blooms, RGB)

You are a junior art director for an advertising agency. You have been working on an ad that promotes milk and milk products. You have started the project, but still have a few details to finish up before it is complete.

1. Open PS E-4.psd, then save it as **Spilled Milk**.
2. Create a type layer above the Milk Glass layer using a catchy phrase, such as "Don't Cry".
3. Use the Eyedropper pointer to sample the white background color for the type layer. (*Hint*: You can use a location such as 40 H/150 V.)
4. Use a 60 pt Arial Black font for the catch phrase type layer. (If necessary, substitute another font.)
5. Create a bevel and emboss style on the "Don't Cry" type layer, setting the angle to 100° and the altitude to 30°.
6. Compare your document to the sample in Figure E-28.
7. Save your work.

FIGURE E-28

Completed Project Builder 2

You are a freelance designer. A local clothing store, Attitude, is expanding and has hired you to work on an advertisement. You have already created the file, and inserted the necessary type layers. Before you proceed, you decide to explore the Internet to find information on using type to create an effective design.

1. Connect to the Internet and go to *www.course.com*, navigate to the page for this book, click the Student Online Companion link, then click the link for this unit.
2. Click the Improve this advert and the Show the bad advert buttons to see how type can be used to make an effective design.
3. Open PS E-5.psd, then save the file as **Attitude**.
4. Modify the existing type by changing fonts, font colors, and font sizes.
5. Edit the type, if necessary, to make it shorter and clearer.
6. Rearrange the position of the type to create an effective design.
7. Add a bevel and emboss style using your choice of settings, then compare your document to the sample in Figure E-29. (The fonts Mistral and Trebuchet MS are used in this document. Make substitutions if you don't have these fonts.)
8. Save your work.

FIGURE E-29
Completed Design Project

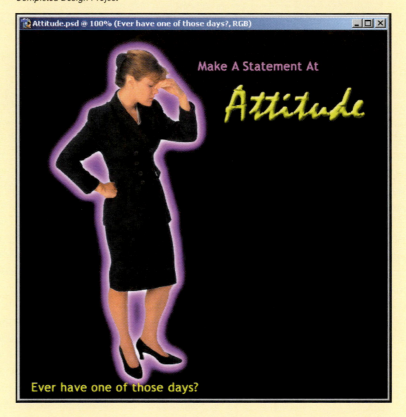

Depending on the size of your group, you can assign individual elements of the project to group members, or work collectively to create the finished product.

You have been hired by your community to create an advertising campaign that promotes tourism. Assemble a team and decide what aspect of the community you want to emphasize. Locate appropriate imagery (already existing on your hard drive, on the Web, your own creation, or using a scanner), then add type to create a meaningful Photoshop document.

1. Create a document with the dimensions 550 pixels × 550 pixels.
2. Save this file as **Community Promotion**.
3. Locate imagery that exists on your hard drive, or from a digital camera or a scanner.
4. Add at least two layers of type in the document, using multiple font sizes. (Use any fonts available on your computer. You can use multiple fonts if you want.)
5. Add a bevel and emboss style to at least one type layer, and add a drop shadow to at least one layer. (*Hint*: You can add both effects to the same layer.)
6. Position type layers to create an effective design.
7. Compare your document to the sample in Figure E-30.
8. Save your work.

FIGURE E-30
Completed Group Project

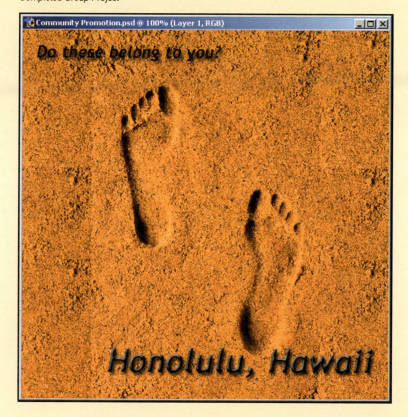

Placing Type in an Image

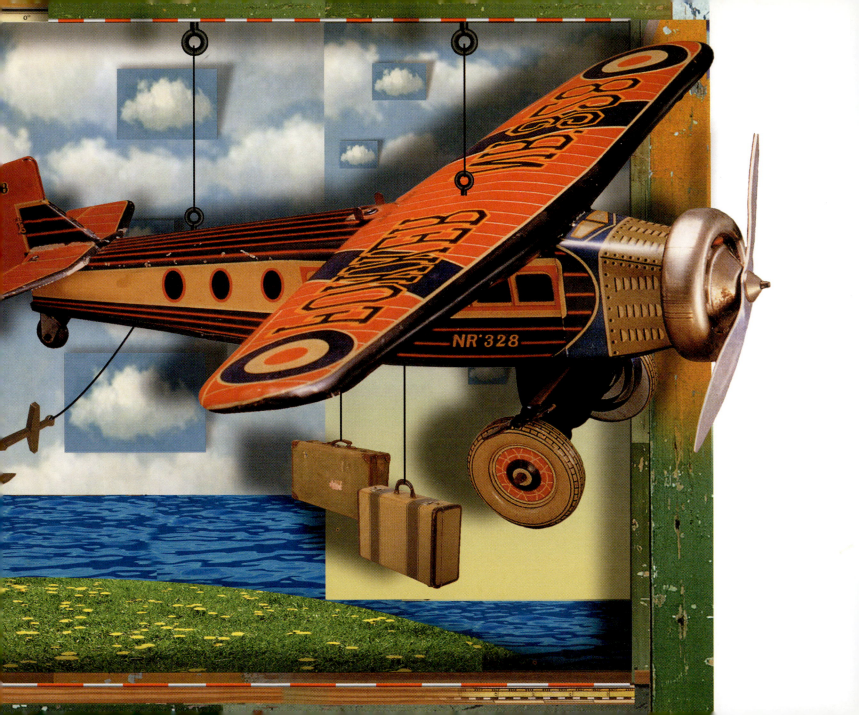

UNIT

USING PAINTING TOOLS

1. Paint and patch an image.

2. Create and modify a brush tip.

3. Smudge colors to create an artistic effect.

4. Use a library and an airbrush effect.

UNIT F
USING PAINTING TOOLS

Painting Pixels

In addition to the color-enhancing techniques you've already learned, Photoshop has a variety of painting tools that let you modify colors. Unlike the tools an oil painter might use to *apply* pigment to a canvas, such as a brush or a palette knife, these virtual painting tools *change* existing colors and pixels.

Understanding Painting Tools

In most cases, you use a painting tool by selecting it, then choosing a brush tip. Just like a real brush, the brush size and shape determines how colors are affected. You paint the image by applying the brush tip to an image, which is similar to the way pigment is applied to a real brush and then applied to a canvas. In Photoshop, the results of the painting process can be deeper, richer colors, bleached or blurred colors, or filter-like effects in specific areas. You can select the size and shape of a brush tip, and control the point at which the brushstroke fades.

Learning About Brush Libraries

Brushes that are used with painting tools are stored within a brush library. Each **brush library** contains a variety of brush tips that you can use, rename, delete, or customize. After you select a tool, you can select a brush tip from the default brush library, which is automatically available from the Brush Preset picker list arrow. Photoshop comes with the following additional brush libraries:

- Assorted Brushes
- Calligraphic Brushes
- Drop Shadow Brushes
- Dry Media Brushes
- Faux Finish Brushes
- Natural Brushes
- Natural Brushes 2
- Special Effect Brushes
- Square Brushes
- Thick Heavy Brushes
- Wet Media Brushes

Tools You'll Use

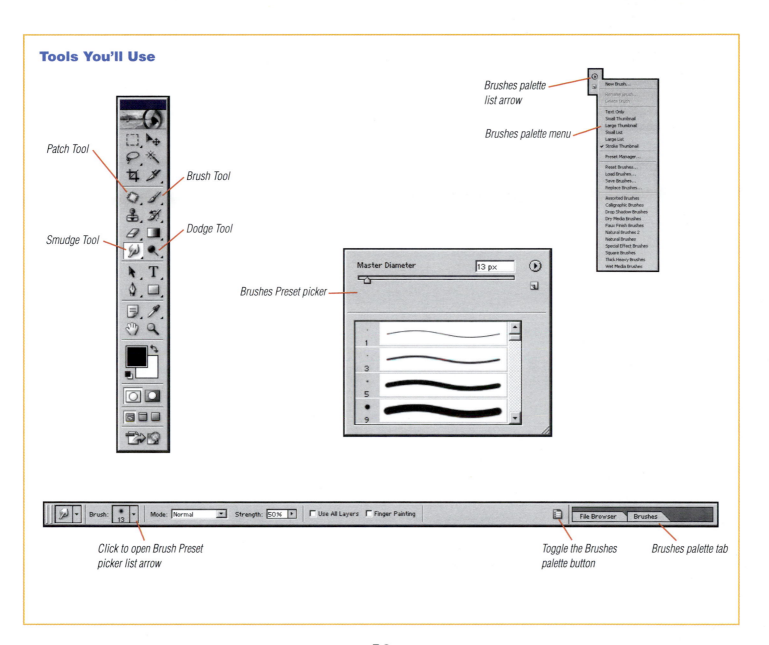

Patch Tool

Brush Tool

Smudge Tool

Dodge Tool

Brushes palette list arrow

Brushes palette menu

New Brush...
Rename brush...
Delete brush

Text Only
Small Thumbnail
Large Thumbnail
Small List
Large List
✔ Stroke Thumbnail

Preset Manager...

Reset Brushes...
Load Brushes...
Save Brushes...
Replace Brushes...

Assorted Brushes
Calligraphic Brushes
Drop Shadow Brushes
Dry Media Brushes
Faux Finish Brushes
Natural Brushes 2
Natural Brushes
Special Effect Brushes
Square Brushes
Thick Heavy Brushes
Wet Media Brushes

Master Diameter   13 px

Brushes Preset picker

1

3

5

9

Brush: 13   Mode: Normal   Strength: 50%   ☐ Use All Layers ☐ Finger Painting

File Browser   Brushes

Click to open Brush Preset picker list arrow

Toggle the Brushes palette button

Brushes palette tab

F-3

PAINT AND PATCH AN IMAGE

What You'll Do

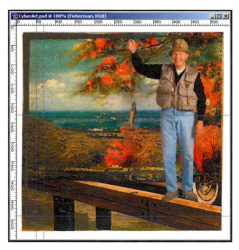

 In this lesson, you'll use the Sharpen Tool to give pixels more definition, the Burn Tool to increase darker areas, then use fade settings to paint an area. You'll also use the Patch Tool to hide unnecessary imagery.

Using Painting Tools

As you've probably realized, you can use many methods to achieve similar effects in Photoshop, and each method isn't necessarily right or wrong. Like a mask, Photoshop painting tools can be used to enhance specific areas of a layer. You can use the painting tools, shown in Table F-1, to create the effects shown in Figure F-1. Unlike a mask that is applied to a defined area within a layer, or a filter that is applied to an entire layer, the effects of painting tools are applied to whatever areas the pointer contacts. Photoshop painting tools are very similar to real painting brushes in the way their effects are applied.

Understanding Fade Options

When you dip a real brush in paint and then apply the brush to canvas, the brushstroke begins to fade as more of the pigment is left on the canvas than on the brush. This effect can be duplicated in Photoshop using fade options. Fade options are brush settings that determine how and when colors fade toward the end of brushstrokes. Fade option settings are measured in steps. A **step** is equivalent to one mark of the brush tip and can be any value from 1—9999. The larger the step value, the longer the fade. You can set fade options for most of the painting tools using the Size Jitter Control option in the Brushes palette.

QUICKTIP

A brush fade is analogous to a skid mark left by a tire.

Using the Patch Tool

Photoshop offers many tools to work with damaged or unwanted imagery. One such tool is the Patch Tool. Although this is not a painting tool, you might find as you work in Photoshop, you have to combine a variety of tool types to achieve the effect you want. The Patch Tool is located on the toolbox and is hidden under the Healing Brush Tool. You can use this tool to cover a selected area with pixels from another area, or a pattern. This tool matches the texture, lighting, and shading of the sampled pixels so your repaired area will look seamless. This tool provides a quick and easy way to repair or remove an area

within an image. You can use the Patch Tool in the following ways:

- Select the area you want to fix, click the Source option button on the tool options bar, then drag the selection over the area you want to replicate.
- Select the area you want replicated, click the Destination option button on the tool options bar, then drag the selection over the area you want to fix.

QUICKTIP

There's not necessarily one "right tool" for any given job: there might be several methods of completing a task. It's up to you to figure out which tool can be used to do the job. Remember, many Photoshop tasks might take several tries before you get the results you want. Hang in there and just keep trying.

FIGURE F-1
Painting samples

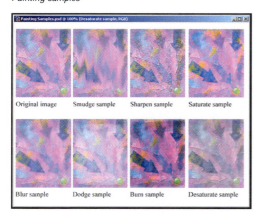

TABLE F-1: Painting Tools

tool	button	effect
Smudge Tool		Smears colors across an image as if you dragged your finger across wet ink. (This tool might be hidden under the Blur Tool.)
Sharpen Tool		Increases contrast between pixels, giving a sharp, crisp look. (This tool might be hidden under the Blur Tool.)
Blur Tool		Decreases contrast between pixels, giving a soft, blurred look.
Dodge Tool		Lightens underlying pixels, giving a lighter, underexposed appearance.
Burn Tool		Darkens underlying pixels, giving a richer, overexposed appearance. (This tool might be hidden under the Dodge Tool.)
Sponge Tool		Increases or decreases the purity of a color by saturating or desaturating the color. (This tool might be hidden under the Dodge Tool.)

Use the Sharpen Tool

1. Start Photoshop, open PS F-1.psd, then save it as **CyberArt**.

2. Display the rulers in pixels, if necessary.

3. Click the Sharpen Tool on the toolbox. △

   TIP   Look under the Blur Tool if the Sharpen Tool is hidden.

4. Click the Click to open the Brush Preset picker list arrow on the tool options bar.

5. Scroll down the list, and double-click 19 (Hard Round 19 pixels).

6. Drag the pointer from 20 H/20 V to 530 H/20 V, to sharpen this area of the image. ◯

7. Press and hold [Shift], then click the image at 530 H/530 V. ◯

   TIP   Instead of dragging to create a line from point to point, you can click a starting point, press and hold [Shift] then click an ending point to create a perfectly straight line.

8. Press and hold [Shift], then click the image at 20 H/530 V. ◯

9. Press and hold [Shift], then click the image at 20 H/20 V. Compare your image to Figure F-2. ◯

You used the Sharpen Tool to focus on the pixels in the perimeter of the image. The affected pixels appear sharper and crisper.

FIGURE F-2
Results of Sharpen Tool

Sharpened areas

Burn an area

1. Click the Burn Tool on the toolbox. ▣

   | TIP   Look under the Dodge Tool if the Burn Tool is hidden.

2. Click the Click to open the Brush Preset picker list arrow on the tool options bar, scroll down, then double-click 27 (Soft Round 27 pixels).

3. Drag the pointer from 20 H/25 V to 550 H/25 V. ◯

4. Drag the pointer back and forth over the upper-right corner from 400 H/25 V to 530 H/120 V. Compare your image to Figure F-3. ◯

You used the Burn Tool to tone down the pixels in the upper-right corner of the image. This technique increases the darker tones, heightening the mood of the document.

Painting with a pattern

Suppose you have an area within an image that you want to replicate on a new or existing layer. You can create a tiled effect using imagery and the Pattern Stamp Tool. To create this effect, select the Rectangular Marquee Tool using a 0 pixel feather setting, then drag the outline around an area in your document. With this area outlined, click Edit on the menu bar, click Define Pattern, type a name in the Name text box, then click OK. Deselect the marquee, click the Pattern Stamp Tool on the toolbox, click the Click to open Pattern picker list arrow on the tool options bar, then click the new pattern. Each time you click the pointer on a layer, the new pattern will be applied. You can delete a custom pattern by right-clicking the pattern swatch in the Pattern picker, then clicking Delete Pattern.

Set fade options and paint an area

1. Click the Eyedropper Tool on the toolbox.

2. Click the image at 50 H/490 V, as shown in Figure F-4.

3. Click the Brush Tool on the toolbox.

4. Click the Click to open the Brush Preset picker list arrow on the tool options bar, then double-click 19 (Hard Round 19 pixels).

5. Click the Toggle the Brushes palette button on the tool options bar.

6. Click the Shape Dynamics text in the Brushes palette, then adjust your settings using Figure F-5 as a guide.

   Available fade options and their locations in the Brushes palette are described in Table F-2.

   TIP   Click the option name in the Brushes palette to see the option settings. Selecting an option's check box turns the option on, but doesn't display the settings.

7. Drag the pointer from 25 H/25 V to 525 H/25 V.

8. Click the image at 25 H/40 V, press and hold [Shift], then click the image at 25 H/520 V, as shown in Figure F-6.

You modified the fade options, then painted areas using the fade settings.

FIGURE F-4
Sample location

FIGURE F-6
Areas painted with fade

Faded areas

FIGURE F-5
Brushes palette

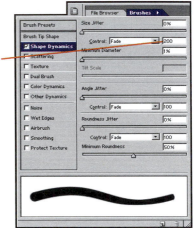

Indicates how many steps it takes for fade to occur

TABLE F-2: Fade Options

option	description	in Brushes palette
Size Jitter	Decreases the brush stroke size toward the end of the stroke.	Shape Dynamics
Opacity Jitter	Decreases the brush stroke opacity toward the end of the stroke.	Other Dynamics
Color	Causes the foreground color to shift to the background color toward the end of the stroke. Available in the following tools: Airbrush , Brush , and Pencil.	Color Dynamics

FIGURE F-7
Marquee surrounding source area

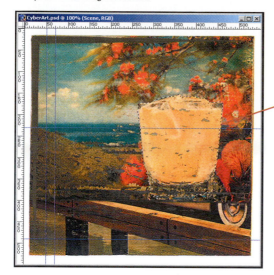

Selection to be patched

FIGURE F-8
Results of Patch Tool

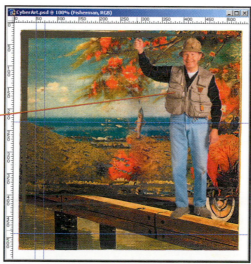

The location of the fisherman might vary slightly

1. Click the Patch Tool on the toolbox.

   TIP Look under the Healing Brush Tool if the Patch Tool is hidden.

2. Drag the pointer around the glass, as shown in Figure F-7.

3. Click the Source option button on the tool options bar, if it's not already selected.

4. Drag the selection so that the outline of the left edge of the glass (the outline source) is at approximately 60 H/170 V.

   The selection is replaced with imagery from the location that you defined with the selection.

5. Click Select on the menu bar, then click Deselect.

6. Click the Fisherman layer on the Layers palette.

7. Click the Move Tool on the toolbox, then press → until the right side of the man covers any remnants of the glass. Compare your image to Figure F-8.

   Selecting and patching are difficult skills to master and your results might differ.

8. Click the Scene layer on the Layers palette.

9. Save your work.

You used the Patch Tool to cover an area within an image.

CREATE AND MODIFY A BRUSH TIP

What You'll Do

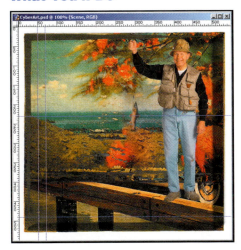

In this lesson, you'll create a brush tip and modify its settings, then you'll use it to paint a border. This new brush tip will be wide and have a distinctive shape that will add an element of mystery to the image.

Understanding Brush Tips

You use brush tips to change the size and pattern of the brush used to apply color. Brushes are stored within libraries. In addition to the default brushes that are available from the Brush Preset picker list, you can also select a brush tip from 11 brush libraries. You can access these additional libraries, shown in Figure F-9, by clicking the Brush Preset picker list arrow on the tool options bar.

Learning About Brush Tip Modifications

You can adjust the many brush tip settings that help determine the shape of a brush. One factor that influences the shape of a brush stroke is jitter. **Jitter** is the randomness of dynamic elements such as size, angle, roundness, hue, saturation, brightness, opacity, and flow. The number beneath the brush tip indicates the diameter, and the image of the tip changes as its values are modified. Figure F-10 shows some of the types of modifications that you can make to a brush tip using the Brushes palette. The shape of the brush tip pointer reflects the shape of the brush tip. As you change the brush tip, its pointer also changes.

QUICK TIP

You can open the Brushes palette to change a brush tip by clicking the Brushes palette tab in the palette well, or by clicking the Toggle the Brushes palette button on the tool options bar.

Applying a tint

You can use brush tips to apply a tint to a grayscale image. By changing the mode of a grayscale image to RGB color, you can use painting tools to tint an image. After you change the image mode, create a new layer, click the Mode list arrow in the New Layer dialog box, click Color, select colors from the Swatches palette, then apply tints to the new layer. See Figure F-11 for a sample.

Creating a Brush Tip

You can create your own brush tip by clicking the Brushes palette list arrow then clicking New Brush to open the Brush Name dialog box, where you can type a descriptive name in the Name text box. All the options on the Brushes palette are available to you as you adjust the settings. As you select settings, a sample appears at the bottom of the palette. You can delete a current brush tip by selecting it from the Brush Preset picker, clicking the Brush Preset picker list arrow, clicking Delete Brush, then clicking OK in the warning box. You can also right-click (Win) or [control] click (Mac) a brush tip in the Brushes palette, then click Delete Brush.

Brush tip libraries

Tinted image

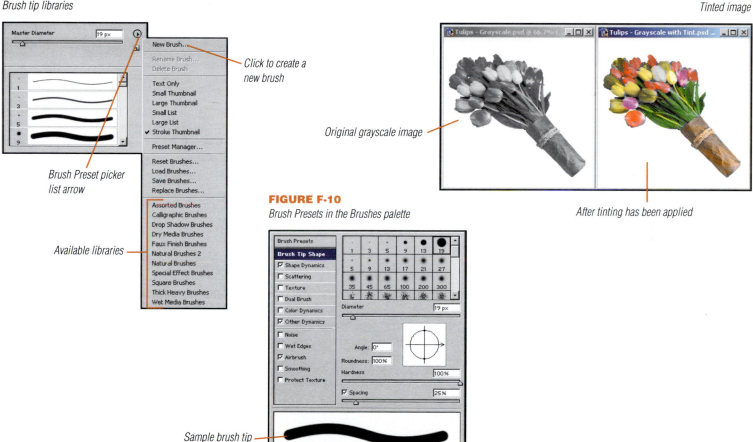

Click to create a new brush

Brush Preset picker list arrow

Available libraries

Original grayscale image

After tinting has been applied

FIGURE F-10
Brush Presets in the Brushes palette

Sample brush tip

Create a brush tip

1. Click the Brushes palette tab in the palette well. `Brushes`

2. Click the Brush Tool on the toolbox, if necessary.

3. Click the arrowhead to the right of the tab, then click Clear Brush Controls.

4. Click the arrowhead to the right of the Brushes palette tab, then click New Brush.

5. Select the contents of the Name text box if necessary, type **Custom oval brush tip**, then click OK.

6. Click Brush Tip Shape in the Brushes palette, then adjust your settings using Figure F-12 as a guide.

7. Click the Brushes palette tab to close the palette.

> TIP A newly added brush tip generally appears at the bottom of the Brushes palette.

The new brush tip appears on the tool options bar.

You created a brush tip, using the Brushes palette. You modified its settings to create a custom brush tip for painting a border.

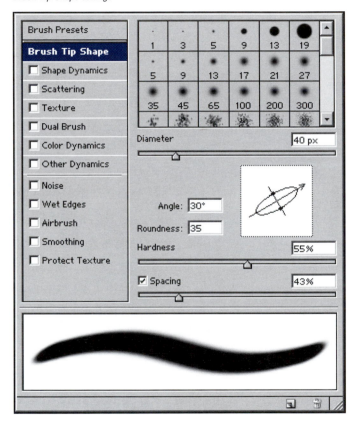

FIGURE F-12
Brush Tip Shape settings

FIGURE F-13

Painted image

CyberArt.psd @ 100% (Scene, RGB)

The smoothness of your
border might differ

Paint a border

1. Click the Mode list arrow on the tool options bar, then click Multiply.

   TIP   The Multiply blend mode creates semitransparent shadow effects and multiplies the value of the base color by the blend color.

2. Double-click the Opacity text box, then type **75**, if necessary.

3. Click the Toggle the Brushes palette button, then click Shape Dynamics.

4. Click the Control list arrow under the Size Jitter section, then click Fade.

5. Type **400**.

6. Click the Brushes palette tab to close the palette.

7. Click the image at 515 H/25 V, press and hold [Shift], then click the image at 515 H/515 V, then release [Shift].

8. Press and hold [Shift], then click the image at 30 H/515 V, then release [Shift].

9. Save your work, then compare your image to Figure F-13.

Using the newly created brush tip, you painted areas of the document. You also made adjustments to the opacity and fade settings to make the brush stroke more dramatic.

SMUDGE COLORS TO CREATE AN ARTISTIC EFFECT

What You'll Do

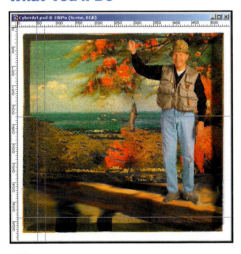

In this lesson, you'll smudge pixels to create a surreal, impressionistic effect.

Blurring Colors

You can create the same finger-painting look in your Photoshop document that you did as a kid. Using the Smudge Tool, you can create the effect of dragging your finger through wet paint. Like the Brush Tool, the Smudge Tool has many brush tips that you can select from the Brushes palette, or you can create a brush tip of your own.

QUICKTIP

You can use the Smudge Tool to minimize defects in an image.

Smudging Options

Figure F-14 shows an original image and three examples of Smudge Tool effects. In each example, the same brush tip is used with different options on the tool options bar. If you select the Smudge Tool with the default settings, your smudge effect will be similar to the image shown in the upper-right corner of Figure F-14.

Using Finger Painting

The image in the lower-right corner of Figure F-14 shows the effect with the Finger Painting check box selected *prior* to the smudge stroke. The image in the upper-right corner did not have the Finger Painting check box selected. The image in the lower-left corner had the Finger Painting option off, but had the Use All Layers check box selected. The Use All Layers check box enables your smudge stroke to affect all the layers beneath the current layer.

QUICKTIP

The Finger Painting option uses the foreground color at the beginning of each stroke. Without the Finger Painting option, the color under the pointer is used at the beginning of each stroke.

FIGURE F-14

Smudge samples

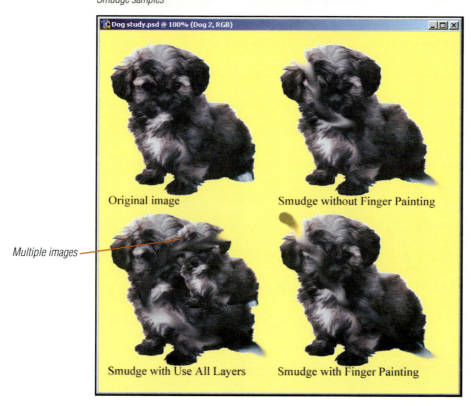

Dog study.psd @ 100% (Dog 2, RGB)

Original image   Smudge without Finger Painting

Multiple images

Smudge with Use All Layers   Smudge with Finger Painting

Modify smudge settings

1. Click the Smudge Tool on the toolbox.

   > TIP The Smudge Tool might be hidden under the Blur Tool.

2. Click the Click to open the Brush Preset picker list arrow on the tool options bar.

3. Double-click 46 (Spatter 46 pixels).

   > TIP This brush tip is located in the upper middle of the list.

4. Select the Finger Painting check box on the tool options bar, if necessary.

5. Make sure your settings match those shown in Figure F-15.

You modified the existing smudge settings.

FIGURE F-15

Tool options bar

Using Painting Tools

FIGURE F-16
Smudged area

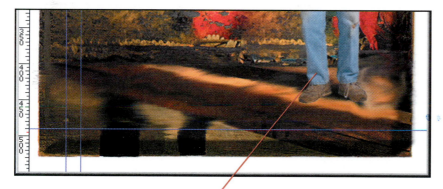

Unchanged imagery

1. Drag the pointer (zigzagging from right to left) from 0 H/400 V to 530 H/500 V.

   TIP   Dragging the pointer back and forth as you move from left to right will create an interesting smudge effect.

   An area on the current layer is smudged. Did you notice that the fisherman layer is unchanged?

2. Save your work, then compare your document to Figure F-16.

You used the Smudge Tool to smear the pixels in the bottom third of the image. That area now has a dreamy quality.

USE A LIBRARY AND AN AIRBRUSH EFFECT

What You'll Do

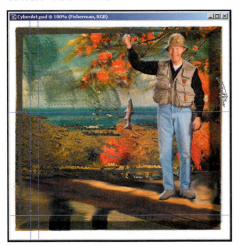

In this lesson, you'll sample an area of the document, then use brush tips from a library to create additional effects. You'll also use an airbrush effect to apply gradual tones.

Learning About the Airbrush Effect

You might have heard of professional photographers using an airbrush to minimize or eliminate flaws in faces or objects. In Photoshop, the airbrush effect simulates the photographer's airbrush technique by applying gradual tones to an image. Airbrushing creates a diffused effect on the edges of pixels. The airbrush effect is located on the tool options bar and on the Brushes palette. You can apply the airbrush effect with any brush tip size, using the Brush Tool, History Brush Tool, Dodge Tool, Burn Tool, and Sponge Tool. The flow setting determines how much paint is sprayed while the mouse button is held.

QUICKTIP

When using the airbrush effect, you can accumulate color by holding the mouse button without dragging. You can use the flow setting to control the speed with which the paint is applied.

Restoring pixel data

You can use the History Brush Tool to restore painted pixels. The History Brush Tool makes a copy of previous pixel data, and then lets you paint with that data, making this tool another good source for undoing painting errors. The Art History Brush Tool also lets you re-create imagery using pixel data, but with more stylized effects. This tool has many more options than the History Brush Tool, including Style, Area, and Tolerance. Style controls the shape of the paint stroke. Area controls the area covered by the brush tip (a higher area value covers a larger area). Tolerance controls the region where the paint stroke is applied, based on color tolerance. A greater spacing value causes paint strokes to occur in areas that differ in color from the original area. Some of the Art History Brush Tool options are shown in Figure F-19.

Using Brush Tip Libraries

Photoshop comes with 11 brush libraries that can replace or be appended to the current list of brushes. All the libraries are stored in a folder called Brushes. Each of the additional libraries is stored in its own file (having the extension .abr). You can load any of the brush libraries by clicking the Click to open the Brush Preset picker list arrow, clicking the Brush Preset picker list arrow, clicking Load Brushes, then clicking one of the libraries, as shown in Figure F-17. Four of the brush libraries are available in the Adobe Photoshop Only folder. When you use the Load Brushes command, the brush tips are added to the end of the brushes list. When you click the name of a brush tip library from the Brush Preset picker list, you are given the option of replacing the existing brush tips with the contents of the library, or adding the brush tips to the existing list.

QUICKTIP

You can restore the default brush tip settings by clicking the list arrow on the Brushes palette, clicking Reset Brushes, then clicking OK.

Managing the Preset Manager

The **Preset Manager** is a Photoshop feature that allows you to manage libraries of preset brushes, swatches, gradients, styles, patterns, contours, custom shapes, and tools. You can display the Preset Manager by clicking Edit on the menu bar, and then clicking Preset Manager. Options for the Preset Manager are shown in Figure F-18. You can delete or rename individual elements for each type of library. Changes that you make in the Preset Manager dialog box are reflected in the corresponding palettes.

FIGURE F-17
Load dialog box

4 additional libraries are available here

FIGURE F-18
Preset Manager dialog box

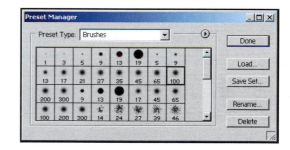

FIGURE F-19
Art History Brush Tool options

Load a brush library

1. Click the Eyedropper Tool on the toolbox.

2. Click the image at 50 H/230 V.

3. Click the Brush Tool on the toolbox.

4. Click the Click to open the Brush Preset picker list arrow on the tool options bar.

5. Click the Brush Preset picker list arrow, then click Load Brushes.

6. Navigate to the Brushes folder, then click Faux Finish Brushes.abr as shown in Figure F-20.

   TIP This brush library is located in the Brushes folder. The Brushes folder is located in the Presets folder in the Adobe Photoshop 7 folder in Applications (Mac).

7. Click Load.

8. Scroll to the end of the list of brush tips, then double-click 75 (Veining Feather 1).

   The active brush tip is from the Faux Finish Brushes library.

You sampled a specific location in the document, then loaded the Faux Finish Brushes library. You selected a brush tip from this new library, which you will use to paint an area.

FIGURE F-21
Brush Tool options

FIGURE F-22
Results of airbrush effect and style

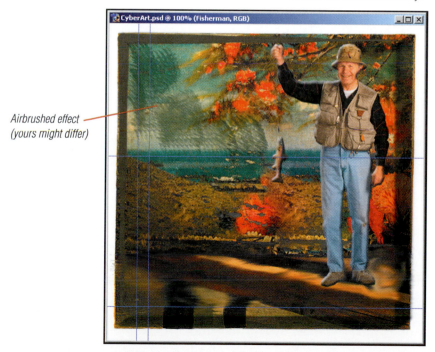

Airbrushed effect
(yours might differ)

Create an airbrush effect

1. Click the Set to enable airbrush capabilities button on the tool options bar.

2. Change the settings on the tool options bar so they match those in Figure F-21.

3. Drag the pointer back and forth over the areas of the image containing the sky (from approximately 30 H/50 V to 250 H/200 V).

4. Hide the rulers.

5. Click the Fisherman layer on the Layers palette.

6. Click the Add a layer style button on the Layers palette.

7. Click Bevel and Emboss, then click OK to accept the existing settings.

8. Save your work, then compare your document to Figure F-22.

You used an airbrush effect to paint the sky in the image. You applied the Bevel and Emboss style to a layer to add finishing touches.

Power User Shortcuts

to do this:	use this method:
Apply tint to grayscale image	Image ➢ Mode ➢ RGB Color, choose color, choose paint tool, then apply color from Swatches palette
Blur an image	⬚ or **Shift R**
Burn an image	⬚ or **Shift O**
Create a brush tip	Brushes , ▶ click New Brush
Define a pattern	Edit ➢ Define Pattern, type name, click OK
Delete brush tip	⬚, then click Delete Brush
Dodge an image	⬚ or **Shift O**

to do this:	use this method:
Load brush library	Click painting tool, ⬚, ⬚, click Load Brushes, choose a library
Paint a straight line	Press and hold [Shift] while dragging pointer
Paint an image	⬚ or **Shift B**
Restore default brushes	⬚, ⬚, click Reset Brushes
Select Fade options	Brushes , then Shape Dynamics
Sharpen an image	⬚ or **Shift R**
Smudge an image	⬚ or **Shift R**

Key: Menu items are indicated by ➢ between the menu name and its command. Bold blue letters are shortcuts for selecting tools on the toolbox.

Using Painting Tools

Paint and patch an image.

1. Open PS F-2.psd, then save it as **The Maze**.
2. Display the rulers in pixels, if necessary.
3. Select the Sharpen Tool.
4. Select brush tip 27 (Soft Round 27 pixels).
5. Drag the pointer back and forth over the maze gates, as shown in Figure F-23; start at 740 H/20 V and finish at 840 H/540 V.
6. Select the Burn Tool.
7. Select brush tip 19 (Hard Round 19 pixels).
8. Drag the pointer back and forth over the two dark red arrows.
9. Sample the image at 50 H/100 V (the ball's shadow) with the Eyedropper Tool.
10. Select the Brush Tool, then use brush tip 17 (Soft Round 17 pixels).
11. Adjust the Size Jitter Fade to 700 steps, then drag the pointer over the inside perimeter of the entire image.
12. Select the Patch Tool.
13. Select the red arrow (at 150 H/350 V).
14. Select the Destination option button, if necessary.
15. Drag the selection to the area at approximately 500 H/140 V.
16. Deselect the selection.
17. Save your work.

Create and modify a brush tip.

1. Create a brush using the Brushes palette called **25 Pixel Sample**.
2. Change the existing settings (using the Brush Tip Shape area in the Brushes palette) to the following: Diameter = 25 pixels, Hardness = 15%, Spacing = 65%, Angle = 15 degrees, and Roundness = 80%.
3. Use the new brush and the current foreground color to fill in the remaining white space surrounding the perimeter of the image.
4. Save your work.

Smudge colors to create an artistic effect.

1. Select the Smudge Tool.
2. Click brush tip 24 (Spatter 24 pixels).
3. Verify that the Finger Painting check box is selected.
4. Use the Normal mode and 70% strength settings.
5. Drag the pointer diagonally (zigzagging from left to right along the way) from the top left to the bottom right of the image.
6. Save your work.

Use a library and an airbrush effect.

1. Use the Eyedropper Tool to sample the aqua arrow in the lower-right corner of the image.
2. Select the Brush Tool and use the airbrush effect.
3. Append the Calligraphic Brushes library to the existing set of brushes.
4. Select brush tip 45 (Oval 45 px) near the bottom of the list.
5. Drag the pointer over the aqua arrowhead.
6. Hide the rulers.
7. Save your work.
8. Compare your document to Figure F-23. The appearance of your document might differ slightly.

FIGURE F-23
Completed Skills Review

A national bank has hired you to create artwork for its new home loan division. The bank wants this artwork to be original. They have instructed you to go wild, and make this ad look like a work of art. You have created a suitable image, but want to add some artistic touches.

1. Open PS F-3.psd, then save it as **Bank Artwork**.
2. Use the Burn Tool and any brush tip you think is appropriate to accentuate the money and the hand that is holding it.
3. Sample a dark brown area within the image (420 H/180 V was used in the sample).
4. Use a painting tool and brush tip of your choice (brush tip 27 is used in the sample) to paint areas within the suits. (*Hint*: In the sample, the suit lapels are painted.)
5. Create a brush tip using a size and shape of your choice, and give the brush tip a descriptive name.
6. Use any painting tool and any color to create a border that surrounds the image. Use the Fade options of your choice.
7. Use the Smudge Tool and the settings of your choice to create an interesting effect in the image.
8. Load a library of your choice, and apply an effect using the Burn Tool and the airbrush effect. (Brush tip 43 from the Drop Shadow library is used in the sample.)

9. Make any color adjustments you want, if necessary. (The Brightness was changed to –26, and the Contrast was changed to +15 in the sample.)

10. Save your work, then compare your document to the sample in Figure F-24.

FIGURE F-24
Completed Project Builder 1

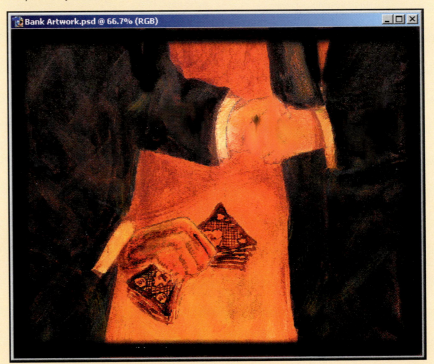

The Robotics Department of a major chip manufacturer is conducting an art contest in the hopes of creating a new image for itself. The contest winner will be used in their upcoming advertising campaign, and they want the ad to be lighthearted and humorous. You have decided to enter the contest and have created a preliminary image. You still need to add the finishing touches.

1. Open PS F-4.psd, then save it as **Robotics Contest Entry**.
2. Use the Sharpen Tool in an area of the image.
3. Burn any area within the image, using any size brush tip.
4. Use the Blur Tool to create an interesting background effect.
5. Use any additional painting tools, libraries, and settings to enhance colors and imagery within the image.
6. Add descriptive type to the image, using the font and wording of your choice. (In the sample, a 36 pt Onyx font is used. A drop shadow effect was added to the type.)
7. Make any color adjustments you want, if necessary. (In the sample, the Hue is modified to −15, the Saturation is modified to +34, and the Lightness is modified to −20.)
8. Save your work, then compare your document to the sample in Figure F-25.

FIGURE F-25
Completed Project Builder 2

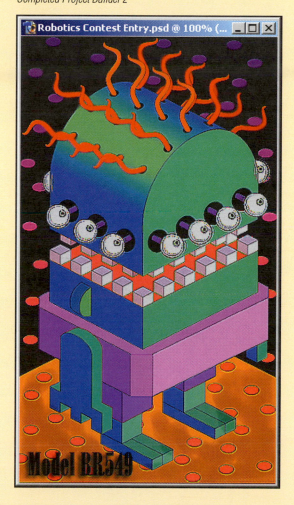

DESIGN PROJECT

You have been hired by a local art gallery, Expressions, to teach a course that describes how Photoshop can be used to create impressionistic artwork. This gallery specializes in offbeat, avant-garde art, and wants you to inspire the attendees to see the possibilities of this important software program. They hired you because you have a reputation for creating daring artwork. As you prepare your lecture, you decide to explore the Internet to see what information already exists.

1. Connect to the Internet and use your browser and favorite search engine to find information on digital art. One possible link is listed in the Student Online Companion. Go to *www.course.com*, navigate to the page for this book, click the Student Online Companion link, then click the link for this unit.
2. Identify and print a page containing an interesting piece of artwork that you feel could be created in Photoshop.

3. Using your word processor, create a document called **Art Course**. A sample document is shown in Figure F-26. (*Tip*: You can capture your image by pressing [Print Scrn], then [Ctrl][V] in your word processor (Win) or pressing [command][shift][3] (Mac).)

4. In the document, analyze the image, pointing out which effects could be created in Photoshop, and which Photoshop tools and features you would use to achieve these effects.
5. Save your work.

FIGURE F-26
Completed Design Project

Art Course Discussion
Expressions Gallery

Using Adobe Photoshop, the document shown here could be created by assembling a variety of images. Adding various images to a rectangular document, such as the red car, clock tower, arch, and flower, could create such a document.

Once the images are positioned within the document, you can use various Photoshop painting tools to create the background stripes and border.

By hiding all the layers except the background, the Brush Tool and the Airbrush option can be used to create the striped effect. (The colors in the background can be obtained from the Swatches palette.) The individual stripes in the background can be made to look less sharp by using the Blur Tool, and the Smudge Tool can be used to muddy the borders of the background stripes.

Once the painting tools have been used, the layers can be displayed and rearranged to achieve the effect you want.

GROUP PROJECT

Depending on the size of your group, you can assign individual elements of the project to group members, or work collectively to create the finished product.

A local car dealer has hired you to create a poster that can be used in magazine ads and highway billboards. The dealership's only requirement is that an automobile be featured within the artwork. Assemble a team and decide what imagery you want to use and who will do the assembly. You can use any appropriate imagery (already existing on your hard drive, from the Web, or your own creation, using a scanner or a digital camera), then compile the artwork and use Photoshop's painting tools to create daring effects. You should create a tag line for the document. You do not need to add a name for the dealership; it will be added at a later date.

1. Start Photoshop and create a document with any dimensions you want.
2. Save this file as **Dealership Ad**.
3. Use any images available from a digital camera or a scanner.
4. Make selections and create a composite image.
5. Use any painting tools and settings to create interesting effects.

6. Add at least one layer of type in the document. (Use any fonts available on your computer. The font shown in the sample is 100 pt Informal Roman.)

7. Make color adjustments, if necessary.
8. Save your work.
9. Compare your document to the sample in Figure F-27.

FIGURE F-27
Completed Group Project

UNIT G

WORKING WITH SPECIAL LAYER FUNCTIONS

1. Use a layer mask with a selection.

2. Work with layer masks and layer content.

3. Control pixels to blend colors.

4. Eliminate a layer mask.

5. Use an adjustment layer.

6. Create a clipping group to act as a mask.

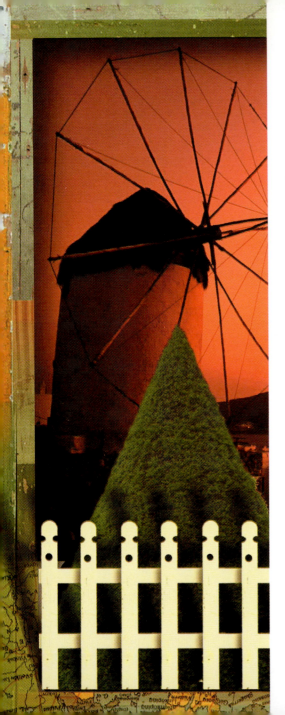

WORKING WITH SPECIAL LAYER FUNCTIONS

Enhancing an Image

Photoshop is rich with tools and techniques that can enhance your document. After the imagery is in place, you can hide and modify objects to create special effects. When used in conjunction with other common functions, such as merging layers or duplicating layers, the results can be dramatic.

Modifying Specific Areas Within a Layer

You can use special layer features to modify the entire document or an entire layer.

For example, suppose that you have a document with objects in multiple layers. Perhaps you want to use elements from each layer, but you also want to hide some imagery. You can *define* the precise area you want to manipulate in each layer, and then accurately adjust its appearance to exactly what you want, without permanently altering the original image. You can turn your changes on or off, align images, blend and adjust color, and combine elements to enhance your image.

Tools You'll Use

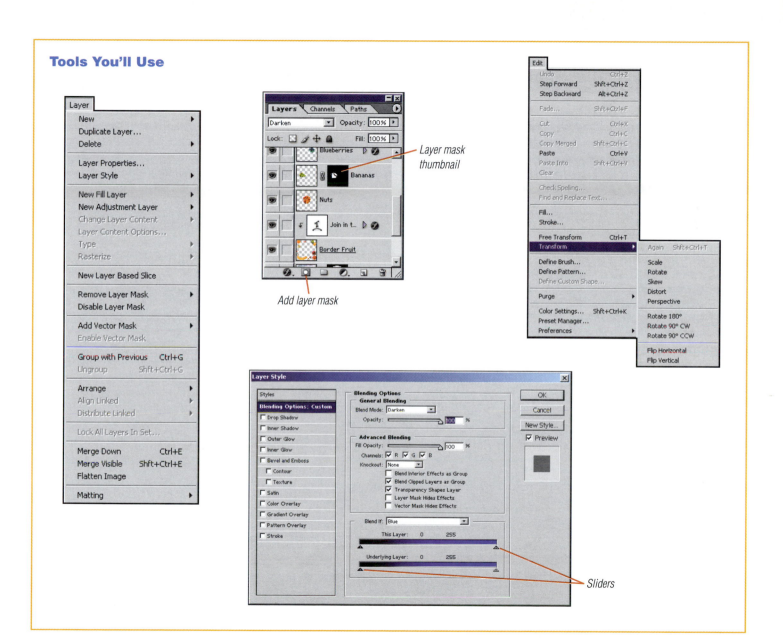

Layer mask thumbnail

Add layer mask

Sliders

USE A LAYER MASK WITH A SELECTION

What You'll Do

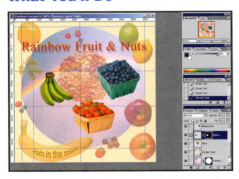

In this lesson, you'll use the Elliptical Marquee Tool to make a selection and create a layer mask on the Rainbow layer and on the Bananas layer. You'll select the Brush Tool and a brush tip, and then paint on the layer mask to hide pixels.

About Layer Masks

You can hide or reveal a selection within a layer by using a layer mask. A **layer mask** can cover an entire layer or specific areas within a layer. When a layer contains a mask, a layer mask thumbnail appears on the Layers palette to the left of the layer name. As you hide or reveal portions of a layer, the layer mask thumbnail mirrors the changes you make to the object. Some Photoshop features are permanent after you implement them. Masks, however, are extremely flexible—you can hide their effect when you view the document, or change them at will. Because you alter the mask and not the image, no actual image pixels are harmed in the creation of your document. You can add an unlimited number of masks to a document, but only one mask to each layer. You can also continue to edit the layer without affecting the layer mask.

Creating a Layer Mask

You can use tools on the toolbox to create the area you want to mask. You can apply a mask to the selection, or you can apply the mask to everything except the selection. You can also feather (control the softness of the selection's edges) by typing pixel values in the Feather text box on the tool options bar.

QUICKTIP

The term "mask" has its origin in printing. Traditionally, a mask was opaque material or tape used to block off an area of the artwork that you did not want to print.

Painting a Layer Mask

After you add a layer mask to a layer, you can reshape it with the Brush Tool and a specific brush size, or tip. Photoshop offers dozens of brush tips, so you can paint just the area you want. For example, you can create a smooth transition between the hidden and visible areas using a soft-edged brush. Here are some important facts about painting a layer mask:

- When you paint the image with a black foreground, the size of the mask *increases*, and each brush stroke hides pixels on the image layer. *Paint with black to hide pixels.*
- When you paint an object using white as the foreground color, the size of the mask *decreases*, and each brush stroke restores pixels of the layer object. *Paint with white to reveal pixels.*

In Figure G-1, the School Bus layer contains a layer mask. The area where the bus intersects with the camera has been painted in black so that the bus appears to be driving through the camera.

Correcting and Updating a Mask

If you need to make a slight correction to an area, you can just switch the foreground and background colors and paint over the mistake. The layer mask thumbnail on the Layers palette automatically updates itself to reflect changes you make to the mask.

FIGURE G-1

Example of a layer mask

Layer mask

Layer mask thumbnail

Create a layer mask using the Layer menu

1. Start Photoshop, open PS G-1.psd, then save it as **Rainbow Fruit**.

2. Reset the default foreground and background colors.

3. Display the rulers in pixels, if necessary.

4. Click the Rainbow layer on the Layers palette.

5. Click the Elliptical Marquee Tool.

   TIP   Look under the Rectangular Marquee Tool if the Elliptical Marquee Tool is hidden.

6. Verify that the Feather setting is set to 0 px.

7. Drag the pointer from 30 H/20 V to 550 H/540 V, using the snap-to feature and the guides, then compare your image to Figure G-2. ✛

8. Click Layer on the menu bar, point to Add Layer Mask, then click Reveal Selection.

   TIP   You can deselect a marquee by clicking Select on the menu bar, then clicking Deselect, or by clicking in another area of the image with the marquee tool that you are using.

You used the Elliptical Marquee Tool to create a selection, and created a layer mask on the Rainbow layer using the Add Layer Mask command on the Layer menu.

Elliptical selection on the Rainbow layer

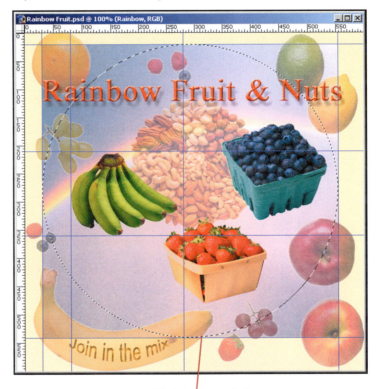

Elliptical marquee selection

FIGURE G-3

Elliptical selection on the Bananas layer

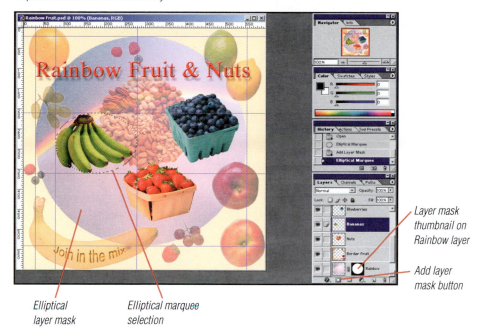

Elliptical
layer mask

Elliptical marquee
selection

Layer mask
thumbnail on
Rainbow layer

Add layer
mask button

FIGURE G-4

Layer mask icons on the Layers palette

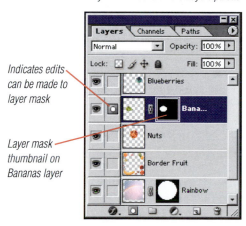

Indicates edits
can be made to
layer mask

Layer mask
thumbnail on
Bananas layer

Create a layer mask using the Layers palette

1. Click the Bananas layer on the Layers palette.

2. Drag the pointer from 80 H/210 V to 280 H/360 V, as shown in Figure G-3. ╶┼╴

3. Click the Add layer mask button on the Layers palette. ▣

The lower-left edge of the bananas is obscured by the layer mask. The layer mask icon replaces the paintbrush icon in the column to the left of the layer thumbnail, and a layer mask thumbnail appears to the right of the layer thumbnail.

> TIP You can press and hold [Alt] (Win) or [option] (Mac) while clicking the Add mask layer button to add a mask that *hides* the selection, rather than reveals it.

4. Click the layer mask thumbnail on the Bananas layer, then compare your Layers palette to Figure G-4.

You used the Elliptical Marquee Tool to create a selection, and then used the Add layer mask button on the Layers palette to create a layer mask on the Bananas layer.

Paint a layer mask

1. Click the Zoom Tool on the toolbox.

2. Select the Resize Windows To Fit check box on the tool options bar if necessary, then click 150 H/300 V until the bananas are centered and the zoom factor is 200%.

3. Click the Brush Tool on the toolbox.

4. Click the Click to open the Brush Preset picker list arrow on the tool options bar if necessary, then double-click the Hard Round 9 pixels brush tip.

5. Verify that the Painting Mode is set to Normal and that the Opacity is set to 100%.

6. Set the default foreground and background colors, then click the Switch Foreground and Background Colors button on the toolbox.

7. Drag the brush pointer along the left-most banana until it is completely hidden. Compare your document to Figure G-5.

   | TIP   Select a different brush tip if the brush is too big or too small.

You used the Zoom Tool to keep a specific portion of the document in view as you increased the zoom percentage, selected a brush tip, and painted pixels on the layer mask to hide a banana.

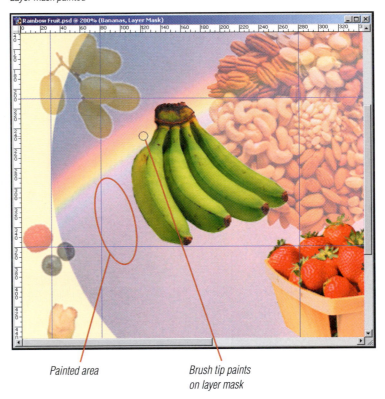

FIGURE G-5
Layer mask painted

Painted area

Brush tip paints on layer mask

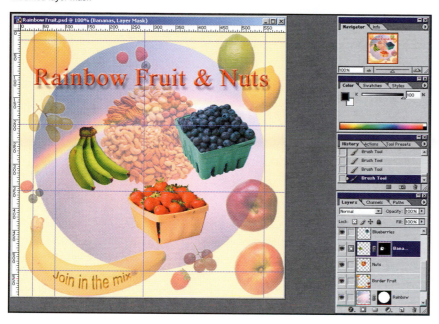

Modify the layer mask

1. Drag the brush pointer along the right edge of the object, until the right-most banana is no longer visible. ⭕

   TIP As you paint, a new History state is created each time you release the mouse button.

2. Click the Zoom Tool on the toolbox. 🔍

3. Press [Alt] (Win) or [option] (Mac), click at 150 H/300 V until the zoom factor is 100%, then release [Alt] (Win) or [option] (Mac). 🔍

4. Save your work, then compare your document to Figure G-6.

You painted pixels to hide the right-most banana, then reset the zoom percentage to 100%.

Editing a layer mask versus editing a layer

Normally, when you click a layer, the paintbrush icon appears in the column to the left of the layer thumbnail. This icon indicates that the changes you make will affect the layer *only*. When you click the layer mask thumbnail, the mask icon appears. It indicates that any changes you make to the layer will affect the mask *only*.

WORK WITH LAYER MASKS AND LAYER CONTENT

What You'll Do

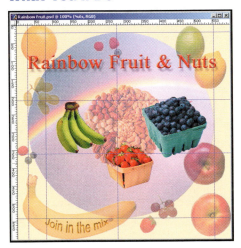

In this lesson, you'll link three layers, align the images on three layers, and then unlink the layers. You'll also scale the strawberries on the Strawberries layer and rotate the nuts on the Nuts layer.

Understanding Layers and Their Masks

The ability to repeatedly alter the appearance of the image without ever disturbing the actual pixels on the layer image makes a layer mask such a powerful editing tool. By default, Photoshop embeds, or links, the mask to the layer. This means that if you move the layer, the mask moves as well.

Understanding the Link Icon

In Photoshop, the link icon performs multiple functions. It automatically appears when you create a layer mask, and it appears when you link layers or layer sets. When you create a layer mask, the link icon appears *in between* the layer thumbnail and the layer mask thumbnail, indicating that the layer and the layer mask are linked together. To unlink the layer mask from its layer, you click the link icon.

Linking Layers

You can group or link layers on the Layers palette so that multiple layers can become one. When you link layers or layer sets, the link icon appears in the column to the left of the layer thumbnail for the affected layers. To link layers, you must verify that the layer, *not the layer mask*, is active, then click the Indicates if layer is linked button on the other layers that you want to link. You can link the active layer to any other layers on the Layers palette, even if they are in different layer sets. You can also link entire layer sets to a single layer or to other layer sets.

Using Linked Layers

After you link layers, you can perform actions that affect the linked group, such as moving their content as a single unit in your document. To unlink layers, click the Indicates if layer is linked button for each layer you want to unlink. When you remove the link, the layers return to their independent state.

Aligning Linked Layers

Suppose you have several type layers in your document and need to align them by their left edges. Rather than individually move and align numerous layers, you can precisely position linked layers in your document. You can align the content in the document by first linking layers on the Layers palette, then selecting one of the six options from the Align Linked command on the Layer menu. Photoshop aligns layers relative to each other or to a selection border. So, if you have four type layers and want to align them by their left sides, Photoshop will align them relative to the leftmost pixels in those layers only, not to any other layers on the Layers palette or to other content that appears in your document.

Distributing Linked Layers

To distribute (evenly space) the content on layers in your document, you must first link three or more layers, verify that their opacity settings are 50% or greater, and then select one of the six options from the Distribute Linked command on the Layer menu. Photoshop spaces out the content in your document relative to pixels in the linked layers. For example, imagine a document that is 700 pixels wide and has four type layers that are 30 pixels wide each and span a range between 100 H and 400 H. If you link the four type layers and click the Horizontal Centers command on the Distribute Linked menu, Photoshop will distribute them evenly, but only between 100 H and 400 H. To distribute the type layers evenly across the width of your document, you must first move the left and right layers to the left and right edges of your document, respectively.

Transforming Objects

You can transform (change the shape, size, perspective, or rotation) of an object or objects on a layer, using 1 of 10 transform commands on the Edit menu. When you use some of the transform commands, eight selection handles, which you drag to transform the layer, surround the contents of the active layer. When you choose a transform command, a bounding box appears around the object you are transforming. A **bounding box** is a rectangle that surrounds an image and contains handles that can be used to change dimensions. You can pull the handles with the pointer to start transforming the object. After you transform an object, you can apply the changes by clicking the Commit transform (Return) button on the tool options bar, or by pressing [Enter] (Win) or [return] (Mac). You can use transform commands individually or in a chain. After you choose your initial transform command, you can try out as many others as you like before you apply the changes by pressing [Enter] (Win) or [return] (Mac). If you attempt another command (something other than another transform command) before pressing [Enter] (Win) or [return] (Mac), a warning box will appear. Click Apply to accept the transformation you made to the layer.

Link and align layers

1. Verify that the Bananas layer on the Layers palette is active.

2. Click the Indicates if layer is linked button on the Nuts layer on the Layers palette. ▢

   TIP The link icon appears in the same column that holds the paintbrush and mask icons.

3. Click the Indicates if layer is linked button on the Blueberries layer on the Layers palette, then compare your Layers palette to Figure G-7. ▢

4. Click Layer on the menu bar, point to Align Linked, then click Vertical Centers.

   The centers of the blueberries and nuts images are aligned with the center of the bananas image. Compare your image to Figure G-8.

5. Click the Indicates if layer is linked button on the Nuts layer and on the Blueberries layer on the Layers palette to unlink these layers from the Bananas layer. ▢

   The objects are no longer linked, but retain their new locations.

You linked three layers on the Layers palette aligned the objects on those layers by their vertical centers using the Align Linked command on the Layer menu, then you unlinked the layers.

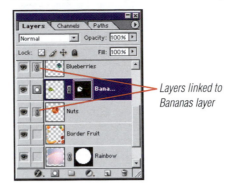

Layers linked to
Bananas layer

Centers of blueberries
and nuts images aligned
with center pixel of
bananas image

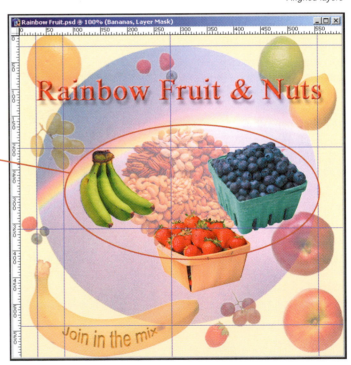

Working with Special Layer Functions

FIGURE G-9
Strawberries layer scaled

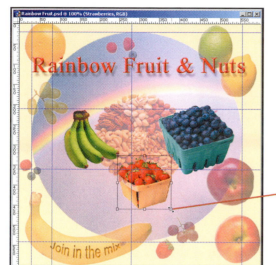

Drag handle to
desired size

FIGURE G-10
Nuts layer rotated

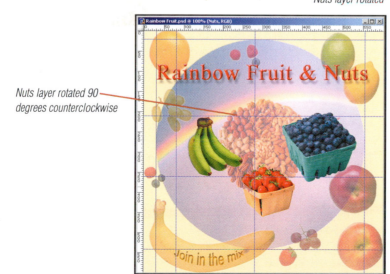

Nuts layer rotated 90
degrees counterclockwise

Transform a layer using scale

1. Click the Strawberries layer on the Layers palette.

2. Click Edit on the menu bar, point to Transform, then click Scale.

3. Position the pointer over the bottom-right sizing handle at approximately 430 H/480 V, then drag to 380 H/460 V, as shown in Figure G-9, then release the mouse button.

4. Click the Commit transform (Return) button on the tool options bar. ✔

   The strawberries image is reduced.

You resized the Strawberries layer using the Scale command.

Transform a layer using rotate

1. Make the Nuts layer active on the Layers palette.

2. Click Edit on the menu bar, point to Transform, then click Rotate 90° CCW.

3. Save your work, then compare your document to Figure G-10.

You rotated the Nuts layer 90° counterclockwise using the Rotate 90° CCW command.

CONTROL PIXELS TO BLEND COLORS

What You'll Do

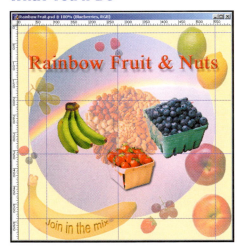

In this lesson, you'll apply styles to layers, using the Layer Style dialog box. You'll also work with blending modes to blend pixels on various layers.

Blending Pixels

You can control the colors and form of your image by blending pixels on one layer with pixels on another layer. You can control *which* pixels from the active layer are blended with pixels from lower layers on the Layers palette. Blending options are found in the Layer Style dialog box. You can control *how* these pixels are blended by choosing a color as the Blend If color, and using the This Layer and Underlying Layer sliders. The **Blend If** color determines the color range for the pixels you want to blend. You use the **This Layer** sliders to specify the range of pixels that will be blended on the active layer. You use the **Underlying Layer** sliders to specify the range of pixels that will be blended on all the lower—but still visible—layers. The color channels available depend on the color mode. For example, an RGB image will have Red, Green, and Blue color channels available.

QUICKTIP

Color channels contain information about colors contained in a document.

Using duplicate layers to blend pixels

You can create interesting effects by duplicating layers. To duplicate a layer, click the layer you want to duplicate to activate it, click the Layers palette list arrow, click Duplicate Layer, then click OK. The duplicate layer is given the same name as the active layer with "copy" attached to it. You can modify the duplicate layer by applying effects or masks to it. In addition, you can alter a document's appearance by moving the original and duplicate layers to different positions on the Layers palette.

Using Color Sliders

The colors that are outside the pixel range you set with the color sliders will not be visible, and the boundary between the visible and invisible pixels will be sharp and hard. You can soften the boundary by creating a gradual transition between the visible and invisible pixels. Normally, you determine the last visible color pixel by adjusting its slider position, just as you can set opacity by dragging a slider on the Layers palette. Photoshop allows you to split the color slider in two. When you move the slider halves apart, you create a span of pixels for the visible boundary. Figure G-11 shows two objects before they are blended and Figure G-12 shows the two objects after they are blended. Do you see how the blended pixels conform to the shape of the underlying pixels?

FIGURE G-11
Pixels before they are blended

All red cap pixels are visible (unblended)

FIGURE G-12
Pixels after they are blended

Red cap pixels blended using sliders in the Layer Style dialog box

Choose a color range to blend

1. Double-click the Strawberries thumbnail on the Layers palette to open the Layer Style dialog box.

   TIP   Move the Layer Style dialog box if it obscures your view of the strawberries.

2. Select the Drop Shadow check box.

3. Click the Blending Options: Custom bar at the top of the list, if necessary.

4. Click the Blend If list arrow, then click Red.

5. Drag the right This Layer slider to 220, as shown in Figure G-13.

   TIP   Slider position determines number of visible pixels for the color channel you've selected.

6. Click OK, then view the fade-out effect on the Strawberries layer.

You opened the Layer Style dialog box for the Strawberries layer, applied the Drop Shadow style, selected Red as the Blend If color, and then adjusted the This Layer slider to change the range of visible pixels.

FIGURE G-13

Layer Style dialog box

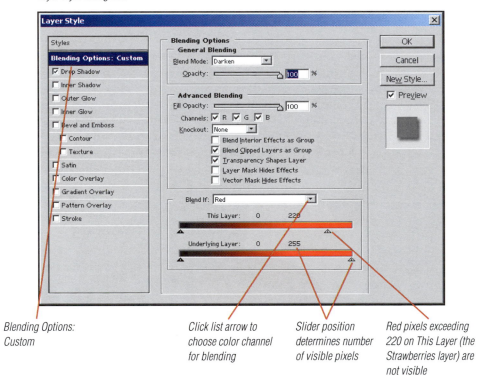

Blending Options: Custom

Click list arrow to choose color channel for blending

Slider position determines number of visible pixels

Red pixels exceeding 220 on This Layer (the Strawberries layer) are not visible

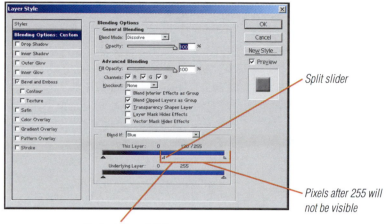

Split slider

Pixels after 255 will
not be visible

Pixels starting at 130
will begin to fade out
of visibility

FIGURE G-15
Blended pixels

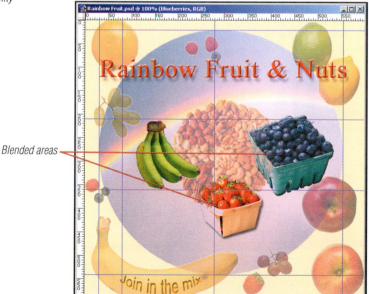

Blended areas

Split sliders to select a color range

1. Double-click the Blueberries thumbnail on the Layers palette.

2. Select the Bevel and Emboss check box.

3. Click the Blending Options: Default bar (Win) or Blending Options: Custom bar (Mac) at the top of the list (if necessary), click the Blend Mode list arrow, then click Dissolve.

4. Click the Blend If list arrow, then click Blue.

5. Press and hold [Alt] (Win) or [option] (Mac), click the right This Layer slider, drag the left split slider to 130, then release [Alt] (Win) or [option] (Mac).

   TIP   Pressing [Alt] (Win) or [option] (Mac) splits the slider.

6. Compare your dialog box to Figure G-14, then click OK.

7. Save your work, then compare your image to Figure G-15.

You opened the Layer Style dialog box for the Blueberries layer, selected the Bevel and Emboss style, changed the blending mode to Dissolve, selected Blue as the Blend If color, and then set a range of pixels that smoothed the transition between visible and invisible pixels by splitting the right This Layer slider.

ELIMINATE A LAYER MASK

What You'll Do

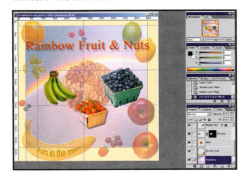

In this lesson, you'll use the Layer menu to temporarily disable a layer mask, and discard a layer mask using the Layers palette.

Disposing of Layer Masks

As you have seen, layer masks enable you to radically change a document's appearance. However, you might not want to keep every layer mask you create, or you might want to turn the layer mask on or off, or you might want to apply the layer mask to the layer and move to another activity. You can turn the layer mask on or off (enable or disable), or remove it from the Layers palette by deleting it from the layer entirely or by permanently applying it to the layer.

Disabling a Layer Mask

Photoshop allows you to temporarily disable a layer mask from a layer to view the layer without the mask. When you disable a layer mask, Photoshop indicates that the layer mask is still in place, but not currently visible, by placing a red X over the layer mask thumbnail, as shown in Figure G-16. Temporarily disabling a layer mask has many advantages. For example, you can create duplicate layers and layer masks, apply different styles and effects to them, and then enable and disable (show and hide) layer masks individually until you decide which mask gives you the look you want.

QUICKTIP

The command available for a layer mask depends on whether the layer is visible or not. If the layer mask is enabled, the Disable Layer Mask command is active on the Layer menu. If the layer mask is disabled, the Enable Layer Mask command is active.

Removing Layer Masks

If you are certain that you don't want a layer mask, you can permanently remove it. Before you remove it, Photoshop gives you the following options:

- You can apply the mask to the layer so that it becomes a permanent part of the layer.
- You can discard the mask and its effect completely.

QUICKTIP

Each layer mask increases the file size, so it's a good idea to perform some routine maintenance as you finalize your document. Remove any unnecessary, unwanted layer masks, and then apply the layer masks you want to keep.

If you apply the mask, the layer will retain the *appearance* of the mask effect, but it will no longer contain the actual layer mask. If you discard the mask entirely, you delete the effects you created with the layer mask, and return the layer to its original state.

QUICKTIP

Before you remove a layer mask, verify that the layer mask is active, *not just the layer*. Otherwise, if you use the Delete layer button on the Layers palette to remove the mask, you will delete the layer, not the layer mask.

FIGURE G-16
Enabled and disabled layer masks

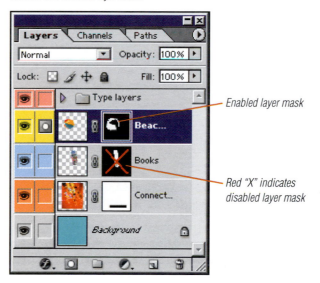

Enabled layer mask

Red "X" indicates disabled layer mask

Disable and enable a layer mask

1. Click the Bananas layer on the Layers palette.

2. Click Layer on the menu bar, then click Disable Layer Mask. See Figure G-17.

   TIP You can also disable a layer mask by pressing [Shift] then clicking the layer mask thumbnail, and then enable it by pressing [Shift] and clicking the layer mask thumbnail again.

You disabled and enabled the layer mask on the Bananas layer, using commands on the Layer menu.

Effect of disabled layer mask

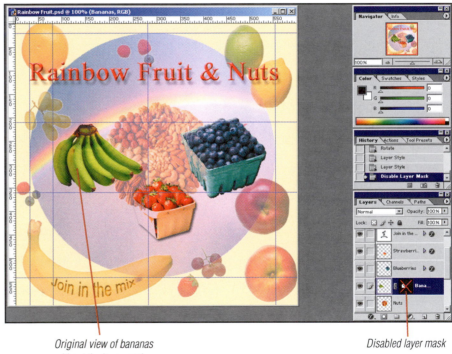

Original view of bananas
without the layer mask

Disabled layer mask

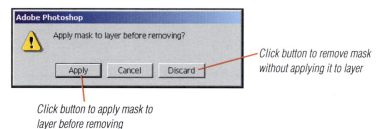

*Click button to remove mask
without applying it to layer*

*Click button to apply mask to
layer before removing*

FIGURE G-19
Rainbow layer with layer mask removed

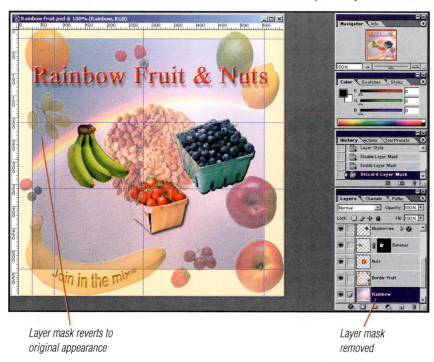

*Layer mask reverts to
original appearance*

*Layer mask
removed*

Remove a layer mask

1. Click the layer mask thumbnail on the Rainbow layer on the Layers palette.
2. Click the Delete layer button on the Layers palette, then compare your warning box to Figure G-18.
3. Click Discard to remove the mask without first applying it to the Rainbow layer. Compare your document to Figure G-19.
4. Click Edit on the menu bar, then click Undo Discard Layer Mask.
5. Save your work.

You used the Delete layer button on the Layers palette to delete a layer mask, chose the Discard option in the warning box to remove the mask without applying it to the Rainbow layer, and then undid the action to restore the layer mask on the Rainbow layer.

USE AN ADJUSTMENT LAYER

What You'll Do

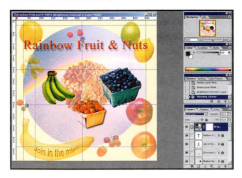

In this lesson, you'll create an adjustment layer, choose Brightness/Contrast as the type of adjustment layer, adjust settings in the Brightness/Contrast dialog box, and then use the Layers palette to change the blending mode of the adjustment layer.

Understanding Adjustment Layers

An adjustment layer is a special layer that acts as a color filter for all the layers beneath it. Just as you can use a layer mask to edit the layer content without permanently deleting pixels on the image, you can create an adjustment layer to adjust color and tone. If you were to make changes to the original layer, the changes would be irreversible. (You could use the Undo feature or the History palette to undo your changes, but only in the current Photoshop session.) However, the color changes you make to the adjustment layer exist only in the adjustment layer.

Creating an Adjustment Layer

You can create an adjustment layer by selecting the layer you want to adjust, then using the Layer menu to click a new adjustments layer command or by clicking the Create new fill or adjustment layer button on the Layers palette. When you create an adjustment layer, you must specify which of the 11 color adjustments you want to use. These adjustments are described in Table G-1.

> **QUICKTIP**
>
> If you use the Create new fill or adjustment layer button on the Layers palette, you'll see 3 additional menu items: Solid Color, Gradient, and Pattern. You use these commands to create fill layers, which fill a layer with a solid color.

Modifying an Adjustment Layer

You can change the adjustment layer settings by double-clicking the layer thumbnail on the adjustment layer. Photoshop identifies the type of adjustment layer on the Layers palette by including the type of adjustment layer in the layer name.

Using Multiple Adjustment Layers

You can use as many adjustment layers as you want, but you must create them one at a time. At first glance, this might strike you as a disadvantage, but when you're working on a document, you'll find it to be an advantage. By adding one or more adjustment layers, you can experiment with a variety of colors and tones, then hide and show each one to determine the one that best suits your needs. Adjustment layers can also contain layer masks, which allow you to fine-tune your alterations by painting just the adjustment layer mask.

Merging Adjustment Layers

You can merge adjustment layers with any *visible* layers in the image, including linked layers. You cannot, however, merge one adjustment layer with another adjustment layer. Merging adjustment layers reduces file size and ensures that your adjustments will be permanent.

QUICKTIP

You can toggle between selecting the layer mask and the entire layer by pressing [Ctrl][\] (Win) or [command][\] (Mac) to select the layer mask, and pressing [Ctrl][~] (Win) or [command][~] (Mac) to select the entire layer.

TABLE G-1: Color Adjustments

color adjustment	description
Levels	Sets highlights and shadows in a document by increasing the tonal range of pixels, while preserving the color balance.
Curves	Makes adjustments to a document's entire tonal range, using three variables: highlights, shadows, and midtones.
Color Balance	Changes the overall mixture of color.
Brightness/Contrast	Makes simple adjustments to a document's tonal range.
Hue/Saturation	Changes position on the color wheel (hue) or purity of a color (saturation).
Selective Color	Increases or decreases the number of process colors in each of the additive and subtractive primary color components.
Channel Mixer	Modifies a color channel, using a mix of current color channels.
Gradient Map	Maps the equivalent grayscale range of an image to colors of a specific gradient fill.
Invert	Converts an image's brightness values to the inverse values on the 256-step color-values scale.
Threshold	Converts images to high-contrast, black-and-white images.
Posterize	Specifies the number of tonal levels for each channel.

Create and set an adjustment layer

1. Click the Rainbow Fruit & Nuts layer on the Layers palette.

   As the top-most layer, all the layers beneath it will be affected by any changes you make.

2. Click Layer on the menu bar, point to New Adjustment Layer, then click Brightness/Contrast. Compare your dialog box to Figure G-20.

   > TIP You can also create a new adjustment layer by clicking the Create new fill or adjustment layer button on the Layers palette, then selecting a color adjustment.

3. Click OK.

4. Type **–15** in the Brightness text box.

5. Type **30** in the Contrast text box.

6. Click OK. Compare your Layers palette to Figure G-21.

   Did you notice that the new adjustment layer appears on the Layers palette above the Rainbow Fruit & Nuts layer, and is named Brightness/Contrast 1 because you chose Brightness/Contrast as the type of color adjustment?

You created a Brightness/Contrast adjustment layer on the Rainbow Fruit & Nuts layer, then adjusted settings in the Brightness/Contrast dialog box.

FIGURE G-20
New Layer dialog box

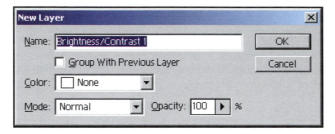

FIGURE G-21
Adjustment layer on Layers palette

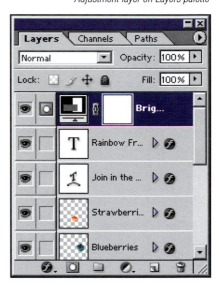

FIGURE G-22

Result of adjustment layer

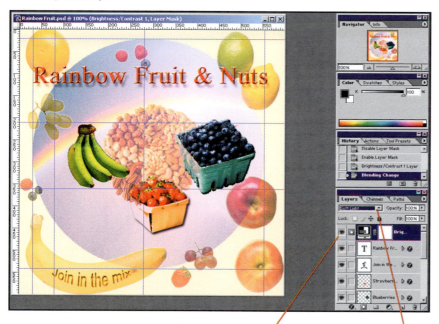

Layer thumbnail for
adjustment layer

Set the blending
mode for the layer
list arrow

1. Make sure that the Brightness/Contrast 1 layer is still the active layer.

2. Click the Set the blending mode for the layer list arrow on the Layers palette, then click Soft Light.

3. Save your work, then compare your image to Figure G-22.

You changed the blending mode for the adjustment layer to Soft Light, using the Layers palette.

CREATE A CLIPPING GROUP
TO ACT AS A MASK

What You'll Do

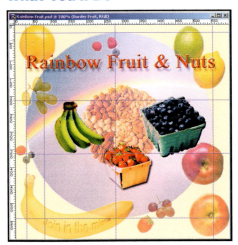

 In this lesson, you'll create a clipping group, adjust the opacity of the base layer, remove and restore the clipping group, then flatten the image.

Understanding Clipping Groups

A **clipping group** is a group of two or more contiguous layers (layers that are next to each other on the Layers palette). Clipping groups are useful when you want one layer to act as the mask for other layers, or if you want an adjustment layer to affect only the layer directly beneath it. The bottom layer in a clipping group is called the base layer, and it serves as the group's mask. For example, you can use a type layer as the base of a clipping group so that a pattern appears through the text on the base layer, as shown in Figure G-23. The properties of the base layer determine the opacity and visible imagery of a clipping group. You can, however, adjust the opacity of the individual layers in a clipping group.

QUICKTIP

You can merge layers in a clipping group with an adjustment layer, as long as the layers are visible.

Creating a Clipping Group

To create a clipping group, you need at least two layers: one to create the shape of the mask, and the other to supply the content for the mask. You can use a type or an image layer to create the clipping group shape, and when the shape is the way you want it, you can position the pointer between the two layers, then press [Alt] (Win) or [option] (Mac). The pointer changes to two circles with a left-pointing arrowhead. Simply click the line between the layers to create the clipping group. You can tell if a clipping group exists by looking at the Layers palette. A clipping group is indicated when one or more layers are indented and appear with a down arrow icon, and the base layer is underlined.

Removing a clipping group

When you create a clipping group, the layers in the clipping group are grouped together. To remove a clipping group, press and hold [Alt] (Win) or [option] (Mac), position the clipping group pointer over the line separating the grouped layers on the Layers palette, then click the mouse. You can also select the base layer, click Layer on the menu bar, and then click Ungroup.

FIGURE G-23
Result of clipping group

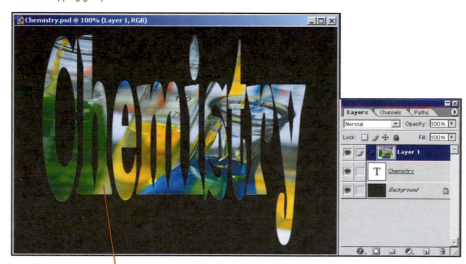

*Clipped texture
appears in layer*

Create a clipping group

1. Click the Join in the mix layer on the Layers palette.

2. Drag the layer below the Nuts layer on the Layers palette.

3. Press and hold [Alt] (Win) or [option] (Mac), then move the clipping group pointer to the line between the Border Fruit and the Join in the mix layers. Compare your Layers palette to Figure G-24.

4. Click the line between the two layers, then release [Alt] (Win) or [option] (Mac).

   The Join in the mix layer (member) is filled with the banana peel from the Border fruit layer (base).

5. Verify that the clipping icon (a small downward pointing arrow) appears in the Join in the mix layer, then compare your Layers palette to Figure G-25.

6. Make sure the Join in the mix layer is active, click the Opacity list arrow on the Layers palette, drag the slider to 100%, then press [Enter] (Win) or [return] (Mac).

You created a clipping group, using the Border Fruit layer as the base and the Join in the mix layer as a member of the clipping group to make the banana peel appear as the fill of the Join in the mix layer, and then you adjusted the opacity of the Join in the mix layer.

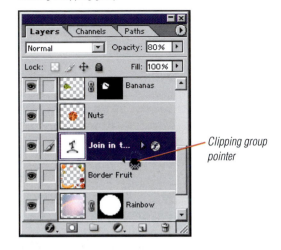

Clipping group pointer

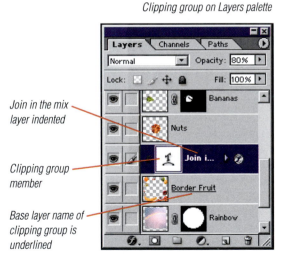

Join in the mix layer indented

Clipping group member

Base layer name of clipping group is underlined

FIGURE G-26

Finished product

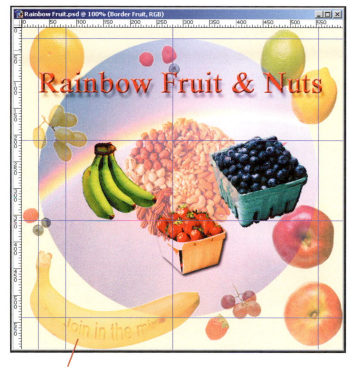

Join in the mix layer
text filled in with
banana texture

1. Click the Border Fruit layer on the Layers palette.

2. Click Layer on the menu bar, then click Ungroup.

3. Click Edit on the menu bar, then click Undo Ungroup. Compare your document to Figure G-26.

4. Click File on the menu bar, click Save As, then, using the name given, select the As a Copy check box, then click Save.

5. Click Layer on the menu bar, then click Flatten Image.

6. Save your work.

You removed the clipping group by using the Ungroup command on the Layer menu, restored the clipping group by using the Undo command on the Edit menu, saved a copy of the document, and then flattened the document.

Power User Shortcuts

to do this:	use this method:	to do this:	use this method:
Activate layer	Press and hold [Ctrl][~] (Win) or [⌘] [~] (Mac)	Create a layer mask that hides the selection	Press and hold [Alt] (Win) or option (Mac) ➤
Activate layer mask	Press and hold [Ctrl][\] (Win) or [⌘] [\] (Mac)	Create a layer mask that reveals the selection	Layer ➤ Add Layer Mask ➤ Reveal Selection
Add an adjustment layer		Delete layer	
Align linked layers by vertical centers	Layer ➤ Align Linked ➤ Vertical Centers	Disable layer mask	Layer ➤ Disable Layer Mask
Blend pixels on a layer	Double-click a layer thumbnail, click Blend If list arrow, choose color, drag This Layer and Underlying Layer sliders	Next or previous brush tip in palette	[,] or [.]
Brush Tool	or **B**	Remove a clipping group	Click a layer in the group ➤ Layer ➤ Ungroup
Change brush tip	Select Brush Tool, right-click (Win) or control (Mac)	Remove a link	Click
Create a clipping group	Press and hold [Alt] (Win) or option (Mac), move the pointer to the line between two layers, then click	Scale a layer	Edit ➤ Transform ➤ Scale
		Rotate a layer 90° to the left	Edit ➤ Transform ➤ Rotate 90° CCW
Create a layer mask		Select first or last brush tip in palette	[Shift][,] or [Shift][.]

Key: Menu items are indicated by ➤ between the menu name and its command. Blue bold letters are shortcuts for selecting tools on the toolbox.

Use a layer mask with a selection.

1. Start Photoshop, open PS G-2.psd, then save it as **Stripes**.
2. Make sure the rulers are displayed in pixels.
3. Zoom in to 150%.
4. Create a type layer title above the Zebra layer and add the drop shadow layer style (using default settings). (*Hint*: A 30-pt Impact font is shown in the sample.)
5. Make the Zebra layer active, then select the Elliptical Marquee Tool.
6. Change the Feather setting on the tool options bar to 5 pixels.
7. Create a marquee selection from 35 H/35 V to 235 H/360 V. (*Hint*: Feel free to add guides, if necessary.)
8. Use the Layers palette to add a layer mask.
9. Save your work.

Work with layer masks and layer content.

1. Select the Brush Tool.
2. Hide the type layer.
3. Change the existing brush tip to Soft Round 9 pixels.
4. Verify that the Painting mode is Normal, and that the flow and opacity are 100%.
5. Use the default foreground and background colors to paint the area from 20 H/70 V to 65 H/290 V. (*Hint*: Make sure the layer mask thumbnail is selected.)
6. Display the type layer.
7. Make the Fern layer active.
8. Unlink the Background layer.

9. Rotate the fern so that its left edge barely touches the zebra's nose.
10. Save your work.

Control pixels to blend colors.

1. Double-click the Fern layer thumbnail.
2. Using green as the Blend if color, drag the right This Layer slider to 200.
3. Split the right This Layer slider, drag the right half to 240, then click OK.
4. Save your work.

Eliminate a layer mask.

1. Click the layer mask thumbnail on the Zebra layer.
2. Use the Layer menu to disable the layer mask.
3. Use the Layer menu to enable the layer mask.
4. Save your work.

Use an adjustment layer.

1. Make the Fern layer active.
2. Using the Layer menu, create a Color Balance adjustment layer called **Modifications**.
3. Make sure the Midtones option button is selected, drag the Cyan, Magenta, and Yellow sliders to +36, +12, and −19, respectively.
4. Create a Brightness/Contrast adjustment layer called **Brightness/Contrast**, above the Modifications layer.
5. Change the Brightness to −25 and the Contrast to +20.
6. Hide the Modifications layer.
7. Hide the Brightness/Contrast layer.

8. Display both adjustment layers.
9. Save your work.

Create a clipping group to act as a mask.

1. Make the Background layer active.
2. Create a clipping group (with the Background layer as the base layer) that includes the type layer. (*Hint*: Move the type layer to a new location, if necessary.)
3. Include the Zebra layer in the clipping group.
4. Save your work, then compare your document to Figure G-27.

FIGURE G-27
Completed Skills Review

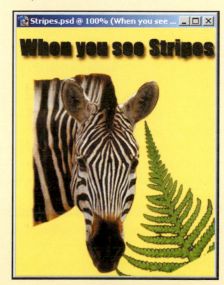

Your cousin has recently bought a beauty shop and wants to increase its numbers of manicure customers. She's hired you to create an image that can be used in print ads and will attract attention. You decided to take an ordinary image and use your knowledge of masks and adjustment layers to make the image look striking.

1. Open PS G-3.psd, then save it as **Manicure**.
2. Duplicate the Polishes layer, then name the new layer Red Polish.
3. Select the red nail polish bottle, then delete everything else in the layer. (*Hint*: You can do this by deleting a selection.)
4. Hide the Red Polish layer.
5. Create a layer mask over the red polish, then brush in the remaining items on the Polishes layer.
6. Use any tools at your disposal to fix the area where the red polish (on the Polishes layer) has been masked.
7. Display the Red Polish layer.
8. Move the Red Polish Layer below the Polishes layer, if necessary.
9. Use the existing layer mask to hide the white polish (with the blue cap).
10. Position the red polish so it appears where the white polish was visible.
11. Use any tools necessary to fix areas, such as the Blur Tool to soften the edges of polish bottles.
12. Add an adjustment layer to the Red Polish layer that makes the polish color violet. (*Hint*: In the sample, a Hue/Saturation adjustment layer was used with the following settings: Hue: –45, Saturation: +35, and Lightness: –5.)
13. Add one or two brief type layers, and apply layer styles to them. (*Hint*: In the sample, the type used is an 80 pt Palace Script MT and a 60-pt Perpetua font.)
14. Save a copy of the document, then flatten the image.
15. Save your work, then compare your image to Figure G-28.

FIGURE G-28
Completed Project Builder 1

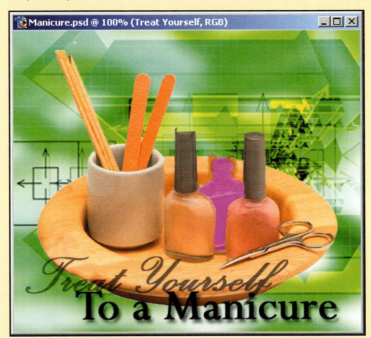

In exchange for free concert tickets, you volunteered to work on the cleanup crew for an outdoor concert facility. After the second concert, the promoter asks you to design a poster to inspire concertgoers to throw trash in the trash barrels. You decide to create a Photoshop document that contains several unique illusions. Using any city or locale but your own as a theme, you'll use your Photoshop skills to create and paint layer masks in a document that conveys a cleanup message.

1. Obtain the following images that reflect the city or locale: a landscape, a sign, one large inanimate object, and two or more other objects. You can use the images that are available on your computer, scan print media, or use a digital camera. (*Hint*: Try to obtain images that fit into your theme.)

2. Create a new Photoshop document and save it as **Cleanup**.

3. Drag the landscape to the Cleanup document above the Background layer, then delete the Background layer.

4. Drag the large object image to the Cleanup document above the landscape layer.

5. Transform the large object as necessary to prepare it to be partially buried in the landscape. (*Hint*: The tower layer in the sample has been rotated and resized.)

6. Apply a layer mask to the large object, then paint the layer mask to reshape the mask and partially obscure the object.

7. Add one or more styles of your choice to the large object.

8. Drag the sign image to the Cleanup document, and then place it below the large object layer.

9. Create a type layer for the sign layer with a message (humor optional), link the layers, then transform the layers as needed to fit in the image. (*Hint*: The sign layer and type layer in the sample have been skewed.)

10. Drag other images as desired to the Cleanup document, and add styles to them or transform them as necessary.

11. Create other type layers (humor optional) as desired, and apply at least one style to each layer. (*Hint*: The title layer in the sample has drop shadow and outer glow styles applied to it. A 12-pt, Agency FB font is used in the sign, and a 35- and 24-pt Arial Black is used in the title.)

12. Add an adjustment layer to the landscape layer, and to any other layer that would benefit from it.

13. Save a copy of your document, then flatten the image.

14. Save your work, then compare your document to Figure G-29.

FIGURE G-29
Completed Project Builder 2

DESIGN PROJECT

As the publishing director for a large accounting firm, you've been asked to design a banner for the new International Monetary Division Web site. They've asked that you include the flag, paper currency, and coinage of the country of your choice. You decide to use Photoshop techniques to create an interesting collage of those three items.

1. Obtain several images of paper currency, coins, and the flag of the country you've chosen. You can use the images that are available on your computer, scan print media, or connect to the Internet and download images. (*Hint*: Try to obtain at least two denominations of both paper and coin.)
2. Create a new document in Photoshop and save it as **Currency**.
3. Add a color to a new Background layer, open the paper money files, then drag the paper money images to the Currency document above the layer.
4. Transform the paper money layers as desired. (*Hint*: The paper money layers in the sample have been rotated and skewed.)
5. Add layer masks as desired.
6. Add an adjustment layer to the paper money layers, and apply at least one color adjustment. (*Hint*: The paper money layers in the sample have a Curves color adjustment applied to them.)

7. Open the flag file, then drag the flag image to the Currency document, and position it to appear on top of the paper money layers, then resize it and adjust opacity, as necessary.
8. Paint the edges of the flag with an unusual brush tip. (*Hint*: Use the Brush Preset picker to access different brush tips.)
9. Open the coin files, drag the coin images to the Currency document, duplicate the coin

layers as desired, position them above the flag layer, then apply at least one transformation and one layer style to them. (*Hint*: The coins in the sample have a Drop Shadow style and have been rotated.)
10. Blend the pixels for two of the coin layers.
11. Save a copy of the document, flatten the image, then close the other files.
12. Save your work, then compare your document to Figure G-30.

FIGURE G-30
Completed Design Project

Depending on the size of your group, you can assign individual elements of the project to group members, or work collectively to create the finished product.

Lost Horizons, a tragically hip coffeehouse, is hosting a regional multimedia Poetry Slam contest. You and your friends, all avid Photoshop users, have teamed up with the Surreal Poetry Enclave, an eclectic poetry group. The contest consists of half of the team reading poetry while the other half creates a visual interpretation using two preselected images and as many elective images as they want. First, though, you must submit an entry design. Assign members in your group to find a poem for inspiration, design the interpretation, obtain images, and write some creative copy (tag line or slogan) to be used in the design.

1. Obtain images for your interpretative design. The images you must include are a picture frame and a background image; the other pieces are up to you. You can use the images that are available on your computer, scan print media, or connect to the Internet and download images.
2. Create a new Photoshop document, then save it as **Lost Horizons**.
3. Open the background image file, drag the background image to the Lost Horizons document above the Background layer, then delete the Background layer.
4. Open the picture frame file, drag it to the Lost Horizons document above the Background layer, transform it as necessary, then apply styles to it. (*Hint*: The frame in the sample has been skewed.)
5. Open the images that will go in or on the picture frame, drag them to the Lost Horizons document, then transform them as necessary.
6. Arrange the image layers on the Layers palette in the configuration you want, and apply styles to them.
7. Apply a layer mask to two or more of the image layers. (*Hint*: The layer mask in the eye layer in the sample has a foreground to background gradient applied to it.)
8. Create a clipping group using two or more of the image layers. (*Hint*: The clipping group in the sample consists of the frame layer as the base and the Lantern and Alarm clock layers as members.)
9. Create type layers as desired and apply styles to them. (*Hint*: The type layer in the sample has an Outer Glow style applied to it.)
10. Close the image files, save your work, then compare your document to Figure G-31.
11. Be prepared to discuss the creative ways you can use clipping groups.

FIGURE G-31
Completed Group Project

UNIT

H

CREATING SPECIAL EFFECTS WITH FILTERS

1. Learn about filters and how to apply them.

2. Create an effect with an Artistic filter.

3. Add unique effects with Stylize filters.

4. Use the Distort and Noise filters.

5. Use a Render filter to alter lighting.

CREATING SPECIAL EFFECTS WITH FILTERS

Understanding Filters

You've already seen some of the dozens of ready-to-use effects and some filters that Photoshop offers. Filters alter the look of an image by altering pixels. This results in a unique, customized appearance. You use filters to apply special effects, such as realistic textures, distortions, changes in lighting, and blurring. Although you can use several categories of filters and options within categories, the most important thing to remember when using filters is subtlety.

Applying Filters

You can apply filters to any layer (except the Background layer) using commands on the Filter menu. Most filters have their own dialog box, where you can adjust filter settings and preview the effect before applying it. The preview window in the dialog box allows you to evaluate the precise effect of the filter on your selection. You can click the Zoom in and Zoom out buttons, and the Hand Tool to pan the image in the dialog box. Other filters apply their effects instantly as soon as you click the command.

QUICKTIP

Does your computer have enough RAM? You'll know for sure when you start using filters because they are *very* memory-intensive.

Tools You'll Use

Colored Pencil... — *Artistic filters*
Cutout...
Dry Brush...
Film Grain...
Fresco...
Neon Glow...
Paint Daubs...
Palette Knife...
Plastic Wrap...
Poster Edges...
Rough Pastels...
Smudge Stick...
Sponge...
Underpainting...
Watercolor...

Blur — *Blur filters*
Blur More
Gaussian Blur...
Motion Blur...
Radial Blur...
Smart Blur...

Filter	
Last Filter	Ctrl+F
Extract...	Alt+Ctrl+X
Liquify...	Shft+Ctrl+X
Pattern Maker...	Alt+Shft+Ctrl+X
Artistic	▶
Blur	▶
Brush Strokes	▶
Distort	▶
Noise	▶
Pixelate	▶
Render	▶
Sharpen	▶
Sketch	▶
Stylize	▶
Texture	▶
Video	▶
Other	▶
Digimarc	▶

Diffuse Glow...
Displace...
Glass...
Ocean Ripple... — *Distort filters*
Pinch...
Polar Coordinates...
Ripple...
Shear...
Spherize...
Twirl...
Wave...
ZigZag...

Render filters —
3D Transform...
Clouds
Difference Clouds
Lens Flare...
Lighting Effects...
Texture Fill...

Add Noise...
Despeckle
Dust & Scratches...
Median...
Noise filters

Stylize filters —
Diffuse...
Emboss...
Extrude...
Find Edges
Glowing Edges...
Solarize
Tiles...
Trace Contour...
Wind...

LEARN ABOUT FILTERS AND HOW TO APPLY THEM

What You'll Do

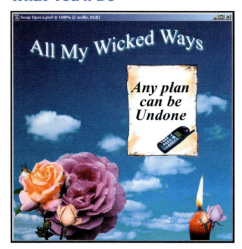

In this lesson, you'll apply the Motion Blur filter to the Candle layer.

Understanding the Filter Menu

The Filter menu sorts the filters into 14 categories and subcategories. Many filters are memory-intensive, so you might need to wait several seconds while Photoshop applies the effect. Using filters might slow down your computer's performance. Figure H-1 shows samples of several filters.

Learning About Filters

In reality, the only *real* way to learn about filters is to use them. You can read about filters all day long, but until you apply a filter to your own image, it's all academic. However, here are a few tips about filters to keep in mind when you apply them.

- Distort filters can completely reshape an image; they are highly resource-demanding filters.
- Photoshop applies Pixelate filters as soon as you click the command; they do not have a preview box.
- Digimarc filters notify users that the image is copyright-protected.

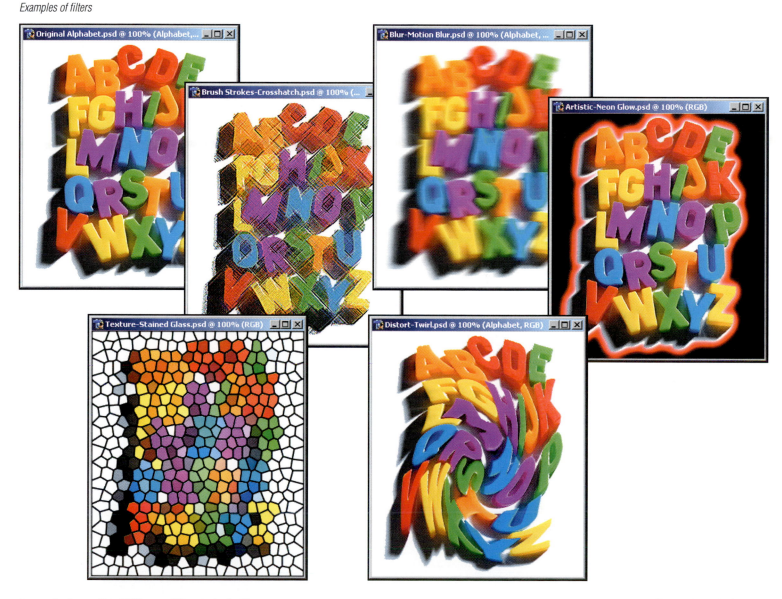

Categorizing Filters

You just won't believe how many filters there are, how much they can do for an image, or just how much fun they can be. Table H-1 lists each filter category and some suggested uses.

TABLE H-1: Filter Categories	
category	**use**
Artistic	Replicates traditional fine arts effects.
Blur	Simulates an object in motion; can use to retouch photographs.
Brush Strokes	Mimics fine arts brushwork and ink effects.
Distort	Reshapes an image.
Noise	Gives an aged look; can use to retouch photographs.
Pixelate	Adds small honeycomb shapes based on similar colors.
Render	Transforms three-dimensional shapes; simulates light reflections.
Sharpen	Refocuses blurry objects by increasing contrast in adjacent pixels.
Sketch	Applies a texture, or simulates a fine arts hard-drawn effect.
Stylize	Produces a painted or impressionistic effect.
Texture	Gives the appearance of depth or substance.
Video	Restricts color use to those that are acceptable for television reproduction and smooth video images.
Other	Creates unique filters, modifies masks, or makes quick color adjustments.
Digimarc	Embeds a digital watermark that stores copyright information.

Creating Special Effects with Filters

FIGURE H-2

Current Layers palette

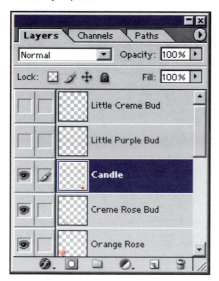

1. Start Photoshop, open PS H-1.psd, then save it as **Soap Opera**.

   TIP If you receive a message stating that some text layers need to be updated before they can be used for vector-based output, click Update.

2. If necessary, click View on the menu bar, point to Show, then click Slices to deselect this option.

3. Click the Default Foreground and Background Colors button on the toolbox to display the default settings.

   TIP It's a good idea to check Photoshop settings and display the rulers before you begin your work.

4. Click the Indicates layer visibility button on the Little Creme Bud layer on the Layers palette.

5. Click the Indicates layer visibility button on the Little Purple Bud layer on the Layers palette.

6. Click the Candle layer on the Layers palette to make it active. Compare your Layers palette to Figure H-2.

7. Click Filter on the menu bar, point to Blur, then click Motion Blur.

   TIP The last filter applied to a layer appears at the top of the Filter menu.

You set default foreground and background colors, hid two layers, then opened the Motion Blur dialog box.

Learning about Motion filters

When you apply a Blur filter, keep in mind how you want your object to appear: as if it's moving. Blur filters smooth the transitions between different colors. The effect of the Blur More filter is four times stronger than the Blur filter. The Gaussian Blur filter produces more of a hazy effect. The direction of the blur is determined by the Angle setting—a straight horizontal path has an angle set to zero. The Motion Blur filter simulates taking a picture of an object in motion, and the Radial Blur filter simulates zooming or rotation. You can use the Smart Blur filter to set exactly how the filter will blur the image.

Apply a Blur filter

1. Drag up and to the left several times in the preview window to display the image in the center of the preview window, if necessary.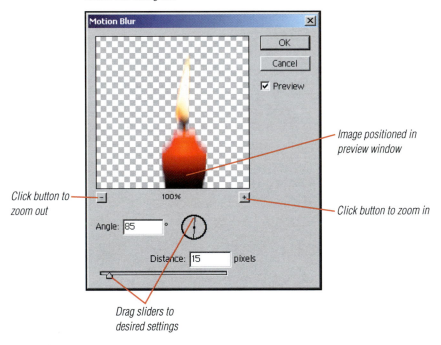

   The candle image is repositioned from the lower-right area to the center of the preview window.

2. Type **85** in the Angle text box.

3. Type **15** in the Distance text box, then compare your dialog box to Figure H-3.

   > TIP You can also adjust the settings in the Motion Blur dialog box by dragging the Angle radius slider and Distance slider.

4. Click OK.

   The Motion Blur filter is applied to the Candle layer and the Motion Blur state appears on the History palette.

   You applied a Motion Blur filter to the Candle layer.

FIGURE H-3
Motion Blur dialog box

Motion Blur

OK

Cancel

☑ Preview

Image positioned in preview window

100%

Click button to zoom out

Click button to zoom in

Angle: 85 °

Distance: 15 pixels

Drag sliders to desired settings

FIGURE H-4
Motion Blur filter applied to layer

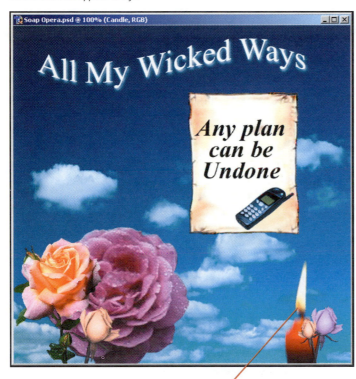

Soap Opera.psd @ 100% (Candle, RGB)

All My Wicked Ways

Any plan can be Undone

*Effect of Motion
Blur filter*

1. Click the Indicates layer visibility on the Little Creme Bud layer on the Layers palette.

2. Click the Indicates layer visibility on the Little Purple Bud layer on the Layers palette.

3. Save your work, then compare your image to Figure H-4.

You restored the visibility of two layers.

CREATE AN EFFECT WITH AN ARTISTIC FILTER

What You'll Do

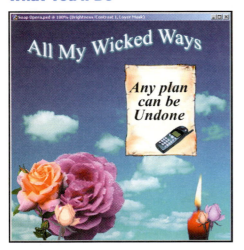

In this lesson, you'll apply the Cutout filter from the Artistic category to the Creme Rose Bud layer and adjust contrast and brightness of the layer.

Learning About Artistic Filters

You can dramatically alter an image by using Artistic filters. Artistic filters are often used for special effects in television commercials and other multimedia venues.

Using Artistic Filters

There are fifteen artistic filters. Figure H-5 shows examples of Artistic filters. The following list contains the names of each of the Artistic filters and their effects.

- Colored Pencil has a colored pencil effect and retains important edges.
- Cutout allows high-contrast images to appear in silhouette and has the effect of using several layers of colored paper.
- Dry Brush simplifies an image by reducing its range of colors.
- Film Grain applies even color variations throughout an object.
- Fresco paints an image with short, rounded dabs of color.
- Neon Glow adds a glow effect to selected objects.
- Paint Daubs gives an image a painterly effect.
- Palette Knife reduces the level of detail in an image, revealing underlying texture.
- Plastic Wrap accentuates surface details and makes the contents of a layer look like it is covered in plastic.

Learning about third-party plug-ins

A plug-in is any external program that adds features and functionality to another while working from within that program. Plug-ins enable you to obtain and work in additional file types and formats, add dazzling special effects, or provide efficient shortcut modules. You can purchase Photoshop plug-ins from third-party companies, or download them from freeware sites. To locate Photoshop plug-ins, you can use your favorite Internet search engine, or check out the sites listed on Adobe's Web site: *www.adobe.com/store/plugins/photoshop/main.html*.

- Poster Edges reduces the number of colors in an image.
- Rough Pastels makes an image look as if it is stroked with colored pastel chalk on a textured background.
- Smudge Stick softens an image by smudging or smearing darker areas.

- Sponge creates highly textured areas, making it look like it was painted with a sponge.
- Underpainting paints the image on a textured background.
- Watercolor simplifies the appearance of an object, making it look like it was painted with watercolors.

Adjusting Filter Effects

You can change the appearance of a filter by using any of the functions listed under the Adjustments command on the Image menu. For example, you can modify the color balance or the brightness/contrast of a layer before or after you apply a filter to it.

FIGURE H-5

Examples of Artistic filters

Apply an Artistic filter

1. Click the Creme Rose Bud layer on the Layers palette.

2. Click Filter on the menu bar, point to Artistic, then click Cutout.

3. Drag the image into the center of the preview window, if necessary.

4. Type **5** in the No. of Levels text box.

5. Type **2** in the Edge Simplicity text box.

6. Type **2** in the Edge Fidelity text box, then compare your dialog box to Figure H-6.

7. Click OK, then compare your image to Figure H-7.

You applied the Cutout filter to the Creme Rose Bud layer.

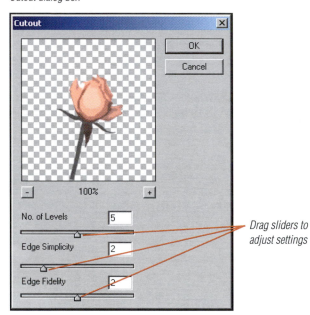

Drag sliders to adjust settings

Effect of Cutout filter

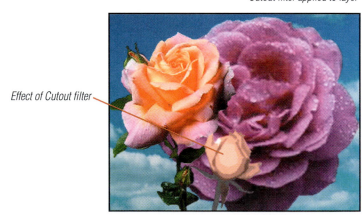

Creating Special Effects with Filters

FIGURE H-8
Image adjusted

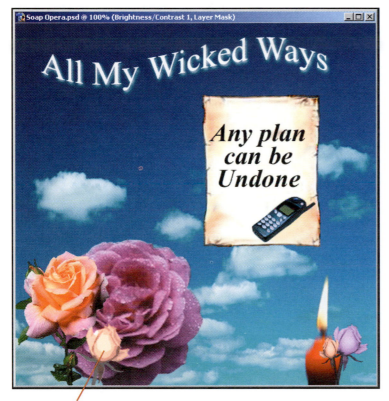

Soap Opera.psd @ 100% (Brightness/Contrast 1, Layer Mask)

All My Wicked Ways

Any plan can be Undone

Brightness and contrast adjusted on layer

1. Click Layer on the menu bar, point to New Adjustment Layer, then click Brightness/Contrast.

2. Select the Group With Previous Layer check box, then click OK.

    The effects of the adjustment layer will be limited to the active layer.

3. Type **20** in the Brightness text box.

4. Type **15** in the Contrast text box, then click OK.

5. Save your work, then compare your image to Figure H-8.

You adjusted the brightness and contrast of the Creme Rose Bud layer.

ADD UNIQUE EFFECTS
WITH STYLIZE FILTERS

What You'll Do

In this lesson, you'll apply a Diffuse filter to the Orange Rose layer and a Wind filter to a selection on the Candle layer. You'll also apply the Wind filter to two layers by using the last filter applied feature.

Learning About Stylize Filters

Stylize filters produce a painted or impressionistic effect by displacing pixels and heightening the contrast within an image. Figure H-9 shows a few Stylize filters. The Diffuse filter breaks up the image so that it looks less focused. The Darken Only option replaces light pixels with dark pixels, and the Lighten Only option replaces dark pixels with light pixels. The Wind filter conveys directed motion. The Extrude filter converts the image into pyramids or blocks.

Applying a Filter to a Selection

Instead of applying a filter to an entire layer, you can specify a particular area of a layer that you want to apply a filter to. You need to first define the area by using a marquee tool, and then apply the desired filter. If you want to apply a filter to a layer that contains a mask, be sure to select the layer name, not the layer mask thumbnail.

Detecting a watermark

Before you can embed a watermark, you must first register with Digimarc Corporation. When Photoshop detects a watermark in an image, it displays the copyright image © in the document's title bar. To check if an image has a watermark, make the layer active, click Filter on the menu bar, point to Digimarc, then click Read Watermark.

FIGURE H-9

Examples of Stylize filters

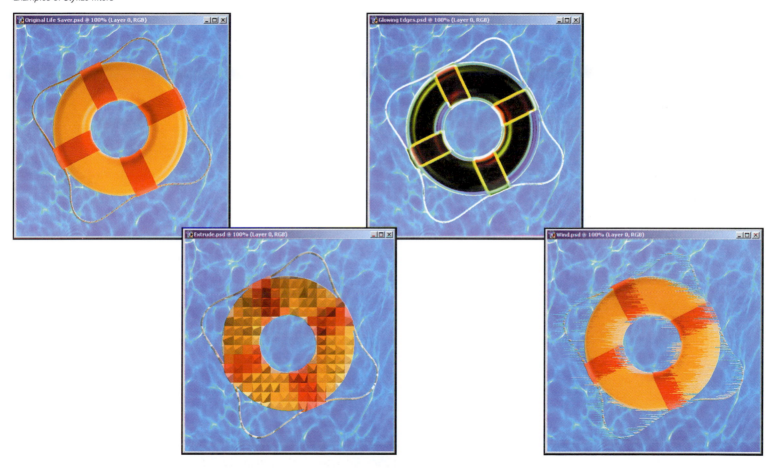

Lesson 3   Add Unique Effects with Stylize Filters

Apply a Stylize filter

1. Click the Orange Rose layer on the Layers palette.

2. Click Filter on the menu bar, point to Stylize, then click Diffuse.

3. Drag the rose into the center of the preview window.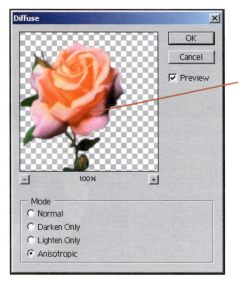

4. Click the Darken Only option button, then view the difference in the preview window.

   Did you see how the Darken Only option button changed the appearance of the image?

5. Click the Anisotropic option button, then compare your dialog box to Figure H-10.

   The Anisotropic mode moves pixels in the direction of the least change in color, resulting in a softened appearance.

6. Click OK, then compare your image to Figure H-11.

You viewed different options in the preview window of the Diffuse dialog box, and applied the Diffuse filter to the Orange Rose layer.

FIGURE H-10
Diffuse dialog box

Image changes as you select different options

FIGURE H-11
Effect of Diffuse filter

Pixels appear softened

Using filters to reduce file size

If you apply a filter to a small area, you can review the effect while conserving your computer's resources. For example, you can test several filters on a small area and then decide which one you want to apply to one or more layers. Alternatively, you can apply a filter to a large portion of a layer, such as applying a slight Motion Blur filter to a grassy background. Your viewers will not notice an appreciable difference when they look at the grass, but by applying the filter, you reduce the number of green colors Photoshop must save in the image, which reduces the size of the file.

Elliptical Marquee selection

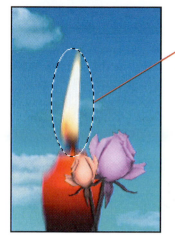

Marquee surrounds
just the flame

FIGURE H-13
Wind dialog box

FIGURE H-14
Effect of Wind filter

Wind filter applied
to candle flame

Apply a filter to a selection

1. Click the Candle layer on the Layers palette.
2. Click the Elliptical Marquee Tool on the toolbox. ⬭
3. Verify that the Feather setting is 30 px.
4. Draw an ellipse around the candle flame, as shown in Figure H-12. ✛
5. Click Filter on the menu bar, point to Stylize, then click Wind.
6. Click the Wind option button in the Method section of the Wind dialog box, if necessary.
7. Click the From the Left option button in the Direction section of the Wind dialog box, then compare your dialog box to Figure H-13.
8. Click OK.
9. Click the marquee to deselect it, then compare your image to Figure H-14. ✛

You used the Elliptical Marquee Tool to select just the flame on the Candle layer, then applied the Wind filter to the selection.

Repeat a filter application

1. Click the Little Creme Bud layer on the Layers palette.

2. Click Filter on the menu bar, then click Wind at the top of the Filter menu, as shown in Figure H-15.

3. Click the Little Purple Bud layer on the Layers palette.

(continued)

FIGURE H-15

Last filter applied on Filter menu

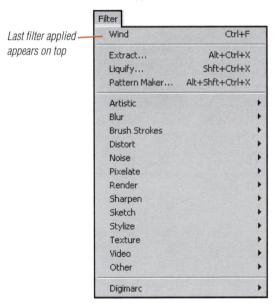

Last filter applied appears on top

FIGURE H-16

Wind filter applied to multiple layers

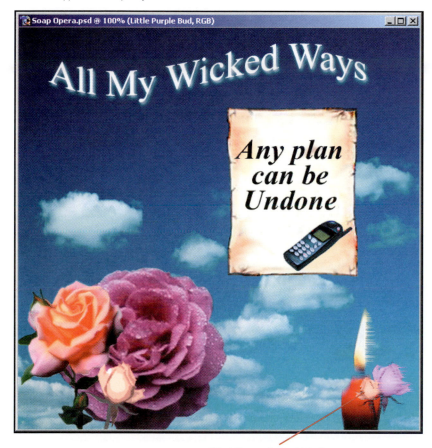

Soap Opera.psd @ 100% (Little Purple Bud, RGB)

All My Wicked Ways

Any plan can be Undone

Wind filter applied to Little Creme Bud and Little Purple Bud layers

4. Click Filter on the menu bar, then click Wind at the top of the Filter menu.

The flame, Little Creme Bud layer, and the Little Purple Bud layer all appear to be blown from the left.

5. Save your work, then compare your image to Figure H-16.

You used the last filter applied feature on the Filter menu to apply the Wind filter to the Little Creme Bud layer and the Little Purple Bud layer.

USE THE DISTORT AND NOISE FILTERS

What You'll Do

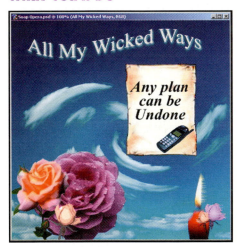

In this lesson, you'll apply the Twirl filter to the Clouds layer and the Noise filter to a type layer.

Understanding Distort and Noise Filters

Distort filters use the most memory, yet even a minimal setting can produce dramatic results. They create a 3-D effect or reshape an object. The Diffuse Glow filter mutes an image, similar to how classic film cinematographers added cheesecloth or Vaseline to the lens of a classic film camera. Others, such as the Ocean Ripple, Glass, Wave, and Ripple filters make an object appear as if it is under or in water. The Twirl filter applies a circular effect to a layer. By adjusting the angle of the twirl, you can make images look as if they are moving or spinning. Figure H-17 shows the diversity of the Distort filters.

Noise filters give an image an appearance of texture. You can apply them to an image layer or to the Background layer. If you want to apply a Noise filter to a type layer, you must rasterize it to convert it to an image layer. You can apply effects to the rasterized type layer; however, you can no longer edit the text.

Optimizing Memory in Photoshop

Many of the dynamic features in Photoshop are memory-intensive, particularly layer masks and filters. In addition to significantly increasing file size, they require a significant quantity of your computer memory to take effect. Part of the fun of working in Photoshop is experimenting with different styles and effects; however, doing so can quickly consume enough memory to diminish Photoshop's performance, or can cause you to not be able to work in other programs while Photoshop is running. You can offset some of the resource loss by freeing up memory as you work in Photoshop, and by adjusting settings in the Preferences dialog box.

Understanding Memory Usage

Every time you change your document, Photoshop stores the previous state in its buffer, which requires memory. You can control some of the memory that Photoshop uses by lowering the number of states available in the History palette. To change the number of states, open the Preferences dialog box, select the General topic, then enter a number in the History States text box. You can also liberate the memory used to store Undo commands, History states, and items on the clipboard by clicking Edit on the menu bar, pointing to Purge, then clicking the area you want to purge. It's a good idea to use the Purge command after you've tried out several effects during a session, but be aware that you cannot undo the Purge command. For example, if you purge the History states, they will no longer appear in the History palette.

Controlling Memory Usage

Factors such as how much memory your computer has, the average size document you work with, and your need to multitask (have other programs open) can determine how Photoshop uses the memory currently allotted to it. To change your memory settings, click Edit on the menu bar, point to Preferences, then click Memory & Image Cache (Win). If you are using a Macintosh, exit Photoshop, select the Photoshop application, click File on the menu bar, click Get Info, click the Show list arrow, click Memory, then change the amount of memory allocated to Photoshop in the Preferred Size text box. You should carefully consider your program needs before changing the default settings. For additional tips on managing resources, search the Adobe Web site Support Knowledgebase: *www.adobe.com/support*.

FIGURE H-17
Examples of Distort filters

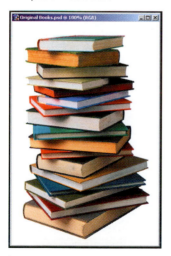   

Apply a Twirl filter

1. Click the Indicates layer visibility button on the Any plan can be Undone type layer on the Layers palette. 👁

2. Click the Indicates layer visibility button on the Cell Phone layer on the Layers palette. 👁

3. Click the Indicates layer visibility button on the Parchment layer on the Layers palette. 👁

4. Click the Clouds layer on the Layers palette.

5. Click Filter on the menu bar, point to Distort, then click Twirl.

6. Drag the Angle slider to 175, as shown in Figure H-18.

7. Click OK.

8. Click the Indicates layer visibility buttons on the Any plan can be Undone type layer, Cell Phone layer, and Parchment layer, then compare your image to Figure H-19. ☐

You applied a Twirl filter to the Clouds layer.

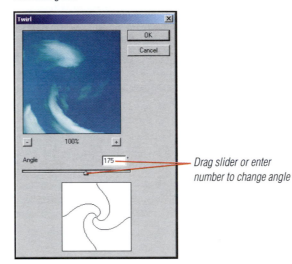

Drag slider or enter number to change angle

FIGURE H-19
Twirl filter applied to Clouds layer

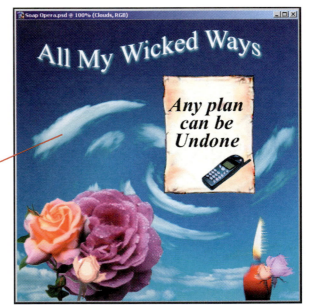

Effect of Twirl filter

Creating Special Effects with Filters

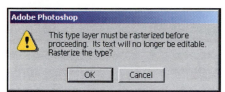

FIGURE H-21
Add Noise dialog box

Light font color is barely visible in preview window

FIGURE H-22
Add Noise filter applied to type layer

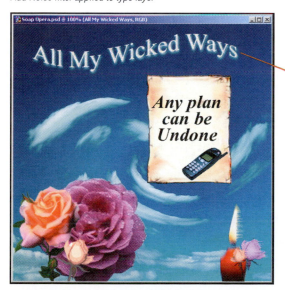

Effect of Add Noise filter

Lesson 4   Use the Distort and Noise Filters

Apply a Noise filter

1. Click the All My Wicked Ways type layer on the Layers palette.

2. Click Filter on the menu bar, point to Noise, then click Add Noise.

   The warning box shown in Figure H-20 appears. You must rasterize a type layer before you can apply a filter to it.

3. Click OK in the warning box.

4. Position the text within the preview window.

5. Drag the Amount slider to 25, then compare your dialog box to Figure H-21.

   TIP Light font colors are not visible in the dialog box preview window.

6. Click OK.

   Flecks of noise are visible in the raster-ized layer.

7. Save your work, then compare your image to Figure H-22.

You rasterized a type layer to apply a Noise filter to it.

USE A RENDER FILTER TO ALTER LIGHTING

What You'll Do

In this lesson, you'll add a lighting effect to the Clouds layer.

Understanding Lighting Effects

The Lighting Effects filter in the Render category allows you to set an atmosphere or highlight elements in your image. You can select the style and type of light, adjust its properties, and texturize it. The preview window displays an ellipse that shows the light settings and allows you to position the light relative to your image. You can drag the handles on each circle, ellipse, or bar to change the direction and distance of the light sources. Figure H-23 shows how you can position the light using the Soft Spotlight style.

Adjusting Light by Setting the Style and Light Type

You can choose from over a dozen lighting styles, including spotlights, floodlights, and full lighting, as shown in Figure H-23. After you select a style, you choose the type of light—Directional, Omni, or Spotlight, and set its intensity and focus. Directional lighting washes the surface with a constant light source, Omni casts

light from the Center, and Spotlight directs light outward from a single point. As shown in Figure H-24, you can adjust the brightness of the light by using the Intensity slider. You can use the Focus slider to adjust the size of the beam of light filling the ellipse. The light source begins where the radius touches the edge of the ellipse. The Light type color swatch lets you modify the color of the light. You can also create custom lighting schemes and save them for use in other documents. Custom lighting schemes will appear in the Style list.

Adjusting Surrounding Light Conditions by Setting Properties

You can adjust the surrounding light conditions using the Gloss, Material, Exposure, or Ambience properties, as shown in Figure H-24. The Gloss property controls the amount of surface reflection on the lighted surfaces. The Material property controls the parts of an image that reflect the light source color. The

Exposure property lightens or darkens the ellipse (the area displaying the light source). The Ambience property controls the balance between the light source and the overall light in an image. The Properties color swatch changes the ambient light around the spotlight.

Adding Texture to Light

The Texture Channel allows you to add 3-D effects to the lighting filter. To use this option, you select one of the three RGB color channels, then drag the Height slider to the relief setting you want. You can also choose whether the black or white areas appear highest in the relief. Figure H-25

shows a lighting effect texture with black colors highest.

QUICKTIP

You can add additional light sources by dragging the light bulb icon onto the preview window, and then adjusting each new light source that you add.

FIGURE H-23

Lighting Effects dialog box

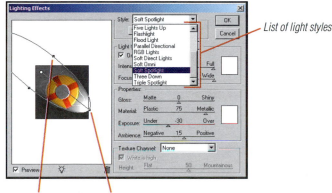

Drag handles to change direction and distance of light source

Light source and direction

FIGURE H-25

Texture added to lighting effect

FIGURE H-24

Settings in the Lighting Effects dialog box

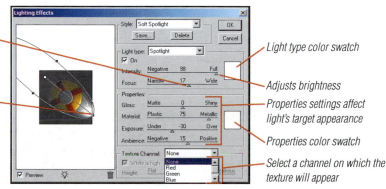

Adjusts the size of the beam of light

Light source begins here

Light type color swatch

Adjusts brightness

Properties settings affect light's target appearance

Properties color swatch

Select a channel on which the texture will appear

Select lighting settings

1. Click the Clouds layer on the Layers palette.

2. Click Filter on the menu bar, point to Render, then click Lighting Effects.

3. Click the Style list arrow, then click Crossing Down.

   The preview window displays the newly selected style.

4. Click the Light type list arrow, then click Spotlight, if necessary.

5. Verify that the On check box is selected.

   The preview window shows the changed Spotlight light source.

6. Drag the top elliptical handle to the upper-left edge of the preview box using Figure H-26 as a guide.

7. Enter the slider settings shown in Figure H-26 in the Lighting Effects dialog box.

   As you drag the ellipse handle, the preview window automatically displays the change in the lighting direction and distance.

   | TIP Lighting effects must include at least one light source.

You selected a lighting style and type, then changed the direction and distance of the lighting.

FIGURE H-26

Light direction and source repositioned

Drag handle to edge of preview window

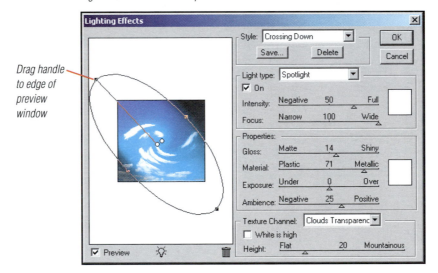

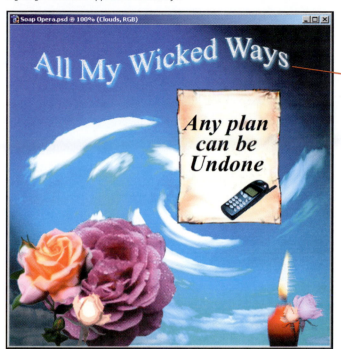

Shadow created
by Lighting
Effects filter

Apply a lighting effect

1. Click OK.

   The light appears brightest in the upper-left corner, and the lower-left and upper-right corners appear to be in shadow.

   > TIP When there are multiple sources of light, you can delete a light source ellipse by dragging its center point over the Delete icon in the Lighting Effects dialog box.

2. Save your work, then compare your image to Figure H-27.

You applied a lighting effect to the Clouds layer.

Creating custom lighting effects

As you modify a style in the Lighting Effects dialog box, you can save the settings as a new style with a unique name. To create a custom style, choose your settings, then click the Save button beneath the Style list arrow. Enter a new name in the Save as dialog box, then click OK. The new style name will appear in the Style list. You can delete an entry by selecting it from the Style list, then clicking the Delete button.

Power User Shortcuts

to do this:	use this method:
Apply a filter	Filter ➤ Filter name
Apply last filter	[Ctrl][F] (Win) or ⌘ [F] (Mac)
Apply last filter, but set new options	[Ctrl][Alt][F] (Win) or ⌘ option [F] (Mac)
Ascend one layer at a time on the Layers palette	[Alt][]] (Win) or option (Mac)

to do this:	use this method:
Descend one layer at a time on the Layers palette	[Alt][[] (Win) or option (Mac)
Fades effect of previous filter	[Ctrl][Shift][F] (Win) or ⌘ [Shift][F] (Mac)
Select bottom layer of Layers palette	[Shift][Alt][[] (Win) or [Shift] option (Mac)
Select top layer of Layers palette	[Shift][Alt][]] (Win) or [Shift] option (Mac)

Key: Menu items are indicated by ➤ between the menu name and its command. Blue bold letters are shortcuts for selecting tools on the toolbox.

Learn about filters and how to apply them.

1. Start Photoshop.
2. Open PS H-2.psd, then save it as **B&B Poster**.
3. Make the Dunes layer active, if necessary.
4. Use the Elliptical Marquee Tool to draw an ellipse around the bend in the driftwood limb.
5. Apply a Gaussian Blur filter (Blur category) with the following settings: Radius = 1px.
6. Create four separate type layers with the text **Fish**, **Swim**, **Hike**, and **Relax**, and arrange them vertically at the left from the bend in the tree limb down to the tree trunk. (*Hint*: A Pure Yellow [color swatch name] 36 pt Copperplate Gothic Bold is used in the sample.)
7. Save your work.

Create an effect with an Artistic filter.

1. Make the B&B layer active.
2. Apply a Film Grain filter (Artistic category) with the following settings: Grain = 3, Highlight Area = 1, Intensity = 10.
3. Save your work.

Add unique effects with Stylize filters.

1. Make the Trout layer active.
2. Apply a Glowing Edges filter (Stylize category), with the following settings: Edge Width = 2, Edge Brightness = 2, Smoothness = 3.
3. Transform the Trout layer by resizing and rotating the trout so that it appears to be jumping, then drag it behind the Fish type layer.
4. Save your work.

Use the Distort and Noise filters.

1. Make the Swim type layer active.
2. Apply a Ripple filter (Distort category) with the following settings: Amount = 55, Size = Medium. (*Hint*: Click OK to rasterize the layer.)
3. Make the Relax type layer active.
4. Recolor the type to the following settings: R = 227, G = 4, B = 178.

FIGURE H-28

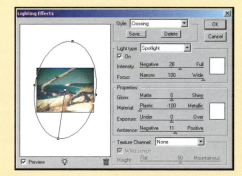

5. Apply an Add Noise filter (Noise category) with the following settings: Amount = 25%, Distribution = Uniform, Monochromatic = Selected.
6. Save your work.

Use a Render filter to alter lighting.

1. Make the Dunes layer active.
2. Apply Lighting Effects (Render category) with the following settings: Style = Crossing, Type = Spotlight.
3. Drag the sliders on the ellipse to match the settings shown in Figure H-28.
4. Save your work, then compare your image to Figure H-29.

FIGURE H-29
Completed Skills Review

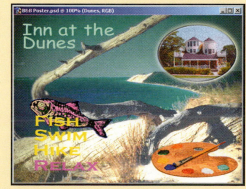

Theatre in the Park, an outdoor production company, is adding Shakespeare's comedies to their summer repertoire. The company has convinced several rollerbladers to wear sandwich boards promoting the event as they blade downtown during the noon hour. You've volunteered to design the board for the Bard. You can use any Shakespearian comedy in the sign.

1. Obtain the following images that reflect the production: a park, an image related to Shakespeare, and other images as desired. You can use the images that are available on your computer, scanned images, or images from a digital camera.
2. Create a new Photoshop document with the dimensions 630 × 450 pixels, then save it as **Play**.
3. Drag or copy the Park image to the Play document above the Background layer, apply at least one style and one filter to it, then rename the Background layer. (*Hint*: The Park layer in the sample has a Render category Lighting Effects filter texture channel, and a Color Overlay applied to it.)
4. Drag the Shakespeare image to the Play document above the Park layer, and modify it as desired. (*Hint*: The face in the sample has an opacity setting of 64%, and has been rotated.)

5. Create a sign announcing the play, and apply at least one style and filter to it. (*Hint*: The sign in the sample was created using the Rectangle Tool, and has the Drop Shadow, Satin, and Bevel and Emboss styles, and a Texture category Craquelure filter applied to it.)
6. Create type layers as desired, and apply at least one style or filter to them. (*Hint*: A 30 pt Broadway font is used in the sample.)

7. Drag or copy the remaining images to the Play document, close the image files, then transform them or apply at least one style or filter to them.
8. Save your work, then compare your image to Figure H-30.

FIGURE H-30
Completed Project Builder 1

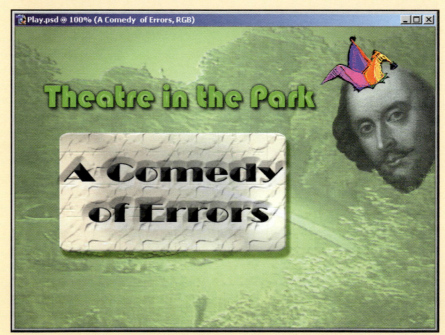

Creating Special Effects with Filters

Local instrument shops in your town are producing a classic jazz and blues event. Last year, the poster was full of sponsor logos and never conveyed the feel of the genre. This year, they've decided on no sponsor logos, and have asked you to design the poster that echoes a bygone era. Use your Photoshop skills to express the sponsors' intent.

1. Obtain images for the design, including at least one instrument that will dominate the image. You can use the images that are available on your computer, scanned images, or images from a digital camera.
2. Create a new Photoshop document using any dimensions, then save it as **Jazz and Blues**.
3. Open the main instrument file, drag it to the Jazz and Blues document above the Background layer, then rename the Background layer.
4. Open the remaining image files, drag or copy them to the Jazz and Blues document, then close the image files.
5. Apply at least one filter to the main instrument layer and transform it or apply any other styles or layer masks as desired. (*Hint*: The Keyboard layer has a Brush Strokes category Crosshatch filter, a Render category Lighting Effects Soft Spotlight filter, and layer mask applied to it.)
6. Apply filters and styles and transform the other image layers as desired. (*Hint*: The Sheet music layer has a Color Overlay layer mask and the Brush Tool applied to it.)
7. Create type layers as desired and apply filters or styles to them. (*Hint*: The Jazz Title type layer has a 48 pt Times New Roman font with the Drop Shadow, Inner Shadow, Bevel and Emboss, and Gradient Overlay styles applied to it. The text in the lower-left corner and lower-right corner has a 14 pt Century Gothic font.)
8. Save your work, then compare your image to Figure H-31.

FIGURE H-31
Completed Project Builder 2

Destined Nations, a local travel agency, is looking to hire a freelance graphic artist to design their marketing pieces. Rather than peruse portfolios, they are holding a contest for a poster design. Each entrant is given the same image to modify as they see fit. As an incentive to get the very best entries, they're offering a week's vacation to the winner. You like vacations, so you decide to enter the contest.

1. Obtain at least one image for the vacation destination design. You can use the images that are available on your computer, scanned images, or images from a digital camera.
2. Open PS H-3.psd, then save it as **Shield**.
3. Make the Shield layer active, open the Lighting Effects dialog box, then apply a lighting style to it.
4. Change the Light type color swatch to yellow. (*Hint*: To change color, double-click the color swatch.)
5. Place at least two other spotlights around the preview window using different colored lights. (*Hint*: To add a spotlight, drag the light bulb icon to the preview window.)
6. Apply a subtle texture to the Shield layer. (*Hint*: The Shield layer in the sample has the Smudge Stick Artistic filter applied to it.)
7. Delete the large black center circle from the Shield layer. (*Hint*: To delete the circle quickly, select the Elliptical Marquee Tool, draw a selection around the black circle,

then press [Delete], or you can apply a layer mask and paint the circle.)
8. Delete the black triangles from the Shield layer. (*Hint*: To delete the triangles quickly, select the Polygonal Lasso Tool, draw a selection around the edges of the triangles, then press [Delete], or you can apply a layer mask and paint the triangles.)
9. Create and name a new layer at the bottom of the Layers palette, and then fill it in black.
10. Create a new layer above the black layer and name it **Blur**.
11. Use a lasso tool or a shape tool to create a shape that fills the left side of the layer, then apply a fill color to the selection.
12. Apply at least one Blur filter to the Blur layer.

13. Transform the shield so that it has dimension, then move it to the left side of the window. (*Hint*: The Shield layer in the sample has been distorted.)
14. Add type layers as desired and apply styles or filters to them. (*Hint*: The mexico layer in the sample has a border applied by clicking the Rasterize command on the Layer menu, and then using the Stroke command on the Edit menu. The feel the magic layer in the sample is a 36 pt Rage Italic.)
15. Open the image files, drag or copy them to the Shield document, close the image files, then apply filters or styles to them.
16. Save your work, then compare your image to Figure H-32.

FIGURE H-32
Completed Design Project

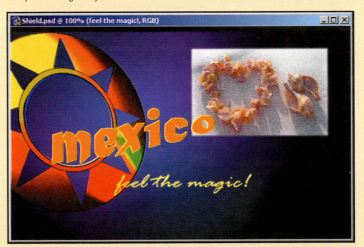

GROUP PROJECT

Depending on the size of your group, you can assign individual elements of the project to group members, or work collectively to create the finished product.

Your group is one of several that has been assigned to put together a presentation on traditional and modern dance styles from around the world. You have first choice on the style you will research, and will lay your claim to that style by using your Photoshop skills to create a title slide. Assign members of your group to research the style of dance you've chosen, and then design an image that conveys the feel of that style.

1. Obtain at least three images that reflect the style of dance you've chosen. You can use the images that are available on your computer, scanned images, images from a digital camera, or images downloaded from the Internet. Try to select images that you can transform and to which you can add styles and apply filters. Make sure that one image can be used as a background.

2. Create a new Photoshop document, then save it as **Dance**.

3. Drag or copy the background to the Dance document above the Background layer, then rename the Background layer and apply a fill color as desired.

4. Drag an image to the Dance document, transform it as desired, then apply a filter to it. (*Hint*: The Swan layer [dancer in lower-left corner] in the sample has an Artistic category Plastic Wrap filter applied to it.)

5. Drag or copy the remaining images, transform as needed, and apply at least one style or filter to them. (*Hint*: The Large Ballerina layer has an Artistic category Palette Knife filter applied to it, and the Shoes layer has the Distort category Diffuse Glow filter applied to it.)

6. Create type layers as desired, and apply at least one style or filter to them. (*Hint*: The Dancing type layer was created in a separate document using an image as a member of a clipping group. The It doesn't matter how— just express yourself type layer in the sample uses a 20 pt Courier New font.)

7. Be prepared to discuss the effects you generate when you add filters to styles and vica versa.

8. Save your work, then compare your image to Figure H-33.

FIGURE H-33
Completed Group Project

UNIT **I**

ENHANCING SPECIFIC SELECTIONS

1. Create an alpha channel.

2. Use Extract to isolate an object.

3. Erase areas in an image to enhance appearance.

4. Fix imperfections in an image.

5. Use the Magic Wand Tool to select objects.

6. Learn how to create snapshots.

7. Create multiple-image layouts.

ENHANCING SPECIFIC SELECTIONS

Modifying Objects

As you have most likely figured out by now, a great part of the power of Photoshop resides in its ability to isolate graphics and text objects and make changes to them. This unit focuses on several of the techniques used to isolate graphics objects and then make changes that enhance their appearance.

Using Channels

Nearly every image you open or create in Photoshop is separated into **channels**. Photoshop uses channels to house the color information for each layer and layer mask in your image. The number of color information channels depends on the color mode of the image. You can also create specific channels for layer masks.

Fixing Imperfections

From time to time, you'll probably work with flawed images. These are not necessarily "bad images," they just might contain imagery that does not fit your needs. Photoshop offers several ways to repair art's imperfections. You can use the following methods—or combinations of these methods—to fix areas within an image that are less than ideal:

- Isolate areas using the Extract feature.
- Erase areas using a variety of eraser tools.
- Take a sample and then paint that sample over an area using the Clone Stamp Tool.

Creating Snapshots

The snapshot command lets you make a temporary copy of any state of an image. The snapshot is added to the top of the History palette and lets you work on a new version of the image. Snapshots are like the states found on the History palette but offer a few more advantages:

- You can name a snapshot to make it easy to identify and manage.
- You can compare changes to documents easily. For example, you can take a snapshot before and after changing the color of a selection.
- You can recover your work easily. If your experimentation with an image doesn't satisfy your needs, you can select the snapshot to undo all the steps from the experiment.

Using Automation Features

After you complete an image that you want to share, you can create a document that contains various sizes of the same image, or several different images. The Picture Package feature, for example, makes it possible to print images in a variety of sizes and shapes on a single sheet. Another example is a contact sheet, a document that contains a collection of images that lets you preview and catalog them by using just thumbnail images.

Tools You'll Use

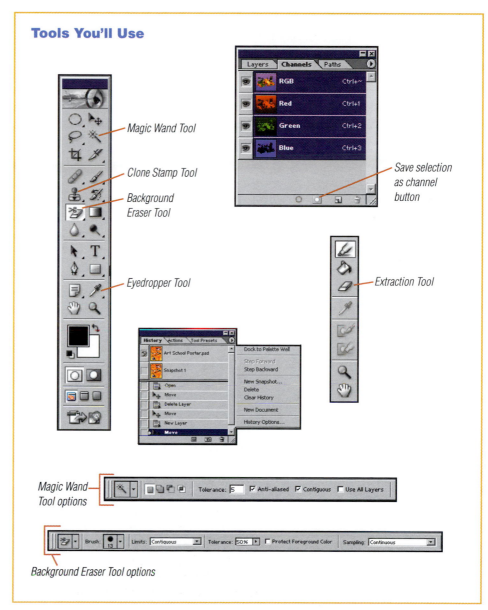

Magic Wand Tool

Clone Stamp Tool

Background Eraser Tool

Eyedropper Tool

Save selection as channel button

Extraction Tool

Magic Wand Tool options

Background Eraser Tool options

CREATE AN ALPHA CHANNEL

What You'll Do

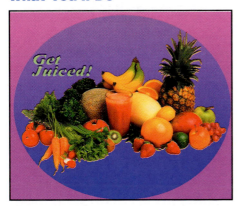

 In this lesson, you'll view the colors in the default color mode on the Channels palette. You'll also use the Elliptical Marquee Tool to create a selection, use the Save selection as channel button on the Channels palette to save it as an alpha channel, and then change the color of the alpha channel.

Defining Channels

Photoshop automatically creates channel information in a new document and uses channels to store color information about images. For example, a CMYK image has at least four channels (one each for cyan, magenta, yellow, and black), whereas an RGB image has three channels (one each for red, green, and blue). Every Photoshop image has at least one channel, and can have a maximum of 24 color channels. The color channels contained in a document are known as **default channels**, which Photoshop creates automatically. You can add specific color information by adding an **alpha channel** or a **spot channel**. You use an alpha channel to create and store masks, which let you manipulate, isolate, and protect parts of an image. A spot channel contains information about special pre-mixed inks used in CYMK color printing. The default number of channels is determined by the color mode you select in the New dialog box that opens when you create a new file, as shown in Figure I-1. You can add channels to documents displayed in all color modes, except the bitmap modes.

Understanding Alpha Channels

You create alpha channels on the Channels palette. You can create an alpha channel that masks all or specific areas of a layer. For example, you can create a selection and then convert it into an alpha channel. Photoshop superimposes the color in an alpha channel onto the document; however, an alpha channel might appear in grayscale in the Channels palette thumbnail. You can use alpha channels to preserve a selection to experiment with, to use later, to create special effects, such as screens or shadows, or to save and reuse them in other documents. Photoshop supports the following formats for saving an alpha channel: PSD, PDF, PICT, TIFF, and Raw. If you use other formats, you might lose some channel information. You can copy the alpha channel to other documents and instantly apply the same information. Alpha channels do not print—they will not be visible in print media.

Understanding the Channels Palette

The Channels palette lists all the default channels contained in a layer and manages all the document's channels. To access this palette, click the Channels tab next to the Layers tab, as shown in Figure I-2. The top channel is a **composite channel**—a combination of all the other default channels. The additional default channels, based on the existing color mode, are shown below the composite channel, followed by spot color channels, and finally by the alpha channels.

Channels have many of the same properties as layers. You can hide channels in the same way as you hide layers: click the Indicates channel visibility button in the column to the left of the channel thumbnail on the Channels palette. Each channel has a thumbnail that mirrors the changes you make to the document's layers. You can also change the order of channels by dragging them to new locations on the Channels palette.

The thumbnails on the Channels palette might appear in grayscale. To view the channels in their actual color, click Edit on the menu bar, point to Preferences, click Display & Cursors, select the Color Channels in Color check box, then click OK. The default channels will appear in the color mode colors; an alpha channel will appear in the color selected in the Channel Options dialog box. You open the Channel Options dialog box by double-clicking the alpha channel on the Channels palette.

FIGURE I-1
New dialog box

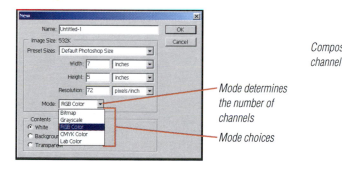

Mode determines the number of channels

Mode choices

FIGURE I-2
Channels on the Channels palette

Composite channel

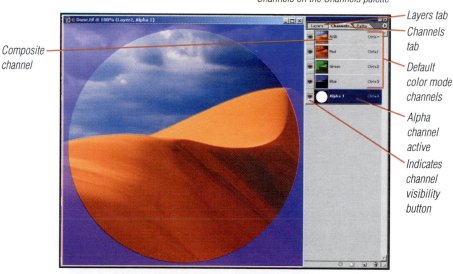

Layers tab

Channels tab

Default color mode channels

Alpha channel active

Indicates channel visibility button

View the Channels palette

1. Start Photoshop, open PS I-1.psd, then save it as **Juiced**.

2. Click the Default Foreground and Background Colors button on the toolbox to display the default settings.

3. Display the rulers in pixels, if necessary.

4. Click the Channels tab next to the Layers tab on the Layers palette, then compare your Channels palette to Figure I-3.

   The Channels palette is active and displays the four channels for RGB color mode: RGB (composite), Red, Green, and Blue.

5. Verify that the default color channels are displayed in color; if not, click Edit on the menu bar, point to Preferences, click Display & Cursors, select the Color Channels in Color check box, then click OK.

   You opened the Channels palette, then, if necessary, displayed colors in the default color channels.

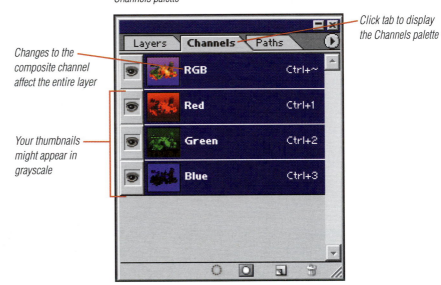

FIGURE I-3
Channels palette

Click tab to display the Channels palette

Changes to the composite channel affect the entire layer

Your thumbnails might appear in grayscale

Changing alpha channel colors

You can change the color that the alpha channel displays by picking a color in the Channel Options dialog box. To open the Channel Options dialog box, double-click the alpha channel on the Channels palette, click the color box, select a color in the Color Picker dialog box, click OK, click an option button in the Channel Options dialog box to choose whether the color includes or excludes the selected area, then click OK.

Enhancing Specific Selections

FIGURE I-4
Selection created

Elliptical marquee

Click to save selection as a channel

FIGURE I-5
Alpha channel created

Alpha 1 channel

Create an alpha channel from a selection

1. Click the Elliptical Marquee Tool on the toolbox, then set the Feather setting on the tool options bar to 0 px, if necessary.

2. Drag the pointer from 10 H/10 V to 685 H/590 V, then compare your image to Figure I-4.

   TIP You might need to resize the document window to make the selection.

3. Click the Save selection as channel button on the Channels palette.

4. Double-click the Alpha 1 thumbnail on the Channels palette, then click the color box in the Channel Options dialog box.

5. Select red in the Color Picker dialog box (R=255, G=0, B=0), then click OK.

6. Verify that the opacity setting is 50% and that the Masked Areas option button is selected, then click OK.

7. On the Channels palette, click RGB, then click the Indicates channel visibility button for the Alpha 1 channel to view the alpha channel, if necessary.

   The combination of the red alpha channel color overlaying blue produces purple.

8. Click Select on the menu bar, click Deselect, then compare your image to Figure I-5.

9. Save your work.

You used the Elliptical Marquee Tool to create a selection and used the Save selection as channel button to save it as an alpha channel. You also changed the alpha channel color.

USE EXTRACT TO ISOLATE AN OBJECT

What You'll Do

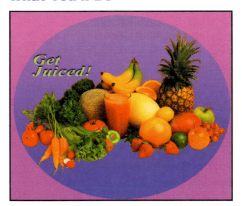

▶ *In this lesson, you'll create a duplicate layer, and use the Extract feature to extract the kiwi from the Fruit and Vegetables layer so that you can adjust the color. You'll adjust the color of the extracted object by applying a Gradient Map to it, and then view the extracted kiwi in the document window.*

Isolating Objects

You can use the Extract feature to isolate a foreground object from its background. This feature lets you define the object you want to extract, even if its edge is vaguely defined. When you extract an object from a layer, Photoshop deletes the non-extracted portion of the image's background to underlying transparency. It's always a good idea to first copy the original layer and then extract an object from the duplicate layer. This preserves the original layer, which you can use as a reference, and helps you to avoid losing any of the original image information. After you extract an image, you will be able to modify the extracted object layer as you wish.

QUICKTIP

The Extract feature is ideally used for objects that have vague edges or in images with low contrast values.

Using the Extract Feature

You isolate objects using tools in the Extract dialog box, listed in Table I-1. You first trace the edge of the object you want to extract with the Edge Highlighter Tool, then you select everything inside of the edge with the Fill Tool. If you make a mistake, you can use the eraser to erase the erroneous parts or you can click Undo on the Edit menu to delete the entire action. It takes practice to become proficient at using the Edge Highlighter Tool. If you do not draw a continuous edge around the object, Photoshop might not fill in the area accurately. You can edit portions of the edge as often as necessary. Depending on the size of the brush tip you select, the dimensions of your extracted object will vary.

TABLE I-1: Extraction Tools

tool	name	use
	Edge Highlighter Tool	Paints an edge around the object you want to extract.
	Fill Tool	Fills the extracted object.
	Eraser Tool	Deletes highlighted edges or filled areas.
	Eyedropper Tool	Active when Force Foreground check box is selected; samples a color in image or in the Color Picker dialog box.
	Cleanup Tool	Makes mask transparent; press keyboard numbers 1–9 (increasing transparency) to change pressure of tool.
	Edge Touchup Tool	Deletes edges of extracted object to sharpen edge; press keyboard numbers 1–9 (increasing transparency) to change pressure of tool.
	Zoom Tool	Changes view of object in dialog box.
	Hand Tool	Positions image in dialog box.

Isolate an object

1. Click the Layers tab on the Layers palette.

2. Verify that the Fruit and Vegetables layer is active.

3. Click the Layers palette list arrow, then click Duplicate Layer.

4. Type **Kiwi** in the As text box in the Duplicate Layer dialog box, then click OK.

   The new layer appears above the Fruit and Vegetables layer on the Layers palette, and is now the active layer.

5. Click Filter on the menu bar, then click Extract.

6. Click the Zoom Tool in the Extract dialog box, then click the center of the kiwi three times.

7. Click the Edge Highlighter Tool in the dialog box.

8. Double-click the Brush Size text box on the right side of the dialog box, then type **5**.

9. Drag the pointer around the edge of the kiwi.

10. Click the Fill Tool in the dialog box, click the center of the kiwi, then compare your dialog box to Figure I-6.

    The kiwi is surrounded by the highlighted border and filled in blue.

You created and named a duplicate layer of the Fruit and Vegetables layer, opened the Extract dialog box, used the Edge Highlighter Tool to outline the kiwi, and filled in the kiwi using the Fill Tool.

FIGURE I-6
Extract dialog box

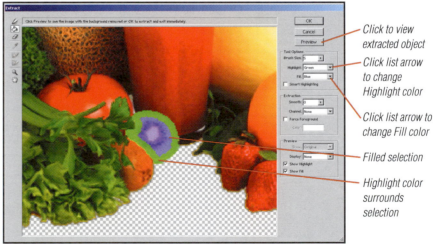

Click to view extracted object

Click list arrow to change Highlight color

Click list arrow to change Fill color

Filled selection

Highlight color surrounds selection

FIGURE I-7
Layer containing the extracted object

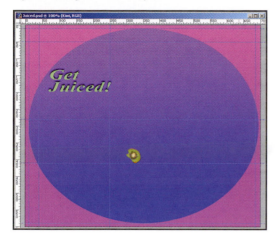

FIGURE I-9
Extracted object with a Gradient Map applied

Gradient Map adjustment
on the extracted object

FIGURE I-8
Sample gradients

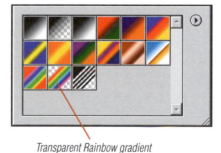

Transparent Rainbow gradient

Extract an object

1. Click Preview in the upper-right corner of the Extract dialog box.

   The highlighted kiwi appears on the layer with a transparent background.

2. Click OK.

3. Click the Indicates layer visibility button on the Fruit and Vegetables layer on the Layers palette so that only the Kiwi layer is visible. See Figure I-7. 👁

You previewed the extracted kiwi in the Extract dialog box, then viewed the layer containing the extracted object.

Enhance an extracted object

1. Click Image on the menu bar, point to Adjustments, then click Gradient Map.

2. Select the Reverse check box, click the Gradient list arrow, click the Transparent Rainbow gradient, as shown in Figure I-8, then click OK.

3. Click the Indicates layer visibility button on the Fruit and Vegetables layer. ▢

4. Save your work, then compare your image to Figure I-9.

You adjusted the color for the extracted kiwi by applying a Gradient Map to the layer, then viewed the color-adjusted image.

Lesson 2   Use Extract to Isolate an Object

ERASE AREAS IN AN IMAGE
TO ENHANCE APPEARANCE

What You'll Do

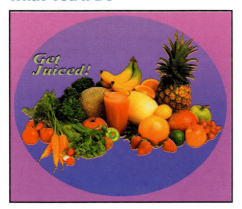

▶ In this lesson, you'll use the Background Eraser Tool to delete pixels on the Fruit and Vegetables layer, then adjust the brightness and contrast of the isolated object.

Learning How to Erase Areas

The Extract feature automatically discards the area of an image that is *not* high-lighted and filled. At times, you might want to simply erase an area *without* going through the extraction process. Photoshop provides three Eraser Tools that can accommodate all your expunging needs. Figure I-10 contains samples of the effects of each eraser tool. The specific use for each eraser tool is reflected in its tool options bar, as shown in Figure I-11.

Understanding Eraser Tools

The **Eraser Tool** has the opposite function of a brush. Instead of brushing *on* pixel color, you drag it *off*. When you erase a layer that has a layer beneath it, and the Lock transparent pixels button is not selected, you'll expose the color of the underlying layer when you erase. If there is no underlying layer, you'll expose trans-parency. If the Lock transparent pixels button *is* selected, you'll expose the cur-rent background on the toolbox, regard-less of the color of an underlying layer.

Setting options for eraser tools

Each eraser tool has its own tool options bar. You can select the brush mode for the Eraser Tool, and the brush tip and size for both the Eraser Tool and Background Eraser Tool. Depending on the tool, you can also set the **tolerance**—how close a pixel color must be to another color to be erased with the tool. The lower the tolerance, the closer the color must be to the selection. You can also specify the opacity of the eraser strength. A 100% opacity erases pixels to complete transparency. To set options, click an eraser tool on the toolbox, then change the tolerance and opacity settings using the text boxes and list arrows on the tool options bar.

The **Magic Eraser Tool** grabs similarly colored pixels based on the tool settings, and then exposes background color in the same way as the Eraser Tool. However, instead of dragging the eraser, you click the areas you want to change. The Magic Eraser Tool will erase all the pixels on the current layer close in values to where you first click the mouse or just those pixels that are contiguous to that area.

The **Background Eraser Tool** contains small crosshairs in the brush tip. When you click the mouse, the tool selects a color in the crosshairs, then erases that particular color anywhere within the brush tip size. The Background Eraser Tool exposes the color of the layer beneath it, or it exposes transparency if there is no layer beneath it. You can preserve objects in the foreground,

while eliminating the background (it works best with a large brush tip size). The Background Eraser Tool will sample the background colors of the current layer as you drag the tool in your image—you can watch the current background color change on the toolbox.

FIGURE I-10

Examples of eraser tools

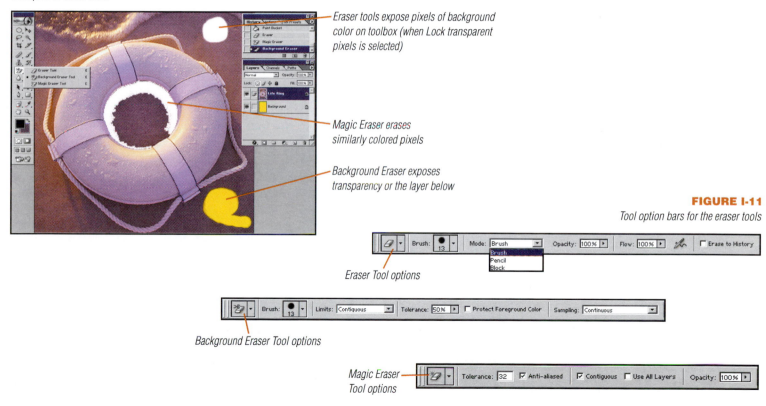

Eraser tools expose pixels of background color on toolbox (when Lock transparent pixels is selected)

Magic Eraser erases similarly colored pixels

Background Eraser exposes transparency or the layer below

FIGURE I-11

Tool option bars for the eraser tools

Eraser Tool options

Background Eraser Tool options

Magic Eraser
Tool options

Use the Background Eraser Tool

1. Click the Indicates layer visibility button on the Kiwi layer to hide the layer.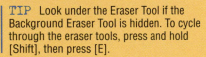

2. Click the Fruit and Vegetables layer.

3. Click the Zoom Tool on the toolbox. 🔍

4. Click the center of the kiwi until the zoom factor is 300%. 🔍

5. Click the Background Eraser Tool.

   TIP Look under the Eraser Tool if the Background Eraser Tool is hidden. To cycle through the eraser tools, press and hold [Shift], then press [E].

6. Click the Click to open the Brush Preset picker list arrow on the tool options bar, set the Diameter to 5 px, the Hardness to 100% and the Spacing to 15% if necessary, as shown in Figure I-12.

7. Press [Enter] (Win) or [return] (Mac).

8. Keeping the crosshairs of the brush tip on the kiwi, drag the brush tip over the kiwi until it is completely erased, as shown in Figure I-13. ⊕

   TIP As you drag the pointer, background colors change on the toolbox when the pointer moves over a different colored pixel in the layer beneath it.

You hid the Kiwi layer, zoomed in on the Fruit and Vegetables layer, selected a brush tip for the Background Eraser Tool, and erased the kiwi on the Fruit and Vegetables layer.

FIGURE I-12
Brush Preset picker

FIGURE I-13
Selection erased on layer

Erased area
exposes pixels on
Background layer

FIGURE I-14
Object adjusted in image

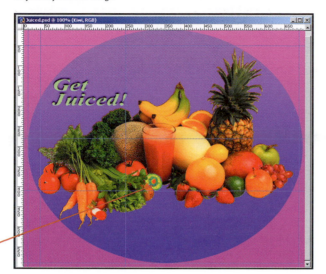

Equalize adjustment
applied to kiwi layer

Equalize brightness and contrast

1. Click the Kiwi layer on the Layers palette.
2. Click the Zoom Tool on the toolbox.
3. Press and hold [Alt] (Win) or [option] (Mac), click the center of the kiwi until the zoom factor is 100%, then release [Alt] (Win) or [option] (Mac).
4. Click Image on the menu bar, point to Adjustments, then click Equalize.

   The Equalize command evens out the brightness and contrast values in the kiwi.
5. Save your work, then compare your image to Figure I-14.

You adjusted the color of the kiwi by equalizing the colors, then viewed the color-adjusted image.

Redistributing brightness values

The Equalize command changes the brightness values of an image's pixels so they more evenly display the entire range of brightness levels. Photoshop changes the brightest and darkest values by remapping them so that the brightest values appear as white and the darkest values appear as black, then it redistributes the intermediate pixel values evenly throughout the grayscale. You can use equalize to "tone down" an image that is too bright. Conversely, you could use it on a dark image that you want to make lighter.

FIX IMPERFECTIONS IN AN IMAGE

What You'll Do

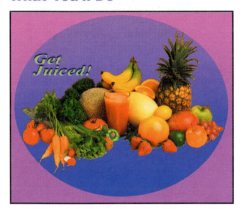

▶ *In this lesson, you'll use the Clone Stamp Tool to sample an undamaged portion of an image and use it to cover up a fly on a tomato.*

Touching Up a Damaged Area

Let's face it, many of the images you'll want to work with will have a visual flaw of some kind, such as a scratch, or an object obscuring what would otherwise be a great shot. While you cannot go back in time and move something out of the way, you can use the Clone Stamp Tool to remove an object or cover up a flaw.

Using the Clone Stamp Tool

The Clone Stamp Tool can copy a sample (a pixel selection) in an image then paste it over what you want to cover up. The size of the sample taken with the Clone Stamp Tool depends on the brush tip size you choose in the Brushes palette. Figure I-15 shows the Clone Stamp Tool in action. In addition to using the Clone Stamp Tool to touch up images, you can use it to copy an image onto another. Using the Clone Stamp Tool to copy an image differs from copying an image because you have extensive control over how much of the cloned area you expose and at what opacity.

FIGURE I-15
Clone Stamp Tool in action

Object to be deleted

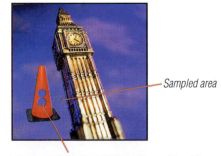

Sampled area

Sampled area applied twice to hide portions of the object

FIGURE I-16
Comparing images

Perfecting your analytical skills

An important step in making an adjustment to any image is to examine it critically for a minute or two to figure out what is wrong. An area that you select for fixing does not necessarily have to look ugly or wrong. An image might be "wrong" because it simply does not convey the right meaning or mood. Compare the two images in Figure I-17. They contain basically the same elements but express entirely different ideas. The figure on the left conveys a more positive image than the one on the right; this is also reflected in the lighter colored paper, which is in pristine condition. The elements that you choose for your content should depend on what you want to convey. For example, if you want to convey a positive mood, using the elements in the image on the right would be inappropriate for your image. Choosing the right content in the beginning can save you a lot of time in the end. It is much easier and quicker to reach a destination if you know where you are going before you begin the journey.

Sample an area

1. Click the Fruit and Vegetables layer on the Layers palette.

2. Click the Zoom Tool on the toolbox.

3. Click the center of the far-left tomato until the zoom factor is 200% so you can clearly see the fly.

4. Click the Clone Stamp Tool on the toolbox.

5. Click the Click to open the Brush Preset picker list arrow on the tool options bar, then double-click the Hard Round 13 pixels brush tip.

6. Verify that the Opacity setting on the tool options bar is 100%.

7. Position the pointer at 60 H/400 V, as shown in Figure I-17.

8. Press [Alt] (Win) or [option] (Mac), click once, then release [Alt] (Win) or [option] (Mac).

   The sample is collected and is ready to be applied to the fly.

You selected the Fruit and Vegetables layer, set the zoom percentage, selected a brush tip for the Clone Stamp Tool, and sampled an undamaged portion of the tomato.

FIGURE I-17
Defining the area to be sampled

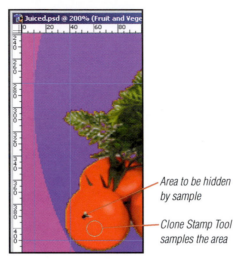

Area to be hidden by sample

Clone Stamp Tool samples the area

FIGURE I-19
Defect corrected

Clone Stamp Tool sample area covers the fly

FIGURE I-18
Clone Stamp Tool positioned over defect

Clone Stamp Tool positioned over the fly

FIGURE I-20
Corrected image

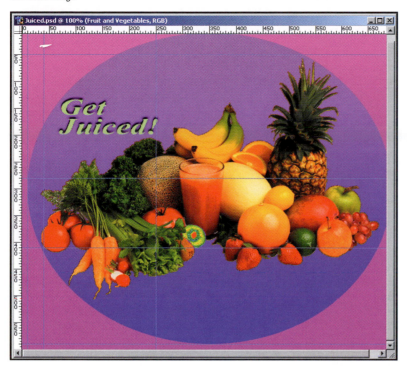

Juiced.psd @ 100% (Fruit and Vegetables, RGB)

Get Juiced!

Use the Clone Stamp Tool to fix an imperfection

1. Position the pointer *directly* over the fly, as shown in Figure I-18. ◯

2. Click the fly, then compare your image to Figure I-19.

   > TIP Select a different brush size if your brush is too small or too large, and then reapply the stamp.

3. Click the Zoom Tool on the toolbox. 🔍

4. Press and hold [Alt] (Win) or [option] (Mac), click the center of the tomato until the zoom factor is 100%, then release [Alt] (Win) or [option] (Mac). 🔍

5. Save your work, then compare your image to Figure I-20.

You fixed the damaged area of the tomato by covering up the fly.

Using pressure-sensitive tablets

For specialized painting that gives you maximum control when you create an image, you can purchase a pressure-sensitive stylus or tablet. A pressure-sensitive device mimics the force you'd use with an actual brush; you paint softer when you press lightly and paint darker when you press harder. You can set the stylus or tablet pressure for the Magnetic Lasso, Magnetic Pen, Pencil, Brush, Airbrush, Eraser, Clone Stamp, Pattern Stamp, History Brush, Art History Brush, Smudge, Blur, Sharpen, Dodge, Burn, and Sponge Tools.

USE THE MAGIC WAND TOOL TO SELECT OBJECTS

What You'll Do

 In this lesson, you'll open a new document, adjust the Eyedropper Tool sample size and the Magic Wand Tool tolerance settings, use the Magic Wand Tool to select an image in the new document, and move it to the Juiced document. You'll also readjust the Eyedropper Tool sample size, reselect and move the image so you can compare the selection difference, then delete the incomplete layer and position the complete layer in the Juiced document.

Understanding the Magic Wand Tool

You can use the Magic Wand Tool to select an object by selecting the color range of the object. The **Magic Wand Tool** lets you choose pixels that are similar to the ones where you first click in an image. You can control how the Magic Wand Tool behaves by specifying tolerance settings and whether or not you want to select only contiguous pixels on the tool options bar.

Learning About Tolerance

The tolerance setting determines the range of colors you select with the Magic Wand Tool. For example, if you select a low tolerance and then click an image of the sky, you will only select a narrow range of blue pixels and probably not the entire sky. However, if you set a higher tolerance, you can expand the range of blue pixels selected by the Magic Wand Tool. Each time you click the Magic Wand Tool, you can choose from one of four buttons on the tool options bar to select a new area, add to the existing area (the effect is cumulative; the more you click, the more

you add), subtract from the existing area, or intersect with the existing area. The settings for the Magic Wand Tool are shown in Figure I-22.

> **QUICKTIP**
>
> You can also press and hold [Shift] and repeatedly click the mouse to add pixels to your selection, or press and hold [Alt] (Win) or [option] (Mac), then click to subtract pixels from your selection.

Using the Eyedropper Tool and the Magic Wand Tool

The Contiguous and Tolerance settings are not the only determinants that establish the pixel area selected by the Magic Wand Tool. The area that the Magic Wand Tool selects also has an intrinsic relationship with the settings for the Eyedropper Tool. The sample size, or number of pixels used by the Eyedropper Tool to determine the color it picks up, affects the area selected by the Magic Wand Tool. To understand this, you need to first examine the Eyedropper Tool settings.

Understanding Sample Size

When the Eyedropper Tool sample size is set to Point Sample, it picks up the one pixel where you click on the image. When the sample size is set to 3 by 3 Average, the Eyedropper Tool picks up the color values of the nine pixels that surround the pixel where you click the image and averages them. The sample area increases exponentially to 25 pixels for the 5 by 5 Average setting. The sample size of the Eyedropper Tool influences the area selected by the Magic Wand Tool. Figure I-22 shows how different Eyedropper Tool sample sizes change the Magic Wand Tool selections, even when you sample an image at the same coordinates and use the same tolerance setting. As you become familiar with the Magic Wand Tool, it's a good idea to verify or change the Eyedropper Tool sample size as needed, in addition to changing the tolerance setting.

FIGURE I-21

Magic Wand Tool options

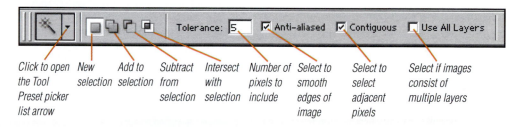

Click to open the Tool Preset picker list arrow

New selection

Add to selection

Subtract from selection

Intersect with selection

Number of pixels to include

Select to smooth edges of image

Select to select adjacent pixels

Select if images consist of multiple layers

FIGURE I-22

Selection affected by Eyedropper Tool sample size

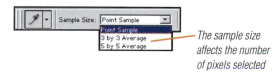

The sample size affects the number of pixels selected

Fewer pixels selected using Point Sample with Magic Wand

More pixels selected using 5 by 5 Average sample with Magic Wand

Select an object using the Magic Wand Tool

1. Click the Background layer on the Layers palette.

2. Open Peppermint.psd, then drag it to the right side of the workspace, as shown in Figure I-23.

3. Click the Eyedropper Tool on the toolbox, then verify that the sample size is set to 5 by 5 Average.

4. Click the Magic Wand Tool on the toolbox.

5. Type **50** in the Tolerance text box on the tool options bar, then press [Enter] (Win) or [return] (Mac).

6. Deselect the Contiguous check box, if necessary.

   > TIP   If the Contiguous check box is selected, you'll select only the pixels sharing the same color values that are adjoining each other.

7. Click the bottom-left leaf at 20 H/175 V to select the peppermint plant, as shown in Figure I-24.

8. Click the Move Tool on the toolbox.

9. Position the pointer over the bottom-left leaf, drag the plant above the bananas in the Juiced document, then compare your image to Figure I-25.

You opened a new document, set the Eyedropper Tool sample size to its largest selection setting, used the Magic Wand Tool to select the image, then moved the selected image into the Juiced document.

FIGURE I-23
New document opened and positioned

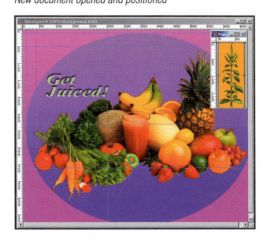

FIGURE I-25
Selected object moved to current document

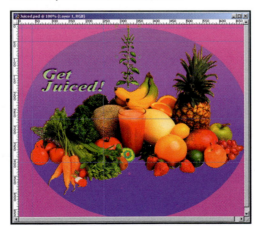

FIGURE I-24
Selection indicated by marquee

FIGURE I-26
Comparison of selections

Selection made
with 5 by 5
Average sample
size captures
more pixels

Selection made
with Point
Sample size
captures fewer
pixels

FIGURE I-27
Selection positioned in document

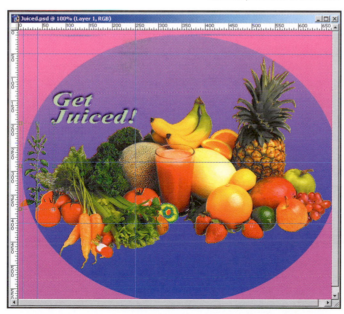

Compare objects selected using different sample sizes

1. Click Window on the menu bar, point to Documents, then click Peppermint.psd.

2. Click Select on the menu bar, then click Deselect.

3. Repeat Steps 3 through 9 in the previous steps, but this time, set the sample size for the Eyedropper Tool to Point Sample in Step 3 and drag the plant above the oranges in Step 9.

4. Verify that the Show Bounding Box check box is selected on the tool options bar, then compare the two plants in the Juiced document, as shown in Figure I-26.

5. Delete Layer 2 on the Layers palette.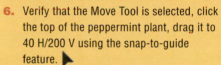

6. Verify that the Move Tool is selected, click the top of the peppermint plant, drag it to 40 H/200 V using the snap-to-guide feature. ▶

7. Save your work, then compare your image to Figure I-27.

8. Close Peppermint.psd without saving changes.

You changed the Eyedropper Tool sample size to its smallest setting, reselected the plant, moved it to the Juiced document, deleted a new layer, then repositioned the image.

LEARN HOW TO CREATE SNAPSHOTS

What You'll Do

 In this lesson, you'll create a snapshot on the History palette, edit a document, then use the snapshot to view the document as it existed prior to making changes.

Understanding Snapshots

As mentioned earlier in this unit, it is a good work habit to make a copy of an original layer to help you avoid losing any of the original image information. Creating snapshots is like creating that new copy. The History palette can only record a maximum of 20 tasks, or states, that you perform. When the History palette reaches its limit, it starts deleting the oldest states to make room for new states. You can create a **snapshot**, a temporary copy of your document that contains the history states made to that point. It's a good idea to take a snapshot of the History palette image before you begin an editing session and after you've made crucial changes because you can use snapshots to revert to or review your image from an earlier stage of development. You can create multiple snapshots in an image, and you can switch between snapshots as necessary.

Creating a Snapshot

To create a snapshot, you can click the Create new snapshot button on the History palette, or click the History palette list arrow and then click New Snapshot, as shown in Figure I-28. Each new snapshot is numbered consecutively; snapshots appear in order at the top of the History palette. If you create a snapshot by clicking the New Snapshot command, you can name the snapshot in the Name text box in the New Snapshot dialog box. Otherwise, you can rename an existing snapshot in the same way as you rename a layer on the Layers palette: double-click the snapshot, then type the name in the Name text box in the Rename Snapshot dialog box. You can create a snapshot based on the full document, merged layers, or just the current layer. A snapshot of the full document includes all layers in the current document. A snapshot of merged layers combines all the layers in the current document on a single layer, and a snapshot of the current layer includes only the layer active at the time you took the snapshot. Figure I-29 shows the New Snapshot dialog box.

Changing Snapshot Options

By default, Photoshop automatically creates a snapshot of an image when you open it. To change the default snapshot option, click the History palette list arrow, click History Options, then select one of the check boxes shown in Figure I-30. You can open files faster by deselecting the Automatically Create First Snapshot check box.

QUICKTIP

Photoshop does not save snapshots when you close the document.

FIGURE I-28

Snapshot commands on the History palette

Default snapshot created when file is opened

New snapshot

Click to open the New Snapshot dialog box

Click to change default snapshot options

Create new snapshot button

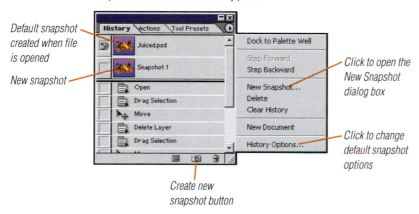

FIGURE I-29

New Snapshot dialog box

Click to select which layers to include in the snapshot

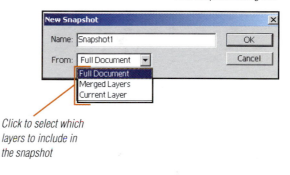

FIGURE I-30

History Options dialog box

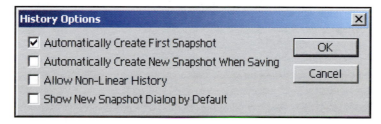

Create a snapshot

1. Open Peppermint.psd.

2. Click Image on the menu bar, point to Adjustments, then click Invert. See Figure I-31.

3. Click the History palette list arrow, then click New Snapshot.

4. Type **After Color** in the Name text box, as shown in Figure I-32.

5. Click OK.

   The newly named snapshot appears on the History palette beneath the snapshot Photoshop created when you opened the document.

   You opened the Peppermint document, edited the document, then created and named a new snapshot.

FIGURE I-31
Inverted image

Original snapshot created when document opened

FIGURE I-32
New Snapshot dialog box

Type snapshot name here

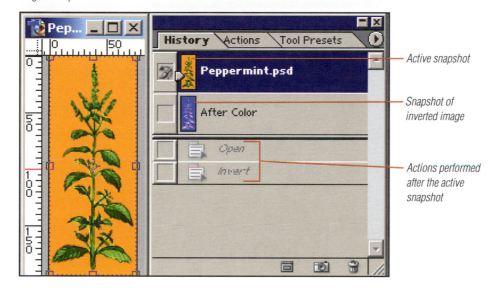

FIGURE I-33

Original snapshot view

Active snapshot

Snapshot of inverted image

Actions performed after the active snapshot

1. Click the Peppermint.psd snapshot on the History palette, then compare your image to Figure I-33.

   The image returns to its original color.

2. Click the After Color snapshot on the History palette.

3. Close Peppermint.psd *without* saving changes.

You used the snapshot to view the document as it was before you made changes.

CREATE MULTIPLE-IMAGE *LAYOUTS*

What You'll Do

In this lesson, you'll create a picture package of the current image and then create a folder containing a contact sheet of images.

Understanding a Picture Package

Photoshop allows you to generate several types of multiple-image layouts. Multiple-image layouts are useful when you need to gather one or more Photoshop documents in a variety of sizes for a variety of uses. For example, if you create an advertisement, you might want to have multiple image layouts for printing in different publications. You can generate a single layout, known as a picture package, which contains multiple sizes of a single document, as shown in Figure I-34. The picture package option lets you choose from 20 possible layouts of the same document, and then places them in a single file.

Creating a Web Photo Gallery

You can display your image files on a Web site by creating a Web Photo Gallery. A Web Photo Gallery contains a thumbnail index page of all files you choose. To create a Web Photo Gallery, click File on the menu bar, point to Automate, then click Web Photo Gallery. You can choose which files to include in the gallery by clicking the Browse button, and choosing the gallery location by clicking the Destination button. Before you click OK to generate the Web Photo Gallery, you can customize the look of your Web Photo Gallery using the options in the Styles and Options lists. You can also choose a font and font size for the gallery, and name the photographer in the Photographer text box.

Assembling a Contact Sheet

You might be getting the feeling that previewing and cataloging images can be a time-consuming and difficult chore.

Photoshop has a feature that helps by allowing you to assemble a maximum of 30 thumbnail images in a specific folder, called a **contact sheet**, as shown in Figure I-36. If the folder used to compile the contact sheet contains more than 30 files, Photoshop automatically creates new sheets so that all the documents appear.

FIGURE I-34

Sample picture package

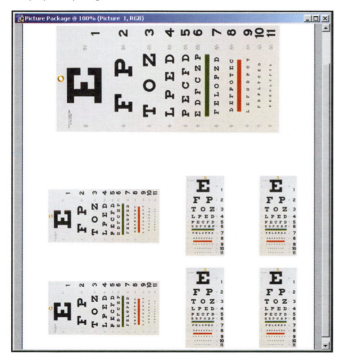

FIGURE I-35

Sample contact sheet

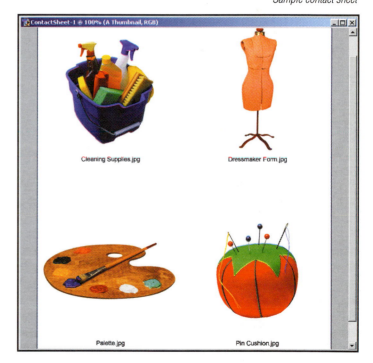

Create a picture package

1. Click File on the menu bar, point to Automate, then click Picture Package.

   The Picture Package dialog box opens.

   | TIP   You can use the Browse button to select the document you want to package.

2. Verify that the Frontmost Document appears in the Use text box, click the Layout list arrow, click (1) 5 × 7 (2) 2.5 × 3.5 (4) 2 × 2.5, then compare your picture package dialog box to Figure I-36.

3. Click OK.

   | TIP   Photoshop creates a temporary storage file (called Juiced copy) while it creates the picture package, then deletes the file when it is complete.

4. Save the picture package where your Unit I project files are stored, and use the default name (Picture Package.psd), then close the file.

5. Save your work, then close Juiced.psd.

You selected the Picture Package option from the Automate command on the File menu, selected a layout for a picture package, then created a picture package using the Juiced document.

FIGURE I-36
Picture Package dialog box

Frontmost document is pictured by default

3 page sizes are available

16 page layouts are available

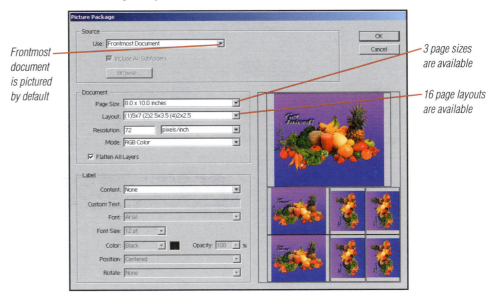

FIGURE I-37

Contact Sheet II dialog box

Images are located by source folder

The placement of images in columns and rows is defined by user

Use of filename as caption makes document easier to retrieve

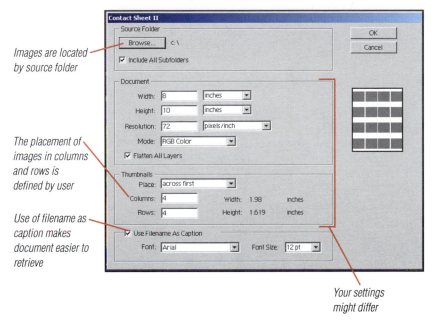

Your settings might differ

1. Create a folder on your computer that contains at least three Photoshop documents you have created, then name it **Contact Sample**.

   TIP See your instructor if you require assistance.

2. Click File on the menu bar, point to Automate, click Contact Sheet II, then compare your dialog box to Figure I-37.

3. Click Browse, navigate to the Contact Sample folder, click OK (Win) or Choose (Mac), then click OK to close the Contact Sheet II dialog box.

   Photoshop opens the documents and places them in a new file called ContactSheet-1.psd.

   TIP Photoshop automatically numbers additional contact sheets consecutively.

4. Save ContactSheet-1.psd where your Contact Sample folder is stored, use the default name (ContactSheet-1.psd), then close the file.

You created a folder and placed images in it, selected the Contact Sheet II option from the Automate command on the File menu, and then created a contact sheet of the images in the folder you created.

Power User Shortcuts

to do this:	use this method:
Clone Stamp Tool	or S
Create a snapshot	
Duplicate selection and move 1 pixel	Press and hold [Ctrl][Alt] (Win) or [control][option] (Mac), then press
Left	←
Right	→
Up	↑
Down	↓
Move selection 10 pixels	Press and hold [Ctrl][Shift] (Win) or [control][shift] (Mac), then press
Left	←
Right	→
Up	↑
Down	↓

to do this:	use this method:
Eraser tools	Shift E
Magic Wand	or W
Move selection 1 pixel	Press and hold [Ctrl] (Win) or [control] (Mac), then press
Left	←
Right	→
Up	↑
Down	↓
Open Extract dialog box	[Ctrl][Alt][X] (Win) or [control][option][X] (Mac)

Key: Menu items are indicated by ➢ between the menu name and its command. Blue bold letters are shortcuts for selecting tools on the toolbox.

Create an alpha channel.

1. Open PS I-2.psd, then save it as **Tool World**.
2. Make sure the rulers appear in pixels, then enlarge the image to 150%.
3. Display the Channels palette.
4. Select the Rectangular Marquee Tool, then change the feathering to **25** on the tool options bar.
5. Create a selection from 70 H/50 V to 400 H/270 V.
6. Save the selection on the Channels palette, then display the Alpha 1 channel.
7. Deselect the selection.
8. Open the Channel Options dialog box, select a blue color swatch at 50% opacity, then close the dialog box.
9. Display the RGB channel.

Use Extract to isolate an object.

1. Display the Layers palette.
2. Duplicate the Tools layer, then name it **Yellow Tape**.
3. Display the Extract dialog box.
4. Enlarge the view of the roll of yellow tape.
5. Change the Edge Highlighter Tool brush size to 1.
6. Draw a tight border around the outer and inner edges of the yellow tape.
7. Fill between the inner and outer edges of your selection, then close the Extract dialog box.

Erase areas in an image to enhance appearance.

1. Hide the Yellow Tape layer.
2. Make the Tools layer active.
3. Magnify the view of the yellow tape.
4. Using the Background Eraser Tool, erase the roll of yellow tape.
5. Make the Yellow Tape layer active.
6. Reduce the view of the yellow tape.
7. Adjust the Color Balance settings on the Yellow Tape layer to +75, +25, and –80. (*Hint*: Click Color Balance on the Adjustment submenu.)

Fix imperfections in an image.

1. Make the Tools layer active.
2. Select the Clone Stamp Tool on the toolbox.
3. Use the Hard round 5 pixels brush tip. (*Hint*: Use the Brush Preset picker.)
4. Sample the area to be *pasted* at 340 H/50 V by pressing [Alt] (Win) or [option] (Mac) over the wire cutters.
5. Click the red dot (at approximately 310 H/85 V).

Use the Magic Wand Tool to select objects.

1. Open PS I-3.psd.
2. Select the Magic Wand Tool, deselect the Contiguous check box if necessary, then set the Tolerance to 0.
3. Click the image at 80 H/20 V.
4. Select the inverse of the selection.

5. Move the selection to the Tool World document.
6. Move the top of the handle of the wrench to 200 H/40 V.
7. Deselect the selection, then close PS I-3.psd without saving your changes.

Learn how to create snapshots.

1. Use the History palette list arrow to create a new snapshot.
2. Name the snapshot **New**.

Create multiple-image layouts.

1. Use the frontmost document to create a 4(4×5) picture package.
2. Save the file as **Picture Package-Tools**, and close it.
3. Create a folder with files to use for a contact sheet.
4. Save this file using the default naming scheme and the next available number, and close it.
5. Save your work, then compare your image to Figure I-38.

FIGURE I-38
Completed Skills Review

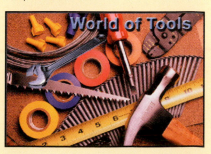

Van O'Puppets, a traveling educational show for children, is planning a piece on earth science. For the first segment, the puppets will teach about different shapes, starting with spheres. You're going to design the spot graphic that will link users to the Van O'Puppets science Web page.

1. Obtain the following images for the graphic: an orb background, at least two images that contain spheres whose content you can select or extract, and any other images as desired. You'll use two of the sphere images for a clipping group.

2. Create a new Photoshop document, then save it as **Spheroid**.

3. Apply a color or style to the Background layer, or use any of the techniques you learned in this unit to select and drag the image that will be the background to the Spheroid document, then apply at least one style to it. (*Hint*: An Adjustment layer is applied to the berries.)

4. Use any of the techniques you learned in this unit to select and drag the image that will be the base of the clipping group to the Spheroid document above the Background layer, and modify it as desired. (*Hint*: The tennis ball in the sample is the base image.)

5. Use any of the techniques you learned in this unit to select and drag the image that will be the target of the clipping group to the Spheroid document, and modify it as necessary. (*Hint*: The golf balls in the sample are the target image.)

6. Create a clipping group using the two images, then modify the result as desired. (*Hint*: The tennis ball has been copied to another layer, which was adjusted to a lower opacity setting and moved above the clipping group to create the illusion that the golf balls are inside it.)

7. Create an alpha channel and ensure that it is visible in the document. (*Hint*: The tennis ball has a selected area alpha channel applied to it.)

8. Create type layers as desired, and apply at least one style or filter to them. (*Hint*: The We have nothing to sphere but sphere itself type has a Dissolve blending mode, and the Drop Shadow and Gradient Overlay styles applied to it.)

9. Drag or copy the remaining images to the Spheroid document, transform them or apply at least one style or filter to them, then close the image files.

10. Save your work, then compare your image to the sample in Figure I-39.

FIGURE I-39
Completed Project Builder 1

Several resort hotels want to accommodate the unique vacation needs of their younger guests. They're going to give each child under 12 a bag full of equipment, books, games, and other items that match their interests. Your job is to design the cover of the information booklet that will be included in the package.

1. Obtain images for the cover that are centered on a beach vacation theme. Include images whose content you can select or extract, and any other images as desired. You can use scanned images or images that are available on your computer, or connect to the Internet and download images. You'll need a background image, at least one image that will serve as the focal point, and at least two other images that will surround the focal point and blend into the background.

2. Create a new Photoshop document, then save it as **Beach It Guide**.

3. Apply a color or style to the Background layer, or use any of the techniques you learned in this unit to select and drag the image that will be the background to the Beach It Guide document, then apply a style to it.

4. Use any of the techniques you learned in this unit to select and drag the image that will be the focal point to the Beach It Guide document, copy it, if desired, apply an elliptical marquee to it, then save the selection as an alpha channel. (*Hint*: The girl has a layer mask applied to it, and has been copied to another layer that has an elliptical marquee with Drop Shadow and Bevel and Emboss styles applied to it.)

5. Open the surrounding image files, then use any of the techniques you learned in this unit to select and drag the images to the Beach It Guide document.

6. Add layer masks, transform, or apply filters or styles to the surrounding images as desired. (*Hint*: The foliage has been enhanced and has a layer mask; the tropical flowers have a layer mask.)

FIGURE I-40
Completed Project Builder 2

7. Create type layers as desired and apply filters or styles to them. (*Hint*: The Beach It Guide type has Drop Shadow, Bevel and Emboss, and Gradient Overlay styles applied to it.)

8. Create a layer set called **Title**, add a color to the layer set, and then add the type layers to it.

9. Save your work, close the image files, then compare your image to the sample in Figure I-40.

DESIGN PROJECT

You're the senior graphics engineer at a 3-D software simulation company and have just hired a few new graphic designers. Some of the work at your company involves reverse engineering, a process that your new artists will need to understand and capture visually. To better orient them to the practice, you've asked them to deconstruct a Photoshop image on the Web, and then reinterpret the image using the techniques they identified. Before you assemble the staff, you want to walk through the process yourself.

1. Connect to the Internet, and go to *www.course.com*, navigate to the page for this book, click the Student Online Companion link, then click the link for this unit to display the Web site shown in Figure I-41.
2. Create a new Photoshop document and save it as **My Vision**.
3. Create a type layer named **Techniques**, then on the layer, type the skills and features that you believe were used to create the appearance of each letter and its background image. In addition to addressing the specifics for each letter, be sure to include the following general analyses:
   - Identify the light source for the image, and how light is handled for each letter and its background.
   - Discuss the relationship between the styles applied to the type and the styles or filters applied to the background image.

- Evaluate any seemingly conflicting or unidentifiable techniques.
4. Complete your analyses and print the document.
5. Hide the Techniques layer, then obtain images to use for your own interpretation of the Web page. You can use scanned images or images that are available on your computer, or download images from the Internet.

FIGURE I-41
Completed Design Project

6. Place the images in your document, create type layers for the letters, and then apply the techniques you identified.
7. Update the Techniques layer as necessary, print the document so that the Techniques layer prints clearly, then compare your before and after analyses. (*Hint*: Hide distracting layers if necessary.)
8. Hide the Techniques layer, make the other layers active, then save your work.

Depending on the size of your group, you can assign individual elements of the project to group members, or work collectively to create the finished product.

After years of catching fish from the gallery, one of the aquatic mammals in an aquatic park near you is being featured in marketing material for the park, and you know that this is a grand public relations opportunity not to be missed. You and the other interns decide to design a poster and a companion bumper sticker that highlights an aquatic mammal. You can use the aquatic mammal of your choice in the design.

1. Obtain images for the poster and bumper sticker. Include those whose content you can select or extract, and any other images as desired. You can use scanned images, or images that are available on your computer, or connect to the Internet and download images. You'll need a background image that might or might not include the animal, at least one small image (such as snack, toy, or flower) to accompany the mammal, and as many other images as desired.

2. Create a new Photoshop document and save it as **Aquatic Mammal**.

3. Drag or copy the background to the Aquatic Mammal document above the Background layer, delete the Background layer, if necessary, then apply styles and filters to it.

(*Hint*: The seal in the sample is both the animal and the background.)

4. Copy the animal image layer, select the animal, then save the selection as an alpha channel. (*Hint*: The seal was selected using the Magic Wand Tool, and then saved as an alpha channel.)

5. Copy the animal layer again if desired, and apply filters or styles to it. (*Hint*: The seal was copied twice and has an Ink Outlines filter applied to one copy and a Motion Blur filter applied to the right side of the other copy.)

6. Drag or copy the small image, transform it as needed, and then apply at least one style or filter to it. (*Hint*: The yellow flower has been scaled, rotated, and erased.)

7. Drag or copy other images as desired, then apply filters or styles to them. (*Hint*: The purple flower has been scaled, rotated, and erased.)

FIGURE I-42
Completed Group Project

8. Create type layers for the bumper sticker as desired, include something unique about the species you selected, and apply at least one style or filter to them. (*Hint*: The background of the bumper sticker was created with the Rectangle Tool and has a stroke applied to it, the heart was created with the Custom Shape Tool, and the cut corners were created with the Eraser Tool.)

9. Be prepared to discuss the effects you can generate when you extract or select an image, copy it, and apply different opacity settings, filters, or styles to each copy.

10. Save your work, then compare your image to the sample in Figure I-43.

UNIT J

ADJUSTING COLORS

1. Correct and adjust color.

2. Enhance colors by altering saturation.

3. Modify color channels using levels.

4. Create color samplers with the Info palette.

UNIT J
ADJUSTING COLORS

Enhancing Color

Photoshop places several color-enhancing tools at your disposal. These tools make it possible to change the mood or "personality" of a color, by changing its tonal values. **Tonal values**, also called color **levels**, are the numeric values of an individual color and are crucial if you ever need to duplicate a color. For example, when you select a specific shade in a paint store that requires custom mixing, a recipe that contains the tonal values is used to create the color.

Using Tools to Adjust Colors

You can use color adjustment tools to make an image that is flat or dull appear to come to life. You can mute distracting colors to call attention to a central image. You can choose from several adjustment tools to achieve the same results, so the method you use depends on which one you *prefer*, not on which one is *better*.

Reproducing Colors

Accurate color reproduction is an important reason to learn about color measurement and modification. Because colors vary from monitor to monitor, and can be altered during the output process, you can specify exactly the way you want them to look. Professional printers know how to take your Photoshop settings and adapt them to get the colors that match your specifications. Color levels, depicted in a **histogram** (a graph that represents the frequency distribution—for example, the number of times a particular pixel color occurs), can be modified by making adjustments in the input and output levels. Moving the input sliders toward the center changes the tonal range, resulting in increased contrast. Moving the output sliders toward the center decreases the tonal range, resulting in decreased contrast.

QUICK TIP

You can make color adjustments directly on a layer, or by using an adjustment layer. Directly applying a color adjustment affects only the layer to which it is applied. Applying a color adjustment using an adjustment layer affects all visible layers beneath it.

Tools You'll Use

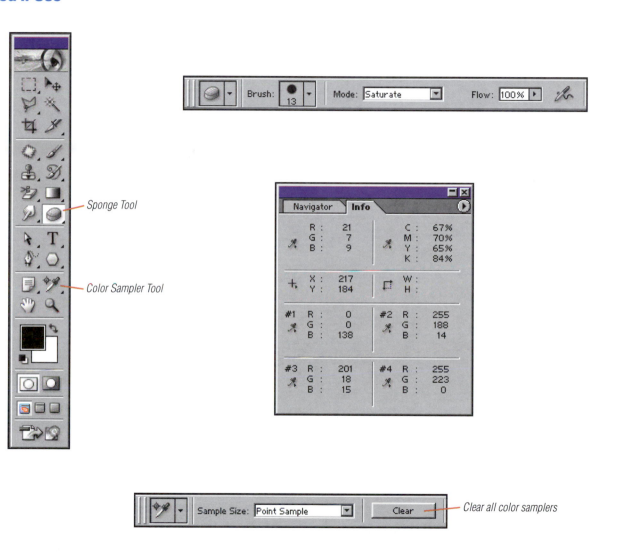

Sponge Tool

Color Sampler Tool

Clear all color samplers

Brush: 13   Mode: Saturate   Flow: 100%

Navigator   Info

R :   21   C :   67%
G :   7   M :   70%
B :   9   Y :   65%
              K :   84%

X :   217   W :
Y :   184   H :

#1 R :   0   #2 R :   255
    G :   0   G :   188
    B :   138   B :   14

#3 R :   201   #4 R :   255
    G :   18   G :   223
    B :   15   B :   0

Sample Size: Point Sample   Clear

CORRECT AND ADJUST COLOR

What You'll Do

Parrot Mania

In this lesson, you'll modify settings for color balance and curves to make dull colors look more vivid.

Making Color Corrections

Learning to recognize which colors need correction is one of the hardest skills to develop. Adjusting colors can be extremely difficult because, although there is a science to color correction, you must also consider the aesthetics of your image. Art is in the eye of the beholder, and you must choose how you want your work to look and feel.

Balancing Colors

You can **balance colors** by adding and subtracting colors from those already existing in a layer. You do this to correct oversaturated or undersaturated color and to remove color casts from an image. The Color Balance dialog box contains three sliders: one for Cyan-Red, one for Magenta-Green, and one for Yellow-Blue. You can adjust colors by dragging each of these sliders or by typing in values in the Color Levels text boxes. You can also use the Color Balance dialog box to adjust the color balance of shadows or highlights by

clicking the Shadows or Highlights option buttons.

Modifying Curves

By using the Curves dialog box, you can alter the output tonal value of any pixel input. Instead of just being able to make adjustments using three variables (highlights, shadows, and midtones), you can change as many as 16 points along the 0–255 scale in the Curves dialog box. The horizontal axis in the Curves dialog box represents the original intensity values of the pixels (the Input levels), and the vertical axis represents the modified color values (the Output levels). The default curve appears as a diagonal line that shares the same input and output values. Each point on the line represents each pixel. You add curves to the line to adjust the tonal values.

Analyzing Colors

When you look at an image, ask yourself, "What's wrong with this picture?" Does the image need more blue than yellow? Preserve your work by creating an adjustment layer, then try adjusting the color sliders, and see how the image changes. Then try modifying the curves. Much of the color correction process involves experimentation—with you, the artist, learning and applying the subtleties of shading and contrast.

FIGURE J-1
Variations dialog box

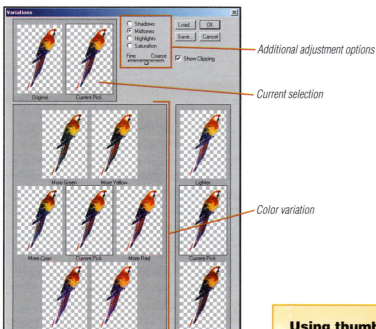

Additional adjustment options

Current selection

Color variation

Modify color balance settings

1. Start Photoshop, open PS J-1.psd, then save the file as **Parrot Mania**.

2. Click the Default Foreground and Background Colors button.

3. Click the Large Parrot layer on the Layers palette.

4. Click Image on the menu bar, point to Adjustments, then click Color Balance.

5. Drag the sliders so that the settings in the Color Levels text boxes are +60, −40, and −50, then click OK to close the dialog box.

6. Compare your image to Figure J-2.

You modified the color balance settings by using the sliders.

FIGURE J-2
Color balanced layer

Intensified reds, magentas, and yellows

Using the Auto Adjustments commands

You can make color adjustments using the Auto Adjustments commands on the Image menu. You can use three Auto Commands (Auto Levels, Auto Contrast, and Auto Color) to make color adjustments automatically without any additional input. The Auto Levels command adjusts the intensity levels of shadows and highlights by identifying the lightest and darkest pixel in each color channel and then redistributing the pixel's values across that range. You can use the Auto Contrast command to make simple adjustments to the contrast and mixture of colors in an RGB image; it works by analyzing the distribution of colors in the composite image, not in the individual color channels. The Auto Color command adjusts the contrast and color mixtures using the image itself to make the adjustment, resulting in neutralized midtones.

Curves dialog box

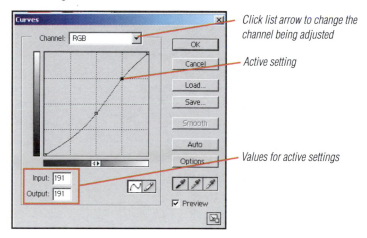

Click list arrow to change the channel being adjusted

Active setting

Values for active settings

Modify curves

1. With the Large Parrot layer still active, click Image on the menu bar, point to Adjustments, then click Curves.

2. Click the center of the graph at the point on the line where the input and output both equal 128.

3. Drag the point down so that the input equals 128 and the output equals 104.

   The image's colors change as you drag the line.

4. Click the point where the curve intersects the right vertical gridline (input equals 193 approximately, and output equals 176 approximately).

   TIP The point that you click in the Curves dialog box is called the **active setting**.

5. Drag the active setting until the input and output values both equal 191, as shown in Figure J-3.

   TIP After you select the active setting, you can also change its location by changing the values in the Input and Output boxes.

6. Click OK.

7. Save your work, then compare your document to Figure J-4.

You modified curves settings by using the Curves dialog box.

FIGURE J-4
Image with modified curves

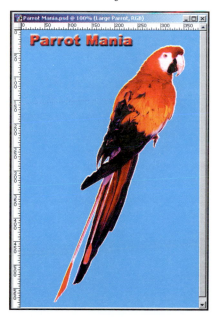

ENHANCE COLORS BY ALTERING SATURATION

What You'll Do

In this lesson, you'll modify the appearance of an image by altering color saturation.

Understanding Saturation

Saturation is the purity of a particular color. A higher saturation level indicates a color that is more intense. To understand saturation, imagine that you are trying to lighten a can of blue paint. For example, if you add some gray paint, you decrease the purity and the intensity of the original color. Photoshop provides two methods of modifying color saturation: the Hue/Saturation dialog box and the Sponge Tool.

Using the Sponge Tool

The Sponge Tool is located on the toolbox, and is used to increase or decrease the color saturation of a specific area within a layer. Settings for the Sponge Tool are located on the tool options bar and include the brush size, whether you want the sponge to saturate or desaturate, and how quickly you want the color to flow into or from the Sponge Tool.

QUICKTIP

You can reset the active tool to its default settings by right-clicking the tool on the tool options bar, then clicking Reset Tool.

Using the Hue/Saturation Dialog Box

Hue is the amount of color that is reflected from an object. In technical terms, hue is assigned a measurement (between 0 and 360 degrees) that is taken from a standard color wheel. In conversation, hue is referred to as red, blue, or gold and described in terms of its tints or shades, such as yellow-green or blue-green. Adjusting hue and saturation is similar to making modifications to color balance. You can make these adjustments by using the Hue, Saturation, and Lightness sliders, which are located in the Hue/Saturation dialog box. When modifying saturation levels using the Hue/Saturation dialog box, you have the option of adjusting the entire color range, or preset color ranges. The available preset color ranges are shown in Figure J-5. To choose any one of these color ranges, click the Edit list arrow in the Hue/Saturation dialog box *before* modifying any of the sliders.

Using Saturation to Convert a Color Layer to Grayscale

Have you ever wondered how a color image can contain a grayscale object, as shown in Figure J-6? You can easily create this effect using the Hue/Saturation dialog box. Click the layer containing the object you want in grayscale, click Image on the menu bar, point to Adjustments, then click Hue/Saturation. Drag the Saturation slider to the extreme left (or type –100 in the Saturation text box), then click OK.

FIGURE J-5

Preset color ranges in the Hue/Saturation dialog box

FIGURE J-6

Grayscale layer

Click list arrow to select colors to alter

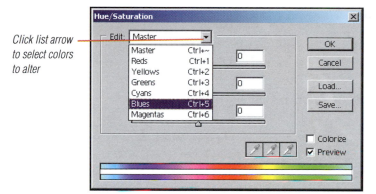

Saturate a color range

1. Click the Small Parrot 1 layer on the Layers palette to make it active.

2. Click the Indicates layer visibility button to hide the Large Parrot layer.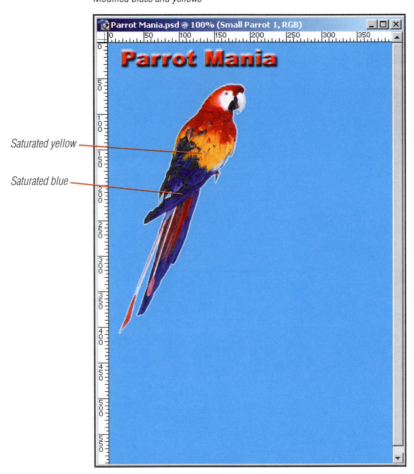

3. Click Image on the menu bar, point to Adjustments, then click Hue/Saturation.

4. Click the Edit list arrow, then click Blues.

5. Drag the Saturation slider to +40.

6. Click the Edit list arrow, then click Yellows.

7. Drag the Saturation slider to +30.

   The image's blues and yellows are intensified.

8. Click OK, then compare your image to Figure J-7.

You changed the saturation of two preset color ranges.

FIGURE J-7
Modified blues and yellows

Parrot Mania.psd @ 100% (Small Parrot 1, RGB)

Parrot Mania

Saturated yellow

Saturated blue

FIGURE J-8

Reds saturated with the Sponge Tool

Saturated red areas

1. Click the Sponge Tool on the toolbox.

   TIP The Sponge Tool might be hidden beneath the Dodge Tool on the toolbox.

2. Click the Click to open Brush Preset picker list arrow, then double-click the Hard Round 13 pixels brush tip.

3. If necessary, click the Mode list arrow on the tool options bar, click Saturate, then set the Flow to 100%.

4. Click and drag the pointer over the red areas (head and tail feathers) of the parrot.

   The red color in the saturated area is brighter.

5. Save your work, then compare your document to Figure J-8.

You used the Sponge Tool to saturate specific areas in an image.

MODIFY COLOR CHANNELS USING LEVELS

What You'll Do

Parrot Mania

In this lesson, you'll use levels to make color adjustments.

Making Color or Tonal Adjustments

You can make color adjustments using the Levels dialog box. This tool lets you make modifications across a tonal range, using the composite color channel or individual channels. Unlike the Curves feature, the Levels feature takes the form of a histogram and displays light and dark color values on a linear scale. The plotted data indicates the total number of pixels for a given tonal value.

There is no "ideal" histogram shape. The image's character and tone determine the shape of the histogram. Some images will be lighter and their histogram will be bunched on the right; some will be darker and their histogram will be bunched on the left. Three triangular sliders appear beneath the histogram representing shadows, midtones, and highlights. Three text boxes appear for input levels (one box each for the input shadows, midtones, and highlights). Two text boxes appear for output levels (one box each for the output shadows and highlights).

Correcting Shadows and Highlights

You can modify the settings for shadows and highlights independently. By moving the output shadows slider to the right, you can decrease contrast and *lighten* the image on an individual layer, as shown in Figure J-9. You can decrease contrast and *darken* an image by moving the output highlights slider to the left in the Levels dialog box.

FIGURE J-9
Output shadows adjusted

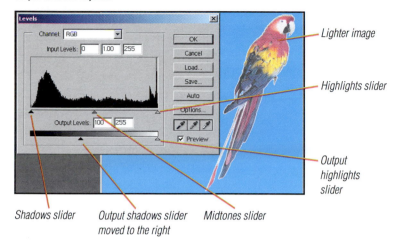

Lighter image

Highlights slider

Output highlights slider

Shadows slider   Output shadows slider   Midtones slider
                      moved to the right

FIGURE J-10
Levels dialog box

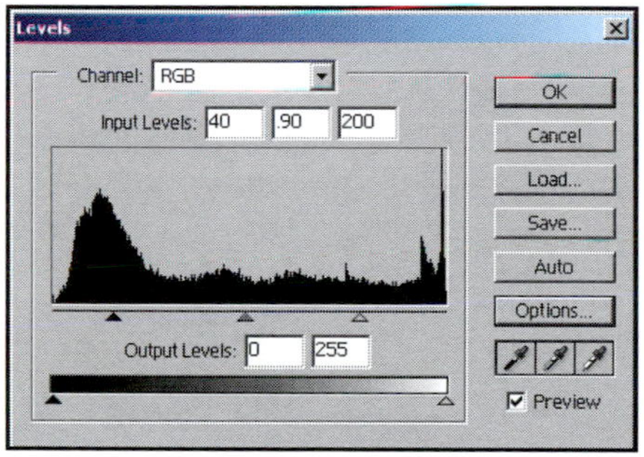

FIGURE J-11
Adjusted levels

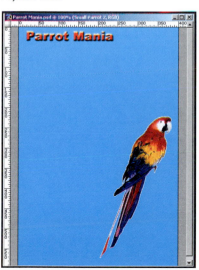

1. Click the Small Parrot 2 layer on the Layers palette to make it active.

2. Click the Indicates layer visibility button to hide the Small Parrot 1 layer. 👁

3. Click Image on the menu bar, point to Adjustments, then click Levels.

4. Drag the Shadows slider to 40, the Midtones slider to 0.90, and the Highlights slider to 200, as shown in Figure J-10.

5. Click OK, then compare your work to Figure J-11.

6. Save your work.

You modified levels for shadows, midtones, and highlights.

Lesson 3   Modify Color Channels Using Levels

CREATE COLOR SAMPLERS WITH THE INFO PALETTE

What You'll Do

In this lesson, you'll take color samples and use the Info palette to store color information.

Sampling Colors

In the past, you've used the Eyedropper pointer to take a sample of an existing color. By taking the sample, you were able to use the color as a background or a font color. Unfortunately, this method limited you to one color sample at a time. Photoshop has an additional feature, the **Color Sampler Tool**, that makes it possible to sample—and store—up to four distinct color samplers.

QUICKTIP

The color samplers are saved with the document in which they were created.

Using Color Samplers

You can apply each of the four color samplers to a document or use the samplers to make color adjustments. Each time you click the Color Sampler Tool, a color reading is taken and the number 1, 2, 3, or 4 appears on the image, depending on how many samplers you have already taken.

See Figure J-12. A color sampler includes all visible layers and is dynamic. This means that if you hide a layer from which a sampler was taken, the next visible layer will contain a sampler that has the same coordinates of the hidden layer, but the sampler will have the color reading of the visible layer.

QUICKTIP

The Color Sampler Tool is on the toolbox and is hidden under the Eyedropper Tool.

Using the Info Palette

The Info palette is grouped with the Navigator palette. The top-left quadrant displays actual color values for the current color mode. For example, if the current mode is RGB, then RGB values are displayed. The Info palette also displays CMYK values, X and Y coordinates of the current pointer location, and the width and height of a selection (if applicable), as shown in Figure J-13. When a color sampler is created, the Info palette expands to show the color measurement information from that sample. Figure J-14 shows an Info palette containing four color samplers. After you have established your color samplers but no longer want them to be displayed, click the Info palette list arrow, then deselect Color Samplers. Display hidden color samplers by clicking the Info palette list arrow, then selecting Color Samplers.

Manipulating Color Samplers

Color samplers, like most Photoshop features, are designed to accommodate change. Each color sampler can be moved by dragging the sampler icon to a new location. After the sampler is moved to its new location, its color value information is updated in the Info palette. You can individually delete any of the samplers by selecting the Color Sampler Tool, holding [Alt] (Win) or [option] (Mac), then clicking

the sampler you want to delete. You can also delete all the samplers by clicking the Clear button on the tool options bar.

QUICKTIP

Each time a color sampler is deleted, the remaining samplers are automatically renumbered. If you have defined four samplers and you want to add another sampler, you will have to clear an existing sampler before you can create another.

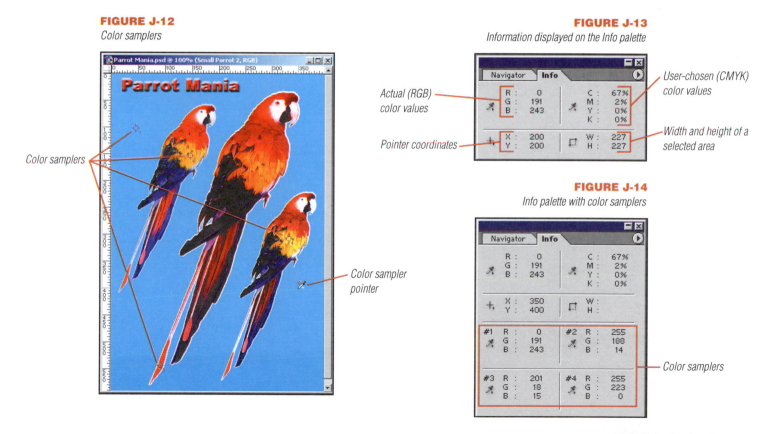

FIGURE J-12
Color samplers

Color samplers

Color sampler pointer

FIGURE J-13
Information displayed on the Info palette

Actual (RGB) color values

Pointer coordinates

User-chosen (CMYK) color values

Width and height of a selected area

FIGURE J-14
Info palette with color samplers

Color samplers

Create color samplers and use the Info palette

1. Click the Indicates layer visibility button on the Layers palette for the Large Parrot and Small Parrot 1 layers. 👁

2. Click Window on the menu bar and select Info to display the Info palette, if necessary.

3. Click the Color Sampler Tool on the toolbox. 🖋

4. Using Figure J-15 as a guide, click the image in four locations.

5. Click the Info palette list arrow, then click Color Samplers to hide the color samplers.

You sampled specific areas in the document, stored that color data in the Info palette, then hid the color samplers.

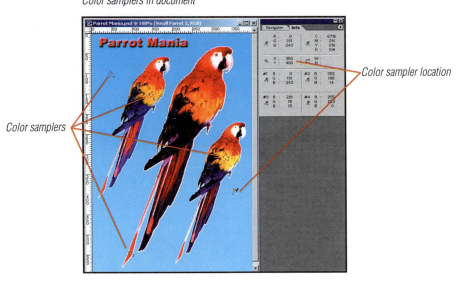

Color sampler location

Color samplers

Creating a spot color channel

Printing a Photoshop image can be a costly process, especially if a spot color is used. A **spot color** is one that can't easily be re-created by a printer, such as a specific color used in a client's logo. By creating a spot color channel, you can make it easier for your printer to create the ink for a difficult color, assure yourself of accurate color reproduction, and save yourself high printing costs. If you use this feature, you won't have to provide your printer with substitution colors: the spot color contains all of the necessary information. You can create a spot color channel by displaying the Channels palette, clicking the Channels palette list arrow, then clicking New Spot Channel. Create a meaningful name for the new spot channel, click the Color box, click the Custom button in the Color Picker dialog box, click the Book list arrow, then click a color-matching system. You can also create a custom color by clicking the Picker button in the Custom Colors dialog box. If you have created a color sampler, you can use this information to create the custom color for the spot color channel. Click OK to close the Custom Color dialog box, then click OK to close the New Spot Channel dialog box.

FIGURE J-16
Unsharp Mask dialog box

FIGURE J-18
Lighting effect applied

Unsharpen Mask changes the appearance of the Large Parrot layer

Lighting effect changes the appearance of the Backdrop layer

FIGURE J-17
Lighting Effects dialog box

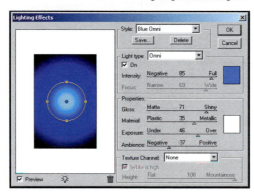

1. Click the Large Parrot layer on the Layers palette.

2. Click Filter on the menu bar, point to Sharpen, then click Unsharp Mask. You are now ready to put the finishing touches on your color-corrected document.

3. Use the settings in the Unsharp Mask dialog box shown in Figure J-16, then click OK. These settings emphasize the edges and create the illusion of a sharper image.

4. Click the Backdrop layer on the Layers palette.

5. Click Filter on the menu bar, point to Render, then click Lighting Effects.

6. Use the settings in the Lighting Effects dialog box shown in Figure J-17, then click OK.

7. Save your work, then compare your document to Figure J-18.

You added the Unsharp Mask and Lighting Effects filters to give the image a more professional appearance.

Power User Shortcuts

to do this:	use this method:
Adjust color with thumbnails	Image ➤ Adjustments ➤ Variations
Adjust saturation	Image ➤ Adjustments ➤ Hue/Saturation
Balance colors	Image ➤ Adjustments ➤ Color Balance
Choose color range	Click Edit list arrow in Hue/Saturation dialog box, click color range
Convert color layer	Image ➤ Adjustments ➤ Hue/Saturation
Create color sampler	Click [icon], click image using [eyedropper] in document
Create spot color channel	Click [Channels], click [▶], New Spot Channel
Delete color sampler	Click [icon], press [Alt] (Win) or [option] (Mac), click sampler using [scissors]

to do this:	use this method:
Modify curves	Image ➤ Adjustments ➤ Curves
Modify levels	Image ➤ Adjustments ➤ Levels
Move color sampler	Click sampler with [pointer]
Open Info palette	[Info]
Saturate with Sponge Tool	[icon] or **0**
Set to grayscale	Image ➤ Adjustments ➤ Hue/Saturation, set Saturation slider to −100
Show/Hide color samplers	Click [▶] ➤ Color Samplers

Key: Menu items are indicated by ➤ between the menu name and its command. Blue bold letters are shortcuts for selecting tools on the toolbox.

Correct and adjust color.

1. Start Photoshop.
2. Open PS J-2.psd, then save it as **Big Bird**.
3. Make the Bird layer active.
4. Open the Color Balance dialog box.
5. Drag the Yellow-Blue slider to –53, then close the dialog box.
6. Open the Curves dialog box.
7. Click the point where the input and output both equal 64.
8. Drag the curve up so that the output equals 128, then close the dialog box.
9. Save your work.

Enhance colors by altering saturation.

1. Open the Hue/Saturation dialog box.
2. Edit the Greens color range.
3. Change the Hue to –70 and the Saturation to –40, then close the dialog box.
4. Use the Sponge Tool to further saturate the green areas of the bird.
5. Use the Sponge Tool to saturate the light and dark blue areas of the bird.
6. Save your work.

Modify color channels using levels.

1. Open the Levels dialog box.
2. Modify the Blue channel Input Levels to 95, 1.60, 185.
3. Modify the Blue channel Output Levels to 0, 200.
4. Modify the Red channel Input Levels to 75, 1.20, 190.
5. Save your work.

Create color samplers with the Info palette.

1. Click the Color Sampler Tool.
2. Display the Info palette.
3. Create samplers for the following areas: the light blue feathers, the red wing, the yellow head, and the gold floor.
4. Compare your document to Figure J-19.
5. Hide the color samplers.
6. Save your work.

FIGURE J-19
Completed Skills Review

The Gray Barn Gallery has commissioned you to create a promotional poster for an upcoming show called Moods and Metaphors, which will be held during November of this year. The only guidance they have provided is that they want a piece that is moody and evocative. You have already begun by creating a basic design, and you want to use color adjustments to create the mood.

1. Open PS J-3.psd, then save it as **Gallery Poster**.
2. Make the Backdrop layer active.
3. Open the Curves dialog box and re-create the settings shown in Figure J-20.
4. Make the Shadow Man layer active.
5. Open the Hue/Saturation dialog box and change the Saturation setting to +60.
6. Create two color samplers: one using the color of the man's tie, and the other using the yellow under the spotlight.
7. Create two type layers: one for the name of the art show and one for the name of the gallery, then position them appropriately in the document. Use either of the colors in the samplers for the font colors. For example, you can enter the color sampler RGB values in the Color Picker dialog box to create that color. (*Hint*: You can use any font and font size you want. The font used in the sample is Footlight MT Light; the font size is 60 for the art show name and 30 for the date information.)

8. Hide the samplers.
9. Apply the following colors to the layer thumbnails: show name = red, date information = green. (*Hint*: Make these modifications using the Layer Properties command.)
10. Apply any styles to the type you feel are appropriate. (*Hint*: The Bevel and Emboss style is applied to the Moods and Metaphors type layer in the sample. The Outer Glow and the Inner Glow styles are applied to the November 1–30, 2003 layer in the sample.)

11. Apply any lighting effect you feel adds to the theme of the show. (*Hint*: The Floodlight style and Spotlight light type are applied to the Backdrop layer in the sample.)
12. Save your work, then compare your document to the sample in Figure J-21.

FIGURE J-20

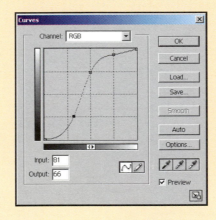

FIGURE J-21
Completed Project Builder 1

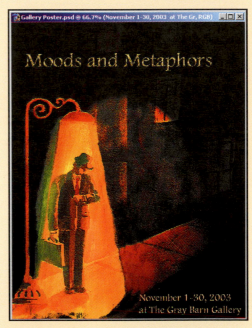

A new, unnamed e-commerce company has hired you to create an advertisement for their upcoming debut. While they are leaving the design to you, the only type they want in the imagery is "Heads Up." They want this ad to be a teaser; more descriptive type will be added in the future. This is a cutting-edge company, and they want something really striking.

1. Open PS J-4.psd, then save it as **Heads Up**.
2. Make the Backdrop layer active.
3. Use the Levels dialog box to modify the Input levels of the RGB color settings. (*Hint*: The settings used in the sample are 82, 1.46, 240.)
4. Make the Head layer active.
5. Use the Hue/Saturation dialog box to modify the Head layer. (*Hint*: The settings used in the sample are Hue = −55, Saturation = +38, Lightness = 0.)
6. Create a color sampler for the color of the head, then hide the sampler.
7. Create a type layer for the name of the document, then position it appropriately in the document. (*Hint*: You can use any font and font size you want. The font used in the sample is OCR A Extended; the font size is 72.)

8. Apply the color yellow to the type layer thumbnail.
9. Apply any styles to the type you feel are appropriate. (*Hint*: The Drop Shadow and Bevel and Emboss styles are applied to the type layer in the sample.)

FIGURE J-22
Completed Project Builder 2

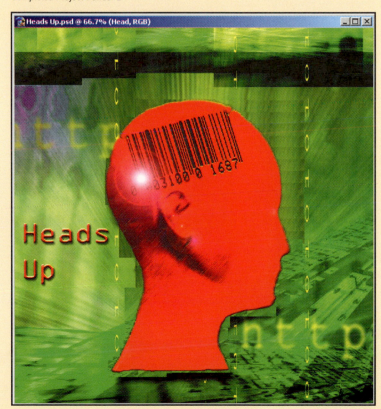

10. Apply any filter you feel adds to the image. (*Hint*: The Lens Flare filter is applied to the Head layer in the sample.)
11. Save your work, then compare your document to the sample in Figure J-22.

DESIGN PROJECT

A friend of yours is a textile artist; she creates artwork that is turned into materials for clothing, curtains, and bedding. She has turned to you because of your Photoshop expertise and wants your advice on how she can jazz up her current project. You love the design, but think the colors need correction so they'll look more dynamic. Before you proceed, you decide to explore the Internet to find information on how Photoshop color correction techniques can be used to create an effective design.

1. Connect to the Internet, go to *www.course.com*, navigate to the page for this book, click the Student Online Companion link, then click the link for this unit.
2. Read about color correction and take notes on any information that will help you incorporate new ideas into the image.
3. Open PS J-5.psd, then save the file as **Puzzle Pieces**.
4. Use any skills you have learned to correct the colors in this document.
5. Create two color samplers from colors used in the document.
6. Apply any filter you feel adds to the image. (*Hint*: The Artistic Sponge filter is applied to the Yellow Pieces layer in the sample.)
7. Save your work, then compare your document to the sample in Figure J-23.

FIGURE J-23
Completed Design Project

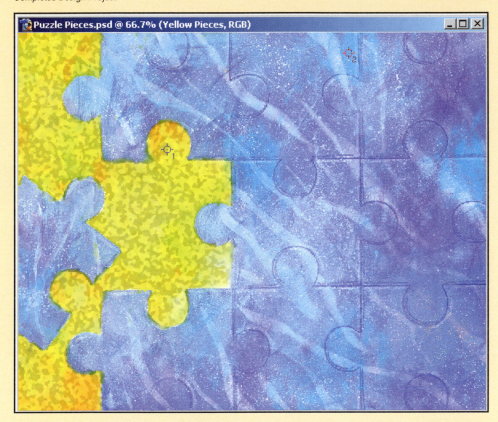

Puzzle Pieces.psd @ 66.7% (Yellow Pieces, RGB)

GROUP PROJECT

Depending on the size of your group, you can assign individual elements of the project to group members, or work collectively to create the finished product.

Each year, your company, CyberNews, has an art contest, and the winning entry is used as the cover of the Annual Report. You have decided that this is the year your entry will be the winner. CyberNews encourages employees to enter the contest. Entries may be produced as a team effort.

1. Create a document with the dimensions 500 pixels × 600 pixels.
2. Locate several pieces of artwork—either on your computer, from scanned images, or on the Internet. Remember that the images can show anything, but you want to show the flexibility of Photoshop and the range of your skills.
3. Save this file as **Annual Report Cover**.
4. Use any skills you have learned to correct the colors in this document.
5. Create a color sampler for at least two colors in the document, then hide the samplers.
6. Create one or two type layers for the name of the document (CyberNews Annual Report), then position the layer(s) appropriately in the document. Use your choice of font colors. (*Hint*: You can use any font and font size you want. The font used in the sample is Tempus Sans ITC; the font size is 60 in the title and 48 in the subtitle.)

FIGURE J-24
Completed Group Project

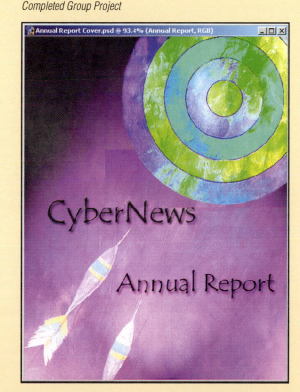

7. Add any necessary effects to the type layer.
8. If necessary, apply any filters you feel add to the image.
9. Apply colors to thumbnails in the document.
10. Save the image, then compare your document to the sample in Figure J-24.

Adjusting Colors

ADOBE PHOTOSHOP J-23

UNIT K

USING CLIPPING GROUPS, PATHS, & SHAPES

1. Use a clipping group as a mask.

2. Use pen tools to create and modify a path.

3. Work with shapes.

4. Convert paths and selections.

UNIT K

USING CLIPPING GROUPS
PATHS, & SHAPES

Working with Shapes

Photoshop provides several tools that help add stylistic elements to enhance your work. For example, you can introduce two different types of shapes to your documents: a shape and a rasterized shape. A **shape** is a vector object that keeps its crisp appearance when it is resized, edited, moved, reshaped, or copied. A **rasterized shape** is converted into a bitmapped object that cannot be moved or copied, but uses a much smaller file size. You can add either kind of shape as a predesigned shape, such as an ellipse, circle, or rectangle, or you can create a unique shape using a pen tool.

Defining Clipping Groups and Paths

A **clipping group** creates an effect in which the bottommost layer acts as a mask for all other layers in the group. You can use a **path** to turn an area defined within an object into a separate individual object; it is defined as one or more straight or curved line segments connected by **anchor points**, small squares similar to fastening points. Paths can be either open or closed. An **open path**, such as an individual line,

has two distinct **endpoints**, anchor points at each end of the open path. A **closed path**, such as a circle, is one continuous path without endpoints. A **path component** consists of one or more anchor points joined by line segments. You can use another type of path called a **clipping path**, to extract a Photoshop object from within a layer, place it in another program (such as QuarkXPress or Adobe Illustrator), and retain its transparent background.

QUICKTIP

A shape and path are basically the same: the shape tools allow you to use an existing path instead of having to create one by hand.

Creating Paths

Using a path, you can manipulate images on a layer. Each path is stored on the **Paths palette**. You can create a path using the Pen Tool or the Freeform Pen Tool. Each **pen tool** lets you draw a path by placing anchor points along the edge of another image, or wherever you need them, to draw a specific shape. As you place anchor points, line segments automatically fall

K-2

between them. The **Freeform Pen Tool** acts just like a traditional pen or pencil. Just draw with it, and it automatically places *both* the anchor points and line segments wherever necessary to achieve the shape you want. With these tools, you can create freeform shapes or use existing edges within an image by tracing on top of it. After you create a path, you can use the **Path Selection Tool** to select the entire path, or the **Direct Selection Tool** to select and manipulate individual anchor points and segments to reshape the path. Unlike selections, multiple paths can be saved using the Paths palette. When first created, a path is called a **work path**. The work path is temporary, but becomes a permanent part of your document when you name it. Paths, like layers, can be named, viewed, deleted, and duplicated.

Tools You'll Use

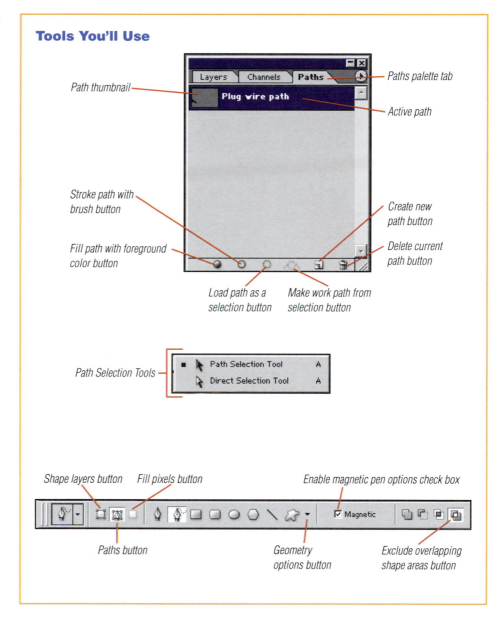

Path thumbnail

Paths palette tab

Plug wire path

Active path

Stroke path with brush button

Create new path button

Fill path with foreground color button

Delete current path button

Load path as a selection button

Make work path from selection button

Path Selection Tools

Path Selection Tool   A
Direct Selection Tool   A

Shape layers button   Fill pixels button

Enable magnetic pen options check box

✓ Magnetic

Paths button

Geometry options button

Exclude overlapping shape areas button

USE A CLIPPING GROUP AS A MASK

What You'll Do

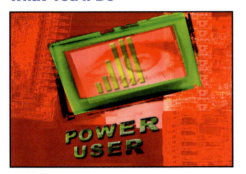

In this lesson, you'll rasterize a type layer, then use a clipping group as a mask for imagery already in a document.

Understanding the Clipping Group Effect

If you've ever wanted to display type in one layer using an interesting image or pattern in another layer as the fill for the type, then look no further. You can create this effect using a clipping group. With a clipping group, you can isolate an area and make images outside the area transparent. This feature works very well with type, but can be used with all types of images. Figure K-1 shows an example of this effect in which type acts as a mask for imagery. In this effect, the (rasterized type) layer becomes a mask for the imagery. The image of the roses is *masked* by the text. For this effect to work, the layer that is being masked (the imagery, in this case) *must* be positioned above the mask layer on the Layers palette.

FIGURE K-1
Sample clipping group effect

Rasterizing Text and Shape Layers

To use typed text or a shape in a clipping group, the type or shape layer must first be rasterized, or changed from vector graphics into a normal layer. Rasterizing changes the vector graphic into a bitmapped object, one that is made up of colored pixels. **Vector graphics** are made up of lines and curves defined by mathematical objects called vectors. The advantage to vector graphics for shapes is that they can be resized and moved without losing image quality.

QUICKTIP

Bitmapped images contain a fixed number of pixels; as a consequence, they can appear jagged and lose detail when resized.

Using Transform Commands

Before you create a clipping group, you might want to use one of the transform commands on the Edit menu to reshape layer contents so the shapes conform to the imagery that will be displayed. The transform commands are described in Table K-1. Samples of the transform commands are shown in Figure K-2. When a transform command is selected, a **bounding box** is displayed around the object. The bounding box contains **handles**, small boxes surrounding the object that are used to modify the selection. A **reference point** is located in the center of the bounding box. This is the point around which the transform command takes place.

QUICKTIP

You can change the location of the reference point by dragging the point to a new location within the bounding box.

TABLE K-1: Transform Commands

command	use
Scale	Changes the image size. Press [Shift] while dragging to scale proportionally. Press [Alt] (Win) or [option] (Mac) to scale from the reference point.
Rotate	Allows rotation of an image 360°. Press [Shift] to rotate in increments of 15°.
Skew	Stretches an image horizontally or vertically, but cannot exceed the image boundary.
Distort	Stretches an image horizontally or vertically, and can exceed the image boundary.
Perspective	Changes opposite sides of an image equally, and can be used to make an oval appear circular, or change a rectangle into a trapezoid.
Rotate 180	Rotates image 180° clockwise.
Rotate 90 CW	Rotates image 90° clockwise.
Rotate 90 CCW	Rotates image 90° counterclockwise.
Flip Horizontal	Produces a mirror image.
Flip Vertical	Produces an upside-down image.

FIGURE K-2
Sample transformations

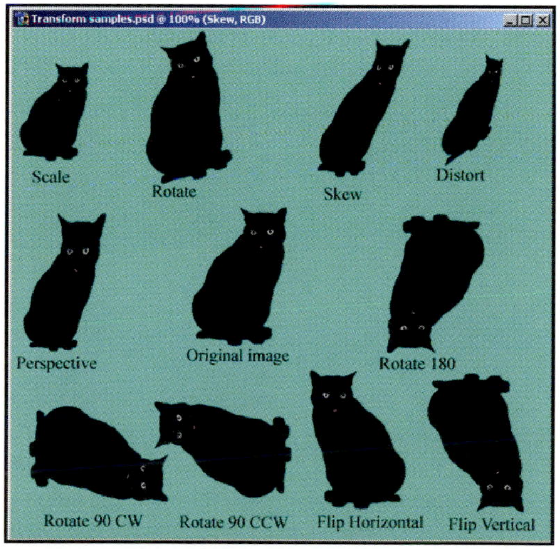

Transform a type layer for use in a clipping group

1. Open PS K-1.psd, then save the file as **Power User**.

   The Power User type layer is active.

2. Click Layer on the menu bar, point to Rasterize, then click Type.

   The active layer is no longer a type layer, as shown in Figure K-3.

3. Click the Move Tool, if necessary.

4. Click Edit on the menu bar, point to Transform, then click Skew.

5. Drag the handles so that they conform to the shape of the keyboard, as shown in Figure K-4. ▶

6. Press [Enter] (Win) or [return] (Mac).

7. Compare your image to Figure K-5.

You rasterized the existing type layer, then altered its shape using the Skew command. This transformation placed the text directly over the keyboard image.

No longer a
type layer

FIGURE K-4
Handles surround text

Handles

Rasterized layer after
being skewed

FIGURE K-5
Skewed layer

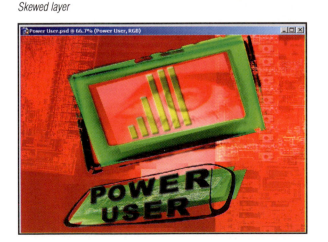

FIGURE K-6

New Layers palette order

Relocated layer

FIGURE K-8

Effect of clipping group

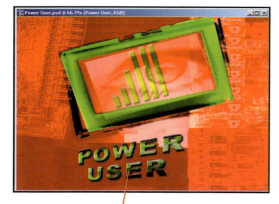

Keyboard background visible through text

FIGURE K-7

Preparing to create the clipping group

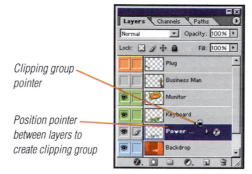

Clipping group pointer

Position pointer between layers to create clipping group

FIGURE K-9

Layers and History palettes

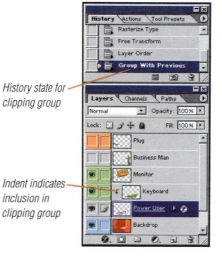

History state for clipping group

Indent indicates inclusion in clipping group

Create a clipping group

1. Drag the Power User layer beneath the Keyboard layer, as shown in Figure K-6.

   TIP   It's a good idea to position the layer that will act as a mask *above* the layer containing the pattern so that you can adjust its size and shape. After the size and shape are the way you want them, reposition the mask layer *beneath* the pattern layer.

2. Position the pointer over the horizontal line between the Power User and Keyboard layers, press and hold [Alt] (Win) or [option] (Mac), then click, as shown in Figure K-7.

   The clipping group is created. The keyboard background becomes visible through the text.

3. Save your work, then compare your document to Figure K-8 and the Layers palette to Figure K-9.

You moved the type layer beneath the Keyboard layer, then created the clipping group effect.

USE PEN TOOLS TO CREATE
AND MODIFY A PATH

What You'll Do

In this lesson, you'll create and name a path, expand the path to give it a wider, more curved appearance, then fill it with the foreground color.

Using Pen and Shape Tools

You have already seen how you can use a clipping group to create a mask effect. You can use any of the shape tools, the Pen Tool, the Freeform Pen Tool, or the Magnetic Pen Tool to create a path. You can modify a path using the Add Anchor Point Tool, Delete Anchor Point Tool, Convert Point Tool, Direct Selection Tool, and the Path Selection Tool. Table K-2 describes some of these tools and their functions. When you select a pen tool, you can choose to create a shape layer or a path by choosing the appropriate option on the tool options bar.

Creating a Path

Unlike selections, paths you create are saved with the document they were created in and stored in the Paths palette. Although you can't print paths unless they are filled or stroked, you can always display a path and make modifications to it. You can create a path based on an existing object, or you can create your own shape with a pen tool. To create a closed path,

you must position the pointer on top of the first anchor point. A small circle appears next to the pointer, indicating that the path will be closed when the pointer is clicked. Figure K-10 shows an image of a young man and the Paths palette containing three paths. The active path (Bust) displays an outline of the man's head and shoulders. Like the Layers palette, each path thumbnail displays a representation of its path. You can click a thumbnail in the Paths palette to see a specific path. The way that you create a path depends on the tool you choose to work with. The Pen Tool requires that you click using the pointer each time you want to add a smooth (curved) or corner anchor point, whereas the Freeform Pen Tool only requires you to click once to begin creating the path, and places the anchor points for you as you drag the pointer.

Modifying a Path

After you establish a path, you can embellish it and convert it into a selection. For example, you can add more width or more curves to an existing path, or fill a path with the foreground color. Before you can modify an unselected path, you must select it with the Direct Selection Tool. When you select a path using the Direct Selection Tool, you can manipulate its individual anchor points without affecting the entire path. Moving an anchor point automatically forces the two line segments on either side of the anchor point to shrink or grow, depending on which direction you move the anchor point. You can also click individual line segments and move them to new locations. If you are working with a curved path, you can shorten or elongate the direction handles associated with each smooth point to adjust the amount of curve or length of the corresponding line segment.

Other methods for modifying a path include adding anchor points, deleting anchor points, and converting corner anchor points into smooth anchor points, or vice versa. Adding anchor points splits an existing line segment into two, giving you more sides to your object. Deleting an anchor point does the reverse. Deleting anchor points is helpful when you have too many anchor points, resulting in a bumpy path. Converting corner points into smooth points can give your drawing a softer appearance, and converting smooth points into corner points will give your drawing a sharper appearance.

QUICKTIP

Each time you click and drag using the Add Anchor pointer, you are adding smooth anchor points. You use two direction handles attached to each anchor point to control the length, shape, and slope of the curved segment.

QUICKTIP

You can press [Alt] (Win) or [option] (Mac) while you click a path thumbnail to view the path and select it at the same time.

FIGURE K-10
Multiple paths for the same image

Current path

Current path thumbnail

TABLE K-2: Pen Tools

tool	button	use
Pen Tool		Creates curved or straight line segments, connected by anchor points.
Freeform Pen Tool		Creates unique shapes by placing anchor points at each change of direction.
Magnetic find Pen Tool	☑ Magnetic	(Option of the Freeform Pen Tool) Lets the tool an object's edge.
Add Anchor Point Tool		Adds an anchor point to an existing path or shape.
Delete Anchor Point Tool		Removes an anchor point from an existing path or shape.
Convert Point Tool		Converts a smooth point to a corner point and a corner point to a smooth point.

Create a path

1. Click the Plug layer on the Layers palette.

2. Click the Indicates layer visibility button on the Backdrop layer on the Layers palette.

3. Click the Indicates layer visibility button on the Power User layer on the Layers palette.

   Hiding layers makes it easier to work on a specific area of the document.

4. Click the Freeform Pen Tool on the toolbox.

5. Click the Paths button on the tool options bar.

6. Adjust the settings on the tool options bar, using Figure K-11 as a guide. Make sure the Enable magnetic pen options check box is selected.

7. Zoom in on the plug, then use the Freeform Pen Tool to trace *the black wire* that leads to the plug, as well as the additional length of wire beneath it.

8. Click the Paths palette tab.

9. Double-click the Work Path layer on the Paths palette.

10. Type **Plug wire path** in the Name text box, as shown in Figure K-12.

    > TIP   Make sure you click the Create new path button on the Paths palette before starting another path, or it will become part of the active path.

11. Click OK, then compare your path and Paths palette to Figure K-13.

You created and named a path using the Freeform Pen Tool.

FIGURE K-11
Freeform Pen Tool settings

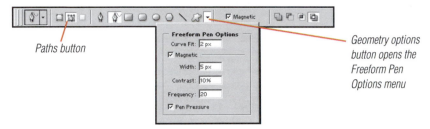

Paths button

Geometry options button opens the Freeform Pen Options menu

FIGURE K-12
Save Path dialog box

FIGURE K-13
Path and Paths palette

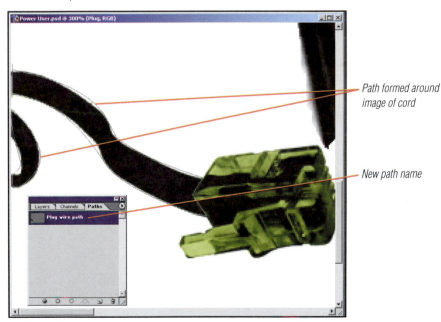

Path formed around image of cord

New path name

FIGURE K-14
Points added to path

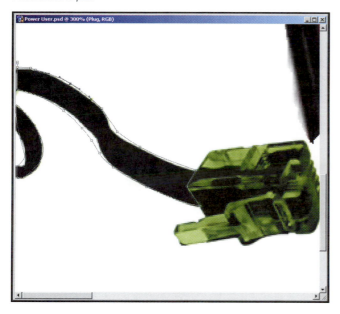

FIGURE K-16
Modified path

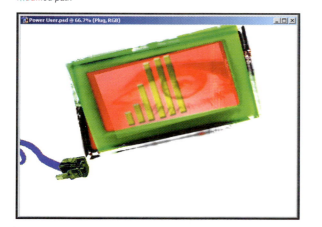

FIGURE K-15
Color choice in Swatches palette

1. Click the Add Anchor Point Tool on the toolbox.

2. Click the path, then drag a few points on the top of the path to create curved line segments, using Figure K-14 as a guide.

   As you drag the new anchor points, direction handles appear, indicating that you have added smooth points instead of corner points.

3. Click the Eyedropper Tool on the toolbox.

4. Click the fifth color box from the left in the first row of the Swatches palette, as shown in Figure K-15.

5. Click the Fill path with foreground color button on the Paths palette.

6. Press [Esc] (Win) or [esc] (Mac) to deselect the path.

   TIP The Plug layer on the Layers palette must be selected or the Fills path with foreground color button on the Paths palette will not be available.

7. Zoom out, if necessary, so the entire image is displayed, save your work, then compare your image to Figure K-16.

You modified an existing path, then filled it with a color from the Swatches palette.

WORK WITH SHAPES

What You'll Do

In this lesson, you'll create two shapes, then modify and add a style to a shape layer.

Using Shape Tools

You might find that the imagery you are working with is not enough, and you need to create your own shapes. There are six shape tools on the toolbox for creating shapes. A shape can occupy its own layer, called a **shape layer**. When you select a shape or pen tool, three buttons appear on the left side of the tool options bar, the Shape layers, Paths, and Fill pixels buttons. These buttons allow you to choose whether you want your shape to be on a new or existing shape layer, be a new work path, or be rasterized and filled with a color. The tools on the tool options bar change depending on what button you select. Shapes and paths contain vector data, meaning that they will not lose their crisp appearance if resized or reshaped. You can create a rasterized shape using the Fill pixel button, but you cannot resize or reshape the rasterized shape.

Creating Rasterized Shapes

You cannot create a rasterized shape on a vector-based layer, such as a type or shape layer. So, to create a rasterized shape, you must first select or create a non-vector-based layer, select the shape you desire, then click the Fill pixels button on the tool options bar. You can change the blending mode to alter how the shape affects existing pixels in the image. You can change the opacity setting to make the shape more transparent or opaque. You can use the anti-aliasing option to blend the pixels on the shape's edge with the surrounding pixels. If you want to make changes to the shape's blending mode, opacity, and anti-aliasing, you must make these changes *before* creating the rasterized shape; however, after you rasterize the shape, you can make changes to blending mode and opacity to the *layer* containing the shape.

Creating Shapes

A path and a shape are essentially the same: you edit them using the same tools. For example, you can modify a path and a shape using the Direct Selection Tool. When selected, the anchor points are white or hollow, and can then be moved to alter the appearance of the shape or path. When you click a shape or path with the Path Selection Tool, the anchor points become solid. In this case, the entire path is selected, and the individual components cannot be moved: the path or shape is moved as a single unit. A shape can be created on its own layer and can be filled with a color. Multiple shapes can also be added to a single layer, and you can specify how overlapping shapes interact. Shape layers are vector objects—not created with pixels—and cannot be edited using brush tools. (Painting tools are used when individual pixels are edited, such as by changing a pixel's color on a rasterized shape.)

Embellishing Shapes

You can apply other features you've learned, such as the Drop Shadow and the Bevel and Emboss style, or filters, to shapes. Figure K-17 shows the Layers palette of a document containing two layer shapes. The top layer (in Yellow) has the Bevel and Emboss style applied to it.

QUICKTIP
A shape is automatically filled with the current foreground color.

FIGURE K-17
Shape layers on Layers palette

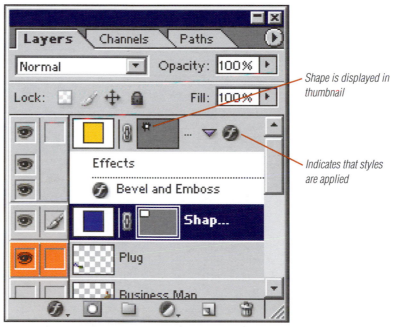

Shape is displayed in thumbnail

Indicates that styles are applied

Create a shape

1. Click the Rectangle Tool on the toolbox.

2. Click the Shape layers button on the tool options bar.

3. Click the Create new shape layer button on the tool options bar.

4. Display the rulers in pixels, if necessary.

5. Drag the pointer from 50 H/50 V to 250 H/200 V. Compare your Paths palette to Figure K-18.

6. Compare your image to Figure K-19.

   The shape is added to the document, and you can create another new shape layer.

You created a new shape layer, using the Rectangle Tool.

FIGURE K-18
Path created by shape

FIGURE K-19
Shape in document

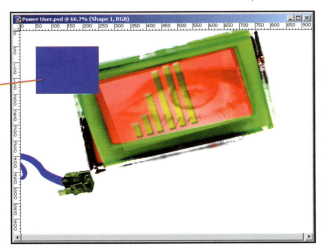

New shape

Export a path into another program

As a designer, you might find yourself working with other programs, such as Adobe Illustrator, Adobe Freehand, or QuarkXPress. Many of the techniques you have learned, such as working with paths, can be used in all these programs. For example, you can create a path in Photoshop, then export it to Illustrator. Before you can export a path, it must be created and named. To export the path, click File on the menu bar, point to Export, then click Paths to Illustrator. The Paths list arrow in the Export Paths dialog box lets you determine which paths are exported. You can export all paths or one specific path. After you choose the path(s) that you want to export, choose a name and location for the path, then click Save.

FIGURE K-20
Additional shape in image

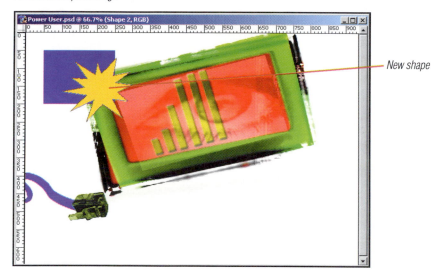

New shape

FIGURE K-21
Style added to shape

Custom shape
with Bevel and
Emboss style

Modify a shape

1. Click the Create new shape layer button, if it's not already selected. ▢

2. Click the Eyedropper Tool on the toolbox, then click the second swatch (RGB Yellow) from the left in the first row of the Swatches palette. ✎

3. Click the Rectangle Tool on the toolbox, then click the Custom Shape Tool button on the tool options bar. ▢

4. Click the Click to open Custom Shape picker list arrow, then double-click the Starburst (the third shape from the left on the fifth row).

5. Drag the pointer from 100 H/70 V to 300 H/250 V. Compare your image to Figure K-20. ┿

6. Hide the rulers.

7. Display the Layers palette, then drag the Shape 1 layer beneath the Monitor layer on the Layers palette.

8. Click Shape 2 on the Layers palette.

9. Click the Add a layer style button on the Layers palette. ●

10. Click the Bevel and Emboss style, then click OK to accept the current settings.

11. Click the Indicates layer visibility button on the Backdrop layer on the Layers palette. ▢

12. Save your work, then compare your image to Figure K-21.

You created an additional shape layer, then applied a style to the shape.

CONVERT PATHS AND SELECTIONS

What You'll Do

▶ *In this lesson, you'll convert a selection into a path, then apply a stroke to the path.*

Converting a Selection into a Path

You can convert a selection into a path so that you can take advantage of clipping paths and other path features, using a button on the Paths palette. First, create your selection using any technique you prefer, such as the Magic Wand Tool, lasso tools, or marquee tools. After the marquee surrounds the selection, press and hold

Understanding print options

During the course of working with an image, you might want some form of output, such as a hard copy printout. Because the monitor is an RGB device and the printer uses CMYK, even a well-calibrated monitor will never match the colors of your printer. Therefore, printers have standardized color systems such as Pantone or Toyo. A multi-layer image prints as a composite image. In addition to selecting the destination printer, you have many options that influence the output of a document.

Before printing a file, you can select your desired print options in the Page Setup dialog box. To open the Page Setup dialog box, click File on the menu bar, then click Page Setup. The relationship of the length to the width of the printed page is called **orientation**. A printed page with dimensions 8½" W × 11" L is called **portrait orientation**. A printed page with dimensions 11" W × 8 ½" L is called **landscape orientation**.

For additional printing options, click File on the menu bar, click Print with Preview, then in the Print dialog box select the Show More Options button. Here you can gain increased control over the way your document prints. For example, pages printed for commercial uses might often need to be trimmed after they are printed. The trim guidelines are called **crop marks**. These marks can be printed at the corners, center of each edge, or both. After you open the Print dialog box, you can select the Corner Crop Marks check box and/or Center Crop Marks check box to print these marks on your document. Click Done to close the Print dialog box.

[Alt] (Win) or [option] (Mac), then click the Make work path from selection button on the Paths palette, as shown in Figure K-22.

Converting a Path into a Selection

You can convert a path into a selection. You can do this by selecting a path on the Paths palette, then clicking the Load path as selection button on the Paths palette.

Deciding Which Method to Use

Are you totally confused about which method to use to make selections? You might have felt equally confused after reading about all the paint tool choices. Well, sometimes the best method to use is the one that works best for you. As you gain experience with Photoshop techniques, your comfort level—and personal confidence—will grow, and you'll learn which methods work for you. In all probability, these are the *right* methods.

FIGURE K-22
Paths created by selection

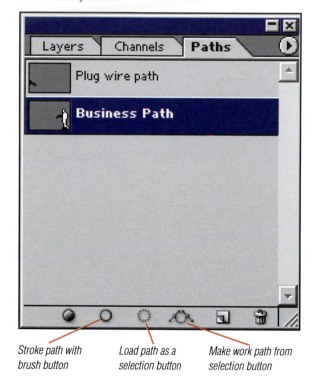

Stroke path with brush button

Load path as a selection button

Make work path from selection button

Convert a selection into a path

1. Click the Indicates layer visibility button on the Layers palette for the following layers: Shape 1, Shape 2, Plug, Monitor, and Backdrop.

2. Click the Business Man layer on the Layers palette.

3. Click the Magic Wand Tool on the toolbox.

4. Click anywhere in the white background area, click Select on the menu bar, then click Inverse. Compare your document to Figure K-23.

5. Click the Paths palette tab. Paths

6. Press and hold [Alt] (Win) or [option] (Mac), then click the Make work path from selection button on the Paths palette.

7. Type **1.0** in the Tolerance text box, if necessary, then click OK.

8. Double-click Work Path on the Paths palette.

9. Type **Business path** in the Name text box of the Save Path dialog box, then click OK. Compare your work to Figure K-24.

You created a selection using the Magic Wand Tool, then converted it into a path using a button on the Paths palette.

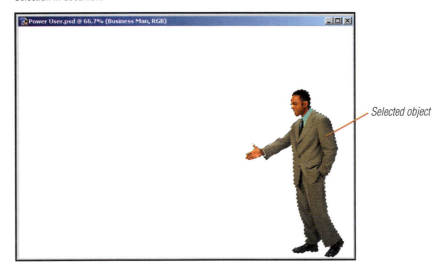

Selected object

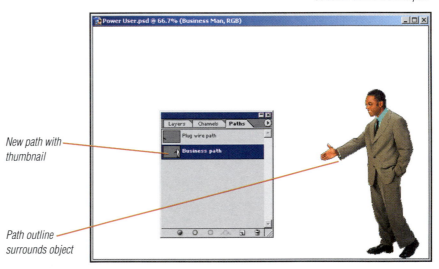

New path with thumbnail

Path outline surrounds object

Using Clipping Groups, Paths, & Shapes

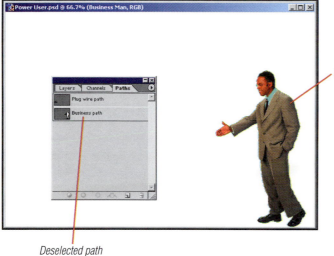

Stroke applied to path

Deselected path

Plug layer (Shape 2 is above this layer)

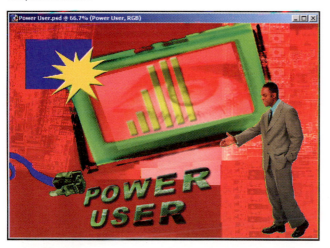

Stroke a path

1. Click the Eyedropper Tool on the toolbox.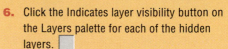

2. Click the third swatch (RGB Green) from the left in the first row of the Swatches palette.

3. Click the Stroke path with brush button on the Paths palette.

4. Click anywhere on the Paths palette to deselect the path, then compare your work to Figure K-25.

5. Click the Layers palette tab. **Layers**

6. Click the Indicates layer visibility button on the Layers palette for each of the hidden layers.

7. Change the layer order, using Figure K-26 as a guide.

   TIP   Be careful not to break the clipping group. If necessary, rebuild the clipping group.

8. Save your work, then compare your document to Figure K-27.

You stroked a path, using a color from the Swatches palette and a button on the Paths palette, displayed the remaining hidden layers, then changed the layer order.

Power User Shortcuts

Key: Menu items are indicated by ➤ between the menu name and its command. Blue bold letters are shortcuts for selecting tools on the toolbox.

to do this:	use this method:
Add an anchor point	[icon]
Change perspective	Edit ➤ Transform ➤ Perspective
Convert a selection into a path	[icon]
Convert a point	[icon]
Create a clipping group	Press and hold [Alt] (Win) or [option] (Mac), position pointer between layers, then click using ◀ [icon]
Create a custom shape	[icon] or **Shift U**
Create a line	[icon] or **Shift U**
Create a new shape layer	[icon]
Create a new work path	[icon]
Create a polygon	[icon] or **Shift U**
Create a rectangle	[icon] or **Shift U**
Create a rounded rectangle	[icon] or **Shift U**
Create an ellipse	[icon] or **Shift U**
Delete an anchor point	[icon]

to do this:	use this method:
Deselect a path	Click within Paths palette
Distort a selection	Edit ➤ Transform ➤ Distort
Draw freeform shapes	[icon] or **Shift P**
Draw paths	[icon] or **Shift P**
Draw along the object's edge	☑ Magnetic
Export a path	File ➤ Export ➤ Paths to Illustrator
Flip a selection	Edit ➤ Transform ➤ Flip Horizontal or Flip Vertical
Load path as a selection	[icon]
Repeat last transform command	Edit ➤ Transform ➤ Again or [Shift][Ctrl][T] or [Shift][T] (Mac)
Rotate a selection	Edit ➤ Transform ➤ Rotate
Scale a selection	Edit ➤ Transform ➤ Scale
Skew a selection	Edit ➤ Transform ➤ Skew
Stroke a path	[icon]

Use a clipping group as a mask.

1. Open PS K-2.psd, then save it as **Mathematics**.
2. Substitute a font available on your computer for the Mathematics type layer, if necessary. (*Hint*: The font used in the sample is a 72 pt Arial Black.)
3. Rasterize the type layer, then click the Move Tool.
4. Transform the rasterized type layer by distorting it, using the ruler guides in the sample document as a guide.
5. Drag the Mathematics layer beneath the Symbols layer on the Layers palette.
6. Create a clipping group with the Mathematics and Symbols layers.
7. Apply the Bevel and Emboss style (using the existing settings) to the Mathematics layer.

Use pen tools to create and modify a path.

1. Make the Man layer active.
2. Click the Freeform Pen Tool on the toolbox.
3. Click the Paths button and verify that the Magnetic check box is selected.
4. Open the Paths palette.
5. Trace the figure, *not the shadow*.
6. Change the name of the Work Path to **Figure path**.
7. Use the Eyedropper Tool on the toolbox to sample the sixth color box from the left in the fifth row (Pure Yellow Green) of the Swatches palette.

8. Fill the path with the foreground color.
9. Deselect the Figure path on the Paths palette.
10. Save your work.

Work with shapes.

1. Make the Megaphone layer active.
2. Use the Eyedropper Tool to sample the second color box (RGB Yellow) from the left in the first row of the Swatches palette.
3. Click the Custom Shape Tool on the toolbox.
4. Click the Shape layers button on the tool options bar.
5. Open the Custom Shape picker on the tool options bar, then select the Checkmark custom shape.
6. Create the shape from 50 H/50 V to 200 H/210 V.
7. Apply a drop shadow (using the existing settings) to the Shape 1 layer.

Convert paths and selections.

1. Make the Megaphone layer active.
2. Hide the Backdrop and Mathematics layers.
3. Use the Magnetic Lasso Tool to select the megaphone. (*Hint*: Try using a 0-pixel feather, a 5-pixel width, and 10% Edge Contrast.)
4. Display the Paths palette.
5. Make a path from the selection.
6. Change the name of the Work Path to **Megaphone path**.
7. Use the Eyedropper Tool to sample the tenth color box from the left (Darker Warm Brown) in the bottom row of the Swatches palette.

8. Fill the megaphone path with a dark brown color.
9. Deselect the path, display the Layers palette, then show all layers.
10. Clear the ruler guides, then hide the rulers.
11. Adjust the contrast of the Symbols layer to +42.
12. Apply a Radial Blur filter, using the Spin method with Good quality and the amount = 10, to the Backdrop layer.
13. Apply a 100% Spherize filter (Distort Filter) to the Backdrop layer.
14. Save your work.
15. Compare your document to Figure K-28.

FIGURE K-28
Completed Skills Review

A cable manufacturer has hired you to create a dynamic image of one of its best-selling products. The client is conducting damage control, and wants to improve its lackluster image—especially after the scandal that occurred earlier in the year. You have been provided with a promotional image of the product, and your job is to create an exciting image.

1. Open PS K-3.psd, then save it as **Power Plug**.
2. Duplicate the Power Plug layer.
3. Add a type layer (using any font available on your computer) that says **Powerful**. (In the sample, a 90 pt Magneto font is used.)
4. Rasterize the type layer.
5. Transform the rasterized type layer, using any method.
6. Apply any layer styles. (In the sample, a textured Bevel and Emboss style is applied.)
7. Move the rasterized layer behind the Power Plug copy layer, then create a clipping group.

8. Adjust the saturation of the Power Plug copy layer to +90.
9. Adjust the Yellow/Blue color balance of the Power Plug copy layer to +65.
10. Adjust the color balance of the (original) Power Plug layer so that the text is more visible. (In the sample, the color levels of the midtones are −80, +80, −80.)

11. Modify the opacity of the Power Plug layer to 85%.
12. Save your work, then compare your document to the sample in Figure K-29.

FIGURE K-29
Completed Project Builder 1

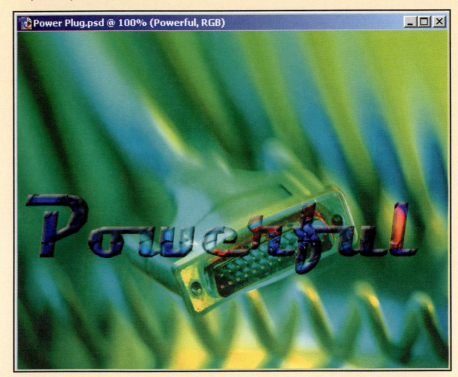

Using Clipping Groups, Paths, & Shapes

The National Initiative to Promote Reading has asked you to come up with a preliminary design for their upcoming season. They have provided you with an initial image you can use, as well as the promise of a fat paycheck if you can finish the project the next day. You can use any additional imagery to complete this task.

1. Open PS K-4.psd, then save it as **Booklovers**.
2. Locate at least one piece of appropriate artwork—either on your computer, in a royalty-free collection, or from scanned images—that you can use in this document.
3. Use any appropriate methods to select imagery from the artwork.
4. After the selections have been made, copy them into Booklovers.
5. Transform any imagery, if necessary.
6. Use your skills to create at least two paths in the document.
7. Add any special effects to a layer, such as a vignette.
8. Add descriptive type to the image, using the font and wording of your choice. (In the sample, an 80 pt Onyx font is used.)
9. Make any color adjustments, or add filters, if necessary.
10. Save your work, then compare your document to the sample in Figure K-30.

FIGURE K-30

Completed Project Builder 2

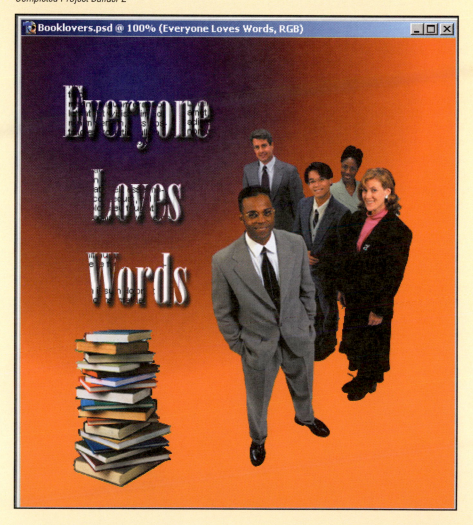

Using Clipping Groups, Paths, & Shapes

You can retrieve a lot of tips and tricks from the Internet. Because you are relatively new to using Photoshop shapes, you decide to see what information you can find about shapes on the Web. Your goal is not only to increase your knowledge of shapes and paths, but to create attractive artwork.

1. Connect to the Internet and use your browser and favorite search engine to find information on Photoshop shapes in design. One possible site is on the Student Online companion. Go to *www.course.com*, navigate to the page for this book, click the Student Online Companion link, then click the link for this unit.

2. Create a new Photoshop document, using the dimensions of your choice, then save it as **Shape Experimentation**.

3. Use paths and shapes to create an attractive document.

4. Create an attractive background, using any of your Photoshop skills.

5. Create at least two paths, using any shapes you want.

6. Add any special effects to the paths.

7. Make any color adjustments, or add filters, if necessary.

8. If you want, add a type layer, using any fonts available on your computer. (In the sample, an 80 pt Elephant font is used.)

9. Save your work, then compare your document to the sample in Figure K-31.

FIGURE K-31
Completed Design Project

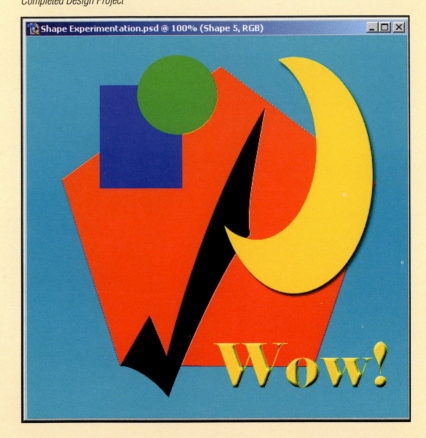

Using Clipping Groups, Paths, & Shapes

Depending on the size of your group, you can assign individual elements of the project to group members, or work collectively to create the finished product.

A Photoshop imagery contest, sponsored by a high-powered advertising agency, has you and your classmates motivated. You know that Photoshop skills can be the key to a great career in design. You have all decided to win the contest. Your entry must be completely original, and can have any imagery available to you.

1. Start Photoshop and create a document with any dimensions you want.
2. Save this file as **Contest Winner**.
3. Locate several pieces of artwork—either on your computer, in a royalty-free collection, or from scanned images. Although the images can show anything, remember that you want to show positive imagery so that the judges will select it.
4. Select imagery from the artwork and move it into Contest Winner.
5. Use your knowledge of shapes and paths to create interesting effects.
6. Use any transformation skills, if necessary.
7. Add any filter effects if you decide they will make your document more dramatic. (In the sample, the Spatter filter was applied to the Computer layer.)
8. Make any color adjustments, if necessary.

9. Add type in any font available on your computer. (A 60 pt Britannic Bold font is shown in the sample. The following styles have been applied: Drop Shadow, and Bevel and Emboss.)

FIGURE K-32
Completed Group Project

10. Save your work, then compare your document to the sample in Figure K-32.

UNIT L

TRANSFORMING TYPE

1. Modify type using a bounding box.

2. Create warped type with a unique shape.

3. Screen back type with imagery.

4. Create a faded type effect.

TRANSFORMING TYPE

Working with Type

Type is usually not the primary focus of most Photoshop documents, but it can be an important element when conveying a message. You have already learned how to create type and to embellish it using styles, such as the Drop Shadow and the Bevel and Emboss styles, and filters, such as the Twirl and Wind filters. You can further enhance type using additional techniques, such as transforming it or warping it.

Transforming and Warping Type

When you want to modify your type's font or size, you simply select the type layer, select the Horizontal Type Tool, then make changes using the tool options bar. Another way to modify type is by using the type's bounding box. A **bounding box** is a rectangle that surrounds type and contains handles that are used to change the dimensions. Without the bounding box, your only method of modifying type is to change the font family, color, or size. Many of the

Photoshop features that can be applied to images can also be applied to type layers. For example, type can be modified using all the transform commands on the Edit menu except Perspective and Distort. Using the transform commands, such as Scale or Skew, you can modify the shape of the type. For more exciting type, you can use the Create warped text button to create unlimited shapes and dimensions. **Warping type** makes it possible to create distortions that conform to a variety of shapes. Some of the distortions possible during the warping process are Arc, Arch, Bulge, Flag, Fish, and Twist. You do not need to rasterize type to use the warp text feature, so you can edit the type, as necessary, after you have warped it.

QUICKTIP

If you want to use the transform commands, Perspective or Distort, or you want to apply a filter to type or create a clipping group, you must first rasterize the type (convert the type into pixels).

Using Type to Create Special Effects

In addition to adding styles to type (such as Bevel and Emboss), you can also create effects with your type and the imagery within your document. One of these effects is **fading type** (the type appears to originate in a dark area, then gradually gets brighter or vice versa). You use the Gradient Tool to fade type. Another is called **screening back**, where imagery is visible through the layer that contains type. One way to create the screened back effect is to convert a type layer into a shape layer, add a mask, and then adjust the levels of the shape layer.

Tools You'll Use

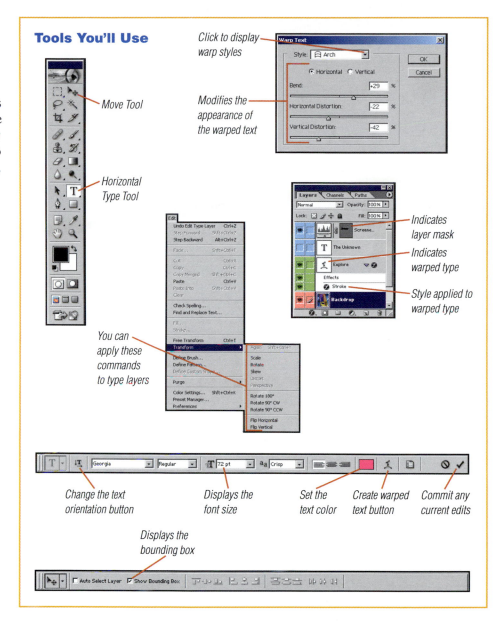

Click to display warp styles

Modifies the appearance of the warped text

Move Tool

Horizontal Type Tool

You can apply these commands to type layers

Indicates layer mask

Indicates warped type

Style applied to warped type

Change the text orientation button

Displays the font size

Set the text color

Create warped text button

Commit any current edits

Displays the bounding box

L-3

MODIFY TYPE USING A BOUNDING BOX

What You'll Do

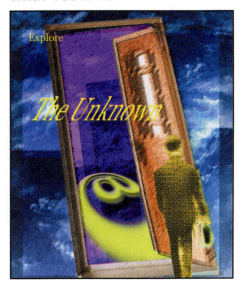

In this lesson, you'll change the dimensions of type using a bounding box.

Using the Bounding Box

A bounding box, like the one shown in Figure L-1, is an additional tool you can use to control the size of existing type. You can display the bounding box by clicking the Move Tool on the toolbox, then selecting the Show Bounding Box check box on the tool options bar. After the bounding box feature is turned on, it will appear around type whenever a type layer is selected. As soon as you click a handle on the bounding box, the dotted lines of the box become solid, as shown in Figure L-2. At the center of the bounding box (by default) is the **reference point**, the location from which distortions and transformations are measured.

QUICKTIP

You can resize the bounding box to visually change type size instead of choosing specific point sizes on the tool options bar.

FIGURE L-1
Bounding box around type

Handle

Bounding box

Reference point

FIGURE L-2
Resizing the bounding box

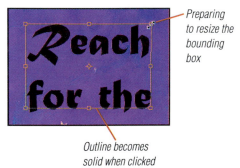

Preparing to resize the bounding box

Outline becomes solid when clicked

Using the Tool Options Bar

When a bounding box is displayed around type, the tool options bar displays additional options for transforming type. Table L-1 describes the bounding box options in detail. You can change the size of the bounding box by placing the pointer over a handle. When you do this, the pointer changes to reflect the direction in which you can pull the box. When you resize a bounding box, the type within it reflows to conform to its new shape. As you can see from the table, some of these tools are buttons and some are text boxes. The text boxes can be used to make entries or will display the results of any changes you have made.

TABLE L-1: Bounding Box Transformation Tools

tool	button	use
Reference point location button		The black dot determines the location of the reference point. Change the reference point by clicking any white dot on the button.
Set horizontal position of reference point text box	X: 210.5 px	Allows you to reassign the horizontal location of the reference point.
Use relative positioning for reference point button	Δ	Determines the point you want used as a reference.
Set vertical position of reference point text box	Y: 228.3 px	Allows you to reassign the vertical location of the reference point.
Set horizontal scale text box	W: 205.9%	Determines the percentage of left-to-right scaling.
Maintain aspect ratio button		Keeps the current proportions of the contents within the bounding box.
Set vertical scale text box	H: 355.6%	Determines the percentage of top-to-bottom scaling.
Set rotation text box	Δ 0.0 °	Determines the angle the bounding box will be rotated.
Set horizontal skew text box	H: -24.4 °	Determines the angle of horizontal distortion.
Set vertical skew text box	V: 0.0 °	Determines the angle of vertical distortion.
Cancel transform (Esc) button	⊘	Returns to the document without carrying out transformations.
Commit transform (Return) button	✓	Returns to the document after carrying out transformations.

Display a bounding box

1. Open PS L-1.psd, click OK if necessary, then save the file as **Exploration**.

   TIP The type in this file is a 24 pt Georgia font. Please substitute another font if this is not available on your computer. To substitute a font, double-click the type layer thumbnail, then click OK.

2. Display the rulers in pixels, if necessary.

3. Click the The Unknown layer, if necessary.

4. Click the Move Tool on the toolbox, if necessary.

5. Select the Show Bounding Box check box on the tool options bar, if necessary. Compare your image to Figure L-3.

   Handles surround the bounding box. When you place the pointer on or near a handle, you can transform the shape of a bounding box. Table L-2 describes the pointers you can use to transform a bounding box.

   You displayed the bounding box to make it easier to adjust the size and shape of the layer contents.

FIGURE L-3
Displayed bounding box

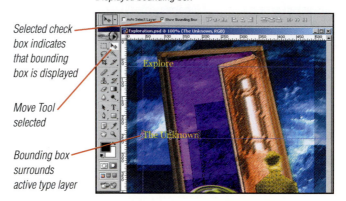

Selected check box indicates that bounding box is displayed

Move Tool selected

Bounding box surrounds active type layer

TABLE L-2: Transformation Pointers

pointer	use to
↗	Resize bounding box contents; drag upper-right and lower-left handles of bounding box.
↖	Resize bounding box contents; drag upper-left and lower-right handles of bounding box.
↔	Resize bounding box contents; drag middle-left and middle-right handles of bounding box.
↕	Resize bounding box contents; drag upper-center and lower-center handles of bounding box.
↲	Rotate bounding box; appears below the lower-right handle.
↳	Rotate bounding box; appears below the lower-left handle.
↰	Rotate bounding box; appears above the upper-right handle.
↱	Rotate bounding box; appears above the upper-left handle.
↻	Rotate bounding box; appears to the right of the middle-right handle.
↵	Rotate bounding box; appears to the left of the lower-center handle.
▶	Skew type. Press and hold [Ctrl] (Win) or [command] (Mac) while dragging a handle.

FIGURE L-4

Modified bounding box

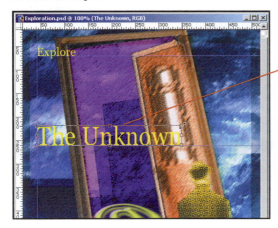

Enlarged type and bounding box

Modify type using a bounding box

1. Press and hold [Shift], drag the upper-right handle to 350 H/220 V, then release [Shift]. Compare your bounding box to Figure L-4.

   TIP Holding [Shift] allows you to resize the bounding box while maintaining its scale.

2. Press and hold [Ctrl] (Win) or [command] (Mac) to skew the type, drag the upper-right handle to 380 H/200 V, then release [Ctrl] (Win) or [command] (Mac).

   Compare your bounding box to Figure L-5 and your tool options bar to Figure L-6. Your settings might differ.

   TIP A skewed transformation distorts a bounding box using an angle other than 90°.

3. Click the Commit transform (Return) button on the tool options bar. ✔

4. Save your work.

Using the bounding box, you modified the type by scaling it, then skewing it.

FIGURE L-5

Skewed bounding box

Skewed (no longer at right angles) bounding box

FIGURE L-6

Transform settings

Current reference point *Horizontal position of reference point* *Vertical position of reference point* *Click to cancel transformations* *Click to accept transformations*

Lesson 1   Modify Type Using a Bounding Box

CREATE WARPED TYPE
WITH A UNIQUE SHAPE

What You'll Do

▶ In this lesson, you'll warp text, then enhance the text with color and a layer style.

Warping Type

Have you ever wondered how designers create those ultra-cool wavy lines of text? The Create warped text feature gives you unlimited freedom to create unique text shapes. You can distort a type layer beyond the limits of stretching a bounding box by using the Create warped text feature. You can choose from 15 warped text styles. These styles are shown in Figure L-7. You can warp type horizontally or vertically.

FIGURE L-7
Warp text styles

Default setting

None

- Arc
- Arc Lower
- Arc Upper

- Arch
- Bulge
- Shell Lower
- Shell Upper

- Flag
- Wave
- Fish
- Rise

- Fisheye
- Inflate
- Squeeze
- Twist

Adding Panache to Warped Text

After you select a warp text style, you can further modify the type using the Bend, Horizontal Distortion, and Vertical Distortion sliders in the Warp Text dialog box. These settings and what they do are described in Table L-3. A sample of warped type is shown in Figure L-8. You adjust the warped type style by using the sliders shown in Figure L-9.

QUICK TIP

You cannot use the Distort and Perspective transform commands on non-rasterized type; however, you can achieve similar results by warping type.

Combining Your Skills

By this time, you've learned that many Photoshop features can be applied to more than one type of Photoshop element. The same is true for warped text. For example, after you warp text, you can apply a style to it, such as the Bevel and Emboss style, or a filter. You can also use the Stroke style to really make the text pop.

FIGURE L-8
Sample of warped type

Bounding box surrounds warped type

FIGURE L-9
Warp Text dialog box

Click to select a new style

Current style

Options are displayed when style other than "None" is selected

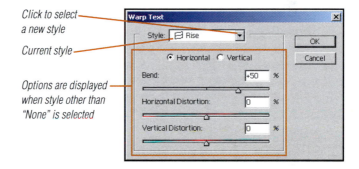

TABLE L-3: Warped Type Settings

setting	use
Horizontal	Determines the left-to-right direction the warp style will take
Vertical	Determines the up-to-down direction the warp style will take
Bend	Determines which side of the type will be affected
Horizontal Distortion	Determines if the left or right side of the type will be warped
Vertical Distortion	Determines if the top or bottom of the type will be warped

Create warped type

1. Click the Explore layer on the Layers palette.

2. Drag the type so its upper-left corner is at 150 H/120 V, as shown in Figure L-10.

3. Double-click the layer thumbnail for the Explore layer on the Layers palette. T

4. Click the Set the font size list arrow on the tool options bar, then click 72 pt.
   T 60 pt

5. Click the Create warped text button on the tool options bar.

6. Click the Style list arrow in the Warp Text dialog box, then click Arch.

7. Verify that the Horizontal option button is selected.

8. Enter the same values for the Bend, Horizontal Distortion, and Vertical Distortion text boxes, using Figure L-11 as a guide.

9. Click OK to close the Warp Text dialog box, then compare your type to Figure L-12.

You transformed existing type into a unique shape using the Create warped text button.

FIGURE L-10
Moved type

Alignment on upper-left corner

FIGURE L-11
Warp Text dialog box

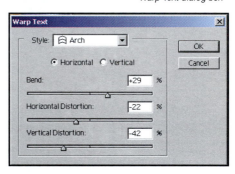

FIGURE L-12
Warped type

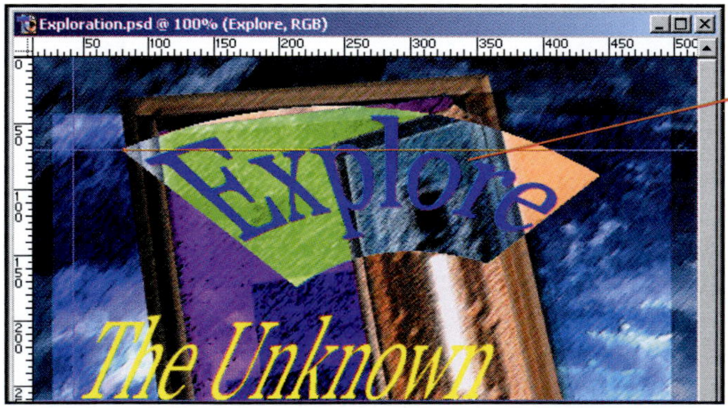

Selected warped text

FIGURE L-13
Sampled area

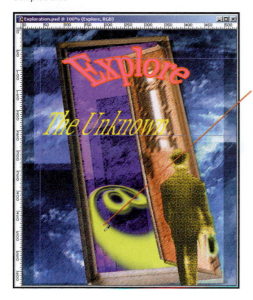

Color from this
location will be
used as color
for stroke

FIGURE L-14
New color applied to warped type

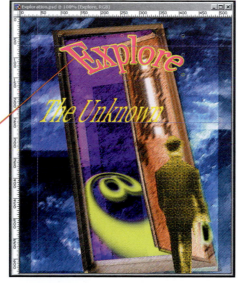

Sampled area used
as stroke color

FIGURE L-15
Layers palette

Thumbnail indicates
warped type

Style applied
to warped type

1. Click the Swatches tab.
2. Click the Set the text color button on the tool options bar. ■
3. Click the sixth swatch from the left (CMYK Magenta) in the second row of the Swatches palette. 🖋

   TIP   You might need to move the Color Picker dialog box out of the way.

4. Click OK to close the Color Picker dialog box.
5. Click the Add a layer style button on the Layers palette. 🗂.
6. Click Stroke.
7. Click the Set color of stroke button in the Layer Style dialog box.
8. Click the document at 200 H/500 V, as shown in Figure L-13.
9. Click OK to close the Color Picker dialog box.
10. Make sure the Size is set to 3 pixels and the Position is set to Outside, then click OK to close the Layer Style dialog box.
11. Save your work, then compare your document to Figure L-14, and the Layers palette to Figure L-15.

You used the Swatches palette to change the color of warped text and added the Stroke style to the warped text.

SCREEN BACK TYPE WITH IMAGERY

What You'll Do

In this lesson, you'll convert type to a shape layer using the Convert to Shape command, then adjust the levels to create a screened back effect.

Screening Type

Using many of the techniques you already know, you can create the illusion that type appears to fade into the imagery below it, also known as **screening back** or simply **screening** type. You can create the screened back effect in many ways. One method is to adjust the opacity of a type layer until you can see imagery behind it. Another method is to convert a type layer into a shape layer, which adds a vector mask, then adjust the levels of the shape layer until you achieve the look you desire. A **vector mask** makes a shape's edges appear neat and defined on a layer. As part of this screening back process, the type assumes the shape of its mask. Figure L-16 contains a sample of screened back type. Notice that the layer imagery beneath the type layer is visible.

FIGURE L-16
Screened back type

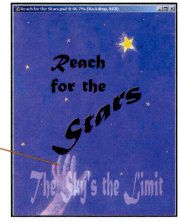

Image visible beneath the shape layer

One of the wonderful aspects of becoming an experienced Photoshop user is that you will figure out other ways of completing tasks. You can always adjust a layer's opacity so you can see more underlying imagery.

Creating the Screened Back Effect

It's a good idea to create a duplicate layer before converting the type layer. That way, if you are not satisfied with the results, you can easily start from scratch with the original type layer. After the duplicate layer is created, you can convert it into a shape layer, using the Layer menu. After the layer is converted, make sure the original layer is hidden. Using the Levels dialog box, you change the midtones and shadows of the content of the shape layer. You can increase or decrease the midtones and shadows levels, as shown in Figure L-17, to create different effects in the screened back text.

QUICK TIP

Whenever you select a shape layer, a path surrounds the shape.

Adding Finishing Touches

You can always add effects to a layer. For example, you can add the Bevel and Emboss style to a screened back shape layer, as shown in Figure L-18. Here, the Bevel and Emboss style serves to accentuate the type. You can also add filter effects such as noise or lighting to make the text look more dramatic.

FIGURE L-17
Levels dialog box

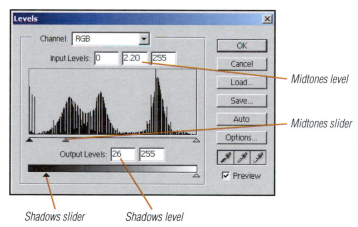

Midtones level

Midtones slider

Shadows slider   Shadows level

FIGURE L-18
Screened back type with Bevel and Emboss style

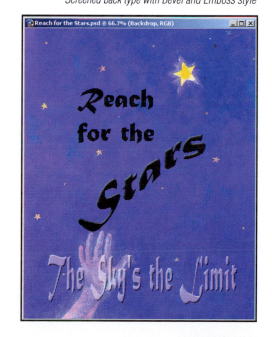

Convert a type layer to a shape layer

1. Click the The Unknown layer on the Layers palette.
2. Click the Layers palette list arrow.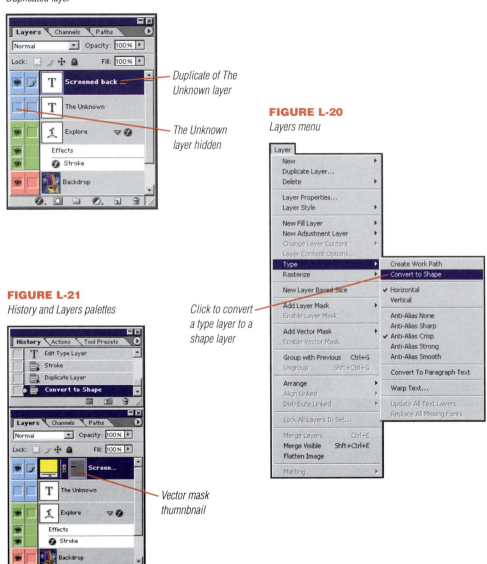
3. Click Duplicate Layer.

   TIP   When duplicating a layer, you have the option of keeping the duplicate in the current document, or placing it in another document that is currently open or in a new document, by clicking the Document list arrow in the Duplicate Layer dialog box, then clicking another filename or New.

4. Type **Screened back type**, then click OK.
5. Click the Indicates layer visibility button on The Unknown layer on the Layers palette, then compare your Layers palette to Figure L-19.
6. Click Layer on the menu bar, point to Type, then click Convert to Shape, as shown in Figure L-20.

   The type layer is converted to a shape layer. Figure L-21 shows the Layers palette (with the converted type layer state and vector mask thumbnail) and the History palette (with the Convert to Shape state).

In preparation for screening back type, you created a duplicate layer, then hid the original from view. You then converted the duplicate layer into a shape layer.

FIGURE L-19
Duplicated layer

Duplicate of The Unknown layer

The Unknown layer hidden

FIGURE L-20
Layers menu

Click to convert a type layer to a shape layer

FIGURE L-21
History and Layers palettes

Vector mask thumnbnail

FIGURE L-22
Levels dialog box

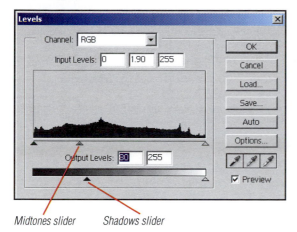

Midtones slider   Shadows slider

Adjust layer content

1. Click Layer on the menu bar, point to Change Layer Content, then click Levels.

After you open the Levels dialog box, the layer becomes transparent.

2. Drag the Input Levels midtones slider to 1.90 so that the content becomes less transparent, as shown in Figure L-22.

3. Drag the Output Levels shadows slider to the right to 80 to make the text brighter, as shown in Figure L-22.

4. Click OK.

5. Click the Backdrop layer on the Layers palette. The path surrounding the text disappears, making the modifications more visible.

6. Save your work, then compare your image to Figure L-23.

You modified the midtones and shadows levels on the shape layer to make the text less transparent. You adjusted the Output Levels shadows slider to make the pixels that make up the text appear lighter and brighter.

FIGURE L-23
Screened back type

Screened
back layer

Click layer to see
screen back effect

CREATE A FADED TYPE EFFECT

What You'll Do

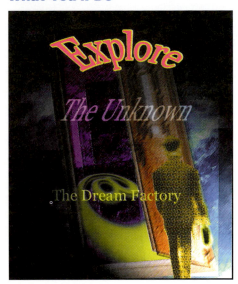

▶ In this lesson, you'll use the Gradient Tool to make text appear faded in one area and brighter in another. You'll also apply a lighting filter.

Creating a Fade Effect

In addition to being able to change the font, size, color, and shape of your text, you might want to create the illusion that type is fading away in order to add an element of mystery to your masterpiece. You can create this effect using a type layer, a layer mask, and the Gradient Tool.

QUICKTIP

Type does not have to be rasterized to create the fade effect.

Using the Gradient Tool

Before you can apply the fade effect, you need to create a layer mask for the type layer. You create the layer mask by clicking the Add layer mask button on the Layers palette. Then, you click the Gradient Tool on the toolbox. You can experiment with different types of gradient styles, but to create simple fading type, make sure Linear Gradient is selected, click the Click to open Gradient picker list arrow, then click the Black, White button on the Gradient palette.

QUICKTIP

The Gradient Tool might be hidden under the Paint Bucket Tool on the toolbox.

Creating semitransparent type

You can use blending options to create what appears to be semitransparent type. To do this, create a type layer and apply any layer styles you want. The Satin style, for example, can be used to darken the type, and the Pattern Overlay style can be used to create a patterned effect. In the Layer Style dialog box, drag the Set opacity of effect slider to the left and watch the preview until you get the amount of transparency you like. The background will be displayed as the contents of the type. So, any background images behind the type will appear to be used for the fill of the type.

Create a fade effect

1. Click the Eyedropper Tool, then click the image at 200 H/500 V.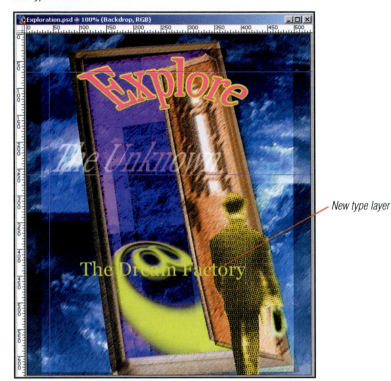

2. Click the Horizontal Type Tool on the toolbox, click at 100 H/450 V, set the font size to 36 pt, then type **The Dream Factory**, as shown in Figure L-24.

3. Click the Add layer mask button on the Layers palette.

4. Click the Gradient Tool on the toolbox.

5. Click the Linear Gradient style on the tool options bar, if necessary.

6. Click the Click to open Gradient picker list arrow on the tool options bar.

7. Click Black, White.

8. Press [Esc] (Win) or [esc] (Mac), then compare the settings on your tool options bar to Figure L-25.

9. Verify that the layer mask is selected, press and hold [Shift], drag the pointer from 50 H/430 V to 200 H/430 V, then release [Shift].

You added a layer mask and a gradient to the left side of the Dream Factory text to create a faded type effect.

FIGURE L-24
New type in document

New type layer

FIGURE L-25
Options for the Gradient Tool

Black, White gradient   *Linear Gradient style*   *Select to reverse the direction of the fade*

FIGURE L-26

Faded text in image

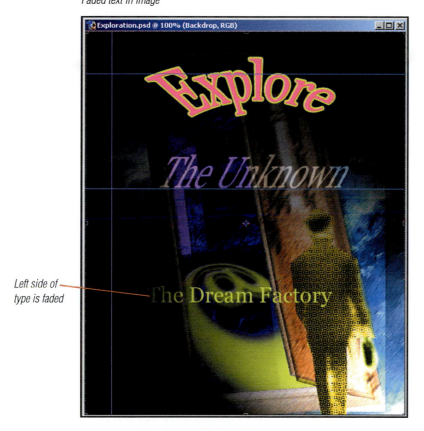

Left side of
type is faded

1. Click the Screened back type layer on the Layers palette, then click the Move Tool on the toolbox.

2. Press and hold [Shift], drag the shape so that the left edge of the bounding box is at 120 H, then release [Shift].

3. Click the Backdrop layer on the Layers palette, click Filter on the menu bar, point to Render, then click Lighting Effects.

4. Select the Default style, select the Spotlight Light type, direct the light source from the lower-right corner, then click OK.

5. Hide the rulers, save your work, then compare your image to Figure L-26.

You added a lighting filter to give the image a more polished appearance.

Power User Shortcuts

to do this:	use this method:
Adjust color levels	Layer ➤ Change Layer Content ➤ Levels
Change warp type color	Double-click [T], click ■
Commit a transformation	✓
Convert type to a shape	Layer ➤ Type ➤ Convert to Shape
Create faded type	⬤ , ▭ , ▭ , Click to open Gradient picker list, then drag pointer over type
Create warped type	Double-click [T], click 工
Display a bounding box	⌖ or **V**, select ☐ Show Bounding Box

to do this:	use this method:
Scale a bounding box	Press [Shift] while dragging handle, click ✓
Screen back type	Duplicate layer, hide original layer, convert type to shape, then adjust Levels
Select Gradient Tool	▭. or **Shift G**
Skew a bounding box	Press [Ctrl] (Win) or [⌘] (Mac) while dragging handle, ✓
Stroke a type layer	🖉. , Stroke, Set color of stroke button
Turn off bounding box display	⌖ or **V**, deselect ☑ Show Bounding Box

Key: Menu items are indicated by ➤ between the menu name and its command. Blue bold letters are shortcuts for selecting tools on the toolbox.

Modify type using a bounding box.

1. Open PS L-2.psd, then save it as **Charge Card**.
2. Substitute a font available on your computer, if necessary. (*Hint*: The fonts used in the sample are a 36 pt and 48 pt Courier New.)
3. Display the rulers in pixels, if necessary.
4. Select the Move Tool, if necessary, then display the bounding box.
5. Make the World-Class Shopper layer active, drag the bounding box to the left so that the left edge of the W is in front of the 90 H guide, then drag the top-middle handle of the bounding box to 290 V.
6. Skew the text by dragging the upper-right handle of the bounding box to 520 H.
7. Commit the transformations.
8. Save your work.

Create warped type with a unique shape.

1. Double-click the layer thumbnail on the Photoshop type layer on the Layers palette.
2. Change the font size to 72 pt.
3. Drag the type's bounding box so that the bottom-left corner is at 135 H/150 V.
4. Open the Warp Text dialog box.
5. Change the Warp Text style to Arch.
6. Click the Horizontal option button, if necessary.
7. Use the following settings for Bend, Horizontal Distortion, and Vertical Distortion: +42, +42, 0, then close the Warp Text dialog box.

8. Move the type so that the bottom-right corner of the bounding box is at 545 H/150 V.
9. Change the type color to the third swatch from the right in the sixth row of the Swatches palette (Dark Violet Magenta).
10. Apply the default Drop Shadow and Bevel and Emboss styles to the Photoshop type layer.
11. Save your work.

Screen back type with imagery.

1. Make the CHARGE layer active.
2. Increase the font size to 80 pt.
3. Move the type layer so the bottom-left corner is at 90 H/275 V.
4. Duplicate this layer, calling the new layer **Screened back type**.
5. Hide the CHARGE layer.
6. Convert the Screened back type layer to a shape layer.
7. Change the layer content by opening the Levels dialog box.

FIGURE L-27
Completed Skills Review

8. Modify the Midtones Input level to 0.45, then close the Levels dialog box.
9. Make the Backdrop layer active.
10. Use the Sponge Tool to saturate the shapes that make up the word Charge.
11. Save your work.

Create a faded type effect.

1. Make the World Class Shopper layer active.
2. Add a mask to this layer.
3. Select the Gradient Tool, set the opacity to 70%, select the Linear Gradient style, then select Black, White on the Gradient picker.
4. Drag a straight line the length of the text, starting at approximately 90 H and 315 V and ending at the right edge of the document.
5. Clear the ruler guides, then hide the rulers.
6. Use the Add Noise filter with a 50% Uniform distribution to the Background layer.
7. Save your work.
8. Compare your document to Figure L-27.

You have been asked to create cover art for a new pop-psychology book entitled *Inner Dilemmas: Outer Struggles*. The author has created some initial artwork that she wants on the cover. You can use any of your Photoshop skills to enhance this image, and add any text.

1. Open PS L-3.psd, then save it as **Inner Dilemmas**.

2. Create two type layers: *Inner Dilemmas* and *Outer Struggles*. (*Hint*: You can use any font available on your computer. In the sample, a 72 and 60 pt Trebuchet MS font is shown.)

3. Position the type layers appropriately.

4. Display the bounding box, if necessary.

5. Warp the Inner Dilemmas type, using the Rise style and the settings of your choice in the Warp Text dialog box.

6. Use the bounding box to enlarge the warped text.

7. Duplicate the Outer Struggles type layer, choosing a suitable name for the duplicate layer.

8. Convert the copied layer to a shape, then change the levels using the settings of your choice. (In the sample, the Midtones input level is 2.26, and the Output shadows level is 20.)

9. Hide the original layer.

10. Add a new type layer using the text of your choice in an appropriate location on the image.

11. Use the bounding box to scale the type layer to a smaller size.

12. Create a mask on this new layer.

13. Use the Gradient Tool and the new type layer to create a fade effect.

14. Change any font colors, and add any enhancing effects to the type layers.

15. Add any filter effects or color adjustments that you determine are necessary. (In the sample, the brightness is adjusted to –15, and the contrast is adjusted to +15 using an adjustment layer).

16. Save your work, then compare your document to the sample in Figure L-28.

FIGURE L-28
Completed Project Builder 1

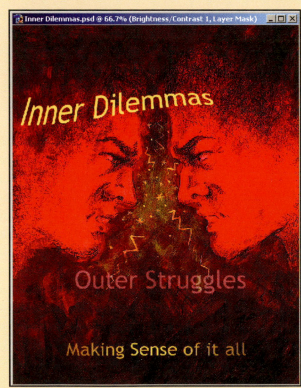

You work for Creativity, a graphic design firm that works almost exclusively with the high-tech business sector. As the newest member of the creative team, you have been assigned the design of the cover for the upcoming Annual Report. You have seen the Annual Reports for previous years, and they always feature dramatic, exciting designs. You have already started on the initial design, but need to complete the project.

1. Open PS L-4.psd, then save it as **Creativity**.
2. Create a new layer just containing the dice. (*Hint*: You can duplicate the Backdrop layer, then use any of your Photoshop skills to isolate the dice in their own layer. Possible alternatives include creating a mask or erasing pixels.)
3. Modify the Backdrop layer so that only the pattern is displayed.
4. Create type layers for text appropriate for an annual report. (*Hint*: You can use any font available on your computer. In the sample, a Georgia font is shown.)
5. Position the type layers appropriately.
6. Warp at least one of the type layers, using the style and settings of your choice. (*Hint*: In the sample, the Bulge style was used.)
7. Enlarge or skew at least one type layer.
8. Create a screened back effect using one of the type layers and the settings of your choice. (In the sample, the Midtones input level is 2.26, and the Output shadows level is 20.)
9. Create a fade effect using one of the type layers.
10. Change any font colors, if necessary, then add any enhancing effects to the type layers.
11. Add any filter effects or color adjustments (using the newly created and modified layers) that you determine are necessary. (In the sample, the brightness is adjusted to +25, and the contrast is adjusted to +10. The area underneath the dice in the Backdrop layer was saturated using the Sponge Tool, and the default Lighting Effects filter was applied to the Backdrop layer.)
12. Save your work, then compare your document to the sample in Figure L-29.

FIGURE L-29
Completed Project Builder 2

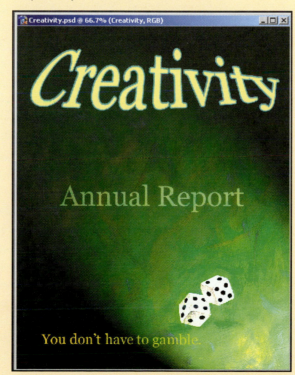

DESIGN PROJECT

You have been asked to design an advertisement for your favorite television station. Before you begin, you decide to see what information you can find about type enhancements on the Internet. You intend to use the information you find to improve your skills and create a dramatic image. Be prepared to discuss the design elements used in this project. (*Hint*: If you don't have a favorite television station, invent call letters that you can use in this exercise.)

1. Connect to the Internet, then use your browser and favorite search engine to find information on warped type. One possible link to a site is in the Student Online Companion. Go to *www.course.com*, navigate to the page for this book, click the Student Online Companion link, then click the link for this unit.

2. Create a new Photoshop document, using the dimensions of your choice, then save it as **Television Station Ad**.

3. Create a type layer, using any font available on your computer, and any text you want. (In the sample, an Onyx font is used.)

4. Create a warped type effect, using any style and settings of your choice. (In the sample, the Arc style is used.)

5. Create an attractive background, using any of your Photoshop skills or any imagery available to you. You can use scanned or digital camera images, purchased imagery, or any images available on your computer.

6. Create any necessary additional type layers.

7. Resize any fonts, if necessary, using the bounding box.

8. Add any special effects to the type layers.

9. If necessary, make color adjustments or add filters.

10. Save your work, then compare your document to the sample in Figure L-30.

FIGURE L-30
Completed Design Project

Depending on the size of your group, you can assign individual elements of the project to group members, or work collectively to create the finished product.

Your favorite band recently ran a contest, and the winning entrant—YOU—gets to design the cover for their next CD. Fortunately for the band, your expert Photoshop skills ensure that the cover will be fabulous. After the document is complete, all members of the group should be prepared to discuss what they did, why they did it, and how their efforts contributed to the overall design of the image.

1. Create a Photoshop document using the dimensions of your choice, then save it as **CD Cover Artwork**.
2. Locate several pieces of artwork—either on your computer, in a royalty-free collection, or from scanned images. Although the images can show anything, you want to show positive imagery in keeping with the band's message.
3. Select imagery from the artwork and move it into CD Cover Artwork.
4. Create a warped type effect using any style and settings of your choice. (In the sample, the Pristina font is used.)
5. Create any necessary additional type layers.
6. Resize any fonts, if necessary, using the bounding box.
7. Add any special effects to the type layers.

8. If necessary, make color adjustments or add filters.
9. Use any transformation skills, if necessary.
10. Add any filter effects, if you decide they will make your document more dramatic. (In the sample, the Wind filter is applied to the Time layer.)
11. Make any color adjustments, if necessary.
12. Save your work, then compare your document to the sample in Figure L-31.

FIGURE L-31
Completed Group Project

UNIT M

LIQUIFYING AN IMAGE

1. Use the Liquify tools to distort an image.

2. Learn how to freeze and thaw areas.

3. Use the mesh feature as you distort an image.

UNIT M
LIQUIFYING AN IMAGE

Distorting Images

If you want to have some fun with Photoshop, try your hand at the Liquify feature. This feature works similarly to the Smudge Tool and distort filters because you can use it to distort an image. Unlike the Smudge Tool and the distort filters, however, the Liquify feature gives you much more control over the finished product. The Smudge Tool is just a single tool, whereas the Liquify feature contains 11 distinct tools that you can use to modify an image, although only nine of these tools create actual distortion effects.

Using the Liquify Feature

The Liquify feature lets you make an image look as if parts of it have been melted. You can apply the nine Liquify distortions with a brush, and like other brush-based Photoshop tools, you can modify both the brush size and pressure to give you just the effect you want. You can use the two non-distortion Liquify tools to freeze and thaw areas within the image. Freezing protects an area from editing and possible editing errors, and thawing a frozen area allows it to be edited. With these two tools, you can protect specific areas from Liquify distortions, and can determine with great accuracy which areas are affected.

Using Common Sense

Because the effects of the Liquify feature are so dramatic, you should take the proper precautions to preserve your original work. You can work on a copy of the original document, or create duplicate layers to ensure that you can always get back to your starting point.

Tools You'll Use

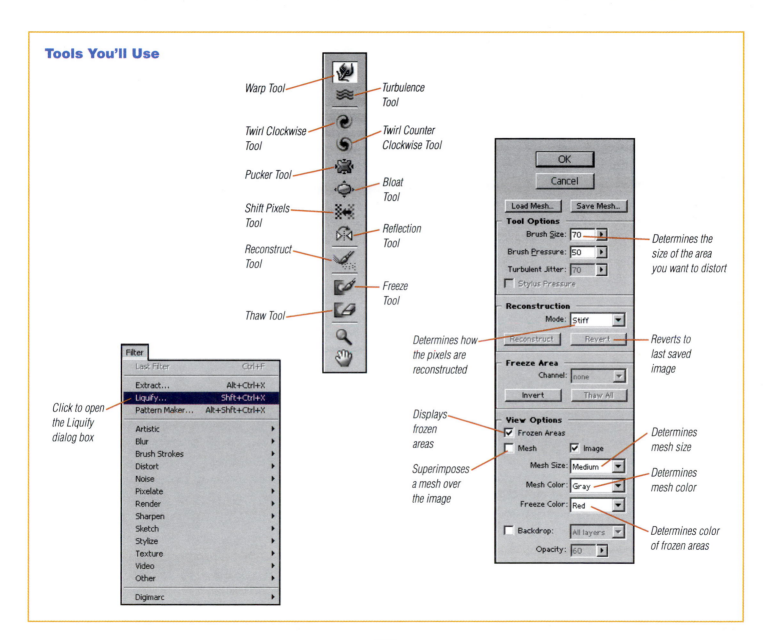

Warp Tool

Turbulence Tool

Twirl Clockwise Tool

Twirl Counter Clockwise Tool

Pucker Tool

Bloat Tool

Shift Pixels Tool

Reflection Tool

Reconstruct Tool

Freeze Tool

Thaw Tool

Filter

Last Filter	Ctrl+F
Extract...	Alt+Ctrl+X
Liquify...	Shft+Ctrl+X
Pattern Maker...	Alt+Shft+Ctrl+X
Artistic	▶
Blur	▶
Brush Strokes	▶
Distort	▶
Noise	▶
Pixelate	▶
Render	▶
Sharpen	▶
Sketch	▶
Stylize	▶
Texture	▶
Video	▶
Other	▶
Digimarc	▶

Click to open the Liquify dialog box

OK

Cancel

Load Mesh...   Save Mesh...

Tool Options
- Brush Size: 70 ▶
- Brush Pressure: 50 ▶
- Turbulent Jitter: 70 ▶
- ☐ Stylus Pressure

Determines the size of the area you want to distort

Reconstruction
- Mode: Stiff
- Reconstruct   Revert

Determines how the pixels are reconstructed

Reverts to last saved image

Freeze Area
- Channel: none
- Invert   Thaw All

View Options
- ☑ Frozen Areas
- ☐ Mesh   ☑ Image
- Mesh Size: Medium
- Mesh Color: Gray
- Freeze Color: Red
- ☐ Backdrop: All layers
- Opacity: 60 ▶

Displays frozen areas

Superimposes a mesh over the image

Determines mesh size

Determines mesh color

Determines color of frozen areas

M-3

USE THE LIQUIFY TOOLS
TO DISTORT AN IMAGE

What You'll Do

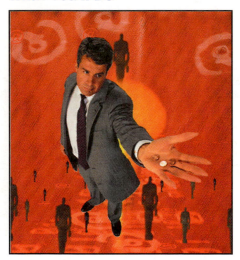

In this lesson, you'll use the Warp Tool in the Liquify dialog box to create distortions.

Using the Liquify Dialog Box

With the Liquify feature, you can apply distortions to any rasterized layer. When you use the Liquify command, the contents of the active layer appear in a large preview window in the Liquify dialog box. The distortion tools—used to apply the Liquify effects—are displayed on the left side of the dialog box; the tool settings are displayed on the right side of the dialog box. Unlike other tools that you use in the document window, you can only access the Liquify tools from the Liquify dialog box. (The Liquify feature is similar to the Extract feature in this respect.) To open this dialog box, select the layer containing the items you want to distort, click Filter on the menu bar, then click Liquify. In this dialog box, you can create nine different types of distortions.

QUICKTIP

As you apply distortions, the effects are immediately visible in the preview window of the Liquify dialog box.

Understanding the Possibilities

When you think of a feature such as Liquify, you might think of creating wild, crazy effects, which is certainly possible. Compare Figures M-1 (the original image) and M-2 (the distorted image). As you can see from the altered image, you can use this feature to make drastic changes in an image. The following Liquify tools were used for the distorted image:

- The Twirl Clockwise Tool was used repeatedly on the topmost book.
- The Twirl Counter Clockwise Tool was used repeatedly on the second book.

- The Pucker Tool was used on the third book eight times. (The Pucker Tool pulls the pixels toward the center of the brush tip.)
- The Bloat Tool was used repeatedly on the fifth book. (The Bloat Tool pushes pixels away from the center of the brush tip, which can create a more subtle effect.)

QUICKTIP

You can use distortions to create wild effects or to make subtle mood changes within an image.

Going Wild with Distortions

Of course, you can create wild, crazy distortions using the Liquify feature, and it is a lot of fun. As you can see from Figure M-2, you can create some rather bizarre effects using these tools, but you can also use the distortion tools very conservatively to just correct a flaw or tweak an image.

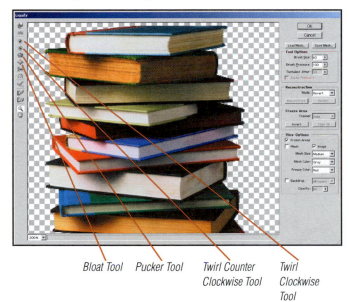

FIGURE M-1
Undistorted image in Liquify dialog box

Bloat Tool   Pucker Tool   Twirl Counter Clockwise Tool   Twirl Clockwise Tool

FIGURE M-2
Distortion samples

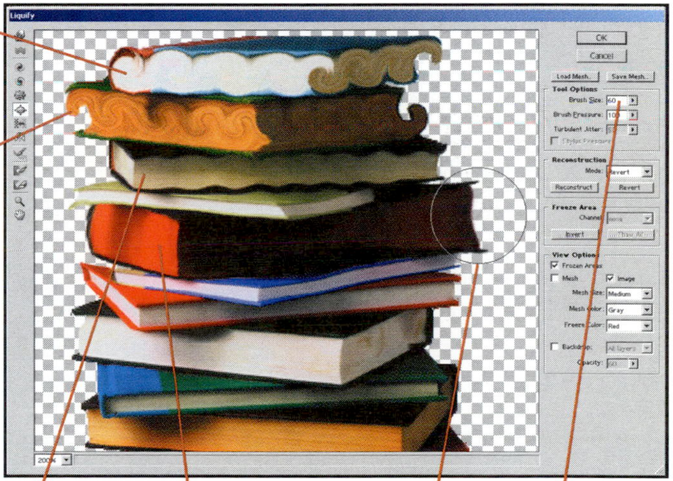

Effect of the Twirl Clockwise Tool

Effect of the Twirl Counter Clockwise Tool

Effect of the Pucker Tool   Effect of Bloat Tool used to increase the size of the book   Brush tip   Brush size

Open the Liquify dialog box and modify the brush size

1. Open PS M-1.psd, then save the file as **Liquidity**.

2. If necessary, click the Change Hand layer on the Layers palette.

3. Click Filter on the menu bar, then click Liquify.

4. Click the Warp Tool in the Liquify dialog box. 🖐

   The Warp Tool is described in Table M-1.

5. Double-click the Brush Size text box, type **10**, then press [Enter] (Win) or [return] (Mac).

   TIP   You can adjust the brush size by typing a value between 1 and 600 in the text box or by clicking the Brush Size list arrow, then dragging the slider to a new value.

6. Compare the settings in the Liquify dialog box to those shown in Figure M-3, and make any necessary adjustments.

You opened the Liquify dialog box, then chose the Warp Tool and a brush size.

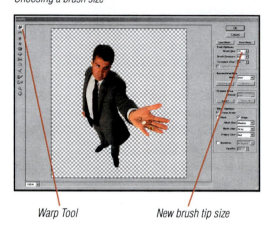

Warp Tool   New brush tip size

TABLE M-1: Liquify Tools

tool	button	use
Warp Tool	🖐	Pushes pixels forward during dragging.
Turbulence Tool	≈	Randomly scrambles pixels.
Twirl Clockwise Tool	↻	Rotates pixels clockwise during dragging.
Twirl Counter Clockwise Tool	↺	Rotates pixels counterclockwise during dragging.
Pucker Tool	✦	Moves pixels toward the center of the active brush tip.
Bloat Tool	◈	Moves pixels away from the center of the active brush tip.
Shift Pixels Tool	⋙	Moves pixels perpendicular to the brush stroke.
Reflection Tool	▨	Copies pixels to the brush area.
Reconstruct Tool	✎	Unpaints recently distorted pixels completely or partially.
Freeze Tool	✔	Protects an area from distortion.
Thaw Tool	✔	Makes a frozen area available for distortions.

FIGURE M-4
Positioned pointer

Warp Tool brush
tip will be used to
distort thumb

FIGURE M-5
Distorted thumb

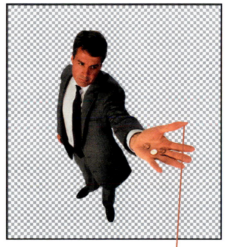

Pixels pushed
using the pointer

FIGURE M-6
Warped fingertips

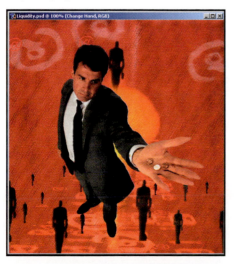

Use the Warp Tool

1. Position the pointer over the thumb on the right side of the image, as shown in Figure M-4. ⬡

2. Drag the tip of the thumb, as shown in Figure M-5.

   > TIP   You can return an image to its former appearance (before you first open the Liquify dialog box) by clicking Revert in the Reconstruction section of the Liquify dialog box.

3. Drag the fingertips of the remaining fingers on the Change Hand layer.

4. Click OK to close the Liquify dialog box.

5. Save your work, then compare your document to Figure M-6.

You used the Warp Tool to distort the pixels of the fingertips in an image. By dragging, you pushed the pixels forward, giving the fingertips a fiendish appearance.

LEARN HOW TO FREEZE AND THAW AREAS

What You'll Do

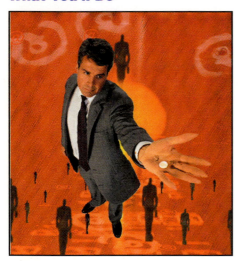

▶ *In this lesson, you'll freeze an area of an image, make distortions, then thaw the areas so that they can be edited.*

Controlling Distortion Areas

Like storing food in the freezer to protect it from spoiling, you can freeze areas within an image so that the Liquify tools leave them unaffected. Using the Liquify dialog box, you can protect areas within an image, then thaw them—or return them to a state that can be edited—and make necessary distortions. You control which areas are distorted by using the Freeze and Thaw Tools in the Liquify dialog box.

Freezing Image Areas

You can selectively freeze areas by painting them with a pointer. The View Options section in the Liquify dialog box lets you display frozen areas in the preview window. By default, frozen areas are painted in red, but you can change this color to make it more visible. For example, in Figure M-7, the frozen area is painted in blue since red would not be visible because of the colors in this image.

QUICKTIP

To isolate the exact areas you want to freeze, try painting a larger area, then using the Thaw Tool to eliminate unwanted frozen areas.

Reconstructing Distortions

No matter how careful you are, you will most likely either create a distortion you don't like, or need to do some sort of damage control. Unlike typical Photoshop states, individual distortions you make using the Liquify feature do not appear in the History palette, and therefore cannot be undone. You can, however, use the History palette to delete the effects of an entire Liquify session (*from the time you open the Liquify dialog box to the time you close it*). How distortions are reconstructed is determined by the mode used. If you want to reconstruct, you can do so by using one of eight different reconstruction modes in the Liquify dialog box. Each mode affects the way pixels are reconstructed, relative to frozen areas in the image. This allows you to redo the changes in new and novel ways.

QUICKTIP

You can use any combination of reconstruction tools and modes to get just the effect you want.

Undergoing Reconstruction

Figure M-8 contains samples of reconstructed areas. Using the Reconstruct Tool and the Stiff mode, the tail feathers of the chicken were restored to their original condition. The Rigid mode was used on the feet, and the beak was reconstructed using the Loose mode. You can use several methods to reconstruct an image:

- Click Revert in the Liquify dialog box
- Choose the Revert mode, then click Reconstruct in the Liquify dialog box
- Click the Reconstruct Tool, choose the Revert mode, then drag the brush over distorted areas in the Liquify dialog box
- Click the Cancel button in the Liquify dialog box
- Make distortions in the Liquify dialog box, then drag the Liquify state to the Delete current state button on the History palette

FIGURE M-7
Frozen areas and distortions in the preview window

FIGURE M-8
Sample reconstructions

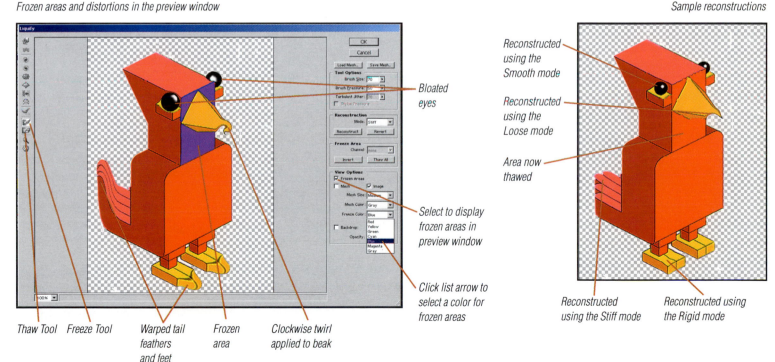

Bloated eyes

Select to display frozen areas in preview window

Click list arrow to select a color for frozen areas

Thaw Tool   Freeze Tool   Warped tail feathers and feet   Frozen area   Clockwise twirl applied to beak

Reconstructed using the Smooth mode

Reconstructed using the Loose mode

Area now thawed

Reconstructed using the Stiff mode   Reconstructed using the Rigid mode

Freeze areas in an image

1. Verify that the Change Hand layer is still selected.
2. Click Filter on the menu bar, then click Liquify.
3. Click the Freeze Tool in the Liquify dialog box.
4. Double-click the Brush Size text box, type **15**, then press [Enter] (Win) or [return] (Mac). 135
5. Click the Freeze Color list arrow, then click Red, if necessary. Compare your Liquify dialog box settings to Figure M-9. Red

   Your Liquify dialog box settings might differ.
6. Drag the pointer over the areas on the fingers, as shown in Figure M-10.

   Table M-2 describes the reconstruction modes available in the Liquify dialog box.

You modified Liquify settings, then froze areas within an image to protect them by using the Freeze Tool.

FIGURE M-9
Liquify settings

FIGURE M-10
Frozen area

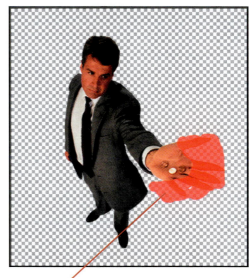

Red area is frozen

TABLE M-2: Reconstruction Modes

mode	use
Revert	Changes areas back to their appearance before the dialog box was opened.
Rigid	Maintains right angles in the pixel grid during reconstruction.
Stiff	Provides continuity between frozen and unfrozen areas during reconstruction.
Smooth	Smoothes continuous distortions over frozen areas during reconstruction.
Loose	Smoothes continuous distortions similar to the Smooth mode.
Displace	Moves distorted pixels in their current location.
Amplitwist	Swirls distorted pixels in a twisted formation.
Affine	Reconstructs pixels based on the distortions of existing pixels.

FIGURE M-11
Distortions in image

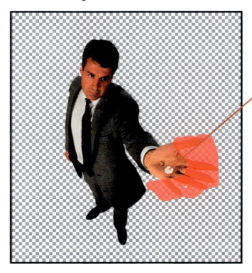

Dime appears
larger than pennies

FIGURE M-12
Distortions applied

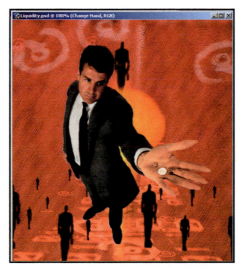

FIGURE M-13
History palette

State indicating
application of
distortions

1. Click the Pucker Tool in the Liquify dialog box. 🖼️

2. Position the center of the pointer over either penny held in the man's palm, then click and hold the mouse button until the penny appears smaller. ⭕

3. Repeat Step 2 on the other penny.

4. Click the Bloat Tool in the Liquify dialog box. 🔘

5. Center the pointer over the dime and click until the dime appears larger. ⭕

6. Compare your image to Figure M-11.

7. Click Thaw All in the Freeze Area section.

8. Click OK.

    The distortions are applied to the image.

9. Save your work, then compare your document to Figure M-12, and the History palette to Figure M-13.

After distorting an area, you thawed a protected frozen area and applied the distortions to the image.

USE THE MESH FEATURE AS YOU DISTORT AN IMAGE

What You'll Do

In this lesson, you'll use the mesh feature when making distortions.

Using the Mesh Feature

As you know, you use the preview window in the Liquify dialog box to view the extent of the distortions being made to your image. You can easily see the effects of your distortions by turning on the mesh. The **mesh** is a series of horizontal and vertical gridlines superimposed on the preview window. Although this feature is not necessary to create distortions, it can be helpful for seeing how much distortion you have added. The mesh can be controlled using the View Options section in the Liquify dialog box, shown in Figure M-14. A distorted image, with the default medium-size, gray mesh displayed, is shown in Figure M-15.

QUICKTIP

Distortions on the gridlines look similar to isobars on a thermal map or elevations on a topographic map.

Changing the Mesh Display

You can modify the appearance of the mesh so that it is displayed in another color or contains larger or smaller gridlines. You may want to use large gridlines if your changes are so dramatic that the use of smaller gridlines would be distracting. As shown in Figure M-16, you can use the large gridlines to see where the distortions occur. If the mesh color and the colors in the image are similar, you may want to change the mesh color. For example, a yellow mesh displayed on an image with a yellow background would be invisible. A blue mesh against a yellow background, as shown in Figure M-16, is more noticeable.

QUICKTIP

You can always turn off the mesh feature if it is distracting.

Visualizing the Distortions

When the mesh feature is on and clearly visible, take a look at the gridlines as you make your distortions. Note where the gridlines have been adjusted and if symmetrical objects have equally symmetrical distortions. For example, distortions of a rectangular skyscraper can be controlled so that they are equivalent on all visible sides. If symmetry is what you want, the mesh gives you one method of checking your results.

Getting a Better View of Distortions

The active layer is always shown in the Liquify dialog box, but you might find it helpful to distort imagery with its companion layers visible. You can do this in two ways. One way is by selecting the Backdrop check box in the Liquify dialog box, and selecting which layer (or all layers) you want to be visible with the selected layer. You can then adjust the opacity of the backdrop layer(s) to make the layer(s) more visible. This technique distorts only the layer selected on the Layers palette. The other way is by merging visible layers: Click the highest layer on the Layers palette, click the Layers palette list arrow, then click Merge Visible. When you open the merged layers in the Liquify dialog box, all the imagery will be visible and can be altered by distortions. One way of ensuring that you can get back to your original layers—in case things don't turn out quite as you planned—is by making copies of the layers you want to combine before you merge the layers.

Mesh display options

Click list arrow to change mesh size

Click list arrow to change mesh color

Select to display mesh

Distorted image with large blue mesh

Larger gridlines

Less detail in mesh

Distorted image with default size and color mesh

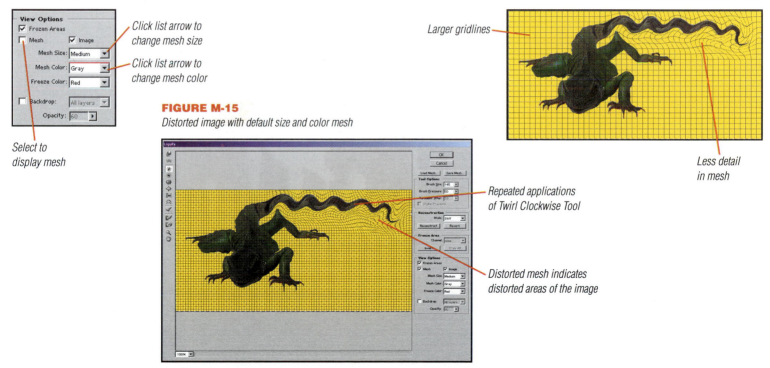

Repeated applications of Twirl Clockwise Tool

Distorted mesh indicates distorted areas of the image

Turn on the mesh

1. Click the Layers palette list arrow, then click Merge Visible.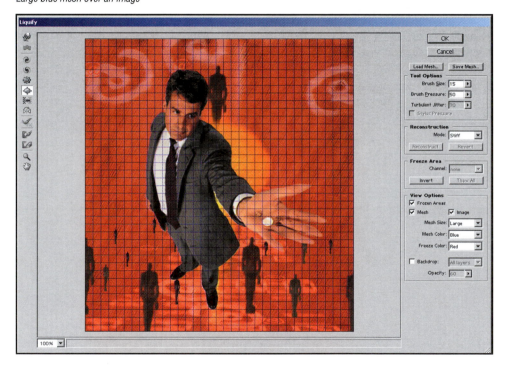

   The two visible layers, Backdrop and Change Hand, are consolidated into the selected layer (Change Hand layer). Any new distortions will now affect both layers.

2. Click Filter on the menu bar, then click Liquify.

3. Verify that the Bloat Tool is selected and 15 appears in the Brush Size text box.

4. Select the Mesh check box. ☐ Mesh

5. Click the Mesh Color list arrow, then click Blue. `Gray ▼`

6. Click the Mesh Size list arrow, then click Large. Compare your image and settings to Figure M-17. `Medium ▼`

Prior to turning on the mesh, you merged the active layer with the layer beneath it. Then, you turned on the mesh and changed the mesh color and size.

FIGURE M-17
Large blue mesh over an image

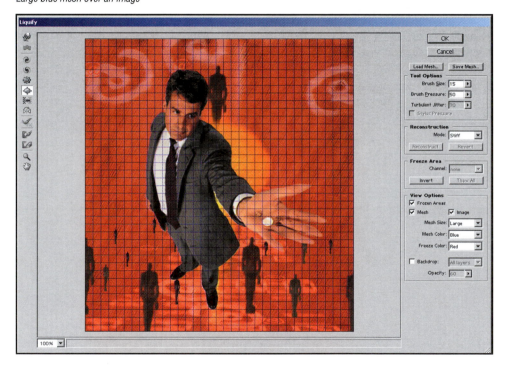

Warped hair

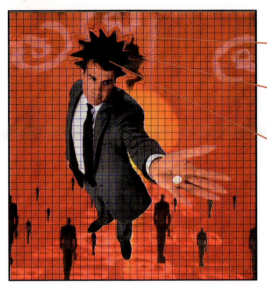

— *Distorted mesh*

— *Distortion affected merged layer*

— *Spikes created with Warp Tool*

FIGURE M-19
Distortions applied to image

Distort an image with the mesh feature activated

1. Click the Warp Tool in the Liquify dialog box.
2. Drag the pointer in the hair so that it forms spikes, as shown in Figure M-18.
3. Click the Mesh Size list arrow, then click Medium. `Large ▼`

    The gridlines appear smaller.
4. Deselect the Mesh check box to turn off the mesh. `☑ Mesh`
5. Click OK.
6. Save your work, then compare your image to Figure M-19.

You added new distortions to the image and modified the mesh size. After viewing the distortions with the smaller mesh, you turned off the mesh and viewed the image.

Power User Shortcuts

to do this:	use this method:
Bloat an area	Filter ➤ Liquify, ⊕ or **B**
Change freeze color	Filter ➤ Liquify, Red ▾
Change mesh color	Filter ➤ Liquify, Gray ▾
Change mesh size	Filter ➤ Liquify, Large ▾
Change brush size	Filter ➤ Liquify, 135 ▸
Freeze pixels	Filter ➤ Liquify, 🖌 or **F**
Open Liquify dialog box	Filter ➤ Liquify or [Shift][Ctrl][X] (Win) or [shift][X] (Mac)
Pucker an area	Filter ➤ Liquify, ▦ or **P**
Reconstruct pixels in an area	Filter ➤ Liquify, 🖌 or **E**
Reflect pixels in an area	Filter ➤ Liquify, ▧ or **M**

to do this:	use this method:
Return image to prewarp state	Click Revert in Liquify dialog box, click Cancel in Liquify dialog box, or drag state to 🗑 in History palette
Shift pixels in an area	Filter ➤ Liquify, ▥ or **S**
Thaw frozen pixels	Filter ➤ Liquify, 🖌 or **T**
Turn mesh on/off	Filter ➤ Liquify, ☑ Mesh
Turn Backdrop on/off	Filter ➤ Liquify, ☐ Backdrop:
Twirl an area clockwise	Filter ➤ Liquify, 🌀 or **R**
Twirl an area counterclockwise	Filter ➤ Liquify, 🌀 or **L**
Warp an area	Filter ➤ Liquify, 🖐 or **W**

Key: Menu items are indicated by ➤ between the menu name and its command. Blue bold letters are shortcuts for selecting tools on the toolbox.

Use the Liquify tools to distort an image.

1. Open PS M-2.psd, then save it as **Blurred Vision**.
2. Open the Liquify dialog box.
3. Change the brush size to 65, if necessary.
4. Select the Twirl Clockwise Tool.
5. Twirl the F in Line 2, as shown in Figure M-21.
6. Select the Twirl Counter Clockwise Tool.
7. Twirl the P in Line 2.
8. Save your work.

Learn how to freeze and thaw areas.

1. Open the Liquify dialog box.
2. Change the freeze color to Green, if necessary.
3. Freeze the O in the middle of Line 3.
4. Select the Bloat Tool.
5. Bloat each letter in Line 3.
6. Thaw all the frozen areas.
7. Save your work.

Use the mesh feature as you distort an image.

1. Open the Liquify dialog box.
2. Turn on the mesh feature.
3. Change the mesh color to Red, if necessary.
4. Change the mesh size to Large.
5. Select the Pucker Tool and change the brush size to 135.

6. Pucker the E on Line 1, as shown in Figure M-20. (*Hint*: Click the mouse button repeatedly until you notice that the grid shows the distortion.)

FIGURE M-20
Skills Review document with mesh

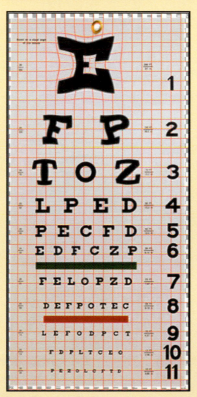

7. Save your work, then compare your document to the sample in Figure M-21.

FIGURE M-21
Completed Skills Review

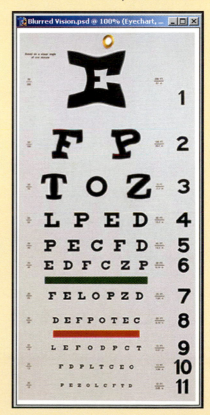

Your lifelong dream to open a restaurant is about to come true. In fact, even though you haven't found a location, you've already chosen a name: the Shooting Star Restaurant. Fortunately, you can use your Photoshop skills to save some money by designing your own promotional advertisements. You've created the initial background art, but need to complete the image.

1. Open PS M-3.psd, then save it as **Shooting Star**.
2. Open the Liquify dialog box.
3. Display a medium-sized, blue mesh.
4. Change the freeze color to Red, if necessary.
5. Use the brush size of your choice to freeze the face in the lower-left corner.
6. Use the Twirl Clockwise Tool and a brush size of 25 to distort the sky area bordering the face.
7. Use the Bloat Tool with a brush size of 250 to distort the shooting star.
8. Use the Twirl Counter Clockwise Tool and the brush size of your choice to distort the bloated shooting star.
9. Turn off the mesh, then close the Liquify dialog box.
10. Add a type layer that says **Shooting Star Restaurant**. (*Hint*: You can use any color and any font available on your computer. In the sample, a Poor Richard font is shown.)
11. Use the bounding box to change the size of the text.

12. Warp the type layer using the style and the settings of your choice. (*Hint*: Do not rasterize the type layer.)
13. Apply the type effects of your choice to the text.
14. Make any color adjustments you feel are necessary. (*Hint*: In the sample, the Brightness was adjusted to –5, and the Contrast was adjusted to +10.)

FIGURE M-22
Completed Project Builder 1

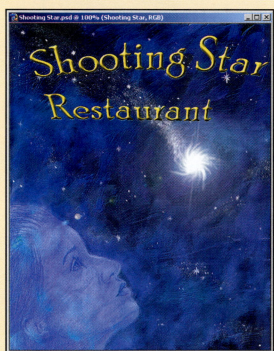

15. Add any filter effects that you determine are necessary. (In the sample, the Lens Flare filter was set at 105mm Prime at 90% Brightness and positioned over the shooting star.)
16. Save your work, then compare your document to the sample in Figure M-22.

Your friend is a film photographer and doesn't understand the power of Photoshop and electronic photography. His birthday is coming soon, and you think it is a great opportunity to show him how useful Photoshop can be and to have a little fun with him. You think it would be fun to use the Liquify tools to turn a photo of him into a caricature. One of the things you like best about your friend is that he has a great sense of humor and can laugh at himself.

1. Open PS M-4.psd, then save it as **Buddy Boy**.
2. Locate at least one piece of appropriate artwork—either a scanned image of a friend, an image on your computer, or an image from a royalty-free collection—that you can use in this document.
3. Use any appropriate methods to select imagery from the artwork.
4. After the selections have been made, copy the selection into Buddy Boy.
5. Transform any imagery, if necessary.
6. Change the colors of the gradient fill in the Backdrop layer to suit the colors in your friend's image.
7. Open the Liquify dialog box.
8. Display any size mesh in any color you find helpful.
9. Change the freeze color to a color you find helpful.

10. Use the brush size of your choice to freeze an area within the image. (*Hint*: In the example, the face was protected while the hair was enlarged and brushed back.)
11. Use any distortion tool in any brush size of your choice to distort an area in the image.
12. Thaw the frozen areas.
13. Use any additional distortion techniques to modify the image.

14. Turn off the mesh, then close the Liquify dialog box.
15. Add a type layer with a clever title for your friend.
16. Save your work, then compare your document to the sample in Figure M-23.

FIGURE M-23
Completed Project Builder 2

Liquifying an Image

DESIGN PROJECT

You really love the Photoshop Liquify feature and want to see other samples of how this tool can be used. You decide to look on the Internet, find a sample, then cast a critical eye on the results.

1. Connect to the Internet, go to *www.course.com*, navigate to the page for this book, click the Student Online Companion link, then click the link for this unit to display the image shown in Figure M-24.
2. Use your browser and favorite search engine to find information about the Liquify feature and design effects. One site that describes how this feature can be used is *http://www.adobe.com/webstudio/ photoshop/phsliquify/main.html.*
3. Ask yourself the following questions.
   - Do you like this image? If so, why?
   - Does the distortion prevent you from determining what the image is?
   - In your opinion, does the distortion make the image more or less effective?
   - How was the distortion created?
   - After seeing this sample, what is your opinion as to the overall effectiveness of the Liquify feature? How can it best be used?
4. Be prepared to discuss your answers to these questions either in writing, in a group discussion, or in a presentation format.

FIGURE M-24
Completed Design Project

GROUP PROJECT

Depending on the size of your group, you can assign individual elements of the project to group members, or work collectively to create the finished product.

You have been asked to give a presentation to a group of students who are interested in taking computer design classes. The presentation should include general topics, such as layers, type, and making selections, and can also include more exotic features, such as Liquify. Make it clear that the Liquify feature can be used on people, objects, or abstract images. Create a document that you can use in your presentation.

1. Create a new Photoshop document with any dimensions.
2. Save the file as **Photoshop Presentation**.
3. Locate several pieces of artwork—either on your computer, in a royalty-free collection, or from scanned images. Remember that the images can show anything, but you want to show the flexibility of Photoshop and the range of your skills.
4. Select imagery from the artwork and move it into Photoshop Presentation. (*Hint*: Make sure your document has multiple layers, so you can demonstrate this feature during the presentation.)
5. Open the Liquify dialog box.
6. Display any size mesh in any color you find helpful.

7. Use the Freeze Tool and the brush size of your choice to isolate areas that you don't want to distort.
8. Use any distortion tool in any brush size of your choice to distort an area in the image.
9. Thaw the frozen areas.
10. Use any additional distortion techniques to modify the image.
11. Turn off the mesh, then close the Liquify dialog box.
12. Use any transformation skills, if necessary.
13. Add any filter effects, if you decide they will make your document more dramatic. (In the sample, the Fresco filter was applied to the Abstract layer.)

FIGURE M-25
Completed Group Project

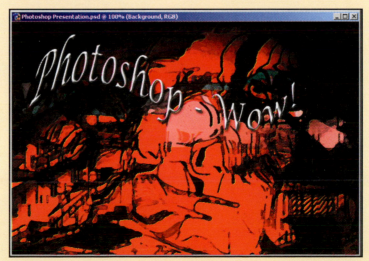

14. Make any necessary color adjustments.
15. Add at least one type layer in any font available on your computer. (A Lucida Calligraphy font is shown in the sample.)
16. Use your knowledge of special effects and the bounding box to enhance the type layer. (The following effects have been applied: Flag-style warped text, Drop Shadow style, and Bevel and Emboss style.)
17. Save your work, then compare your document to the sample in Figure M-25.

UNIT N

PERFORMING DOCUMENT SURGERY

1. Delete unnecessary imagery.

2. Correct colors in an image.

3. Fix a background.

UNIT N
PERFORMING DOCUMENT SURGERY

Understanding the Realities

By now you've realized that the practical use of Photoshop is not always cut and dried. In fact, a fair amount of problem solving may be required. You don't always have access to perfect images with objects that can be easily selected and placed into existing images. If you did, you wouldn't need the arsenal of tools that Photoshop provides. Often, we find ourselves with images that need some "help." Perhaps an image has colors that are washed out, or perhaps it would be perfect except for an element that you don't want or need. By the time your document is finished, you may feel as if it has undergone major surgery.

Assessing the Situation

In some situations, there may be many ways to achieve the look you want. A smart Photoshop user knows what tools are at his/her disposal, evaluates a document to see what is needed, then decides which method is best to fix a problem area in a Photoshop image.

Applying Knowledge and Making Decisions

A lot of Photoshop work requires the ability to assess what is needed and then apply the appropriate tools. You've probably already figured out that you can approach the same problem in many ways; that's one reason that someone with savvy Photoshop skills is in demand in today's job market. Your job is to determine the best approach to take to make an image look right. And it is up to you to determine what "right" is.

QUICKTIP

Your hardest work may never be seen. You may spend a significant amount of time cleaning up edges and eliminating "dirt" and smudges.

Tools You'll Use

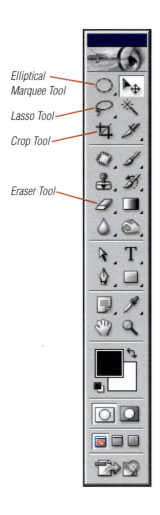

Elliptical Marquee Tool

Lasso Tool

Crop Tool

Eraser Tool

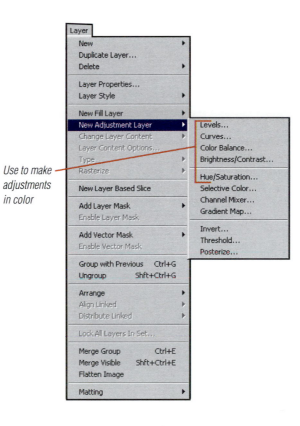

Use to make adjustments in color

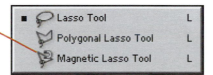

Use to select objects with complex edges

DELETE UNNECESSARY IMAGERY

What You'll Do

In this lesson, you'll use your skills and a variety of tools to remove unwanted imagery. You'll also add a new layer from a selection and add a layer mask.

Evaluating the Possibilities

Now that you have some experience creating and editing images, your assessment abilities have probably sharpened. Your ability to decide what imagery is necessary and what is not is improved. You may also find that as you become more experienced using Photoshop, you'll start looking at images with a more discerning eye. You might, for example, see a great image and think, "That has a great crisp edge. I could isolate that object using the Magnetic Lasso Tool."

QUICKTIP

Don't be surprised when a simple touch-up job takes hours when you thought it would take only minutes. Photoshop is a powerful program, and some tasks take longer than others.

Performing Surgery

Removing unwanted imagery can be time-consuming and frustrating, but it can also be extremely gratifying (after you're finished). It's detailed, demanding, and sometimes complicated work. For example, Figures N-1 and N-2 show the same image *before* and *after* it underwent the following alterations:

- The TIFF file was saved as a Photoshop document.
- Selection tools were used to create separate layers for the background, the backdrop, and the candles.
- The candles layer was duplicated, as insurance—just in case it became necessary to start over. See the Layers palette in Figure N-3.
- The background color was changed from black to pure blue violet.
- The candles on the left and right sides were eliminated by using eraser tools.
- Extraneous "dirt" and smudges were eliminated by using eraser tools.
- Contrast was added to the candles by using an adjustment layer.
- The Liquify feature was used to extend the individual flames and to smooth out the candle holder at the bottom of the image.
- The Noise filter was applied to the Backdrop layer, to give it more texture and dimension.

Understanding the Alternatives

Could these effects be achieved using other methods? Of course. For example, the bottom of the image was modified using the Warp Tool in the Liquify dialog box, but a similar effect could have been created using a painting tool such as the Smudge Tool. The effect of the Noise filter could also have been created using the Grain filter. And how many different ways can you think of to get the imagery from Figure N-1 into the separate layers in Figure N-2? It's possible that you can create individual effects in many ways. For example, you might want to use the Magnetic Lasso Tool to select areas with clearly defined edges, then zoom in and use the Eraser Tool to clean up dirt and smudges.

Preparing for Surgery

You've got it all figured out, right? And things always go the way you plan them, right? Wrong. We purchase car and home insurance to protect us from unforeseen events. Doesn't it make sense to take the time to prepare for a worst-case scenario when using Photoshop? Of course. You can easily protect yourself against disaster by building in some safety nets as you work. For example, you can duplicate your original image (or images) just in case things go awry. By creating a copy, you'll never have to complain that your original work got clobbered. You can also save interim copies of your document at strategic stages of your work. Above all, make sure you plan your steps. To do this, perform a few trial runs on a practice image before starting on the *real* project. Until you get comfortable reading the states in the History palette, write down what steps you took and what settings you used. All that work will pay off.

FIGURE N-1
Original TIFF file

FIGURE N-2
Modified image

Flames extended using the Liquify feature's Warp Tool

Noise filter added to new background color to give texture

Eraser Tool used to delete candles from left and right edges and to eliminate smudges

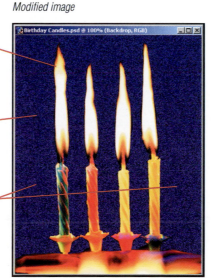

FIGURE N-3
Layers palette of modified image

Contrast applied using an Adjustment layer

Original candles layer is hidden

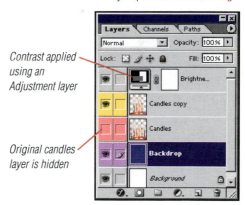

Prepare the document for surgery

1. Open PS N-1.jpg, then save the file as **Runners.psd**.

   | **TIP** Use the Format list arrow to change the file from a JPG to the Photoshop format.

2. Click Layer on the menu bar, point to New, then click Layer From Background.

3. Type **Runners** in the Name text box.

4. Click the Color list arrow, then click Violet.

5. Click OK.

6. Drag the Runners layer on the Layers palette to the Create a new layer button.

   A copy of the Runners layer (called Runners copy) is created. Compare your document and History and Layers palettes to Figure N-4.

7. Click the Runners layer on the Layers palette.

8. Click the Indicates layer visibility button on the Runners copy layer. 👁

   Table N-1 reviews some of the possible selection methods you can use to remove unwanted imagery. You can use many more methods.

You saved a JPG file in the Photoshop format, converted a Background layer into an image layer, then made a copy of the image layer.

New file format

Copied layer

TABLE N-1: Image Removal Methods

tool	name	method
	Magnetic Lasso Tool	Trace an object along its edge, then click Edit ➢ Clear.
	Magic Wand Tool	Select by color, then click Edit ➢ Clear.
	Clone Stamp Tool	Press and hold [Alt] (Win) or [option] (Mac), click sample area, release [Alt] (Win) or [option] (Mac), then click areas you want to remove.
	Rectangular Marquee Tool	Select area, press and hold [Alt] (Win) or [option] (Mac), select Move Tool, drag selection to new location.
	Elliptical Marquee Tool	Select area, press and hold [Alt] (Win) or [option] (Mac), select Move Tool, drag selection to new location.
	Eraser Tool	Drag over pixels to be removed.
	Patch Tool	Select source/destination, then drag to destination/source.

Imagery surrounded
by marquee

FIGURE N-6
Cleared selection

Area with
deleted pixels

Remove imagery with the Magnetic Lasso Tool

1. Click the Zoom Tool on the toolbox. 🔍

> **TIP** Make sure the Resize Windows To Fit check box is selected.

2. Click the woman in the pink jogging suit until the zoom level is 200%.

3. Click the Magnetic Lasso Tool on the toolbox. 🔗

4. Drag the pointer around the woman in pink. 🔗

5. Click to close the selection (when the "o" appears on the pointer, indicating that you have reached the starting point). Compare your selection to Figure N-5.

> **TIP** You can also use the Eraser Tool to delete the woman in pink, although it would be difficult to erase all the nooks and crannies.

6. Click Edit on the menu bar, then click Clear.

> **TIP** You can also cut a selection by clicking Edit on the menu bar, then clicking Cut, which allows you to paste the selection elsewhere by clicking Edit on the menu bar, then clicking Paste.

7. Click Select on the menu bar, then click Deselect.

8. Click the Eraser Tool on the toolbox. 🧽

9. Drag the pointer (using any brush size) over remaining pixels. Compare your image to Figure N-6. ⭕

You used the Zoom Tool to get a closer look at an image, then used a combination of the Magnetic Lasso Tool and the Eraser Tool to eliminate unwanted imagery.

Duplicate imagery

1. Display the rulers in pixels, if necessary.

2. Click the Lasso Tool on the toolbox.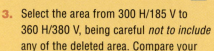

3. Select the area from 300 H/185 V to 360 H/380 V, being careful *not to include* any of the deleted area. Compare your selection to Figure N-7.

4. Press and hold [Ctrl][Alt] (Win) or [command][option] (Mac), drag the selection to the deleted object, then release [Ctrl][Alt] (Win) or [command][option] (Mac).

   The selection is duplicated over the deleted pixels.

   > TIP Pressing and holding [Ctrl] (Win) or [command] (Mac) lets you temporarily convert the current tool to the Move Tool.

5. Click Select on the menu bar, then click Deselect.

6. Repeat Steps 3 through 5 (using different selections as you see fit) as many times as necessary until all the deleted pixels are covered.

   The deleted pixels are covered with duplicated pixels. Compare your document to Figure N-8.

   > TIP You can use pixels from anywhere in the image. For example, you can create a selection from approximately 130 H/315 V to 145 H/360 V to create a more natural-looking background area.

You selected areas within the image and then duplicated them to cover deleted imagery and make the image look more natural.

Your selection size and shape will be different

FIGURE N-8
Image with duplicated pixels

Cloned pixels

Sampled area

Fooling the eye

You can replace pixels in an image, even though they may not be an exact match. Even if the replacement pixels are not technically accurate, the eye can be tricked into thinking that the image looks reasonable. For example, you can duplicate ground and sky pixels, and while they might not be perfect, a reader's eye will accept them as looking "right." However, the reverse is not necessarily true. If you remove a woman from an image, but you neglect to remove all the pixels for the woman's hair, the reader's eye would probably recognize the incongruity of hair with no person attached. Remnants of dangling hair would almost certainly bring into question the accuracy of the image.

Image with new layer and mask

Layer
created
from
selection

Create a layer from a selection

1. Click the Elliptical Marquee Tool on the tool-box, then verify that the Feather setting is set to 0 px. ⬭

2. Drag the pointer from 135 H/195 V to 220 H/440 V. ┼

3. Click Layer on the menu bar, point to New, then click Layer via Copy.

   A new layer containing the selection is created and is the active layer.

4. Click the Runners layer on the Layers palette.

5. Drag the pointer from 140 H/200 V to 215 H/435 V. ┼

6. Click Layer on the menu bar, point to Add Layer Mask, then click Hide Selection.

   A layer mask is placed over the selection on the Runners layer. The mask will be used to highlight the image of the woman runner.

7. Hide the rulers.

8. Click the Zoom Tool on the toolbox. 🔍

9. Press and hold [Alt] (Win) or [option] (Mac), click the image until the zoom level is 100%, then release [Alt] (Win) or [option] (Mac). 🔍

10. Save your work, then compare your document to Figure N-9.

You created a new layer from a selection, then added a layer mask to a selection.

Correcting color

You can make color corrections on a layer in a number of ways. One option is to make your corrections directly on the original layer. Another option is to make a copy of the original layer *before* making the corrections on the layer. You can also make your corrections using adjustment layers, and then merge the layers down when you are satisfied with the results. You can add an adjustment layer to the current layer by clicking Layer on the menu bar, pointing to New Adjustment Layer, then clicking the type of adjustment you want to make.

CORRECT COLORS IN AN IMAGE

What You'll Do

In this lesson, you'll add zip to an image that appears bleached out by making color adjustments to a specific layer.

Revitalizing an Image

You may find that you are working with an image that is perfectly fine except that it seems washed out or just in the doldrums. You may be able to spice up such an image by adjusting the color settings. By modifying the color balance, for example, you can increase the red tones while decreasing the green and blue tones to make the image look more realistic and dramatic. After you select the layer that you want to adjust, you can make color-correcting adjustments by clicking Image on the menu bar, pointing to Adjustments, then clicking the type of color adjustment you want to make.

Making Color Adjustments

So, the image you're working with seems to need *something*, but you're not quite sure what. Until you become comfortable making color corrections, do everything in your power to provide yourself with a safety net. Create duplicate layers and use adjustment layers instead of making corrections directly on the original layer. Before you begin, take a long look at the image and ask yourself, "What's lacking?" Is the problem composition, or is it truly a color problem? Do the colors appear washed out rather than vibrant and true to life? Is the color deficiency really a problem, or does the image's appearance work with what you're trying to accomplish?

Assessing the Mood

Not every image will be a vision of happiness. For example, if you are trying to create a sad mood, maybe all you have to do is correct the color. After you establish that your image does need color correction, start slow. Try balancing the color and see if that gives you the effect you want. Keep experimenting with the various color correction options until you find the method that works for you.

FIGURE N-10
Color Balance dialog box

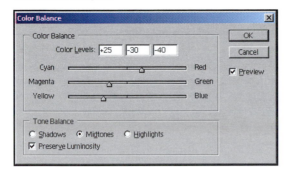

FIGURE N-12
Color-corrected image

Corrected pixels
created from
selection

FIGURE N-11
Brightness/Contrast dialog box

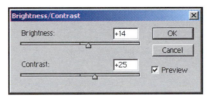

FIGURE N-13
Layers palette

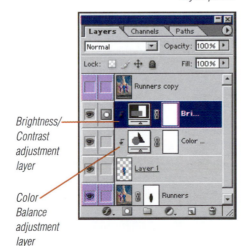

Brightness/
Contrast
adjustment
layer

Color
Balance
adjustment
layer

Correct colors in an image

1. Click Layer 1 on the Layers palette.

2. Click Layer on the menu bar, point to New Adjustment Layer, then click Color Balance.

3. Select the Group With Previous Layer check box, then click OK.

4. Change the settings in the Color Balance dialog box, using Figure N-10 as a guide, then click OK.

5. Click Layer on the menu bar, point to New Adjustment Layer, then click Brightness/Contrast.

6. Select the Group With Previous Layer check box, then click OK.

7. Change the settings, using Figure N-11 as a guide, then click OK.

8. Save your work, then compare your document to Figure N-12 and the Layers palette to Figure N-13.

You adjusted the color balance and brightness/contrast in the layer created from a selection, making the image of the woman stand out. You made color adjustments using adjustment layers, which you grouped with the Runners layer.

FIX A BACKGROUND

What You'll Do

Runners.psd @ 100% (Layer 1, R...

In this lesson, you'll crop out unnecessary imagery. You'll also add a layer style to enhance the image, and draw attention away from the background.

Cropping an Image

Sometimes an image can have too much imagery. For example, in the image of the runners, there's too much sky and road. Of course, *you* have to determine the central focus of the image and what it is you want the reader to see. Is the subject of the image the road, the sky, or the runners? Is it both of the runners or one in particular? If your image suffers from too much of the wrong imagery, you can help your reader by getting rid of those images that are not needed and possibly distracting. This type of deletion not only removes imagery, but changes the size and shape of the document. You can make this type of change using the Crop Tool on the toolbox. When you make a selection within an image, you can use cropped area settings (the Shield check box and the Opacity list arrow) on the tool options bar to see how the document will appear after it has been cropped.

Adding Layer Styles

Image layers—in the background and elsewhere—can also benefit from the styles that are usually applied to type layers, such as Drop Shadow and Inner Shadow. After you have selected the layer you want to modify, click the Add a layer style button on the Layers palette. You can add one or more of the styles simultaneously in the Layer Style dialog box. Each of the added styles will appear on the Layers palette.

Taking an image from weak to wild

Suppose you have an image that would be really terrific to use, but it has some "problems." Maybe the colors are wrong, or there are imperfections that are just beyond your Photoshop abilities. Should you just get rid of it and look for a better image, or can it be salvaged? Perhaps you can turn these imperfections into features. Try using a combination of filters and distortions to turn negative aspects into positive attributes.

FIGURE N-14
Cropped area in image

— *Darker area will be deleted during cropping*

— *Dotted line indicates new image boundaries*

FIGURE N-16
Layers palette for completed image

— *Style applied to layer*

FIGURE N-15
Completed image

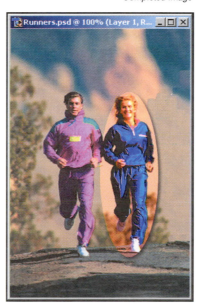

1. Display the rulers in pixels.

2. Click the Crop Tool on the toolbox. ⊟

3. Drag the pointer from 5 H/100 V to 270 H/500 V. ⊟

   The area that will be cropped from the image appears darker, as shown in Figure N-14.

4. Click the Commit current crop operation button on the tool options bar. ✔

   The cropped imagery is discarded from the document.

5. Hide the rulers.

6. Click Layer 1 on the Layers palette.

7. Click the Add a layer style button on the Layers palette. ⊘.

8. Click Drop Shadow, use the default settings, then click OK.

9. Save your work, then compare your image to Figure N-15 and the Layers palette to Figure N-16.

You cropped the image, then applied the Drop Shadow style to the layer created from a selection.

Power User Shortcuts

to do this:	use this method:
Add layer style	⬦ , click style(s)
Clear selection	Edit ➤ Clear
Clone an area	🖿 or **Shift S**, press and hold [Alt] (Win) or option (Mac), click sample area, release [Alt] (Win) or option (Mac), then click areas you want cloned
Create an adjustment layer	Layer ➤ New Adjustment Layer ➤ type of adjustment
Create layer from selection	Layer ➤ New ➤ Layer via Copy
Crop an image	⬚
Cut selection	Edit ➤ Cut, or [Ctrl][X] (Win) or ⌘ [X] (Mac)
Deselect selection	Select ➤ Deselect, or [Ctrl][D] (Win) or ⌘ [D] (Mac)

to do this:	use this method:
Duplicate a layer	Drag layer to 🖿
Duplicate a selection and move it to a new location	⬚ or ◯ or **Shift M**, create selection, press and hold [Ctrl][Alt] (Win) or ⌘ option (Mac), then drag selection to new location
Erase pixels	⬦ or **Shift E**, drag pointer over pixels to be removed
Magnify an area	🔍 or **Z**, then click image
Paste selection	Edit ➤ Paste, or [Ctrl][V] (Win) or ⌘ [V] (Mac)
Select a complex object	⬦ or **Shift L**
Select by color	⬦ or **W**, then click Edit ➤ Clear

Key: Menu items are indicated by ➤ between the menu name and its command. Blue bold letters are shortcuts for selecting tools on the toolbox.

Delete unnecessary imagery.

1. Open PS N-2.psd, then save it as **Treasure Shop**.
2. Zoom into the metronome.
3. Use the Magnetic Lasso Tool to select as much of the metronome as possible *without* selecting the toy boat or telephone. (*Hint*: You can use the Add to selection button on the tool options bar, or you can make multiple selections.)
4. Clear the metronome selection from the image.
5. Deselect the selection.
6. Use the Eraser Tool and any size brush tip to get rid of the remnants of the metronome.
7. Create a selection around the telephone and its cord using the Magnetic Lasso Tool. (*Hint*: You can use multiple selections to select this object.)
8. Clear the selection. (*Hint*: You will repair the defects created by this step later.)
9. Deselect the marquee.
10. Use the Eraser Tool and any size brush tip to get rid of the remnants of the telephone.
11. Sample the red in the damaged area of the toy boat.
12. Use the Brush Tool and any size brush tip to repair the damaged toy boat (where the telephone was removed).
13. Zoom out to the original magnification.
14. Save your work.

Correct colors in an image.

1. Make the Whistle layer active.
2. Create a Color Balance adjustment layer that is grouped with the previous layer. (Accept the default layer name.)
3. Correct the Cyan/Red level to +73, and the Magenta/Green level to –57.
4. Create a Brightness/Contrast adjustment layer that is grouped with the previous layer. (Accept the default layer name.)
5. Change the Brightness slider to –10 and the Contrast slider to +15.
6. Use the bounding box feature to rotate the whistle, then nudge the object up using the sample in Figure N-17 as a guide.
7. Make the Toy Boat layer active.
8. Create a Hue/Saturation adjustment layer that is grouped with the previous layer. (Accept the default layer name.)
9. Change the Hue slider to +15 and the Saturation slider to +35.
10. Save your work.

Fix a background.

1. Hide the Background layer.
2. Make the Push Pins layer active.
3. Use the Magnetic Lasso Tool and the Patch Tool to remove the two shadows to the left and right of the body of the whistle using Figure N-17 as a guide. (*Hint*: You can magnify the area, if necessary.)

4. Apply the Ocean Ripple (Distort) filter using the following settings: Ripple Size = 3, Ripple Magnitude = 6.
5. Display the Background layer.
6. Change the opacity of the Push Pins layer to 90%.
7. Apply the Drop Shadow style to the Toy Boat layer using the default settings.
8. Make the Push Pins layer active.
9. Use the Horizontal Type Tool to create a red type layer in the upper-right corner of the image that says Treasure Shop. (In the sample, a Tempus Sans ITC font is used.)
10. Add the following styles to the type: Drop Shadow and Bevel and Emboss.
11. Save your work, then compare your document to the sample in Figure N-17.

FIGURE N-17
Completed Skills Review

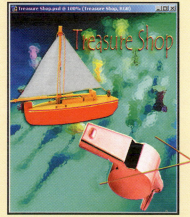

Shadow removed here

An exclusive women's clothing shop, Only The Best, has hired you to revamp its image by creating the first in a series of advertisements. Only The Best has been known for some time as a stuffy clothing store that sells pricey designer originals to the over-60 set. The time has come to increase its customer base to include women between the ages of 30 and 60. Their advertising agency recommended you, having seen samples of your work. They want you to inject some humor into your creation. They have provided you with some whimsical images they want to see in the ad.

1. Open PS N-3.psd, then save it as **Only The Best**.
2. Separate each of the items in the Glasses, Necklace, Bags layer into their own layers. (*Hint*: You can use the selection method(s) of your choice.)
3. Rename the layers using appropriate names.
4. Apply colors to each renamed thumbnail on the Layers palette.
5. Rearrange the objects as you see fit.
6. Use the bounding box feature to resize the glasses, bags, or neckace, using your discretion.
7. Transform the size of the fan so it is smaller. (*Hint*: You can use the Scale command.)

8. Make a duplicate of the Glasses layer, accepting the default name.
9. Hide the original Glasses layer.
10. Use the Liquify feature on the duplicate Glasses layer using your choice of effects.
11. Add at least one adjustment layer, as you feel necessary. (*Hint*: In the sample, the brightness was adjusted to –8, and the contrast was adjusted to +35 in the Bags layer. In the Necklace layer, the following color balance adjustments were made: Cyan/Red level to +53, the Magenta/Green level to –65, and the Yellow/Blue level to –49. In the Roses layer, the brightness was adjusted to –55, and the contrast to –1.)

FIGURE N-18
Completed Project Builder 1

12. Add a type layer that says **Only The Best**. (*Hint*: You can use any color and any font available on your computer. In the sample, a 48 pt Script MT Bold font is shown.)
13. Warp the type layer using the style and the settings of your choice.
14. Apply the styles of your choice to the text.
15. Adjust the opacity of the Roses layer using any setting you feel is appropriate.
16. Add any filter effects you want. (In the sample, the Smudge Stick filter is applied to the Roses layer, and the Lens Flare filter is applied to the Glasses copy layer.)
17. Save your work, then compare your document to the sample in Figure N-18.

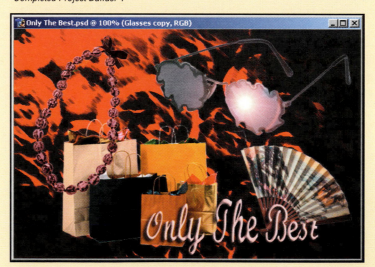

Your local chamber of commerce has asked you to volunteer your services and design a new advertisement for the upcoming membership drive. The theme of this year's membership drive is "The Keys to the City." They have supplied you with an initial image, but the rest is up to you.

1. Open PS N-4.psd, then save it as **Membership Drive**.
2. Convert the Background layer into an image layer.
3. Rename the layer using any name you want, then apply a color to the thumbnail.
4. Create a new layer, then convert it into a Background layer.
5. Locate at least one piece of appropriate artwork—either a scanned image, an image on your computer, one from a digital camera, or an image from a royalty-free collection—that you can use in this document.
6. Use any appropriate methods to select imagery from the artwork.
7. After the selections have been made, copy them into Membership Drive.
8. Transform any imagery, if necessary.
9. Use any method to eliminate some of the keys in the image. (In the sample, the third key from the bottom is eliminated.)
10. Add a type layer that contains a snappy phrase using the text of your choice. (*Hint*: You can use any color and any font available on your computer. In the sample, a Perpetua font in various sizes is shown.)
11. Add another type layer that contains the chamber of commerce name. (*Hint*: You can use the name of the town in which you live.)
12. Add an adjustment layer to at least one of the layers.
13. Modify the layer containing the keys using any method(s) you want. (In the sample, the opacity is lowered to 86%, and the Tiles filter is applied.)
14. Save your work, then compare your document to the sample in Figure N-19.

FIGURE N-19
Completed Project Builder 2

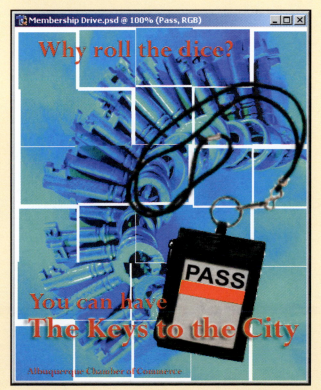

DESIGN PROJECT

You have seen how Photoshop can take ordinary photographs and manipulate them into exciting artistic creations. The Museum of Computer Art features many new and exciting artists who specialize in photo manipulation; among them is Pablo Rios. As a final project in Photoshop usage, your instructor has asked you to examine an artistic work, then *deconstruct it* to speculate as to how it was accomplished.

1. Connect to the Internet and go to *www.course.com*, navigate to the page for this book, click the Student Online Companion link, then click the link for this unit.
2. Click the link for Montage Work, then click Montage 3. A sample image is shown in Figure N-20.
3. Examine the image, then ask yourself the following questions.
   - What images would you need to create this montage? In what format would you need them (electronic file, hard-copy image, or photograph)?
   - What techniques would you use to create this effect?
   - Do you like this image? If so, why?

4. Be prepared to discuss your answers to these questions, either in writing, in a group discussion, or in a presentation format. Using your favorite word processor, create a document called Montage Analysis that records your observations.

FIGURE N-20
Completed Design Project

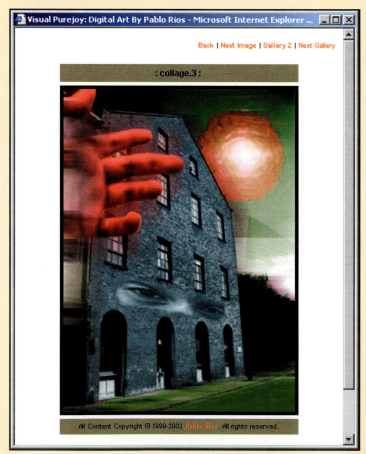

Depending on the size of your group, you can assign individual elements of the project to group members, or work collectively to create the finished product.

You are about to graduate from The Art School, a local, independently owned school that trains artists in the use of all art media. Because of your talent, you have been asked to create next year's poster for the school. Because this can be a complex undertaking, you have decided to determine the individual tasks necessary to complete this assignment, assemble a team, and distribute the tasks.

1. Create a new Photoshop document with any dimensions you want.
2. Save this file as **Art School Poster**.
3. Locate several pieces of artwork—either on your hard disk, in a royalty-free collection, from a digital camera, or from scanned images. The images can show anything that is art-related and can be part of other images.
4. Name each layer and apply a color to each layer thumbnail.
5. Transform any imagery, if necessary.

6. Add a type layer that contains a phrase you like. (*Hint*: You can use any color and any font available on your computer. A Pristina font in various sizes is used in the sample.)
7. Add an adjustment layer to at least one of the layers.

8. Add any filter effects, if you decide they will make your document more dramatic.
9. Save your work, then compare your document to the sample in Figure N-21.

FIGURE N-21
Completed Group Project

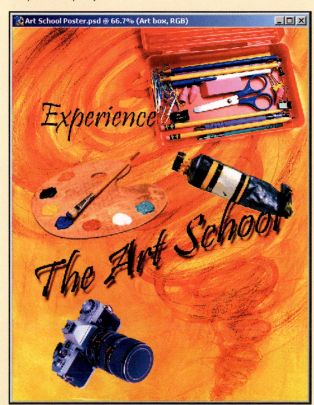

UNIT O

ANNOTATING AND AUTOMATING A DOCUMENT

1. Add annotations to a document.

2. Learn about actions and how they are created.

3. Modify an action.

4. Use a default action and create a droplet.

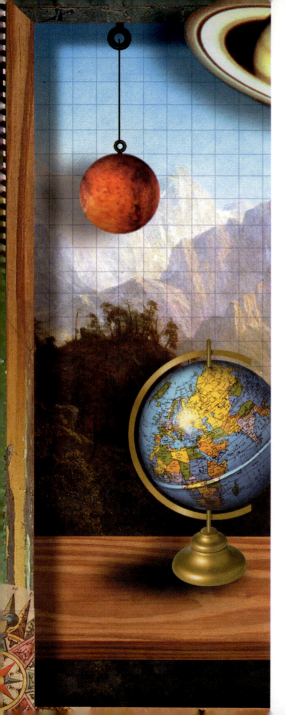

UNIT O

ANNOTATING AND AUTOMATING A DOCUMENT

Creating Annotations

Have you ever wished you could paste a sticky note on an electronic file, or wished that you could actually speak to the person looking at your document? Well, in Photoshop you can do both by using visual and audio annotations.

Communicating Directly to Your Audience

By creating written notes and audio **annotations**, you can communicate directly to the person viewing your document. You can place written comments—like electronic sticky notes—right in a document. If your computer has sound input capabilities, you can place spoken comments in the document as well. For both types of annotations, anyone viewing your document can double-click the text or sound icon, and then read or hear your comments.

Using Automation

Have you ever performed a repetitive task in Photoshop? Suppose you create a document with several type layers containing different fonts, and then you decide that

each of those type layers should use the same font family. To make this change, you would have to perform the following steps on each type layer:

- Select the layer
- Double-click the layer thumbnail
- Click the Set the font family list arrow
- Click the font you want
- Click the Commit any current edits button

Surely, there must be an easier way to speed up commonly performed tasks. Using the Actions feature in Photoshop, you can record these five steps in one action. Then, rather than having to repeat each of the steps, you can just play the action.

Simplifying Common Tasks

An **action** is a series of tasks that can be recorded and saved for future use. Suppose you are responsible for maintaining the ad slicks for all your company's products (and there are a lot of them). What would you do if the company decided to change each existing advertisement so that each product would be shown with Drop Shadow and Inner Shadow styles? (*Hint:* Resigning your position is *not* an option.) You could create an action that would considerably speed up this monumental task.

QUICKTIP

Many programs have a feature that records tasks. Other programs call this feature a macro, script, or behavior.

Ensuring Consistency

You can create and modify actions, and use them in other Photoshop documents. Using actions not only speeds up boring, repetitive tasks, but more importantly, ensures consistency among documents. Repeating the same tasks can cause you to accidentally make the wrong selections or make omissions, which can make you and your work look sloppy and unprofessional.

QUICKTIP

Think of an action as a double-edged tool: it helps you complete tasks easier and faster, and it helps you look more professional.

Tools You'll Use

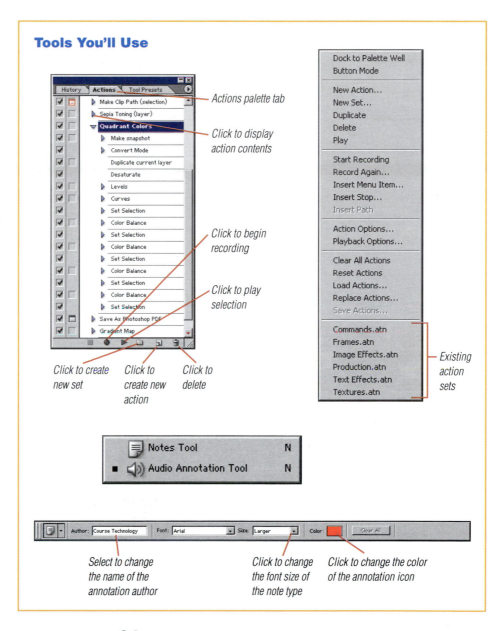

ADD ANNOTATIONS TO A DOCUMENT

What You'll Do

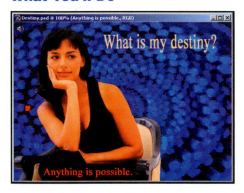

In this lesson, you'll create a text and audio annotation.

Creating a Written Annotation

You use the Notes Tool to create written annotations, which are similar to the yellow sticky notes you might attach to a printout. You can create a note by clicking the Notes Tool on the toolbox, clicking where you want the note to appear in your document, then typing the contents. Each note within a file has an icon that is displayed on the document, as shown in Figure O-1 (although neither the icon nor the note itself can be printed). To open a closed note, double-click the note icon. You can also right-click (Win) or [control]-click (Mac) the note icon, then click Open Note, as shown in Figure O-1. Although you can adjust the size of the note's window, scroll bars will appear if the amount of text exceeds the window size. You can move the note within the document by dragging the note's title bar or icon.

QUICK TIP

You can delete a selected note by pressing [Delete] or by right-clicking the note (Win) or [control]-clicking the note (Mac), then clicking Delete Note.

Personalizing a Note

By default, the title bar of a note is pale yellow. You can change the color of the note's title bar by clicking the Annotation color color box on the tool options bar. When the Color Picker dialog box opens, you can use any method to change the color, such as sampling an area within an existing document. You can also change the author of the note by selecting the contents in the Name of author for annotations text box, typing the information you want, then pressing [Enter] (Win) or [return] (Mac).

Creating an Audio Annotation

Sometimes the next best thing to an in-person presentation is the use of an audio annotation. An **audio annotation** is a sound file that is saved within a document. This feature lets you use your own voice to describe exactly what you want to say. You create an audio annotation by using the Audio Annotation Tool on the toolbox. After this tool is active, click the location in the document where you want the annotation, then click the Start button in the Audio Annotation dialog box (Win) shown in Figure O-2. Like the note icon, the audio icon can be moved within the document by dragging it. To play the audio annotation, double-click the audio icon, shown in Figure O-3. You can tell the difference between written and audio annotations by the appearance of the icons.

FIGURE O-1
Open note in a document

FIGURE O-2
Audio Annotation dialog box

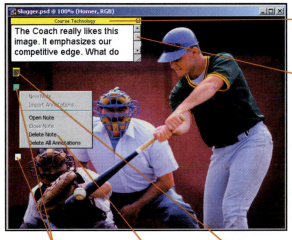

Name of author appears here

Scroll bar indicates additional text

Solid color indicates closed notes

Click to delete note

Color outline indicates open or selected note

FIGURE O-3
Audio icon

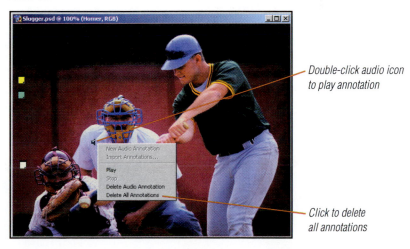

Double-click audio icon to play annotation

Click to delete all annotations

Create a text annotation

1. Open PS O-1.psd, then save the file as **Destiny**.

2. Click the Notes Tool on the toolbox.

3. If your name does not appear in the Name of author for annotations text box on the tool options bar, select the contents of the text box, type your name, then press [Enter] (Win) or [return] (Mac).

4. Click the Font size used for notes list arrow on the tool options bar, then click Largest, if necessary. Size: [Medium ▾]

5. Click the Annotation color color box on the tools options bar. Color: [ ]

6. Click the red letter "p" in the word "possible."

7. Click OK. Compare your tool options bar to Figure O-4.

   The Annotation color color box is red.

8. Click to the left of the woman's right shoulder.

9. Type the text shown in Figure O-5.

10. Click the Note close button at the top of the note.

    | **TIP** You can open a note by double-clicking the icon.

11. Click the note icon. Compare your image to Figure O-6.

You used the Notes Tool to create a written annotation within a document. You also specified an author and type size for the note, and you changed the color of the note title bar and icon by sampling a color in the document.

Your name will be different

FIGURE O-5
Notes annotation in document

Your title bar will be different

Note icon

I think our client will like this image. It's fresh and colorful, and contains an important message.

Note close button (this might appear on the left [Mac])

FIGURE O-6
Note icon

Closed note icon has the same color as the note title bar

FIGURE O-7

Options for the Audio Annotation Tool

FIGURE O-8

Audio annotation in document

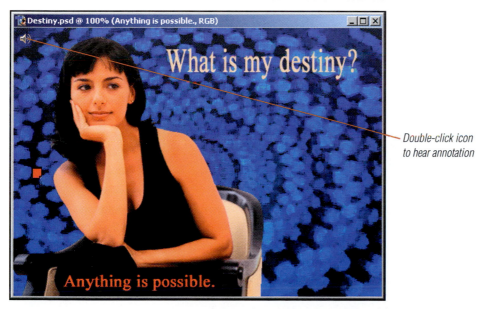

Double-click icon
to hear annotation

Create an audio annotation

1. Click and hold the Notes Tool on the toolbox until a list of tools appears. 📝

2. Click the Audio Annotation Tool on the toolbox. 🔊

   TIP   These steps will only work if you have the necessary sound hardware.

3. Click the Annotation color color box on the tool options bar, then click anywhere in the beige chair fabric. 🖋

4. Click OK. Compare your tool options bar to Figure O-7.

5. Click in the upper-left corner of the image. 🔊

6. Click Start (Win) or Record (Mac) in the Audio Annotation dialog box.

7. Record the following message: "The woman in the image is looking forward to the future."

8. Click Stop (Win) or Stop, then Save (Mac) in the Audio Annotation dialog box.

9. Double-click the audio icon.

10. Save your work, then compare your document to Figure O-8.

You used the Audio Annotation Tool to create an embedded sound message. You also changed the color of the audio icon.

LEARN ABOUT ACTIONS AND HOW THEY ARE CREATED

What You'll Do

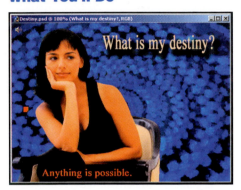

In this lesson, you'll create an action.

Understanding Actions

Most Photoshop tasks that can be performed using a button or menu command can be recorded as an action. Each action can contain one or more steps and can also contain a **stop**, which lets you complete a command that can't be recorded (for example, the use of a painting tool). Actions can be stored in sets, which are saved as .atn files and are typically named by the category of actions they contain. For example, you can create multiple type-related actions, then store them in a set named Type Actions. You access actions from the Actions palette, which is normally grouped with the History palette. You can view actions in list mode or in button mode on the Actions palette. The **list mode**, the default, makes it possible to view the details within each action. The **button mode** displays each action without details.

QUICKTIP

The act of creating an action is not recorded in the History palette; however, the steps you record to define a new action are recorded in the History palette.

Knowing Your Options When Using Actions

You use commonly recognizable VCR-like buttons to operate an action. These buttons are located at the bottom of the Actions palette and let you play, record, stop, and move forward and backward in an action.

Recording an Action

When recording is taking place, the red Recording button on the Actions palette appears. The action set also opens as soon as you begin recording, to show all the individual actions in the set.

QUICKTIP

You can create a snapshot of your image before you work on an action, make any changes, or record new steps, then use the snapshot to restore the document to its original state. After the document is restored, you can play the action to verify that the steps work. This is a handy way to test your actions.

Playing Back Actions

You can modify how actions are played back using the Playback Options dialog box, as shown in Figure O-9. All the playback options are described in Table O-1. You can open the Playback Options dialog box by clicking the Actions palette list arrow, then clicking Playback Options. The Accelerated, Step by Step, and Pause For options control the speed at which the steps are performed.

QUICKTIP

You can reset the actions to their default settings by clicking the Actions palette list arrow, then clicking Reset Actions. Click OK to delete new actions, or Append to add new actions to the set of default actions.

Resizing the Actions Palette

By default, the Actions palette window is quite small. You can enlarge it by dragging the bottom edge of the palette to a more comfortable length.

QUICKTIP

You can return the Actions palette to its original size and location by clicking Window on the menu bar, pointing to Workspace, then clicking Reset Palette Locations.

FIGURE O-9
Playback Options dialog box

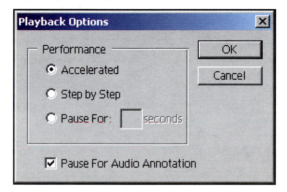

TABLE O-1: Action Playback Options

option	description
Accelerated	Plays all steps within an action, then makes all changes.
Step by Step	Completes each step in an action and redraws the image before advancing to the next step.
Pause For	Lets you specify the number of seconds that should occur between steps in an action.
Pause For Audio Annotation	If audio annotations are in use, this option ensures that the annotation is played before the action advances to the next step.

Create a snapshot and an action

1. Click the Create new snapshot button on the History palette.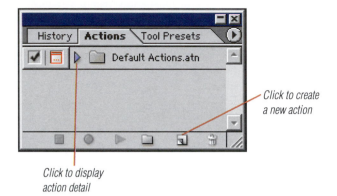

   Snapshot 1 is created and appears in the History palette.

2. Click the Actions palette tab. `Actions`

3. Click the collapse detail triangle to the left of the Default Actions.atn set on the Actions palette, to close the set, if necessary. Compare your palette to Figure O-10.

   You can click the triangle next to a *set* to show or hide the actions in it. You can also click the triangle next to an *action* to show or hide the steps in it.

   > **TIP** When you create an action in the Default Actions.atn set, this action will be available in all your Photoshop documents.

4. Click the Create new action button on the Actions palette.

   The New Action dialog box opens.

5. Type **Modify Type** in the Name text box.

6. Click the Color list arrow, then click Orange. Compare your New Action dialog box to Figure O-11.

7. Click Record. Did you notice that the red Recording button is displayed on the Actions palette? See Figure O-12.

You created a snapshot to make it possible to easily test the new action. You used the Create new action button on the Actions palette to create an action called Modify Type.

FIGURE O-10
Actions palette with detail hidden

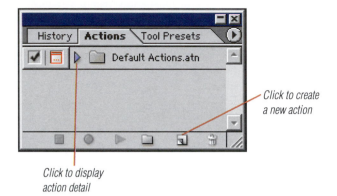

Click to create
a new action

Click to display
action detail

FIGURE O-11
New Action dialog box

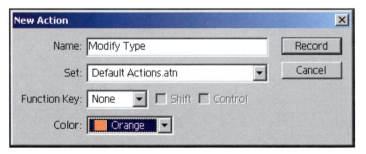

FIGURE O-12
New action

The location of the
action in the list
might be different

Indicates recording
in progress

FIGURE O-13
Layer Style dialog box

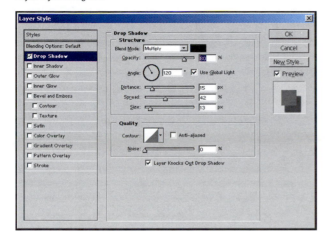

FIGURE O-14
Selected action

FIGURE O-15
Modified document

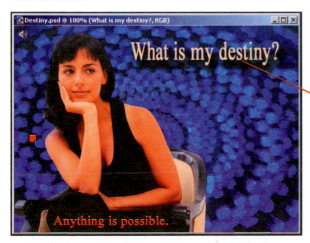

Drop shadow
behind text

Lesson 2   Learn About Actions and How They Are Created

1. Click the What is my destiny? layer on the Layers palette.

2. Click the Add a layer style button on the Layers palette, click Drop Shadow, then change your Layer Style dialog box settings to match those shown in Figure O-13.

3. Click OK.

4. Click the Stop playing/recording button on the Actions palette.

5. Click the Modify Type action. See Figure O-14.

6. Click the History palette tab. History

7. Scroll to the top of the History palette if necessary, then click Snapshot 1.

   The type layer returns to its original appearance.

8. Click the Actions palette tab. Actions

9. Click the Play selection button on the Actions palette.

10. Save your work, then compare your document to Figure O-15.

You recorded steps for the Modify Type action. After the recording was complete, you used a snapshot to restore the image to its original state, then you played the action to verify its accuracy.

MODIFY AN ACTION

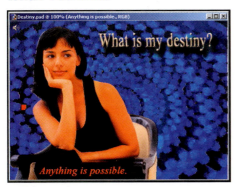

In this lesson, you'll add new steps to the recently created action.

Getting It Right the First Time

If you're like most people, you rarely get things right on the first shot. This is not an insult, but reality. After you create an action, you might think of other steps to include in it, an order of steps to change, or an option you want to alter. The beauty of Photoshop actions is that you can make modifications and additions to them with little effort.

Revising an Action

You can modify an existing action by clicking the step that will come after or before the new steps that you want to add. After you have selected the step, click the Begin recording button on the Actions palette, record your steps (just as you do when you initially create the action), then click the Stop playing/recording button when you're finished.

Understanding a stop

In addition to containing any Photoshop task, an action can include a stop, which is a command that interrupts playback to allow you to perform other operations. You insert a stop by clicking the step *just above* where you want the pause to take place. Click the Actions palette list arrow, then click Insert Stop. The Record Stop dialog box opens, allowing you to enter a text message that appears when the action is stopped, as shown in Figure O-19. You select the Allow Continue check box to include a Continue button in the message that appears when the action is stopped. You can resume the action by clicking this button. An action that contains a dialog box—such as an action that contains a stop—displays a toggle dialog on/off icon to the left of the action name on the Actions palette. This icon indicates a **modal control**, which means that dialog boxes are *used* in the action, but are not displayed. When the action is resumed, the tasks begin where they were interrupted. You can resume the action by clicking the Play selection button on the Actions palette.

Changing the Actions Palette View

In addition to elongating the Actions palette, you can also change the appearance of its contents. By default, actions are displayed in list mode, in which you can display the steps included in them. Figure O-16 shows the actions in the Default Actions set in list mode in which all the detail is accessible but hidden. (Remember that you can display the detail for each action by clicking the triangle next to the action, to expand it.)

Using the Button Mode

In button mode, each of the actions is displayed as a button—without the additional detail found in the list mode. Each button is displayed in a color, if you chose this option when the action was created. Figure O-17 shows the same actions in button mode. You can toggle between these two modes by clicking the Actions palette list arrow, then clicking Button Mode, as shown in Figure O-18.

QUICKTIP

Because users may not know how to resume playback after encountering a stop, it's a good idea to include a helpful tip that tells them to click the Play selection button after encountering the stop.

Click to toggle a dialog on and off

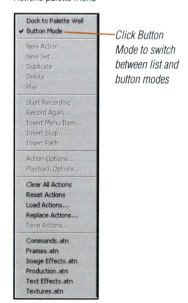

Click Button Mode to switch between list and button modes

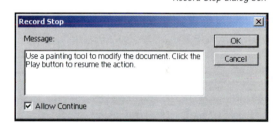

Add steps to an action

1. Verify that the What is my destiny? layer is active.

2. Click the Set Layer Styles of current layer step (the second step) in the Modify Type action on the Actions palette.

3. Click the Begin recording button on the Actions palette. ⬤

4. Click the Anything is possible. layer on the Layers palette.

5. Double-click the layer thumbnail for the active layer.

6. Click the Set the font style list arrow on the tool options bar, then click Italic. Compare your tool options bar to Figure O-20.

7. Click the Commit any current edits button on the tool options bar. ✔

8. Click the Stop playing/recording button on the Actions palette. Compare your Actions palette to Figure O-21. ■

   The Modify Type action has new steps added to it.

9. Click the History palette tab, then click Snapshot 1. History

10. Click the Actions palette tab. Actions

11. Click the Modify Type action, then click the Play selection button on the Actions palette. Compare your screen to Figure O-22. ▶

You added new steps (which modified type in another layer) to the Modify Type action.

FIGURE O-22
Result of modified action

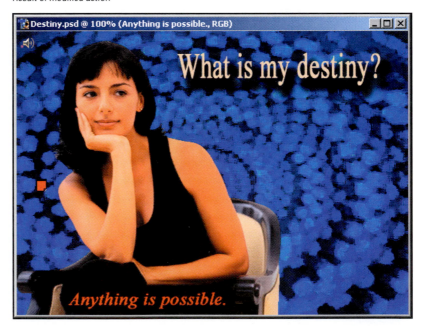

Annotating and Automating a Document

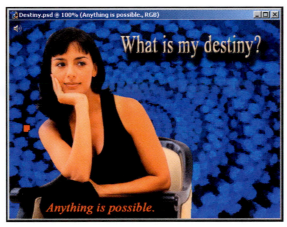

Modify steps in an action

1. Click the What is my destiny? layer on the Layers palette.

2. Click the Set Layer Styles of current layer step in the Actions palette (the second step), as shown in Figure O-23.

3. Click the Begin recording button on the Actions palette. ●

4. Click the Add a layer style button on the Layers palette. ⊘

5. Click Bevel and Emboss, then click OK to accept the existing settings.

6. Click the Stop playing/recording button on the Actions palette. ■

   The new steps are added to the existing action. Table O-2 describes other ways to modify actions.

7. Click the History palette tab, then click Snapshot 1. History

8. Click the Actions palette tab.

9. Click the Modify Type action, then click the Play selection button on the Actions palette. ▶

10. Save your work, then compare your document to Figure O-24.

You added the Bevel and Emboss style to an action, then you replayed the action.

TABLE O-2: Modifications for Actions

option	description
Rearrange steps	Move an existing step by dragging the step to a new location in the action.
Add new commands	Click the step above or below where you want the new step to appear, then click ●.
Rerecord existing commands	Click the step you want to duplicate, click ⊙, then click Record Again.
Duplicate existing commands	Click the step you want to duplicate, click ⊙, then click Duplicate.
Delete actions	Click the action you want to delete, then click 🗑.
Delete a step in an action	Click the step you want to delete, then click 🗑.
Change options	Click the step that has options you want to change, click ⊙, then click Action Options or Playback Options.

LESSON 4

USE A DEFAULT ACTION
AND CREATE A DROPLET

What You'll Do

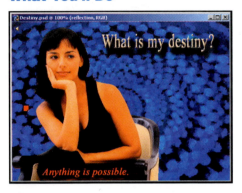

In this lesson, you'll use actions from other sets, and create a droplet.

Taking Advantage of Actions

Photoshop actions are too good to be true, right? But wait: it gets better. You can add a default action to any action you've created. This feature enables you to incorporate some of the nifty actions that come with Photoshop into those you create.

Identifying Default Actions

The default actions that come with Photoshop include Vignette, Frame Channel, Wood Frame, Cast Shadow, Water Reflection, Custom RGB to Grayscale, Molten Lead, Make Clip Path (selection), Sepia Toning (layer), Quadrant Colors,

Save As Photoshop PDF, and Gradient Map. In addition, there are six action sets that come with Photoshop: Commands, Frames, Image Effects, Production, Text Effects, and Textures. You can load any of these action sets by clicking the Actions palette list arrow, then clicking the name of the set you want to load.

Understanding a Droplet

A **droplet** is basically a stand-alone action in the form of an icon. You can drag one or more Photoshop files onto the droplet icon to perform the action on the file. You can store droplets on your hard drive,

Automating using batches

There may be times when you might need to perform the same action on multiple documents. Rather than dragging each document onto a droplet, one at a time, you can combine all of the documents into a batch. A **batch** is a group of documents designated to have the same action performed on them simultaneously. You can create a batch using all of the files in one specific folder or using all of the Photoshop documents that are currently open. When you have organized the files you want to include in a batch, click File on the menu bar, point to Automate, then click Batch. The Batch dialog box opens, offering you options similar to those used for creating droplets.

place them on your desktop, or distribute them to others. Figure O-25 shows an example of a droplet on the desktop. Droplets are a great feature that let you further automate your repetitive tasks.

Creating a Droplet

You can create a droplet by using the Automate command on the File menu, an existing action, and the Create Droplet dialog box. In the Create Droplet dialog box, you use the Set list arrow to choose the set that contains the action you want to use to create the droplet, then use the Action list arrow to choose the action. Finally, you can choose the location on your computer where you'll store the droplet.

QUICKTIP

When placed on the desktop, a droplet has a unique down-arrow icon filled with the Photoshop eye logo. The droplet name appears below the icon.

Using Default Actions

You can incorporate any of the default actions that come with Photoshop—or those you get from other sources—into a new action by playing the action you created while recording a new one. Each time an existing action is played, a new snapshot is created in the History palette, so don't be surprised when you see additional snapshots that you never created. To incorporate an existing action into a new action, first select the step that is above where you want the new action to occur. Click the Begin recording button, then scroll through the Actions palette until you find the action you want to use. Click the action, then click the Play selection button. When the action has completed all steps, you can continue recording other steps or click the Stop playing/recording button if you are done. That's it: all of the steps in the default action will be performed when you play your new action.

Loading Sets

In addition to the Default Actions set, the six additional sets of actions are listed at the bottom of the Actions palette menu. If you store actions from other sources on your hard drive, you can load those actions by clicking the Actions palette list arrow, clicking Load Actions, then choosing the action you want from the Load dialog box. The default sets that come with Photoshop are stored in the Photoshop Actions folder that is in the Presets folder of the Photoshop 7.0 folder.

QUICKTIP

If you want to save actions to distribute to others, you must first put them in a set. You create a set by clicking the Create new set button on the Actions palette (just like creating a Layer set). Place the action or actions in a set, select the set, click the Actions palette list arrow, then click Save Actions.

FIGURE O-25
A droplet on the desktop

Photoshop droplet

Insert an existing action within an action

1. Click the Set current text layer step at the bottom of the Actions palette (in the Modify Type action).

2. Verify that the Anything is possible. layer is selected.

3. Click the Begin recording button on the Actions palette.

   TIP If your Actions palette becomes too messy, you can clear all actions by clicking the Actions palette list arrow, then clicking Clear All Actions. The Default Actions set will be gone but can be restored by clicking the Actions palette list arrow, then clicking Reset Actions.

4. Scroll to the top of the Actions palette, then click the Water Reflection (type) action, as shown in Figure O-26.

   TIP The Water Reflection action adds a blurred shadow beneath the text (like a reflection), then rasterizes the type layer.

You selected the Water Reflection action from the Default Actions set to insert it into the Modify Type action.

FIGURE O-26

Action to be added to the Modify Type action

Click to play the selected action while recording

Water Reflection action in the Modify Type action

FIGURE O-28

Document with action replayed

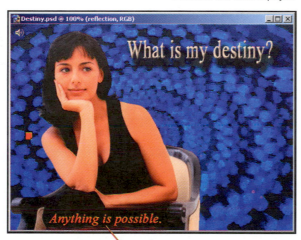

Reflection effect
from Water
Reflection action

FIGURE O-29

Modified Layers palette

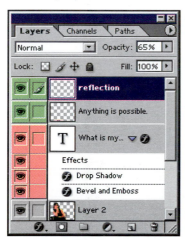

Play an existing action in a new action

1. Click the Play selection button on the Actions palette. ▶

2. Click the Stop playing/recording button on the Actions palette. Compare your Actions palette to Figure O-27. ■

3. Click the History palette tab, then click Snapshot 1. History

   TIP Some default actions create a snapshot as their initial step. For this reason, you might see multiple snapshots in your document.

4. Click the Actions palette tab. Actions

5. Click the Modify Type action.

6. Click the Play selection button on the Actions palette. ▶

7. Save your work, then compare your document to Figure O-28 and your Layers palette to Figure O-29.

   The Water Reflection action added a red blurred shadow beneath the text before rasterizing the type layer.

You played the Water Reflection action in the Modify Type action. You used the snapshot to revert to the document's original appearance and replayed the action, which modified the document.

Create a droplet

1. Click File on the menu bar, point to Automate, then click Create Droplet.

2. Click Choose in the Create Droplet dialog box.

   The Save dialog box opens.

3. Type **Modify Type** in the File name text box (Win) or Name text box (Mac) in the Save dialog box.

4. Click the Save in list arrow (Win) or Where list arrow (Mac), then click Desktop, as shown in Figure O-30.

   > TIP You can create a droplet on your hard drive by clicking the Save in list arrow (Win) or Where list arrow (Mac), and clicking the location where you want to store the file.

5. Click Save.

6. Click the Action list arrow, then click Modify Type, if necessary. Compare your dialog box settings to Figure O-31.

7. Click OK.

You created a droplet using the Modify Type action and saved it on the desktop.

FIGURE O-30
Save dialog box

Choose Desktop to save the droplet on the desktop

Your list will be different

FIGURE O-31
Create Droplet dialog box

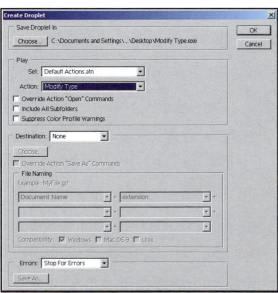

Icons on your
desktop will be
different

New droplet icon
on desktop

FIGURE O-33
Image updated by droplet

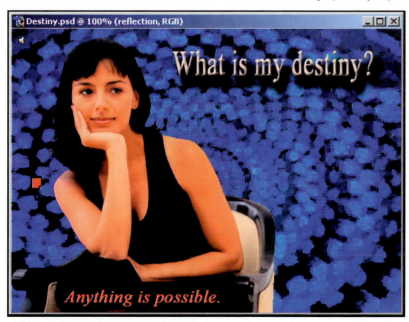

Run a droplet

1. Minimize all open windows so the desktop is visible, then compare your desktop to Figure O-32.

2. Maximize the Photoshop window.

3. Click the History palette tab, then click Snapshot 1. [History]

4. Save your work, close the Destiny document, then minimize Photoshop.

   TIP If Photoshop is *not* running, it is automatically launched when a droplet is activated.

5. Locate the Destiny document (keeping it closed) on your hard drive, and adjust the window so you can see the Destiny file and the droplet icon on the desktop.

6. Drag the Destiny file onto the droplet (on the desktop).

   The Photoshop window is restored and the action is replayed.

   TIP Sometimes a file automatically closes after a droplet has been applied to Photoshop. To see the applied droplet, you must reopen the file.

7. Save your work, then compare your document to Figure O-33.

You returned the document to its original appearance by using Snapshot 1 on the History palette, and closed the document. Then you tested the droplet by dropping the Destiny file onto the droplet.

SKILLS REFERENCE

Power User Shortcuts

to do this:	use this method:
Apply droplet	Drag closed Photoshop file onto droplet
Change audio annotation icon color	🔊 or **Shift N**, click Annotation color color box, choose color, then click OK
Change author display	📝 or **Shift N**, then type name in Name of author for annotations text box
Change Note icon color	📝 or **Shift N**, click Annotation color color box, choose color, then click OK
Close an open note	Click Note close button
Collapse action detail	🔻
Create a batch	File ➤ Automate ➤ Batch
Create a droplet	File ➤ Automate ➤ Create Droplet
Create a note	📝 or **Shift N**, then click where you want the note to appear
Create a snapshot	📷 on the History palette
Create an action	🔲 on the Actions palette, select options, then click Record

to do this:	use this method:
Create an audio annotation	🔊 or **Shift N**, click where you want the icon to appear, click Start (Win) or Record (Mac), record annotation, then click Stop (Win) or Stop then Save (Mac)
Delete a note	Select note, press [Delete]
Expand action detail	▷
Open a closed note	Double-click note icon
Play an action	▶
Play audio annotation	Double-click audio icon
Record an action	⬤, then perform tasks
Record an action from another set	⬤, click existing action in another set, click ▶, then click ⬛
Return Actions palette to original size and location	Window ➤ Workspace ➤ Reset Palette Locations
Revert document to original appearance using a snapshot	History , click snapshot
Stop recording	⬛
Toggle Actions palette between list and button modes	▶, then click Button Mode

Add annotations to a document.

1. Open PS O-2.psd, then save it as **Team Member**.
2. Select the Notes Tool.
3. If necessary, enter your name as the author of the note.
4. Change the Note color to Pure Magenta (the second box from the right in the fifth row of the Swatches palette).
5. Display the rulers, if necessary.
6. Click the image at 30 H/650 V, then type the following: **This will make a great motivational poster for our department**.
7. Close the note.
8. Select the Audio Annotation Tool.
9. Click the image at 800 H/800 V.
10. Record the following message, "Everyone's going to love this."
11. Close the Audio Annotation dialog box.
12. Play the Audio Annotation.
13. Hide the rulers, then save your work.

Learn about actions and how they are created.

1. Make the Each one an integral part of the system. layer active, if necessary.
2. Create a new snapshot using the History palette, then display the Actions palette.
3. Collapse the Default Actions.atn set.
4. Create a new action using the Actions palette.
5. Name the new action **Motivation**, and apply the color Violet to it.

6. Record the action using the following steps.
   a. Make the Team Members layer active.
   b. Change the font in this layer to an 85 pt Impact (or another font available on your computer).
   c. Stop recording.
7. Click Snapshot 1 on the History palette to restore the original appearance of the image.
8. Replay the Motivation action.

Modify an action.

1. Select Set current text layer of the Motivation action at the bottom of the Actions palette.
2. Begin recording the following steps.
   a. Make the Each one an integral part of the system. layer active.
   b. Change the font in this layer to a 36 pt Impact (or another font available on your computer).
   c. Make the Team Members layer active.
   d. Add the default Bevel and Emboss style with Texture to the layer.
   e. Stop recording.
3. Click Snapshot 1 on the History palette to restore the original appearance of the image.
4. Replay the Motivation action.

Use a default action and create a droplet.

1. Make the Each one an integral part of the system. layer active.
2. Select the Set Layer Styles of current layer step (the last step in the Motivation action).

3. Begin recording the following steps.
   a. Make the Team Members layer active.
   b. Play the Water Reflection action in Default Actions.atn.
   c. Stop recording.
4. Click Snapshot 1 on the History palette to restore the original appearance of the image.
5. Replay the Motivation action.
6. Create a droplet on the desktop called **Motivation** using the Motivation action, then exit Photoshop.
7. Drag the Team Member document onto the Motivation droplet. See Figure O-34.

FIGURE O-34
Completed Skills Review

As the newest member of the Game Corporation design team, you have noticed that some of your fellow designers perform many repetitive tasks and don't seem to know about actions. One of the tasks that the designers frequently perform is taking a single-layer document, creating a layer from the Background layer, creating a new layer, then turning the new layer into the Background layer. This way, they can preserve the Background layer and be able to modify the image that was on the existing Background layer. You want to make their lives easier, so you decide to create an action that completes this task. You also create a droplet for this action and circulate it among your co-workers.

1. Open PS O-3.psd, then save it as **New Layers**.
2. Create a snapshot of the current document using the default name.
3. Hide any displayed action details, if necessary.
4. Write down the steps you will need to perform to create this action. (You can use your favorite word processor or a sheet of paper.)
5. Create a new action in the Default Actions.atn set called **New Layers**.
6. Apply the yellow color to the action.
7. Record the steps you wrote down.

8. Use the snapshot to return the document to its original condition.
9. Play the action to verify that it works as you expected.
10. If the action does not perform as expected, make any necessary corrections to it.
11. Save your work, then compare your document, Layers palette, and Actions palette to the sample in Figure O-35.
12. Create a droplet named **Layer Conversion**, and save it on your desktop.

FIGURE O-35
Completed Project Builder 1

Annotating and Automating a Document

An anniversary is coming up for some friends of your family. You and your twin have decided to collaborate on a gift, even though you live at opposite sides of the country. You both have a great photo of the couple that you'd like to modify the same way, using Photoshop. Because your twin does not have much Photoshop experience and has a slow Internet connection, you decide to create a droplet (which is significantly smaller in size than a completed Photoshop document), then e-mail the droplet as an attachment. The droplet can be used to apply your proposed modifications to the picture.

1. Open PS O-4.psd, then save it as **Anniversary Gift**.
2. Create a snapshot of the current document using the default name.
3. After examining the image, decide what changes you want to make. Write down the steps you will need to perform to create this action. (*Hint*: You can use any of your Photoshop skills and any Photoshop features. It is recommended that you create a layer from the Background layer, then create a new layer to be used as the Background layer. Include any necessary color corrections in adjustment layers.)
4. Create a new action in the Default Actions.atn set called **Image Modifications**.
5. Apply the yellow color to the action.

6. Record the steps you wrote down. (*Hint*: In the sample, a 48 pt Trebuchet MS font is used. You do not have to include a type layer, but if you do, use any font available on your computer.)
7. Use the snapshot to return the document to its original condition.
8. Play the action to verify that it works as you expected.

FIGURE O-36
Completed Project Builder 2

9. If the action does not perform as expected, make any necessary corrections to it.
10. Save your work, then compare your document, Layers palette, and Actions palette to the sample in Figure O-36.
11. Create a droplet called **Gift image**.

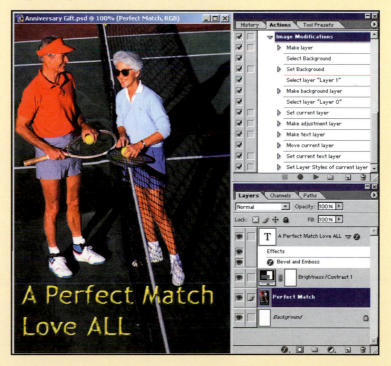

DESIGN PROJECT

The Internet is a great resource for actions and droplets. You can find many actions that have very well thought out design features. Some Web sites let you download actions for free, while others might charge a subscription fee. As you perfect your skills using actions, you decide to scour the Web and see what cool actions you can find.

1. Connect to the Internet and go to *www.course.com*, navigate to the page for this book, click the Student Online Companion link, then click the link for this unit. After you have reached this site, click the link for Photoshop Actions.
2. Download an action that you want to try.
3. Create a new Photoshop document called **Action Sample** using any dimensions.
4. Supply any imagery by using any electronic images you can acquire through purchase, from your hard disk, or by using a scanner, and use any fonts available on your computer.
5. Duplicate image and type layers to preserve your original image.
6. Create a written note anywhere on the document, indicating the source of the action (include the URL).
7. Create a snapshot of the document.
8. Load and play the action in the document. If necessary, click Continue or OK to accept any messages or settings in dialog boxes that open.

9. Create a droplet called **Play Downloaded Action**.
10. Save your work, then compare your document (and the partial view of the downloaded action) to the sample in Figure O-37.

FIGURE O-37
Completed Design Project

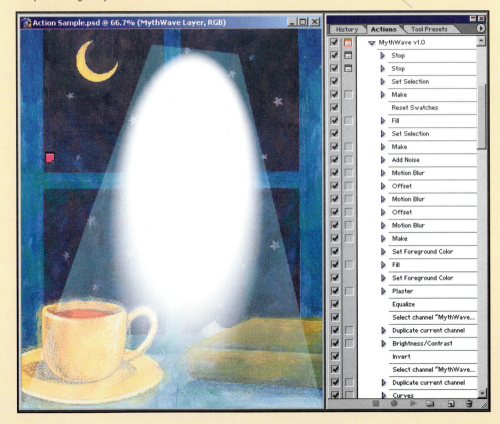

11. Be prepared to discuss the design features used in your downloaded action.

Annotating and Automating a Document

Depending on the size of your group, you can assign individual elements of the project to group members, or work collectively to create the finished product.

Creating an interesting design in a group environment can be a challenge. As a motivational exercise, the head of your department has asked you to work as a group to create an interesting document to inspire a positive working environment using Photoshop, actions, and your raw creativity and imagination. You can choose any topic for the artwork, work with any existing or scanned imagery, and use any new or existing actions. As you determine what actions to create, think about why a series of tasks is worthy of an action. How will automating a task benefit you, your co-workers, and your organization? Think efficiency; think quality.

1. Create a new Photoshop document with any dimensions.
2. Save this file as **Game Plan**.
3. Locate artwork—either on your hard disk, in a royalty-free collection, or from scanned images.
4. Decide on a game plan. What will the image look like? Depending on the number of group members, you can choose to have each member contribute an action, or you can have several members collaborate on multiple actions.

5. Assign a group member who is artistically inclined to sketch a rough draft of your layout.
6. Add any necessary type layers using any fonts available on your computer. (*Hint*: In the sample, a Colonna MT font is used.)
7. Create a written note that lists the actions you used. (*Hint*: You can use actions created in this unit, or you can create one or more new actions, if necessary.)
8. Write down the steps that were used in any new actions. Be prepared to answer the following questions: Why did you create the actions that you did? What factors determined that a task should be converted into an action?
9. Be prepared to demonstrate to others that the actions work correctly.
10. Save your work, then compare your document, Layers palette, and Actions palette to the sample in Figure O-38.

FIGURE O-38
Completed Group Project

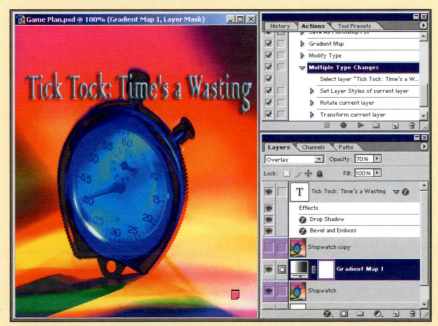

Unit	Lesson	Steps title	Summary	Page
A	Start Adobe Photoshop 7.0	Start Photoshop (Windows)	You started Photoshop for Windows, then created a file with custom dimensions.	A-6
		Start Photoshop (Macintosh)	You started Photoshop for the Macintosh, then created a file with custom dimensions.	A-7
	Learn how to open and save a document	Open a file using the File menu	You used the Open command on the File menu to locate and open a file.	A-10
		Open a file using the File Browser	You used the File Browser to locate and open a file.	A-10
		Use the Save As command	You used the Save As command on the File menu to save the file with a new name.	A-11
	Examine the Photoshop window	Select a tool	You selected the Lasso Tool on the toolbox and used its shortcut key to cycle through the Lasso tools.	A-15
		Select a tool from the Tool Preset Picker	You selected the Magnetic Lasso Tool using the Tool Preset Picker.	A-16
		Add a tool to the Tool Preset Picker	You added the Move Tool to the Tool Preset Picker.	A-17
		Show and hide palettes	You used the Window menu to show and hide the Swatches palette.	A-18
		Create a customized workspace	You created a customized workspace, then reset the palette locations.	A-19
	Use the Layers and History palettes	Hide and display a layer	You made the Azaleas layer active on the Layers palette, then clicked the Indicates layer visibility button to hide and display a layer.	A-22
		Move a layer on the Layers palette and delete a state on the History palette	You moved the Easter Lily layer to the top of the Layers palette, then returned it to its original position by dragging the Layer Order state to the Delete current state button on the History palette.	A-23
	Learn about Photoshop by using Help	Find information in Contents	You used the Photoshop Help command on the Help menu to open the Help window and viewed a topic in Contents.	A-25
		Find information in the Index	You clicked an alphabetical listing and viewed an entry in the Help index.	A-26
		Find information in the Site Map	You clicked a link in the site map to find information on Photoshop.	A-26
		Find information using Search	You entered a search term, viewed search results, and exited the Help window.	A-27

Unit	Lesson	Steps title	Summary	Page
	View and print a document	Use the Zoom Tool	You selected the Zoom Tool on the toolbox and used it to zoom in to and out of the image.	A-30
		Modify print settings	You used the Print command on the File menu to open the Page Setup dialog box, changed the page orientation, then printed the document.	A-31
	Close a document and exit Photoshop	Close the document and exit Photoshop	You closed the current document and exited the program by using the Close and Exit (Win) or Quit (Mac) commands.	A-33
B	Examine and convert layers	Convert an Image layer into a Background layer	You displayed the rulers, deleted the Background layer, then converted an image layer into the Background layer.	B-7
	Add and delete layers	Add a layer using the Layer menu	You created a new layer above the Fall in New England layer using the New command on the Layer menu.	B-10
		Delete a layer	You used the Delete layer button on the Layers palette to delete a layer.	B-11
		Add a layer using the Layers palette	You used the Create a new layer button on the Layers palette to add a new layer.	B-11
	Add a selection from one document to another	Make a color range selection	You opened a document and used the Color Range dialog box to select the image pixels by selecting the image's inverted colors.	B-14
		Move a selection to another document	You dragged a selection from one document to another.	B-15
		Defringe the selection	You removed the fringe from a selection.	B-15
	Organize layers with layer sets and colors	Create a layer set	You used the Layers palette menu to create a layer set, then named and applied a color to it.	B-18
		Move layers to the layer set	You moved two layers into a layer set, then defringed a layer.	B-18
		Rename a layer and adjust opacity	You renamed the new layer, adjusted opacity, and rearranged layers.	B-19
		Flatten an image	You saved the document as a copy, and then flattened the document.	B-19
C	Make a selection using shapes	Create a selection with the Rectangular Marquee Tool	Using the Rectangular Marquee Tool, you created a selection within an image. After the selection was defined, you dragged the object into another document.	C-7
		Position a selection with the Move Tool	You used the Move Tool to reposition the selection in an existing document.	C-8

Unit	Lesson	Steps title	Summary	Page
		Deselect a selection	You hid the active layer, then eliminated the marquee from the source document using the Deselect command on the Select menu.	C-9
		Create a selection with the Magnetic Lasso Tool	You created a selection with the Magnetic Lasso Tool.	C-10
		Move a complex selection to an existing document	You dragged a complex selection into an existing Photoshop document. You positioned the object using ruler guides and deleted an unnecessary layer.	C-11
	Modify a marquee	Move a marquee	You created a marquee, then dragged the marquee to reposition it.	C-14
		Enlarge a marquee	You enlarged a selection marquee using the Grow, Similar, and Expand commands, then you dragged the selection into an open document.	C-15
	Select using color and modify a selection	Select using color range	You made a selection within an image using the Color Range command on the Select menu, and dragged the selection to an existing document.	C-18
		Select using the Magic Wand Tool	You made a selection using the Magic Wand Tool, then dragged it into an existing document.	C-19
		Flip a selection	You flipped and repositioned a selection.	C-20
		Fix imperfections with the Healing Brush Tool	You used the Healing Brush Tool to fix imperfections in an image.	C-21
	Add a vignette effect to a selection	Create a vignette	You created a vignette effect by adding a feathered layer mask. You also rearranged layers and defringed a selection.	C-23
D	Work with color to transform a document	Set the default foreground and background colors	You set the default foreground and background colors and displayed rulers in pixels.	D-7
		Change the background color using the Color palette	You set new values in the Color palette, used the Paint Bucket Tool to change the background to that color, then undid the change.	D-8
		Change the background color using the Eyedropper Tool	You used the Eyedropper Tool to sample a color as the foreground color and then used the Paint Bucket Tool to change the background color to the color you sampled.	D-9
	Use the Color Picker and the Swatches palette	Select a color from the Color Picker	You opened the Color Picker dialog box, selected a different color palette, and then selected a new color.	D-12

Unit	Lesson	Steps title	Summary	Page
		Select a color from the Swatches palette	You opened the Swatches palette, selected a color, and then used the Paint Bucket Tool to change the background to that color.	D-12
		Add a new color to the Swatches palette	You used the Eyedropper Tool to sample a color, and then added the color to the Swatches palette.	D-13
	Place a border around an image	Create a border	You hid a layer, changed the foreground color to black, locked transparent pixels, then used the Stroke dialog box to apply a border to the image.	D-15
	Blend colors using the Gradient Tool	Create a gradient from a sample color	You sampled a color on the image to set the background color, changed the foreground color using an existing swatch, selected the Gradient Tool, and then chose a gradient fill and style.	D-18
		Apply a gradient fill	You applied the gradient fill to the background.	D-19
	Add color to a grayscale image	Change the color mode	You converted the image to Grayscale, then you changed the mode to RGB color.	D-22
		Colorize a grayscale image	You colorized a grayscale image by adjusting settings in the Hue/Saturation dialog box.	D-23
	Use filters, opacity, and blending modes	Adjust brightness and contrast	You adjusted settings in the Brightness/Contrast dialog box.	D-27
		Work with a filter, blending mode, and an opacity setting	You applied the Sharpen More filter, then adjusted the opacity and changed the color mode in the Fade dialog box.	D-28
		Adjust color balance	You switched to the Chili Shop document, and then adjusted settings in the Color Balance dialog box.	D-29
E	Learn about type and how it is created	Create and modify type	You created a type layer by using the Horizontal Type Tool on the toolbox, then modified the font family, alignment, and font size.	E-6
		Change type color using an existing document color	You changed the font family, then modified the color of the font by using the Eyedropper pointer and an existing document color. You also moved the type within the document.	E-7
	Change spacing and adjust baseline shift	Kern characters	You modified the kerning between characters by using the Characters palette.	E-10
		Shift the baseline	You changed the type color, then adjusted the baseline of the first character in each word.	E-11

Unit	Lesson	Steps title	Summary	Page
	Use the Drop Shadow style	Add a drop shadow	You changed the color of the type and created a drop shadow by using the Add a layer style button on the Layers palette.	E-14
		Modify drop shadow settings	You used the Layer Style dialog box to modify the default settings for the drop shadow.	E-15
	Apply anti-aliasing to type	Apply anti-aliasing	You applied the None anti-aliasing setting to see how the setting affected the appearance of type.	E-18
		Undo anti-aliasing	You deleted a state in the History palette to return the type to its original appearance.	E-19
	Modify type with the Bevel and Emboss style	Add the Bevel and Emboss style and modify settings	You applied the Bevel and Emboss style by using the Layer menu, then modified the default settings.	E-22
	Apply special effects to type using filters	Rasterize a type layer	You rasterized a type layer in preparation for filter application.	E-26
		Modify filter settings	You modified the Gaussian Blur filter settings to change the blur effect.	E-27
F	Paint and patch an image	Use the Sharpen Tool	You used the Sharpen Tool to focus on the pixels in the perimeter of the image. The affected pixels appeared sharper and crisper.	F-6
		Burn an area	You used the Burn Tool to tone down the pixels in the upper-right corner of the image. This technique increased the darker tones, heightening the mood of the document.	F-7
		Set fade options and paint an area	You modified the fade options, then painted areas using the fade settings.	F-8
		Patch an area	You used the Patch Tool to cover an area within an image.	F-9
	Create and modify a brush tip	Create a brush tip	You created a brush tip, using the Brushes palette. You modified its settings to create a custom brush tip for painting a border.	F-12
		Paint a border	Using the newly created brush tip, you painted areas of the document. You also made adjustments to the opacity and fade settings to make the brush stroke more dramatic.	F-13
	Smudge colors to create an artistic effect	Modify smudge settings	You modified the existing smudge settings.	F-16
		Smudge an image	You used the Smudge Tool to smear the pixels in the bottom third of the image. That area now has a dreamy quality.	F-17

Unit	Lesson	Steps title	Summary	Page
	Use a library and an airbrush effect	Load a brush library	You sampled a specific location in the document, then loaded the Faux Finish Brushes library. You selected a brush tip from this new library, which you will use to paint an area.	F-20
		Create an airbrush effect	You used an airbrush effect to paint the sky in the image. You applied the Bevel and Emboss style to a layer to add finishing touches.	F-21
G	Use a layer mask with a selection	Create a layer mask using the Layer menu	You used the Elliptical Marquee Tool to create a selection, then created a layer mask on the Rainbow layer using the Add Layer Mask command on the Layer menu.	G-6
		Create a layer mask using the Layers palette	You used the Elliptical Marquee Tool to create a selection, then used the Add layer mask button on the Layers palette to create a layer mask on the Bananas layer.	G-7
		Paint a layer mask	You used the Zoom Tool to keep a specific portion of the document in view as you increased the zoom percentage, selected a brush tip, then painted pixels on the layer mask to hide a banana.	G-8
		Modify the layer mask	You painted pixels to hide the right-most bananas, then reset the zoom percentage to 100%.	G-9
	Work with layer masks and layer content	Link and align layers	You linked three layers on the Layers palette, aligned the objects on those layers by their vertical centers using the Align Linked command on the Layer menu, then unlinked the layers.	G-12
		Transform a layer using scale	You resized the Strawberries layer using the Scale command.	G-13
		Transform a layer using rotate	You rotated the Nuts layer 90° counterclockwise using the Rotate CCW command.	G-13
	Control pixels to blend colors	Choose a color range to blend	You opened the Layer Style dialog box for the Strawberries layer, applied the Drop Shadow style, selected Red as the Blend If color, then adjusted the This Layer slider to change the range of visible pixels.	G-16

Unit	Lesson	Steps title	Summary	Page
		Split sliders to select a color range	You opened the Layer Style dialog box for the Blueberries layer, selected the Bevel and Emboss style, changed the blending mode to Dissolve, selected Blue as the Blend If color, then set a range of pixels that smoothed the transition between visible and invisible pixels by splitting the right This Layer slider.	G-17
	Eliminate a layer mask	Disable and enable a layer mask	You disabled and enabled the layer mask on the Bananas layer, using commands on the Layer menu.	G-20
		Remove a layer mask	You used the Delete layer button on the Layers palette to delete a layer mask, chose the Discard option in the warning box to remove the mask without applying it to the Rainbow layer, then undid the action to restore the layer mask on the Rainbow layer.	G-21
	Use an adjustment layer	Create and set an adjustment layer	You created a Brightness/Contrast adjustment layer on the Rainbow Fruit & Nuts layer, then adjusted settings in the Brightness/Contrast dialog box.	G-24
		Set the blending mode	You changed the blending mode for the adjustment layer to Soft Light, using the Layers palette.	G-25
	Create a clipping group to act as a mask	Create a clipping group	You created a clipping group, using the Border Fruit layer as the base and the Join in the mix layer as a member of the clipping group to make the banana peel appear as the fill of the Join in the mix layer, then you adjusted the opacity of the Join in the mix layer.	G-28
		Remove a clipping group	You removed the clipping group by using the Ungroup command on the Layer menu, restored the clipping group by using the Undo command on the Edit menu, saved a copy of the document, then flattened the document.	G-29
H	Learn about filters and how to apply them	Open a Blur filter	You set default foreground and background colors, hid two layers, and opened the Motion Blur filter dialog box.	H-7
		Apply a Blur filter	You applied a Motion Blur filter to the Candle layer.	H-8
		Display layers	You restored the visibility of two layers.	H-9

Unit	Lesson	Steps title	Summary	Page
	Create an effect with an Artistic filter	Apply an Artistic filter	You applied the Cutout filter to the Creme Rose Bud layer.	H-12
		Adjust the filter effect	You adjusted the brightness and contrast of the Creme Rose Bud layer.	H-13
	Add unique effects with Stylize filters	Apply a Stylize filter	You viewed different options in the preview window of the Diffuse dialog box, and applied the Diffuse filter to the Orange Rose layer.	H-16
		Apply a filter to a selection	You used the Elliptical Marquee Tool to select just the flame on the Candle layer, then applied the Wind filter to the selection.	H-17
		Repeat a filter application	You used the last filter applied feature on the Filter menu to apply the Wind filter to the Little Creme Bud layer and the Little Purple Bud layer.	H-18
	Use the Distort and Noise filters	Apply a Twirl filter	You applied a Twirl filter to the Clouds layer.	H-22
		Apply a Noise filter	You rasterized a type layer to apply a Noise filter to it.	H-23
	Use a Render filter to alter lighting	Select lighting settings	You selected a lighting style and type, then changed the direction and distance of the lighting.	H-26
		Apply a lighting effect	You applied a lighting effect to the Clouds layer.	H-27
I	Create an alpha channel	View the Channels palette	You opened the Channels palette, then, if necessary, displayed colors in the default color channels.	I-6
		Create an alpha channel from a selection	You used the Elliptical Marquee Tool to create a selection and used the Save selection as channel button to save it as an alpha channel. You also changed the alpha channel color.	I-7
	Use Extract to isolate an object	Isolate an object	You created and named a duplicate layer of the Fruit and Vegetables layer, opened the Extract dialog box, used the Edge Highlighter Tool to outline the kiwi, then filled in the kiwi using the Fill Tool.	I-10
		Extract an object	You previewed the extracted kiwi in the Extract dialog box, then viewed the layer with the extracted object.	I-11
		Enhance an extracted object	You adjusted the color for the extracted kiwi by applying a Gradient Map to the layer, then viewed the color-adjusted image.	I-11

Unit	Lesson	Steps title	Summary	Page
	Erase areas in an image to enhance appearance	Use the Background Eraser Tool	You hid the Kiwi layer, zoomed in on the Fruit and Vegetables layer, selected a brush tip for the Background Eraser Tool, and erased the kiwi on the Fruit and Vegetables layer.	I-14
		Equalize brightness and contrast	You adjusted the color of the kiwi by equalizing the colors, then viewed the color-adjusted image.	I-15
	Fix imperfections in an image	Sample an area	You selected the Fruit and Vegetables layer, set the zoom percentage, selected a brush tip for the Clone Stamp Tool, then sampled an undamaged portion of the tomato.	I-18
		Use the Clone Stamp Tool to fix an imperfection	You fixed the damaged area of the tomato by covering up the fly.	I-19
	Use the Magic Wand Tool to select objects	Select an object using the Magic Wand Tool	You opened a new document, set the Eyedropper Tool sample size to its largest selection setting, used the Magic Wand Tool to select it, then moved the selected image into the Juiced document.	I-22
		Compare objects selected using different sample areas	You changed the Eyedropper Tool sample size to its smallest setting, reselected the plant, moved it to the Juiced document, deleted the new layer, then repositioned the image.	I-23
	Learn how to create snapshots	Create a snapshot	You opened the Peppermint document, edited the document, then created and named a new snapshot.	I-26
		Use a snapshot	You used the snapshot to view the document as it was before you made changes.	I-27
	Create multiple-image layouts	Create a picture package	You selected the Picture Package option from the Automate command on the File menu, selected a layout for a picture package, then created a picture package using the Juiced document.	I-30
		Create a contact sheet	You created a folder and placed images in it, selected the Contact Sheet II option from the Automate command on the File menu, then created a contact sheet of the images in the folder you created.	I-31
J	Correct and adjust color	Modify color balance settings	You modified the color balance settings by using the sliders.	J-6
		Modify curves	You modified curves settings by using the Curves dialog box.	J-7

Unit	Lesson	Steps title	Summary	Page
	Enhance colors by altering saturation	Saturate a color range	You changed the saturation of two preset color ranges.	J-10
		Saturate using the Sponge Tool	You used the Sponge Tool to saturate specific areas in an image.	J-11
	Modify color channels using levels	Adjust color using the Levels feature	You modified levels for shadows, midtones, and highlights.	J-13
	Create color samplers with the Info palette	Create color samplers and use the Info palette	You sampled specific areas in the document, stored that color data in the Info palette, then hid the color samplers.	J-16
		Apply a filter and add a lighting effect	You added the Unsharp Mask and Lighting Effects filters to give the image a more professional appearance.	J-17
K	Use a Clipping Group as a Mask	Transform a type layer for use in a clipping group	You rasterized the existing type layer, then altered its shape using the Skew command. This transformation placed the text directly over the keyboard image.	K-6
		Create a clipping group	You moved the type layer beneath the Keyboard layer, then created the clipping group effect.	K-7
	Use pen tools to create and modify a path	Create a path	You created and named a path using the Freeform Pen Tool.	K-10
		Modify a path	You modified an existing path, then filled it with a color from the Swatches palette.	K-11
	Work with shapes	Create a shape	You created a new shape layer, using the Rectangle Tool.	K-14
		Modify a shape	You created an additional shape layer, then applied a style to the shape.	K-15
	Convert paths and selections	Convert a selection into a path	You created a selection using the Magic Wand Tool, then converted it into a path using a button on the Paths palette.	K-18
		Stroke a path	You stroked a path, using a color from the Swatches palette and a button on the Paths palette, displayed the remaining hidden layers, then changed the layer order.	K-19
L	Modify type using a bounding box	Display a bounding box	You displayed the bounding box to make it easier to adjust the size and shape of the layer contents.	L-6
		Modify type using the bounding box	Using the bounding box, you modified the type by scaling it, then skewing it.	L-7

Unit	Lesson	Steps title	Summary	Page
	Create warped type with a unique shape	Create warped type	You transformed existing type into a unique shape using the Create warped text button.	L-10
		Enhance warped type with color and effects	You used the Swatches palette to change the color of warped text and added the Stroke style to the warped text.	L-11
	Screen back type with imagery	Convert a type layer to a shape layer	In preparation for screening back type, you created a duplicate layer, then hid the original from view. You then converted the duplicate layer into a shape layer.	L-14
		Adjust layer content	You modified the midtones and shadows levels on the shape layer to make the text less transparent. You adjusted the Output Levels shadows slider to make the pixels that make up the text appear lighter and brighter.	L-15
	Create a faded type effect	Create a fade effect	You added a layer mask and a gradient to the left side of the Dream Factory text to create a faded type effect.	L-18
		Add a lighting effect	You added a lighting filter to give the image a more polished appearance.	L-19
M	Use the Liquify tools to distort an image	Open the Liquify dialog box and modify the brush size	You opened the Liquify dialog box, then chose the Warp Tool and a brush size.	M-6
		Use the Warp Tool	You used the Warp Tool to distort the pixels of the fingertips in an image. By dragging, you pushed the pixels forward, giving the fingertips a fiendish appearance.	M-7
	Learn how to freeze and thaw areas	Freeze areas in an image	You modified Liquify settings, then froze areas within an image to protect them, using the Freeze Tool.	M-10
		Distort unprotected areas of an image with frozen sections	After distorting an area, you thawed a protected frozen area and applied the distortions to the image.	M-11
	Use the mesh feature as you distort an image	Turn on the mesh	Prior to turning on the mesh, you merged the active layer with the layer beneath it. Then you turned on the mesh and changed the mesh color and size.	M-14
		Distort an image with the mesh feature activated	You added new distortions to the image and modified the mesh size. After viewing the distortions with the smaller mesh, you turned off the mesh and viewed the image.	M-15

Unit	Lesson	Steps title	Summary	Page
N	Delete unnecessary imagery	Prepare the document for surgery	You saved a JPG file in the Photoshop format, converted a Background layer into an image layer, then made a copy of the image layer.	N-6
		Remove imagery with the Magnetic Lasso Tool	You used the Zoom Tool to get a closer look at an image, then used a combination of the Magnetic Lasso Tool and the Eraser Tool to eliminate unwanted imagery.	N-7
		Duplicate imagery	You selected areas within the image and then duplicated them to cover deleted imagery and make the image look more natural.	N-8
		Create a layer from a selection	You created a new layer from a selection, then added a layer mask to a selection.	N-9
	Correct colors in an image	Correct colors in an image	You adjusted the color balance and brightness/contrast in the layer created from a selection, making the image of the woman stand out. You made color adjustments using adjustment layers, which you grouped with the Runners layer.	N-11
	Fix a background	Crop the image	You cropped the image.	N-13
O	Add annotations to a document	Create a text annotation	You used the Notes Tool to create a written annotation within a document. You changed the color of the note title bar and icon by sampling a color in the document.	O-6
		Create an audio annotation	You used the Audio Annotation Tool to create a sound message that is embedded in the document.	O-7
	Learn about actions and how they are created	Create a snapshot and an action	You created a snapshot to make it possible to easily test the new action. You used the Create new action button on the Actions palette to create an action called Modified Type.	O-10
		Record an action	You recorded steps for the Modify Type action. Once the recording was complete, you used a snapshot to restore the image to its original state, then you played the action to verify its accuracy.	O-11
	Modify an action	Add steps to an action	You added new steps (which modify type in another layer) to the Modify Type action.	O-14
		Modify steps in an action	You added a Bevel and Emboss style to an action, then replayed the action.	O-15

Unit	Lesson	Steps title	Summary	Page
	Use a default action and create a droplet	Insert an existing action within an action	You selected the Water Reflection action from the Default Actions set to insert into the Modify Type action.	O-18
		Play an existing action in a new action	You played the Water Reflection action in the Modify Type action. You used the snapshot to revert to the document's original appearance and replayed the action, resulting in a modified document.	O-19
		Create a droplet	You created a droplet using the Modify Type action and saved it on the desktop.	O-20
		Run a droplet	You returned the document to its original appearance, using Snapshot 1 on the History palette, then closed the document. Then you tested the droplet by dropping the Destiny file onto the droplet.	O-21
Bonus A	Learn about ImageReady	Jump to ImageReady	You opened a document in Photoshop, then jumped to ImageReady	Bonus A-6
		Adjust the view and exit ImageReady	You adjusted your view of the document, then exited the program.	Bonus A-7
	Optimize images for Web use	Optimize an image in Photoshop	You opened a file, used the Save For Web command on the File menu to open the Save For Web dialog box, then selected JPEG Medium as an optimization format.	Bonus A-11
		Optimize an image in ImageReady	You jumped to ImageReady, saved an optimized file, then closed the file and exited ImageReady. In Photoshop, you closed the PSD version of the Day Lily file.	Bonus A-12
		Place an optimized image	You opened an optimized file in Photoshop, dragged it into the Bloom Island document, adjusted the opacity setting, then renamed the layer.	Bonus A-13
	Create a button for a Web page	Create a button	You jumped from Photoshop to ImageReady, verified settings, created a new layer, selected the Rounded Rectangle Tool, selected a button style on the tool options bar, and then created a button.	Bonus A-16
		Add type to a button	You added type to the button, applied a style to it, and then linked the QuickGift type layer and the button shape layer.	Bonus A-17

Unit	Lesson	Steps title	Summary	Page
	Create slices in a document	Create a slice using the Slice Tool	You viewed the existing slices in the Bloom Island document, and created a slice for Flowers and a slice for Plants.	Bonus A-22
		Create a layer-based slice	You made the Day Lily layer active on the Layers palette, then created a slice.	Bonus A-23
		Resize a slice	You resized the Plants slice.	Bonus A-24
		Assign a Web address to a slice	You assigned a Web address to a slice using the Slice palette, then deselected the slice.	Bonus A-25
	Create a rollover effect	Create a rollover state	You selected the Jobs slice and made the Jobs layer active on the Layers palette. You created a new Over state, then changed its appearance by applying a new color to it.	Bonus A-28
		Preview a rollover	You used the Preview Document button to preview the rollover effect in the document.	Bonus A-29
	Create and play basic animation	Create a rollover state	You created a new Over state on the Rollovers palette, and then used the Toggle Slices Visibility button to hide the slices.	Bonus A-32
		Create and duplicate animation frames	You created an animation frame, duplicated existing frames, then adjusted the visibility of the layers.	Bonus A-33
		Adjust animation frames	You adjusted the opacity of frames using the Layers palette.	Bonus A-34
		Play animation in the document and browser	You played the animation in your document, then viewed it in a browser.	Bonus A-35
	Add tweening and frame delay	Tween animation frames	You used the Tweens animation frames button on the Animation palette to insert two new frames, then played the animation to view the results.	Bonus A-38
		Set frame delay	You changed the frame delay for frame 2, then previewed the animation in ImageReady and in your browser.	Bonus A-39

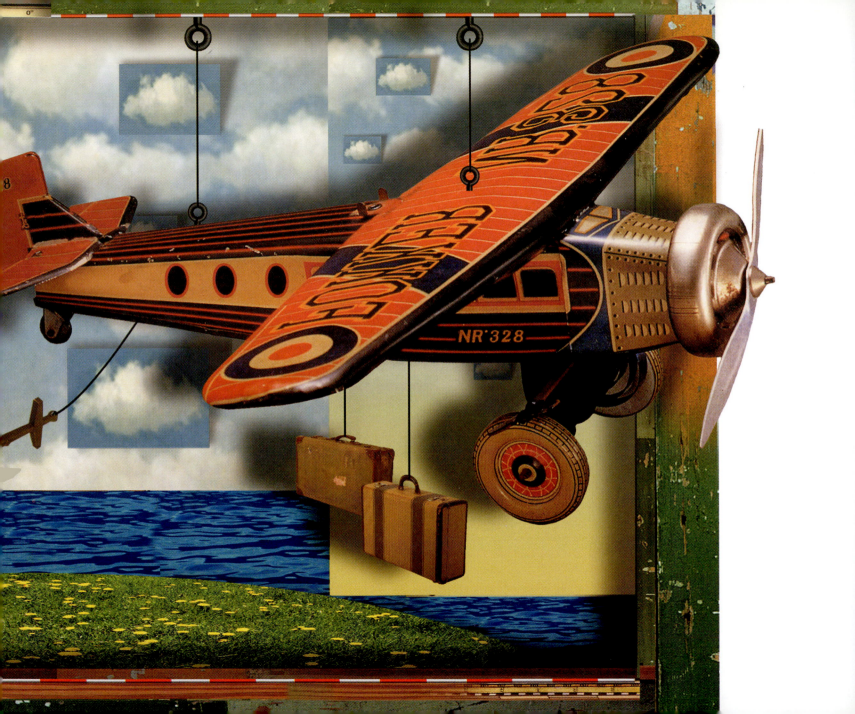

CREATING WEB DOCUMENTS

1. Learn about ImageReady.

2. Optimize images for Web use.

3. Create a button for a Web page.

4. Create slices in a document.

5. Create a rollover effect.

6. Create and play basic animation.

7. Add tweening and frame delay.

CREATING WEB DOCUMENTS

Using Photoshop for the Web

In addition to creating exciting images that can be professionally printed, you can use the tools in Photoshop to create images for use on the Web. Once you have a Photoshop image, you can use an additional program called Adobe ImageReady 7.0 to add the dimension and functionality required by today's Web audience. ImageReady is an integral part of Photoshop.

Understanding Web Graphics

With ImageReady you can tailor images and graphics specifically for the Web by creating buttons and other features unique to Web pages. Using these two programs, you can combine impressive graphics with interactive functionality to create an outstanding Web site.

QUICKTIP

ImageReady provides the capabilities for dividing one image into smaller, more manageable parts, and for creating more efficient Web-ready files.

Jumping Between Programs

Photoshop and ImageReady are designed to work together, so you can jump between the two programs to make changes in each program. Each program updates changes made in the other. This means you can work in ImageReady, return to Photoshop to tweak an image, then jump back to ImageReady to preview what your work will look like in your Web browser.

Tools You'll Use

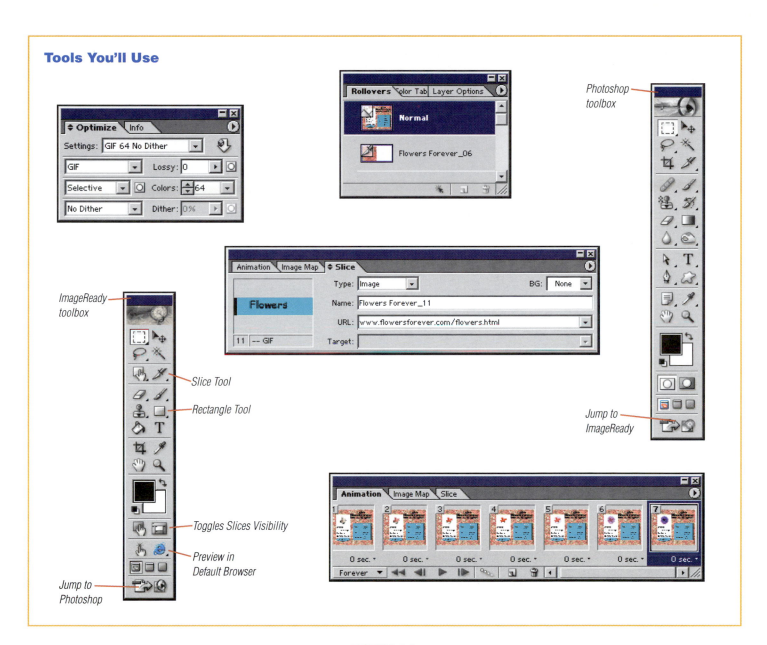

LEARN ABOUT IMAGEREADY

What You'll Do

 In this lesson, you'll open and rename a file in Photoshop, then use the Jump to feature to view the document in ImageReady. You'll also change your view of the document, exit ImageReady, then return to Photoshop.

Using Photoshop and ImageReady

Photoshop and ImageReady share similar tools and features, such as the toolbox, the tool options bar, and many palettes. Most features work identically, but some are found in different locations. For example, in Photoshop, the History palette appears above the Layers palette, but in ImageReady, the History palette is grouped with the Layers and Actions palettes. Figure A-1 shows the ImageReady workspace. You can use the Jump to ImageReady button (in Photoshop) or the Jump to Photoshop button (in ImageReady) to switch between the two programs.

Previewing Files for the Web

You can add many sophisticated Web effects to the files you create in ImageReady. To insert and view them in a Web page, you need to follow the procedures dictated by your HTML editor. HTML (Hypertext Markup Language) is the language used for creating Web pages. You can preview most Web effects directly in Photoshop or ImageReady. ImageReady also allows you to preview your files in your Web browser by clicking the Preview in Default Browser button on the toolbox (you can preview in Internet Explorer or Netscape Navigator).

QUICKTIP

Because monitor quality, operating systems, and Web browsers will vary from user to user, you should preview your images on as many different systems as possible before you finalize an image for the Web.

Updating Files

Each time you jump between Photoshop and ImageReady, the active program will automatically update the current file. This ensures that you always work with the most current version of the document.

QUICKTIP

A History state is created whenever Photoshop or ImageReady is automatically updated. This new state lets you know that an update occurred.

Creating Navigational and Interactive Functionality

You can divide a document you create for a Web site into many smaller sections, or slices. You use a **slice** to assign special features, such as rollovers, links, and animation, to specific areas within a document. A **rollover** changes an object's appearance when the pointer passes over (or the user clicks) a specific area of the document. An image sequence, or **animation**, simulates an object moving on a Web page. You can create an animation by making slight changes to several images, and then adjusting the timing between their appearances. When you convert a document to HTML, slices become cells in an HTML table, and rollovers and animations become files in object folders.

Jumping Between ImageReady and Other Programs

You can jump from ImageReady to other graphics programs or HTML programs, and then automatically update those files. To set up the programs that you want to jump to, click File on the menu bar, point to Jump To, click Other Graphics Editor or Other HTML Editor, then locate the program you want. To set up automatic file updating in Photoshop, click Edit on the menu bar, point to Preferences, click General, select the Auto-update open documents check box, then click OK. To set up automatic file updating in ImageReady, click Edit on the menu bar, point to Preferences, click General, select the Auto-Update Files check box, then click OK.

FIGURE A-1
ImageReady workspace

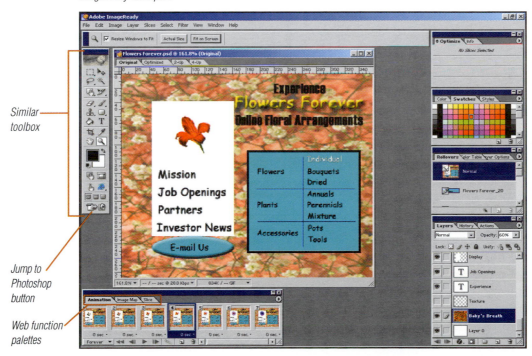

Similar toolbox

Jump to Photoshop button

Web function palettes

Jump to ImageReady

1. Start Photoshop, open PS Bonus A-1.psd, then save it as **Bloom Island**.

   TIP   If you receive a message stating that some text layers need to be updated before they can be used for vector-based output, click Update (Mac).

2. Click the Default Foreground and Background Colors button on the toolbox.

3. Display the rulers in pixels, if necessary.

4. Click the Jump to ImageReady button on the toolbox.

   Click the Toggle Slices Visibility button on the toolbox if the slices are not visible. The Bloom Island document opens in ImageReady. Compare your screen to Figure A-2.

You opened a document in Photoshop, then jumped to ImageReady.

FIGURE A-2
Document in ImageReady

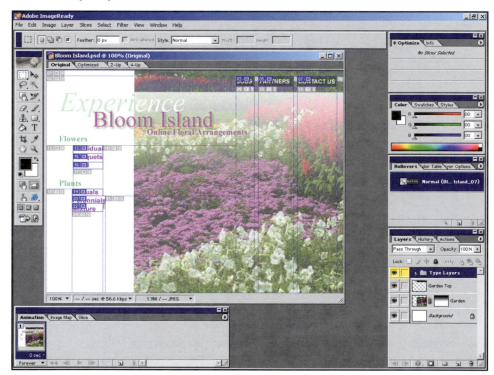

FIGURE A-3
Adjusted document view in ImageReady

Click button to change view

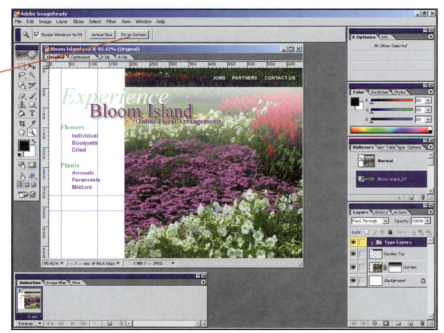

1. If necessary, click View on the menu bar, then click Rulers.

   TIP Many commands, such as displaying rulers, and many shortcut keys are the same in ImageReady and Photoshop.

2. Click View on the menu bar, then deselect Extras, if necessary.

3. Click View on the menu bar, point to Show, then click Guides.

4. Click the Zoom Tool on the toolbox.

5. Verify that the Resize Windows To Fit check box is selected.

6. Click the Fit on Screen button on the tool options bar, then compare your document to Figure A-3.

7. Click File on the menu bar, then click Exit (Win) or click ImageReady on the menu bar, then click Quit ImageReady (Mac) to close the document in ImageReady and return to Photoshop.

   ImageReady closes, and you are returned to the Bloom Island document in Photoshop.

You adjusted your view of the document, then exited the program.

OPTIMIZE IMAGES FOR WEB USE

What You'll Do

 In this lesson, you'll open a file in Photoshop, and then use the Save for Web command on the File menu to select a JPEG optimization format. You'll also jump to ImageReady and select a GIF optimization format, save the file as a GIF, then exit ImageReady. In Photoshop, you'll close the PSD version of the file, open the GIF version, drag it into the document, adjust the opacity setting of a layer, then rename it.

Understanding Optimization

You can create an awesome image in Photoshop and merge and flatten layers in the document, but still have a file so large that no one will wait for it to download from the Web. Both ImageReady and Photoshop contain features that let you precisely optimize an image. An **optimized** file is just as beautiful as a non-optimized file; it's just a fraction of its original size.

Optimizing a File

When you optimize a file, you save it in a Web format that balances the need for detail and accurate color against file size. Photoshop and ImageReady allow you to compare an image in the following common Web formats:

- JPEG (Joint Photographic Experts Group)
- GIF (Graphics Interchange Format)
- PNG (Portable Network Graphics)
- WBMP (a Bitmap format used for mobile devices, such as cell phones)

In Photoshop, the Save For Web dialog box has four view tabs: Original, Optimized, 2-Up, and 4-Up. See Figure A-4. The Original view displays the graphic without any optimization. The Optimized, 2-Up, and 4-Up views display the document in its original format, as well as other file formats. You can change the file format by

Exporting an image

You can export an image with transparency in Photoshop using the Export Transparent Image command on the Help menu. The Export Transparent Image Wizard guides you in selecting the area you want to be transparent. Most commonly, the background becomes transparent instead of white. By default, Photoshop saves the file as an Encapsulated PostScript (EPS) file.

clicking one of the windows in the dialog box, then clicking the Settings list arrow. In ImageReady, a document opens in the optimization window, where you can change views and formats the same way you do in Photoshop. See Figure A-5.

QUICKTIP

You can also use the Photoshop Save As command on the File menu to quickly save a file under a different graphics format by using Photoshop's default settings.

Understanding Compression

GIF, JPEG, and PNG compression create compressed files without losing substantial components. Figuring out when to use which format can be a puzzle. Often, the decision may rest on whether color or image detail is most important. JPEG files are compressed by discarding image pixels; GIF and PNG files are compressed by limiting colors. GIF is an 8-bit format (the maximum number of colors a GIF file can

contain is 256) that supports one transparent color; JPEG does not support transparent color. Having a transparent color is useful if you want to create a fade-out or superimposed effect. Because the JPEG format discards, or *loses*, data when it compresses a file, it is known as **lossy**. GIF and PNG formats are **lossless**—they compress solid color areas but maintain detail.

FIGURE A-4
Optimizing files in Photoshop

FIGURE A-5
Optimizing files in ImageReady

Hand Tool
Slice Select Tool
Zoom Tool
Eyedropper Tool
Eyedropper color
Toggle Slices Visibility Tool
Original image format and size

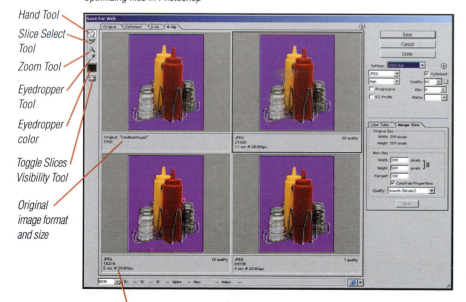

Settings indicate size and download time

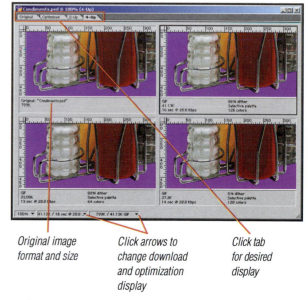

Original image format and size

Click arrows to change download and optimization display

Click tab for desired display

Comparing Image Types

Figure A-6 compares optimization of a photograph with a solid color background optimized in both GIF and JPEG formats. If you look very closely, you'll see that the GIF colors are streaky and broken-up, and the JPEG colors are crisp and appear seamless. Table A-1 lists optimization format considerations. Because you cannot assume that other users will have access to the latest software and hardware, it's a good idea to compare files saved under different formats and optimization settings, and preview them in different browsers and on different computers.

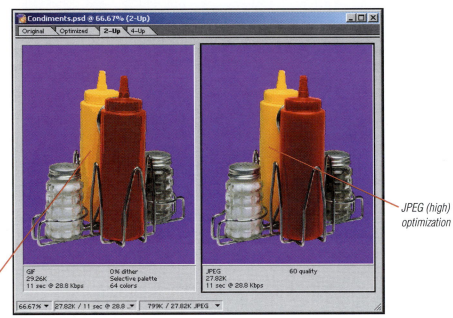

GIF (64 no dither) optimization

JPEG (high) optimization

TABLE A-1: Optimization Format Considerations

format	file format	use with
JPEG (very common)	All 24-bit (works best with 16 M colors)	Photographs, solid colors, soft edges
GIF (very common)	8-bit (256 colors)	Detailed drawings, sharp edges (logos, vector graphics), animation
PNG (less common)	24-bit (16 M colors)	Detailed drawings, logos, bitmap graphics
WBMP (less common)	1-bit (2 colors)	Cell phones and other mobile devices

FIGURE A-7

Save For Web dialog box

Outline surrounds optimal format

Your formats may differ

Magnification level

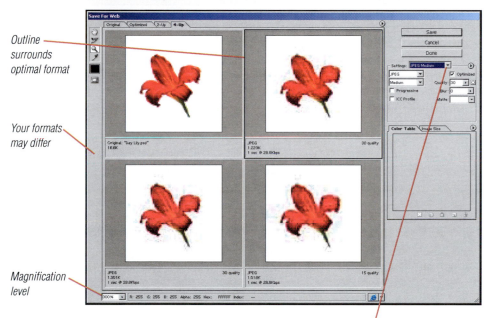

Click list arrow to change format

Optimize an image in Photoshop

1. Open Day Lily.psd.

   TIP Minimize the Bloom Island document if it gets in your way.

2. Click File on the menu bar, then click Save for Web.

3. Click the 4-Up tab, if necessary.

4. Click the Zoom Tool in the Save For Web dialog box.

5. Click the top-right image until all four images are enlarged to 300%.

   TIP The zoom level is displayed in the lower-left corner of the Save For Web dialog box. You can also click the Zoom Level list arrow and select a magnification.

6. Click the Settings list arrow, click JPEG Medium, then compare your dialog box to Figure A-7.

   Photoshop automatically selects the optimal format setting by highlighting it with a black border.

   TIP To optimize the file, click the desired format in the dialog box, click Save, enter a new name (if necessary) in the Save Optimized As dialog box, then click Save.

7. Click Cancel in the Save For Web dialog box.

You opened a file, used the Save for Web command on the File menu to open the Save For Web dialog box, then selected JPEG Medium as an optimization format.

FIGURE A-7

Save For Web dialog box

Outline surrounds optimal format

Your formats may differ

Magnification level

Click list arrow to change format

Optimize an image in ImageReady

1. Click the Jump to ImageReady button on the toolbox.

   The Day Lily document is opened in ImageReady.

2. Verify that the 4-Up tab is selected.

   > TIP   To create a new view of the current image, drag any view tab to a new location in the workspace.

3. Click the Zoom Tool, if necessary.

4. Click Fit on Screen on the tool options bar.

5. Click the Settings list arrow on the Optimize palette, then click GIF 128 Dithered. Compare your image to Figure A-8.

   Did you notice that the optimized size of the file is 1.852K? The original file size was approximately 21K.

6. Click File on the menu bar, then click Save Optimized As.

7. Navigate to the folder where you want to save the file as **Day-Lily.gif**, then click Save.

   The optimized file is saved in the designated location.

8. Close ImageReady, then close Day Lily.psd in Photoshop without saving changes.

You jumped to ImageReady, saved an optimized file, then exited ImageReady. In Photoshop, you closed the PSD version of the Day Lily file.

FIGURE A-8
Document optimized in ImageReady

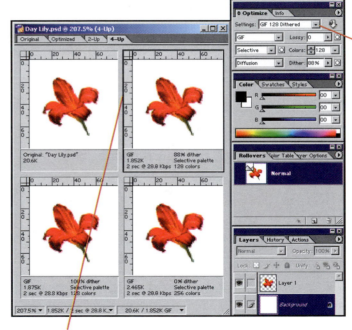

Click list arrow to change format

Outline surrounds optimal format

FIGURE A-9

Optimized image moved to document

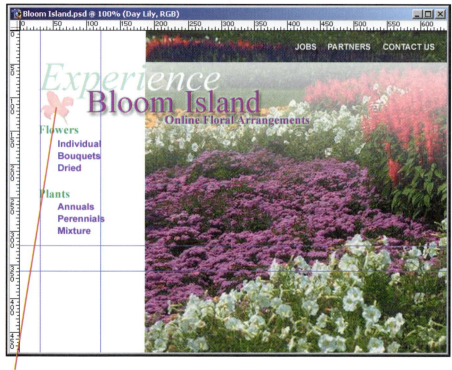

GIF image in
document

1. Verify that the Type Layers layer set is selected in the Bloom Island document.

2. Open Day-Lily.gif in Photoshop.

3. Click Select on the menu bar, click Color Range, then verify that the Image option button is selected and that the Fuzziness text box is set to 0.

4. Click the white background of the image in the Color Range dialog box, select the Invert check box, then click OK.

5. Click the Move Tool on the toolbox, then drag the selection to the Bloom Island document.

6. Drag the top of the day lily to 30 H/90 V.

7. Set the Opacity setting to 25% on the Layers palette.

8. Click the Layers palette list arrow, then click Layer Properties.

9. Type **Day Lily** in the Name text box, then click OK.

10. Make Day-Lily.gif the active document, then close this document.

11. Save your work, then compare your document to Figure A-9.

You opened an optimized file in Photoshop, dragged it into the Bloom Island document, adjusted the opacity setting, then renamed the layer.

CREATE A BUTTON FOR A WEB PAGE

What You'll Do

 In this lesson, you'll create and name a layer in ImageReady, then use the Rounded Rectangle Tool to create a button based on the style you select on the tool options bar. You'll also add type to the button, apply a style to the type, and then link the type and button layers.

Learning About Buttons

A **button** is a graphical interface that helps visitors navigate through and interact with a Web site with ease. ImageReady provides several ways for you to create and use buttons. You can create your own shape, apply a preformatted button style, or import a button you've already created. You can assign a variety of actions to a button so that the button reacts to changes initiated by the visitor.

Creating a Button

You can create a button by drawing a shape with a shape tool, such as a rectangle, on a layer. After you create the shape, you can add interest to it by applying a color or style, and then you can add some text that will explain what will happen when it's clicked.

Saving a file for the Web and defining Web output

Before you can use Photoshop or ImageReady files on the Web, you must first convert them to the HTML format. You can convert all of the slices in ImageReady to HTML by clicking Edit on the menu bar, pointing to Copy HTML Code, and then clicking For All Slices. ImageReady stores the HTML code on the Clipboard so that you can then paste it into your Web page using an HTML editor. Photoshop and ImageReady use default settings when you save optimized images for the Web. You can specify the output settings for HTML format, your HTML editor, and the way image files, background files, and slices are named and saved. To change the output settings in Photoshop, click the Optimize Menu list arrow in the Save For Web dialog box, then click Edit Output Settings. In ImageReady, click an option you want to change from the Output Settings command on the File menu.

Applying a Button Style

You can choose from 29 predesigned ImageReady button styles on the Styles palette, or you can create your own. To apply a style to a button, you must first create a button shape. After you create the button, double-click one of the button styles on the Styles palette, which appear as thumbnails, or click a style name from the Set style for new layer list arrow on the tool options bar. Figure A-10 shows the button styles on the ImageReady Styles palette. You can also modify a button with a style already applied to it by first clicking one of the shape tools, and then choosing a new style from the Styles palette.

FIGURE A-10
Button styles in ImageReady

Style thumbnail

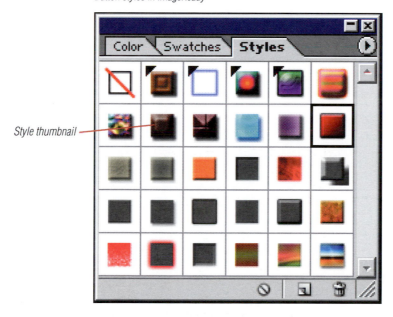

Create a button

1. Jump to ImageReady.
2. Click the Zoom Tool on the toolbox.
3. Click the Fit on Screen button on the tool options bar.
4. If necessary, display the rulers in pixels, and view Guides and Extras.
5. Click the Day Lily layer on the Layers palette, if necessary.
6. Click the Create a new layer button on the Layers palette.

   A new layer, Layer 1, appears at the top of the Layers palette.

7. Double-click the name Layer 1 on the Layers palette, type **QuickGift Button**, then press [Enter] (Win) or [return] (Mac).
8. Click the Rounded Rectangle Tool on the toolbox.

   > TIP Look under the Rectangle Tool if the Rounded Rectangle Tool is hidden.

9. Click the Set style for new layer list arrow on the tool options bar, then click Button-Stone, as shown in Figure A-11.
10. Drag the pointer from 30 H/320 V to 120 H/360 V.

    You created the shape that will be used for a button.

You jumped from Photoshop to ImageReady, verified settings, created a new layer, selected the Rounded Rectangle Tool, selected a button style on the tool options bar, and then created a button.

FIGURE A-11

Button style selected from style list

Click list arrow to display style list

Check mark indicates currently selected style

FIGURE A-12
Button created in document

Blue text baseline indicates that layer is active and can be edited

Shape layer is linked to type layer

1. Click the Type Tool on the toolbox. T

2. Click the button shape at approximately 40 H/345 V.

3. Click the Set the text color list arrow on the tool options bar, then select the third color swatch from the left in the third row from the bottom.

4. Click the Set the font family list arrow on the tool options bar, then click Arial, if necessary.

5. Click the Set the font size list arrow on the tool options bar, then click 18 px, if necessary.

6. Type **QuickGift**.

7. Click the Move Tool on the toolbox, then center the type on the button, if necessary.

8. Click the Add a layer style button on the Layers palette, then click Drop Shadow.

9. Click the Indicates if layer is linked button on the QuickGift Button (shape) layer. See Figure A-12.

    The type and button shape layers are linked.

10. Save your work.

You added type to a button, applied a style to it, and then linked the QuickGift type layer and the button shape layer.

CREATE SLICES IN A DOCUMENT

What You'll Do

 In this lesson, you'll view the existing slices in the Bloom Island document, create slices around the Flowers and Plants type, resize a slice, and assign a Web address to the slice. You'll also use the New Layer Based Slice command on the Layer menu to create a new slice from the Day Lily layer on the Layers palette.

Understanding Slices

Using ImageReady, you not only have the ability to work with layers, but you can divide an image into unlimited smaller sections, or slices. ImageReady uses slices to determine the appearance of special effects in a Web page. A slice is a rectangular section of an image that you can use to apply features, such as rollovers and links, and can be created automatically or by using any marquee tool or the Slice Tool.

QUICKTIP

A slice is rectangular, even if you create it using an elliptical marquee.

Using Slices

ImageReady uses two kinds of slices: a **user-slice**, which you create, and an **auto-slice**, which ImageReady creates in response to your user-slice. You can use the Slice Tool to create a slice by dragging the pointer around an area. Every time you

Creating an image map

In addition to assigning a Web address (URL) to a slice, you can select an area in a document and assign it a Web address. This area, known as a hotspot, is invisible to the user, just as a slice is. When you click the hotspot, the browser opens a different Web page. The areas that link to different Web pages are known collectively as an **image map**. Unlike a slice, an image map can be a circle, rectangle, or polygon. You can create an image map in ImageReady by selecting the Rectangle Image Map Tool, the Circle Image Map Tool, or the Polygon Image Map Tool from the toolbox. Use any of these tools to create a selection, click the Image Map palette tab, then type a Web address in the URL text box. When you position the mouse over the hotspot in your browser, the Web address appears on the status bar.

create a slice, ImageReady automatically creates at least one auto-slice, which fills in the area around the newly created slice. ImageReady automatically numbers user- and auto-slices and updates the numbering according to the location of the new user-slice. User-slices have a solid line border, auto-slices have a dotted line border, and selected slices have a yellow border. A selected user-slice contains a bounding box and sizing handles. You can resize a slice by dragging a handle to a new location, just as you scale an image in Photoshop.

QUICKTIP

When two slices overlap, a **subslice** is automatically created.

Learning About Slice Components

By default, a slice consists of the following components:

- A colored line that helps you identify the slice type.
- An overlay that dims the appearance of the unselected slices.

- A number that helps you identify each individual slice.
- A symbol that helps you determine the type of slice.

Identifying and Adjusting Slice Attributes

You can adjust slice attributes by clicking Slices under the Preferences command on the Edit menu. Figure A-13 shows slice preferences. You can choose whether to display slice lines and numbers and symbols. You can also specify line color and

FIGURE A-13
Preferences dialog box

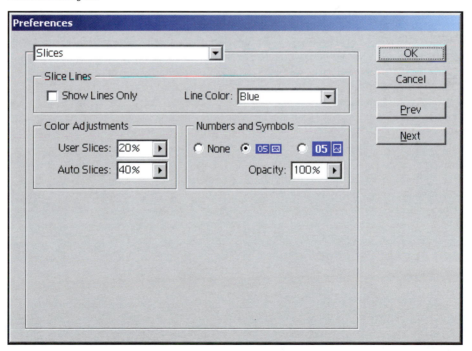

number and symbol opacity. Slice numbering changes as you add or delete slices. Each user-slice contains a symbol indicating if it is an image slice or a layer-based slice, if the slice is linked, or if it includes a rollover effect. See Table A-2 to see the symbols used to identify user slices.

QUICKTIP

It doesn't matter which layer, if any, is active when you create slices using the Slice Tool or the marquee tools.

Using a Layer-Based Slice

In addition to drawing a slice using the Slice Tool, you can use the New Layer Based Slice command on the Layer menu to create a slice from a layer on the Layers palette. This is an easy way of creating a slice *without* having to draw an outline.

Creating a Layer-Based Slice

Creating a layer-based slice automatically surrounds the image on the layer with a slice, which can be useful if you want to create a slice quickly or if you want a large slice. ImageReady updates the slice whenever you modify the layer or its content. For example, the slice automatically adjusts if you move its corresponding layer on the Layers palette, or you erase pixels on the layer.

QUICKTIP

To delete a layer-based slice, user-slice, or auto-slice, select the slice, then press [Delete] (Win) or [delete] (Mac) or click Slices on the menu bar, then click Delete Slice.

TABLE A-2: User Slice Symbols

symbol	used to identify
▢	Image slice
▢	Layer-based slice
▢	No image slice
▢	Slice containing a rollover

Using the Slice Palette

The Slice palette, shown in Figure A-14, is grouped with two other Web function palettes in ImageReady. You activate the palettes just as you do in Photoshop by clicking the tab of the palette you want to use. You use the features on the Slice palette to assign individual settings, features, and effects to the slices you've created in your document. For example, you could set a slice to initiate an action, such as opening another Web page or an e-mail response window when a user clicks the slide on a Web page.

Assigning a Web Address to a Slice

You can assign a Web page to a selected slice by typing its Uniform Resource Locater (URL) in the URL text box. The URL is the Web page's address that appears in the Address (Internet Explorer) or Location (Netscape) text box in your browser. You can designate how that Web page will be displayed in your browser by choosing one of the options on the Target list.

FIGURE A-14
Slice palette

User-slice

Selected slice

Auto-slice

Web address of Web page that will open when user clicks on slice in Web page

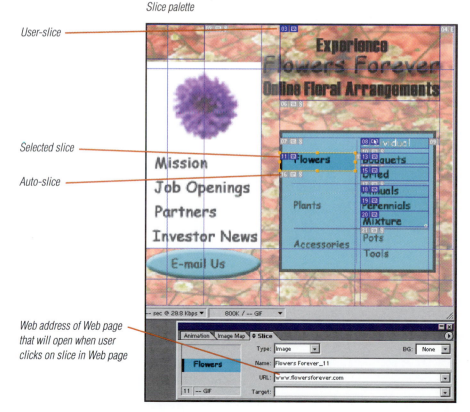

Create a slice using the Slice Tool

1. Click the Zoom Tool on the toolbox.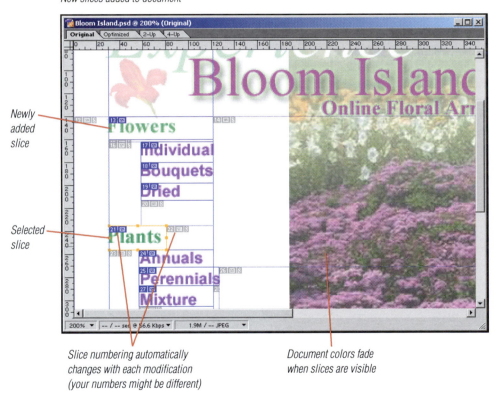

2. Click the document at 50 H/200 V until the zoom percentage is 200%.

3. Click the Slice Tool on the toolbox.

   The existing slices in the document are visible, and the document colors appear faded.

   > **TIP** You can also create a slice by creating a selection with any marquee tool, clicking Select on the menu bar, then clicking Create Slice from Selection.

4. Drag the pointer around the Flowers type (from approximately 30 H/140 V to 120 H/160 V).

5. Drag the pointer around the Plants type (from approximately 30 H/235 V to 80 H/255 V), then compare your slices to Figure A-15.

You viewed the existing slices in the Bloom Island document, and created a slice for Flowers and a slice for Plants.

FIGURE A-15
New slices added to document

Newly added slice

Selected slice

Slice numbering automatically changes with each modification (your numbers might be different)

Document colors fade when slices are visible

1. Click the Day Lily layer on the Layers palette.
2. Click Layer on the menu bar, click New Layer Based Slice, then compare your slice to Figure A-16.

A new slice surrounds the Day Lily layer object.

> TIP You can also create a layer-based slice by right-clicking (Win) or [control] clicking (Mac) the layer, and then clicking New Layer Based Slice.

You made the Day Lily layer active on the Layers palette, then created a slice.

FIGURE A-16
New layer-based slice

Layer-based slice does not display sizing handles

Resize a slice

1. Click the Slice Select Tool on the toolbox.

   TIP Look under the Slice Tool to find the Slice Select Tool. You can also press and hold [Shift], then press [K] to select the Slice Select Tool.

2. Click the Plants slice.

3. Drag the right-middle sizing handle to 120 H, compare your slice to Figure A-17, then release the mouse button.

   TIP Because a layer-based slice is fitted to pixels on the layer, it does not contain sizing handles when you select it.

You resized the Plants slice.

FIGURE A-17
Resized slice

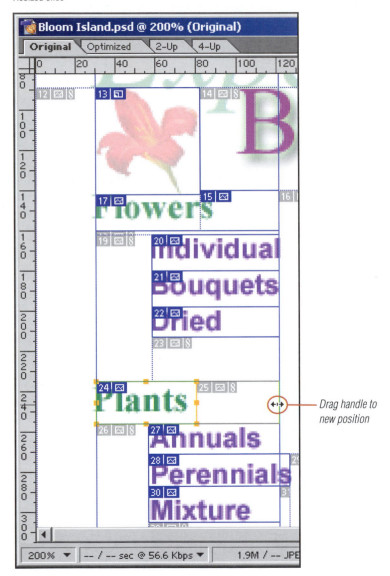

Drag handle to new position

Type Web address here

FIGURE A-19
Deselected slices

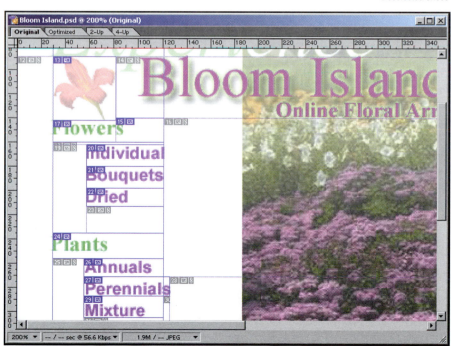

Assign a Web address to a slice

1. Click the Slice palette tab. Slice

2. Type **plants.usda.gov** in the URL text box, then compare your Slice palette to Figure A-18.

   | TIP   Your slice numbers might vary.

3. Click Select on the menu bar, then click Deselect Slices to deselect the Plants slice.

   TIP   To hide slices in your document, click the Toggle Slices Visibility button on the toolbox, or click View on the menu bar, point to Show, then click Slices.

4. Save your work, then compare your document to Figure A-19.

You assigned a Web address to a slice using the Slice palette, then deselected the slice.

CREATE A ROLLOVER EFFECT

What You'll Do

In this lesson, you'll use the Slice Select Tool to select a slice, make the corresponding type layer active on the Layers palette, view the Rollovers palette, and then create a new Over state. You'll also change the font color of the Over state and preview the rollover effect in the document.

Learning About Rollovers

You might have noticed in your own Web surfing that user-initiated actions have become standard features in Web page design. Web sites that contain many inter-active features are more interesting and useful to users. How you introduce and present your content is important to maintaining your visitors' interest, and ultimately, the amount of time they spend viewing your Web site. A rollover is one of the easiest features you can add to a Web page. You can use **rollovers** to respond to a user's action, such as clicking or pointing to (rolling on) an area in your Web page. The change in the Web page can serve as a navigational aid, or it can provide addi-tional choices to the user.

Making Rollovers Happen

The activity of the pointer determines the appearance, or **state**, of the rollover. You can add and modify states on the Rollovers palette. The Rollovers palette is a live sto-ryboard of the image's journey as you first position the pointer on the image, click it, then leave the image.

Learning About Rollover States

You can add the following states to the Rollovers palette: Normal, Over, Down, Click, Out, Up, and None. By default, every slice you create has a Normal state. The Normal state is how an image appears when it is inactive and without any user intervention. Most rollovers have Normal,

Over, and Down states. You can create a rollover out of images of almost any size, and you can control the appearance of each state by using tools and applying styles to its corresponding layer on the Layers palette. After a rollover is created, you can change the type of rollover effect by double-clicking the rollover state on the Rollovers palette. When you do this, the Rollover State Options dialog box opens. Click the type of rollover you want, then click OK. Figure A-20 shows several states on the Rollovers palette with different effects applied to them, and the Rollover State Options dialog box.

QUICKTIP

Because layer-based slices are automatically updated when you alter the layer, they offer the most flexibility when you use them to create rollovers.

Previewing Rollover Effects

You can preview the effects of a rollover in ImageReady or in your browser. To obtain immediate feedback on your rollover actions, click the Preview Document button on the toolbox, then move your mouse in the document, and observe the rollover behavior. For a complete review of how the rollover works, you can also click the Preview in Default Browser button on the toolbox. Your browser will open the document in an optimized format and display relevant HTML code in a box below the image. Exit your browser window when you have completed your rollover test. You can test the rollover in both Internet Explorer and Netscape Navigator, assuming you have both programs loaded on your computer.

FIGURE A-20
Rollover states

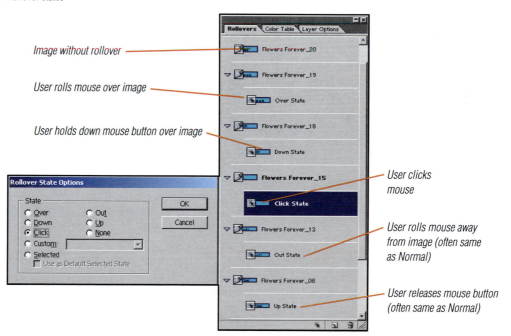

Image without rollover

User rolls mouse over image

User holds down mouse button over image

User clicks mouse

User rolls mouse away from image (often same as Normal)

User releases mouse button (often same as Normal)

Create a rollover state

1. Click the Hand Tool on the toolbox. 🖐

2. Drag the document down to the lower-left corner so that the Jobs type is visible. 🖐

3. Click the Slice Select Tool on the toolbox. 📐

4. Click the Jobs slice.

5. Click the Indicates a layer set arrow for the Type Layers layer set on the Layers palette. ▷

6. Click the JOBS layer on the Layers palette.

7. Click the Rollovers tab, if necessary.

8. Click the Create rollover state button on the Rollovers palette, then compare your Rollover and Layers palettes to Figure A-21. 🔲

   TIP When you create a rollover, you must select the layer on the Layers palette where you want the rollover effect to occur.

9. Click Layer on the menu bar, point to Layer Style, then click Color Overlay.

   The type in the Over state and in the document becomes the default color (red), or the last color selected in the Color Overlay palette.

10. Click the Set color of overlay list arrow on the Color Overlay palette, then click the sixth swatch from the left on the seventh row, as shown in Figure A-22.

You selected the Jobs slice and made the JOBS layer active on the Layers palette. You created a new Over state, and then changed its appearance by applying a new color to it.

FIGURE A-21
Rollovers and Layers palettes

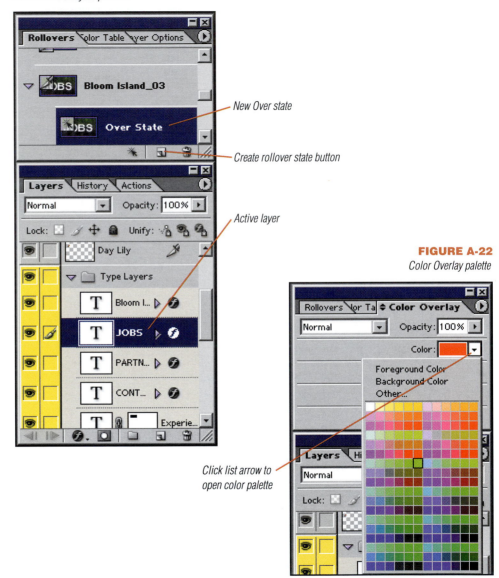

New Over state

Create rollover state button

Active layer

FIGURE A-22
Color Overlay palette

Click list arrow to open color palette

FIGURE A-23

Over state appearance changed

New color of Over
state type

FIGURE A-24

Rollover preview in ImageReady

Type changes color
when mouse rolls
over it

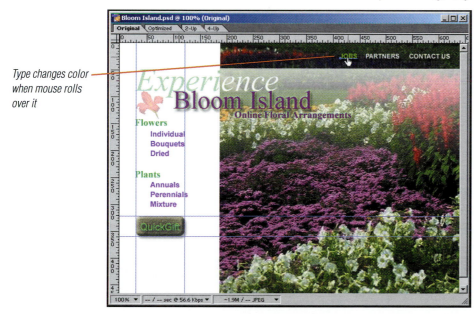

1. Click the Rollovers tab, then compare your palette to Figure A-23.

2. Click the Zoom Tool on the toolbox.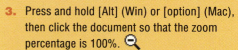

3. Press and hold [Alt] (Win) or [option] (Mac), then click the document so that the zoom percentage is 100%.

4. Click the Toggle Slices Visibility button on the toolbox.

   The individual slices are no longer visible in the document.

   > TIP   The Toggle Slices Visibility button remains on until you click it again to turn it off.

5. Click the Bloom Island_03 state on the Rollovers palette.

6. Click the Preview Document button on the toolbox.

7. Roll the mouse over Jobs in the document, then compare your document to Figure A-24.

   The Jobs type changes from white to green when the mouse rolls over it.

8. Click the Cancel Preview (Esc) button on the tool options bar.

9. Save your work, then close the Bloom Island document *leaving ImageReady open.*

You used the Preview Document button to preview the rollover effect in the document.

CREATE AND PLAY BASIC ANIMATION

What You'll Do

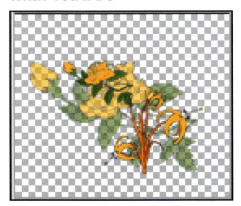

 In this lesson, you'll create a rollover for the Rose layer. You'll also create animation frames. For each newly created frame, you'll modify the layers on the Layers palette by hiding and showing them, and changing their opacity, which will result in an animation sequence. You'll also play the animation in your document, and preview the animation in your browser.

Understanding Animation

You can use nearly any type of graphics image to create interesting animation effects in ImageReady. You can move objects in your document or overlap them so that they blend into one another. Once you place the images that you want to animate in a document, you can determine when and how you want the animation to play. If you want your users to initiate the animation, you can create different animations for each rollover state that you create on the Rollovers palette.

Creating Animation on the Animation Palette

Remember that animation is nothing more than a series of still images displayed rapidly. The Animation palette displays a thumbnail of the animation image in each frame. A **frame** is an individual image that is used in animation. When you create a frame on the Animation palette, you create a duplicate of the current frame, and can then modify it as desired. The layers that

are visible on the Layers palette appear in the selected frame, and thus, in the animation. Here's all that's involved in creating animation:

- Place images on layers in the document.
- Hide all but one layer.
- Duplicate the frame, turn off the displayed layer, then turn on the layer you want to see.

Animating Images

If you look at the Layers palette in Figure A-25, you'll see that there are images on two layers. The Animation palette contains two frames: one for each of the layers. When frame 1 is selected, the man appears in the document; when frame 2 is selected, the woman appears. When the animation is played, the images of the man and woman alternate in the document.

Moving and Deleting Frames

To move a frame to a different spot, click the frame in the Animation palette, and drag it to a new location. To select contiguous frames, press and hold [Shift], and then click the frames you want to include. To select noncontiguous frames, press and hold [Ctrl] (Win) or [command] (Mac), and then click the frames you want to include. You can delete a frame by clicking it in the Animation palette, then dragging it to the Deletes selected frames button on the Animation palette.

Looping the Animation
You can set the number of times the animation plays by clicking the Selects looping options list arrow on the Animation palette, then clicking Once, Forever, or Other. When you select Other, the Set Loop Count dialog box opens, where you can enter the loop number you want.

Previewing the Animation
You can preview the animation in a variety of ways:
- You can use the buttons on the bottom of the Animation palette. When you click the Plays/stops animation button, the animation plays.
- You can also view the animation as it occurs for the user by clicking the Preview Document button on the toolbox

and then initiating the animation based on the rollover state you selected.
- You can preview and test the animation as it functions in your browser by clicking the Preview in Default Browser button on the toolbox.

QUICKTIP
You can change the size of the Rollovers palette and Animation palette thumbnails by clicking the palette list arrow, clicking Palette Options, clicking a thumbnail size, and then clicking OK. You can select a different-sized thumbnail for each palette.

FIGURE A-25
Sample of basic animation

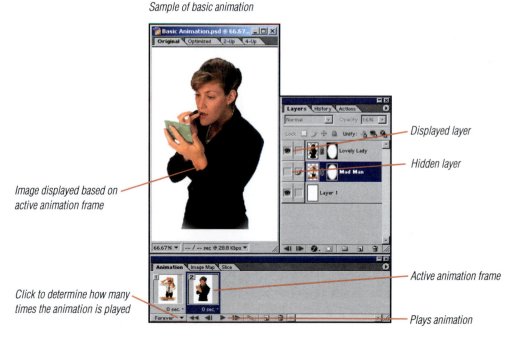

Displayed layer

Hidden layer

Image displayed based on active animation frame

Active animation frame

Click to determine how many times the animation is played

Plays animation

Create a rollover state

1. Open PS Bonus A-2.psd in ImageReady, then save it as **Rose Morph**.

2. Click the Indicates layer visibility button on the Stems layer on the Layers palette.

3. Click the Indicates layer visibility button on the Little Rose layer on the Layers palette.

4. Click the Toggle Slices Visibility button on the toolbox.

5. Click the Create rollover state button on the Rollovers palette.

   A new Over state is created on the Rollovers palette, as shown in Figure A-26.

6. Click the Toggle Slices Visibility button on the toolbox.

   | TIP You can create different animations for each rollover state.

You created a new Over state on the Rollovers palette, and then used the Toggle Slices Visibility button to hide the slices.

New Over state

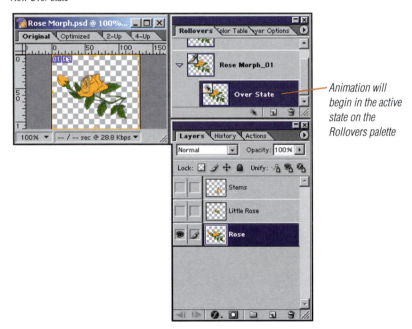

Animation will begin in the active state on the Rollovers palette

FIGURE A-27

Frames created on Animation palette

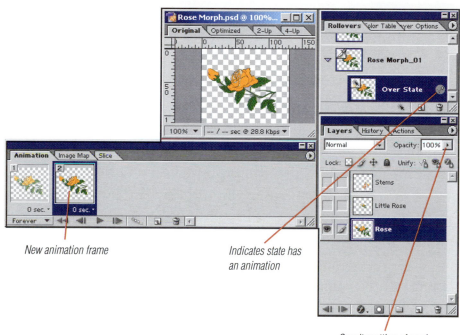

New animation frame

Indicates state has an animation

Opacity setting of newly created animation frame

1. Click the Animation palette tab.

   Animation

2. Adjust the opacity setting of the Rose layer to 50% on the Layers palette.

   The opacity of the active layer changes.

3. Click the Duplicates current frame button on the Animation palette.

   A new Animation frame is created and is now the active frame.

4. Adjust the opacity setting of the Rose layer to 100%, then compare your Animation palette to Figure A-27.

5. Click the Duplicates current frame button on the Animation palette.

6. Click the Indicates layer visibility button on the Rose layer on the Layers palette.

7. Click the Stems layer to make it active, then click the Indicates layer visibility button on the Layers palette for this layer.

   The content from the Stems layer appears in frame 3 of the Animation palette.

You created an animation frame, duplicated existing frames, and adjusted the visibility of the frames.

Adjust animation frames

1. Set the opacity setting of the Stems layer to 30%.

   The opacity of the active layer is changed to 30%.

2. Click the Duplicates current frame button on the Animation palette, then adjust the opacity setting of the Stems layer to 100%.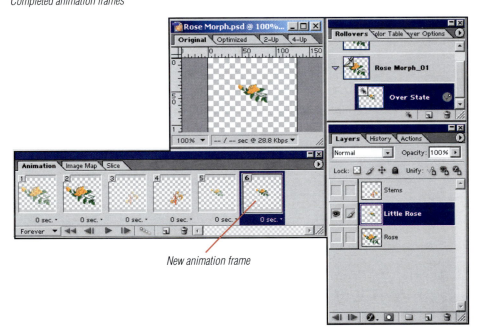

   The content of the new animation frame has an opacity of 100%.

3. Click the Duplicates current frame button on the Animation palette.

4. Click the Indicates layer visibility button on the Stems layer to hide it.

5. Click the Little Rose layer to make it active, then click the Indicates layer visibility button on the Layers palette for this layer.

6. Adjust the opacity setting to 50%.

7. Click the Duplicates current frame button on the Animation palette, then adjust the opacity setting of the Little Rose layer to 100%. Compare your screen to Figure A-28.

You adjusted the opacity of frames using the Layers palette.

FIGURE A-28
Completed animation frames

New animation frame

FIGURE A-29

Animation displayed in browser

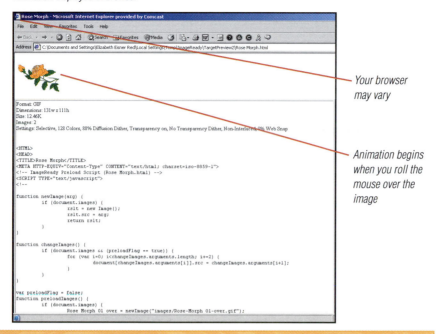

Your browser may vary

Animation begins when you roll the mouse over the image

TABLE A-3: Animation Tools

tool	tool name	description
Forever ▼	Selects looping options	Determines how many times the animation plays.
◀◀	Selects first frame	Makes the first frame in the palette active.
◀▮	Selects previous frame	Makes the previous frame in the palette active.
▶	Plays/stops animation	Plays the animation.
■	Plays/stops animation	Stops the animation.
▮▶	Selects next frame	Makes the next frame to the right in the palette active.
◌	Tweens animation frames	Creates frames in slight increments.

Lesson 6   Create and Play Basic Animation

1. Click the Plays/stops animation button on the Animation palette. ▶

   The Plays/stops animation button changes its appearance depending on the current state of the animation. See Table A-3 for a description of the buttons in the Animation palette.

2. Click the Plays/stops animation button on the Animation palette. ■

   The animation stops, displaying the currently active frame.

3. Save your work.

4. Click the Preview Document button on the toolbox. 🖑

5. Move the pointer over the image, view the animation, then move the pointer off the document. 🖑

   The animation begins when you roll the mouse over the image and stops when you roll it off the image.

6. Click the Preview in Default Browser button on the toolbox, then compare your preview to Figure A-29. 🌐

7. Move the pointer over the image, then move the pointer off the image. 🖑

8. Close your browser.

   TIP   The animation might play differently in ImageReady than in your browser, which is why it is important to preview your files on as many different systems as possible.

You played the animation in your document, then viewed it in a browser.

ADD TWEENING AND FRAME DELAY

What You'll Do

 In this lesson, you'll add tweening to animation and adjust the frame delay for a frame on the Animation palette.

Understanding Tweening

To create animation, you assemble a series of frames, then play them quickly to create the illusion of continuous motion. Each frame represents a major action point. Sometimes the variance between actions creates erratic or rough motion. To blend the motion *in between* the frames, you can tween your animation. Tweening adds frames that change the action in slight increments from one frame to the next. In traditional animation (before computer-generated images), an artist known as an *inbetweener* hand-drew the frames that linked major action frames (at 24 frames per second!).

Using Tweening on the Animation Palette

You can add tweening to a frame by clicking the Tweens animation frames button on the Animation palette, and then entering the number of in-between frames you want in the Tween dialog box. You can choose whether you want the tweening to affect all layers or just the selected layer, and if you want the image to change position or opacity. You can also specify the frame on which you want the tweening to start, and specify the number of frames to add in between the frames (you can add up to 100 frames in a single tween). Figure A-30 shows a two-frame animation after five tween frames were added. The opacity of the man is 100% in the first frame and 0% in the last frame. Adding five tween frames causes the two images to blend into each other smoothly, or **morph** (metamorphose).

QUICKTIP

You can select contiguous frames and apply the same tweening settings to them simultaneously.

Understanding Frame Delays

When you create frames on the Animation palette, ImageReady automatically sets the **frame delay**, the length of time that each frame appears. You can set the delay time in whole or partial seconds by clicking the Selects frame delay time list arrow below each frame. You can set the frame delay you want for each frame, or you can select several frames and apply the same frame delay to them.

Setting Frame Delays

To change the delay for a single frame, click a frame, click the Selects frame delay time list arrow, then click a time. To select contiguous frames, press and hold [Shift], click the frames you want to include, and then click the Selects frame delay time list arrow on *any* of the selected frames. To select noncontiguous frames, press and hold [Ctrl] (Win) or [command] (Mac), click the frames you want to include, then click the Selects frame delay time list arrow on any of the selected frames.

FIGURE A-30
Animation palette

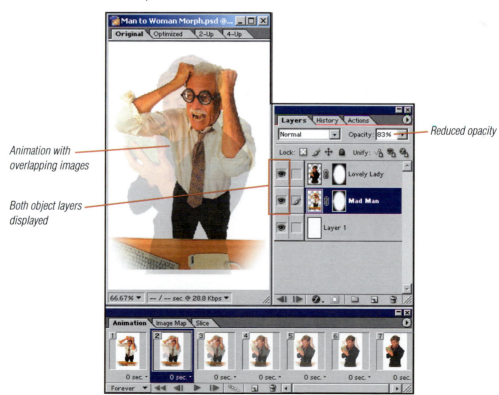

Animation with overlapping images

Both object layers displayed

Reduced opacity

Tween animation frames

1. Click the Cancel Preview (Esc) button on the tool options bar.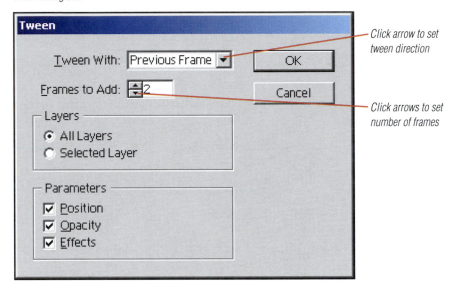

2. Click the Over State on the Rollovers palette.

3. Click frame 3 on the Animation palette.

4. Click the Tweens animation frames button on the Animation palette.

5. Adjust the settings in your Tween dialog box using Figure A-31 as a guide.

6. Click OK.

   Two additional frames are added after frame 2.

7. Click the Plays/stops animation button on the Animation palette, then view the animation.

8. Click the Plays/stops animation button on the Animation palette, then compare your palette to Figure A-32.

You used the Tweens animation frames button on the Animation palette to insert two new frames, then played the animation to view the results.

FIGURE A-31
Tween dialog box

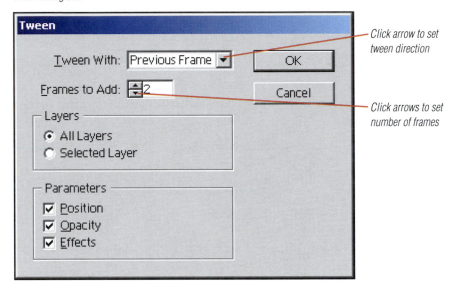

Click arrow to set tween direction

Click arrows to set number of frames

FIGURE A-32
Tweening frames inserted

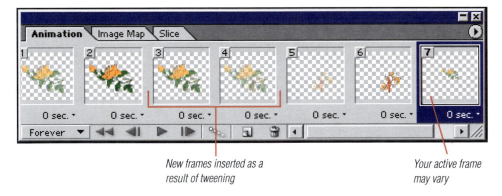

New frames inserted as a result of tweening

Your active frame may vary

FIGURE A-33
Frame delay menu

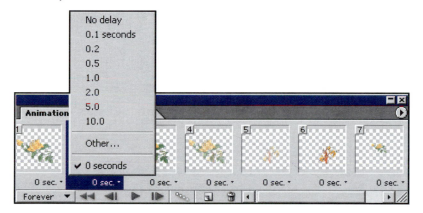

1. Click frame 2 on the Animation palette.

2. Click the Selects frame delay time list arrow at the bottom of the selected frame. ⊞

3. Compare your frame delay menu to Figure A-33, then click 0.2.

   The frame delay for frame 2 changes to 0.2.

4. Click the Plays/stops animation button on the Animation palette, then view the animation. ▶

5. Click the Plays/stops animation button on the Animation palette. ▣

6. Click the Preview in Default Browser button on the toolbox. 🖳

7. Move the pointer over the image to see the effect of the rollover, then close your browser. 🖑

   TIP Frame delays behave very differently in your browser than in ImageReady—be sure to preview them in your browser to ensure that they play the way you intend them to play.

8. Save your work.

You changed the frame delay for frame 2, then previewed the animation in ImageReady and in your browser.

Power User Shortcuts

to do this:	use this method:
Create a slice	
Cycle shape tools	**Shift U**
Cycle through optimize tabs	[Ctrl][Y] (Win) ⌘ [Y] (Mac)
Deselect slices	[Ctrl][D] (Win) ⌘ [D] (Mac)
Hide/show rulers (ImageReady)	[Ctrl][R] (Win) ⌘ [R] (Mac)
Jump to ImageReady	
Jump to Photoshop	
Preview Document	or **Y**
Preview in Browser	or

to do this:	use this method:
Save Optimized	[Ctrl][Alt][S] (Win) ⌘ option [S] (Mac)
Save Optimized As	[Ctrl][Shift][Alt][S] (Win) ⌘ [Shift] option [S] (Mac)
Select all slices	[Ctrl][A] (Win) ⌘ [A] (Mac)
Select a slice	
Show Animation palette	[F11]
Start animation playback	
Stop animation playback	
Toggle Slices Visibility	or **Q**

Key: Menu items are indicated by ➤ between the menu name and its command. Blue bold letters are shortcuts for selecting tools on the toolbox.

Learn about ImageReady.

1. Start Photoshop, open PS Bonus A-3.psd, then save it as **Optimal Dolphin**.
2. Set the background and foreground colors to their default values.
3. Jump to ImageReady.
4. Fit the document to the screen.

Optimize images for Web use.

1. Jump to Photoshop.
2. Open the Save For Web dialog box.
3. Display the 4-Up tab.
4. Change the settings of the original image to GIF 64 Dithered.
5. Save the file as **Optimal-Dolphin-GIF.gif**.
6. Jump to ImageReady.
7. Display the 4-Up tab, then zoom in or out of the image, if necessary.
8. Click the first GIF image after the original image, change the settings to JPEG High, then compare your image to Figure A-34.
9. Use the Save Optimized As command to save the file as **Optimal-Dolphin-JPG.jpg**.
10. Exit (Win) or quit (Mac) ImageReady.
11. Close Optimal Dolphin *without* saving changes, and leave Photoshop open.

FIGURE A-34
Completed Skills Review 1

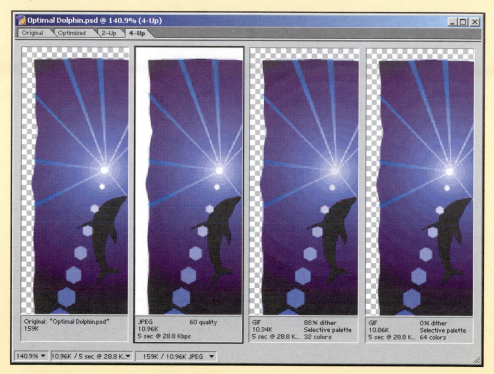

Create a button for a Web page.

1. Open PS Bonus A-4.psd, then save it as **Pet-U-Nation**.

2. If necessary, update the text layers.

3. Set the background and foreground colors to the default.

4. Jump to ImageReady.

5. Fit the document to the screen, and display the rulers, if necessary.

6. Select the Rounded Rectangle Tool.

7. Activate the Board layer.

8. Draw a button from 15 H/340 V to 135 H/390 V using the Button-Wood style.

9. Select the Type Tool.

10. Click the document at approximately 40 H/ 370 V, then type **Rescue** (use a white, bold 18 px Arial font).

11. Save your work.

Create slices in a document.

1. Draw a slice from 15 H/150 V to 135 H/200 V.

2. Draw a slice from 15 H/210 V to 135 H/260 V.

3. Draw a slice from 15 H/275 V to 135 H/320 V.

4. Draw a slice from 15 H/340 V to 135 H/390 V.

5. Resize the Afghan slice (the image of the dog in the top-right portion of the document) so that the top is 90 V and the bottom is 320 V.

6. Type the following (fictitious) URL for the Afghan slice: **www.petunation.com/breed/ afghan_faq.html**.

7. Save your work.

Create a rollover effect.

1. Display the Rollovers palette.

2. Select the Dog Bone layer on the Layers palette, then create a layer-based slice.

3. Create an Over state.

4. Apply a stroke style that has a width of 10 and is light yellow (use the second color swatch from the left in the first row of the color palette). (*Hint*: You can do this by using the Layer Style command on the Layer menu, or the Add a layer style button on the Layers palette.)

5. Hide the slices and rulers.

6. Preview the rollover.

7. Save your work, compare your image to Figure A-35, then close Pet-U-Nation, *leaving ImageReady open*.

FIGURE A-35
Completed Skills Review 2

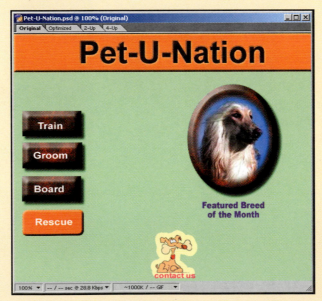

Create and play basic animation.

1. Open PS Bonus A-5, then save it as **The Old Soft Shoe** in ImageReady.
2. Display the rulers, if necessary.
3. Create an Over rollover state for the Cat Dancing layer.
4. Duplicate frame 1, make the Cat Forward layer active, then drag the Cat Forward image to approximately 250 H.
5. Duplicate frame 2, then hide the Cat Forward layer and make the Cat Dancing layer visible.
6. Duplicate frame 3, then hide the Cat Dancing layer and make the Cat Forward layer visible.
7. Duplicate frame 4, hide the Cat Forward layer, make the Cat Dancing layer visible, then change the opacity setting of the Cat Dancing layer to 0%.
8. Play the animation.
9. Save your work, then hide the rulers, if necessary.

Add tweening and frame delay.

1. Tween frame 2 using the previous frame and adding 2 frames.
2. Tween frame 5 using the previous frame and adding 1 frame.
3. Tween frame 6 using the previous frame and adding 5 frames.
4. Play the animation.
5. Set the frame delay for frames 1, 4, 6, and 7 to 0.2 seconds.
6. Play the animation.
7. Preview the animation in your Web browser.
8. Save your work, then compare your image to Figure A-36.

FIGURE A-36

Completed Skills Review 3

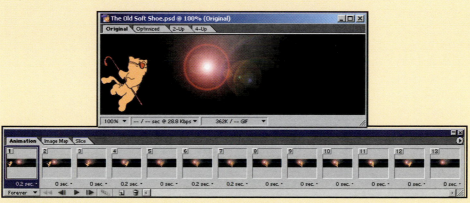

A local long-distance runners group is sponsoring a cross-country run for charity. The event will offer short cross-country races for all ages and fitness levels. You've volunteered to use your ImageReady skills to design an animation for their Web page that echoes the broad accessibility of the event.

1. Obtain the following images for the animation: an object that conveys the idea of movement and an obstacle it moves over, around, or through. You can also obtain a background and any other images, as desired. You can draw your own images, use the images that are available on your computer, scan print media, create images using a digital camera, or connect to the Internet and download images.

2. Create a new Photoshop document and save it as **Xtream Charity**.

3. Apply a color or style to the Background layer, then jump to ImageReady. (*Hint*: The Background layer in the sample has a Pattern Overlay style applied to it.)

4. Create at least two new states on the Rollovers palette.

5. Add animations to each of the states you created on the Rollovers palette. Make one a motion animation and the other a fade-out effect.

6. Tween each animation and add frame delays as necessary.

FIGURE A-37
Completed Project Builder 1

7. Preview the animation in your document and in your browser.

8. Save your work, then compare your screen to the sample shown in Figure A-37.

You've just been elected to the board of directors of a community access TV station. Each board member is expected to serve on at least one committee. You've chosen the Community Involvement Committee, and have been asked to design a snappy, numeric countdown animation that will introduce public service announcements.

1. Obtain images appropriate for a countdown. You can draw your own numbers, use the images that are available on your computer, scan print media, create images using a digital camera, or connect to the Internet and download images. You must include at least one other image, and can include any other images, as desired.

2. Create a new Photoshop document, then save it as **Countdown**.

3. Apply a color or style to the Background layer, add images as desired, and apply effects to them. (*Hint*: The Background layer in the sample has a Pattern Overlay style applied to it.)

4. Create at least three type layers with numbers for a countdown, and apply styles or filters to them as desired. (*Hint*: Each number in the sample has a duplicate with different opacities.)

5. Jump to ImageReady, then create a new rollover state.

6. Create an animation to the state you created on the Rollovers palette. Make the numbers move across the document and fade into one another.

7. Duplicate the last number so that it changes appearance at least twice.

8. Tween each animation and add frame delays as necessary.

9. Preview the animation in your document and in your browser.

10. Save Countdown as **Countdown Browser**, then adjust tweening and frame delays so that it plays perfectly in your Web browser.

11. Save your work, then compare your screen to the sample shown in Figure A-38.

FIGURE A-38
Completed Project Builder 2

DESIGN PROJECT

After your first experience with creating your own animation, you and your friends are hooked. You want to peruse the full range of animation on the Web. Each of you will study one aspect of Web animation. Your first stop will be to check out the latest in animated banner ads.

1. Connect to the Internet and go to *www.course.com*, navigate to the page for this book, click the Student Online Companion link, then click the link for this unit to display the Web page shown in Figure A-39.
2. Create a new Photoshop document and save it as **Banners et al**.
3. Identify an animation that interests you by scrolling down the page or linking to one of the sites listed on the page.
4. Create a type layer named **Animation Techniques**, then type the animation techniques and Photoshop skills and features that you believe were used to create the appearance of the animation.
5. Be sure to add the following points to the Animation Techniques layer:
   - Identify how many different animations are active throughout the sequence and at any one time.
   - Identify the rollover state that initiates the animation.
   - Identify instances of tweening and frame delay.
   - Give examples of techniques unknown to you.
6. When your analysis is complete, print the document.
7. Hide the Animation Techniques layer, then obtain images to use for your own interpretation of the animation. You can use the images that are available on your computer, scan print media, or download images from the Internet.

8. Place the images in your document, create type layers as needed, and then use ImageReady to apply the animation techniques you identified.
9. Update the Animation Techniques layer as necessary, print the document so that the Animation Techniques layer prints clearly, then compare your before and after analyses. (*Hint*: Hide distracting layers.)
10. Hide the Animation Techniques layer, make the other layers active, then save your work.

FIGURE A-39
Completed Design Project

Depending on the size of your group, you can assign individual elements of the project to group members, or work collectively to create the finished product.

Your team handles new product presentations for Never Too Late (NTL), an online message service that sends daily reminders to clients. NTL is teaming with an automated home electronics company to offer a new home-based service. They're going to provide an automatic wake-up call that turns on a client's computer, plays a wake-up message until the client responds, and then lists the day's important activities. The team wants to demonstrate at your next staff meeting a prototype that really shows off the product. You're going to transform a black and white image into a color image. You'll add appropriate sounds later.

1. Obtain images for the wake-up call. One image should be a black and white image that you can easily transform to color. You can draw your own images, use the images that are available on your computer, scan print media, create images using a digital camera, or connect to the Internet and download images.
2. Create a new Photoshop document, then save it as **Wake Up**.
3. Apply a color or style to the Background layer, add other images as desired, and apply effects to them. (*Hint*: The sample has three color layers that alternate as the background, two of which have gradients applied to them.)
4. Place the images in the document. (*Hint*: The black and white line art is a cartoon line drawing that was filled in to colorize it. You can color a similar image by choosing background colors on the toolbox, selecting the Eraser Tool, and then clicking the Lock transparent pixels button on the Layers palette.)
5. Create at least one type layer as desired and at least one other image or background.

FIGURE A-40
Completed Group Project

6. Jump to ImageReady, make the black and white image the Normal state, then add the color image to the new rollover state of your choice.
7. Create an animation for the state you created on the Rollovers palette.
8. Tween each animation, and add frame delays as necessary.
9. Preview the animation in your document and in your browser.
10. Save your work, then compare your screen to the sample shown in Figure A-40.

Adobe Photoshop 7.0 Certified Expert Program
Product Proficiency Exam

Topic Area	Objectives	Unit(s)
1. General Knowledge	1.1 Explain differences between vector graphics and raster (bitmap) images.	D, K
	1.2 Given a color mode, describe the color mode, and explain when you would use the color mode.	D
	1.3 Given a type of output, discuss attributes that affect image quality.	D
	1.4 Given a file format, explain when you would use that format in Photoshop.	A, Bonus A
2. Using the Work Area and Work Spaces	2.1 Manage the work area by setting options for palettes.	A
	2.2 Given a palette, explain the purpose of the palette.	A–E, G–O
	2.3 Describe the functionality provided from the status bar and the tool options bar.	A
	2.4 Manage libraries by using the Preset Manager.	F
	2.5 Given a scenario, configure, save, and load workspaces.	A
3. Importing, Exporting, and Saving	3.1 Discuss issues associated with scanning images.	A
	3.2 Import and manipulate files by using the Place command.	B*
	3.3 Import files from a digital camera.	A
	3.4 Given a scenario, determine the appropriate file format to output to.	A
	3.5 Given a file format, describe options available for saving.	A, Bonus A
	3.6 Given a scenario, rasterize a file that is imported into Photoshop.	H*
	3.7 Describe the functionality provided by the File Browser.	A
4. Working with Selections	4.1 Select an area of an image by using a selection tool.	B, C, I
	4.2 Modify selections by using a selection tool.	C
	4.3 Explain how anti-aliasing and feathering affect selections.	C
5. Creating and Using Layers	5.1 Discuss layers and layer sets, and explain how they can be used.	A, B
	5.2 List and describe the options provided for working with layers in the Layers palette.	A, B, E
	5.3 Use the appropriate tools and commands to create and manage layers.	B
	5.4 Edit layers by using the editing, vector and painting tools; and applying styles and filters.	B, F, H
	5.5 Use the appropriate tools and commands to create and modify clipping groups and layer masks.	K
	5.6 Apply blending modes to layers.	G
	5.7 Use layer effects to manipulate images within a layer.	K

Content covered in the Instructor's Manual for the indicated unit.

Topic Area	Objectives	Unit(s)
6. Using Masks and Channels	6.1 Given a channel, describe the channel, and explain when you would use it.	I
	6.2 Create, manage and use channels by using the Channels palette.	I
	6.3 Explain how masks are used to work with images.	G, I, K
	6.4 Explain how to create a temporary mask by using the Quick Mask command.	G*
	6.5 Given a mask, describe the functionality and when you would use the mask.	G, I
7. Managing Color	7.1 Discuss the color management workflow process that is used in Adobe Photoshop.	D, J
	7.2 Discuss issues associated with color management.	D
	7.3 Given an option on the Color Settings dialog box, describe the option.	J*
	7.4 Explain the purpose and how to use the Proof Setup command.	A*
8. Adjusting Images	8.1 Identify areas of tonal range that may need correcting by viewing a Histogram.	J
	8.2 Adjust the tonal range of an image by using the Image Adjustment commands.	J
	8.3 Adjust the tonal range of an image by setting numerical values.	J
	8.4 Adjust the tonal range of an image by using the Hue/Saturation dialog box.	J
	8.5 Discuss issues associated with changing the size and resolution of images.	D, J
	8.6 Crop images by hiding or deleting specific areas of the image.	N
9. Drawing and Editing	9.1 Create shapes by using the Pen and Shape tools.	K
	9.2 Select and modify paths.	K
	9.3 Save and export paths.	K
	9.4 Transform objects by using the Transform tools.	L
10. Painting	10.1 Paint objects by using a specific tool.	F
	10.2 Given an option from the Brushes palette, explain the purpose of that option.	F
	10.3 Given a tool, create and apply patterns.	E
	10.4 Use the Gradient tools to blend colors.	D
11. Retouching	11.1 Manipulate objects by using filters.	H
	11.2 Use the Liquify command to distort an image.	M
	11.3 Retouch an image by using a specific tool.	C, N
12. Using Actions	12.1 Create an action by using options in the Actions palette.	O
	12.2 Play an action by using the Batch command, including using File Browser as the source.	O
	12.3 Create a droplet from an action.	O
	12.4 Describe the purpose of specific Automate commands.	I

*Content covered in the Instructor's Manual for the indicated unit.

Topic Area	Objectives	Unit(s)
13. Working with Type	13.1 Given a palette, explain how type is used in Photoshop.	E, L
	13.2 Create, enter, and edit type by using a type tool.	E, L
	13.3 Explain and utilize functionality provided by the Check Spelling and Find and Replace Text commands.	E*
	13.4 Describe the composition methods available in Photoshop.	L
14. Outputting to Print	14.1 Given a scenario, select and explain when to use a specific Print command.	A
	14.2 Describe the options available for outputting to print in the Output and Color management pop-up menus in the Print Options dialog box.	K
	14.3 Discuss issues associated with printing duotones.	D*
15. Outputting for the Web	15.1 Given a scenario, choose the appropriate file format to optimize images for the Web.	Bonus A
	15.2 Describe the optimization options available for saving files for the Web.	Bonus A
	15.3 Create transparent and matted images by using the Save for Web command.	Bonus A*
	15.4 Link an image to a URL by using image maps.	Bonus A
	15.5 Explain how slices can be used to optimize images for the Web.	Bonus A
	15.6 Explain when you would use ImageReady versus Photoshop to prepare output for the Web.	Bonus A

*Content covered in the Instructor's Manual for the indicated unit.

Read the following information carefully!!

Find out from your instructor the location of the Data Files you need and the location where you will store your files.

- To complete many of the units in this book, you need to use Data Files. Your instructor will either provide you with a copy of the Data Files or ask you to make your own copy.

- If you need to make a copy of the Data Files, you will need to copy a set of files from a file server, standalone computer, or the Web to the drive and location where you will be storing your Data Files.

- Your instructor will tell you which computer, drive letter, and folders contain the files you need, and where you will store your files.

- You can also download the files by going to *www.course.com*. See the inside back cover of the book for instructions to download your files.

Copy and organize your Data Files.

- Use the Data Files List to organize your files to a zip drive, network folder, hard drive, or other storage device.

- Create a subfolder for each unit in the location where you are storing your files, and name it according to the unit title (e.g., Photoshop Unit A).

- For each unit you are assigned, copy the files listed in the **Data File Supplied** column into that unit's folder.

- Store the files you modify or create in each unit in the unit folder.

Find and keep track of your Data Files and completed files.

- Use the **Data File Supplied** column to make sure you have the files you need before starting the unit or exercise indicated in the **Unit** column.

- Use the **Student Saves File As** column to find out the filename you use when saving your changes to a provided Data File.

- Use the **Student Creates File** column to find out the filename you use when saving your new file for the exercise.

Files used in this book

Unit	Data File Supplied	Student Saves File As	Student Creates File	Used in
A	PS A-1.psd Butterfly.tif	Vacation.psd		Lesson 2-7
	PS A-2.psd	Zenith Design Logo.psd	Review.psd	Skills Review
	PS A-3.psd	Kitchen World.psd		Project Builder 2
			Critique 1.psd Critique 2.psd	Design Project
B	PS B-1.psd Gourds.psd	New England Fall.psd New England Fall copy.psd		Lesson 1-4
	PS B-2.psd Horn.psd	Music World.psd Music World copy.psd		Skills Review
	PS B-3.psd Cell Phone.psd	Fraud Magnet.psd		Project Builder 1
	PS B-4.psd Gorilla.psd	Zoo Billboard.psd		Project Builder 2
	PS B-5.psd Coffee Cups.psd	Coffee Cover.psd		Design Project
	PS B-6.psd	Harvest Market.psd		Group Project
C	PS C-1.psd Sheepdog.tif Butterfly.tif Photographer.tif	Family Portrait.psd		Lesson 1-4
	PS C-2.psd Block cat.tif Calico cat.tif Kitten.tif	Everything Feline.psd		Skills Review
	PS C-3.psd Plug.tif Satellite.tif Headphones.tif	FBI.psd		Project Builder 1
	PS C-4.psd	Marathon Contest.psd		Project Builder 2
			Sample Compositing.psd	Design Project
	PS C-5.psd	Totally Sports.psd		Group Project

Unit	Data File Supplied	Student Saves File As	Student Creates File	Used in
D	PS D-1.psd	Chili Shop.psd		Lesson 1-6
	PS D-2.psd	Chili Shop Colorized.psd		Lesson 5-6
	PS D-3.psd	Firetruck.psd		Skills Review
	PS D-4.psd	Firetruck Colorized.psd		
	PS D-5.psd	Restoration.psd		Project Builder 1
	PS D-6.psd	Preschool.psd		Project Builder 2
	PS D-7.psd	Cornucopia.psd		Design Project
	PS D-8.psd	Rubberband.psd		Group Project
E	PS E-1.psd	Fresh Ideas.psd		Lesson 1-6
	PS E-2.psd	ZD–Logo.psd		Skills Review
	PS E-3.psd	Beautiful Blooms Ad.psd		Project Builder 1
	PS E-4.psd	Spilled Milk.psd		Project Builder 2
	PS E-5.psd	Attitude.psd		Design Project
			Community Promotion.psd	Group Project
F	PS F-1.psd	CyberArt.psd		Lesson 1-4
	PS F-2.psd	The Maze.psd		Skills Review
	PS F-3.psd	Bank Artwork.psd		Project Builder 1
	PS F-4.psd	Robotics Contest Entry.psd		Project Builder 2
			Art Course.doc	Design Project
			Dealership Ad.psd	Group Project
G	PS G-1.psd	Rainbow Fruit.psd		Lesson 1-6
		Rainbow Fruit copy.psd		
	PS G-2.psd	Stripes.psd		Skills Review
	PS G-3.psd	manicure copy.psd		Project Builder 1
			Cleanup.psd	Project Builder 2
			Cleanup copy.psd	
			Currency.psd	Design Project
			Currency copy.psd	
			Lost Horizons.psd	Group Project

Unit	Data File Supplied	Student Saves File As	Student Creates File	Used in
H	PS H-1.psd	Soap Opera.psd		Lesson 1-5
	PS H-2.psd	B&B poster.psd		Skills Review
			Play.psd	Project Builder 1
			Jazz and Blues.psd	Project Builder 2
	PS H-3.psd	Shield.psd		Design Project
			Dance.psd	Group Project
I	PS I-1.psd	Juiced.psd	ContactSheet-1.psd	Lesson 1-7
	Peppermint.psd	Picture Package.psd		
	PS I-2.psd	Tool World.psd	ContactSheet-2.psd	Skills Review
		Picture Package-Tools.psd		
			Spheroid.psd	Project Builder 1
			Beach It Guide.psd	Project Builder 2
			My Vision.psd	Design Project
			Aquatic Mammal.psd	Group Project
J	PS J-1.psd	Parrot Mania.psd		Lesson 1-4
	PS J-2.psd	Big Bird.psd		Skills Review
	PS J-3.psd	Gallery Poster.psd		Project Builder 1
	PS J-4.psd	Heads Up.psd		Project Builder 2
	PS J-5.psd	Puzzle Pieces.psd		Design Project
			Annual Report Cover.psd	Group Project
K	PS K-1.psd	Power User.psd		Lesson 1-4
	PS K-2.psd	Mathematics.psd		Skills Review
	PS K-3.psd	Power Plug.psd		Project Builder 1
	PS K-4.psd	Booklovers.psd		Project Builder 2
			Shape Experimentation.psd	Design Project
			Contest Winner.psd	Group Project

Unit	Data File Supplied	Student Saves File As	Student Creates File	Used in
L	PS L-1.psd	Exploration.psd		Lesson 1-4
	PS L-2.psd	Charge Card.psd		Skills Review
	PS L-3.psd	Inner Dilemmas.psd		Project Builder 1
	PS L-4.psd	Creativity.psd		Project Builder 2
			Television Station Ad.psd	Design Project
			CD Cover Artwork.psd	Group Project
M	PS M-1.psd	Liquidity.psd		Lesson 1-3
	PS M-2.psd	Blurred Vision.psd		Skills Review
	PS M-3.psd	Shooting Star.psd		Project Builder 1
	PS M-4.psd	Buddy Boy.psd		Project Builder 2
			Photoshop Presentation.psd	Group Project
N	PS N-1.jpg	Runners.psd		Lesson 1-3
	PS N-2.psd	Treasure Shop.psd		Skills Review
	PS N-3.psd	Only The Best.psd		Project Builder 1
	PS N-4.psd	Membership Drive.psd		Project Builder 2
			Montage Analysis.doc	Design Project
			Art School Poster.psd	Group Project
O	PS O-1.psd	Destiny.psd	Modify Type.exe	Lesson 1-4
	PS O-2.psd	Team Member.psd	Motivation.exe	Skills Review
	PS O-3.psd	New Layers.psd	Layer Conversion.exe	Project Builder 1
	PS O-4.psd	Anniversary Gift.psd	Gift Image.exe	Project Builder 2
			Action Sample.psd MythWavev1nv.atn Play Downloaded Action.exe	Design Project
			Game Plan.psd	Group Project

Unit	Data File Supplied	Student Saves File As	Student Creates File	Used in
Bonus A	PS Bonus A-1.psd Day Lily.psd PS Bonus A-2.psd	Bloom Island.psd Day Lily.gif Rose Morph.psd		Lesson 1-5 Lesson 2 Lesson 6-7
	PS Bonus A-3.psd	Optimal Dolphin.psd Optimal-Dolphin-GIF.gif Optimal-Dolphin-JPG.jpg		Skills Review
	PS Bonus A-4.psd PS Bonus A-5.psd	Pet-U-Nation.psd The Old Soft Shoe.psd		
			Xtream Charity.psd	Project Builder 1
			Countdown.psd Countdown Browser.psd	Project Builder 2
			Banners et al.psd	Design Project
			Wake Up.psd	Group Project

A

Action
A series of tasks that you record and save to play back later as a single command using buttons on the Actions palette.

Active layer
The layer highlighted in the Layers palette that appears in parentheses in the document window title bar.

Additive colors
When the values of R, G, and B are zero, the result is black; when the values are all 255, the result is white.

Adjustment layer
An additional layer for which you can specify 11 specific color adjustments. The adjustment layer acts as a screen, allowing underlying layer objects to appear.

Adobe ImageReady
An integral part of Photoshop used to create buttons, rollovers, and animations.

Alpha channel
Specific color information added to a default channel.

Altitude
Bevel and Emboss setting that affects the amount of visible dimension.

Ambience property
Controls the balance between the light source and the overall light in an image.

Anchor points
Small squares similar to fastening points that connect straight or curved line segments.

Angle
Setting that determines where a drop shadow falls relative to the text.

Animation
The phenomenon of moving images created by placing images in the same location and adjusting the timing between their appearances.

Annotation
Written and auditory notes embedded into a Photoshop document.

Anti-aliasing
Partially fills in pixel edges, resulting in smooth-edge type and is recommended for large type. This feature lets your type maintain its crisp appearance.

Artistic filters
Replicates natural or traditional media effects.

Audio annotation
A sound file that is saved within a Photoshop document.

Auto-slice
A slice created by ImageReady. An auto-slice has a dotted line border.

B

Background color
Used to make gradient fills and to fill in areas of an image that have been erased. The default background color is white.

Background Eraser Tool
Lets you selectively remove pixels from a document, just as you would use a pencil eraser to remove unwanted written marks. The erased areas become transparent.

Balance colors
Process of adding and subtracting colors from those already existing in a layer.

Base color
The original color of the image.

Base layer
The bottom layer in a clipping group, which serves as the group's mask.

Baseline
An invisible line on which type rests.

Baseline shift
The distance type appears from its original position.

Batch
A group of documents designated to have the same action performed on them simultaneously.

Bitmap
A geometric arrangement of different color dots on a rectangular grid.

Bitmap mode
Uses black or white color values to represent image pixels; a good choice for images with subtle color gradations, such as photographs or painted images.

Bitmap type

Type that is composed of pixels and may develop jagged edges when enlarged.

Blend color

The color that is applied to the base color when a blending mode is applied to a layer.

Blend If color

Determines the color range for the pixels you want to blend.

Blending mode

Affects the layer's underlying pixels or base color. Used to darken or lighten colors, depending on the colors in use.

Blur filters

Used to soften a selection or image.

Bounding box

A rectangle with handles that appears around an object or type and can be used to change dimensions.

Brightness

The measurement of relative lightness or darkness of a color (measured as a percentage from 0% [black] to 100% [white]).

Brush library

Contains a variety of brush tips that you can use, rename, delete, or customize.

Brush Strokes filters

Mimic fine arts effects such as a brush and ink stroke.

Button

A graphical interface that helps visitors navigate and interact with a Web site easily.

Button mode

Optional action display in which each of the actions is displayed as a button—without additional detail.

C

Channels

Used to store information about the color elements contained in each channel.

Channels palette

Lists all channel information. The top channel is a composite channel—a combination of all the default channels. You can hide channels in the same manner as you hide layers: click the Indicates layer visibility button.

Character palette

Helps you control type properties. The Character palette is located on the tool options bar.

Clipboard

Temporary storage area provided by your operating system.

Clipping group

A group of two or more contiguous layers that are linked for the purposes of masking.

Clipping path

Used when you need to extract a Photoshop object from within a layer, then place it in another program (such as QuarkXPress or Adobe Illustrator), while retaining its transparent background.

Closed path

One continuous path without endpoints, such as a circle.

CMYK image

Has at least four channels (one each for cyan, magenta, yellow, and black).

Color channel

An area where color information is stored. Every Photoshop image has at least 1 channel and can have a maximum of 24 color channels.

Color mode

Used to determine how to display and print an image. Each mode is based on established models used in color reproduction.

Color Picker

Feature that lets you choose a color from a color spectrum.

Color Range command

Used to select a particular color contained in an existing image.

Color Sampler Tool

Feature that samples—and stores—up to 4 distinct color samplers. This is used when you want to save specific color settings for future use.

Color separation

Result of converting an RGB image into a CMYK image.

Composite channel

The top channel in the Channels palette that is a combination of all the default channels.

Compositing
Combining images from sources such as other Photoshop documents, royalty-free images, pictures taken from digital cameras, and scanned artwork.

Contact sheet
Compilation of thirty thumbnail images (per sheet) from a specific folder.

Contiguous
Items that are next to one another.

Crisp
Anti-aliasing setting that gives type more definition and makes it appear sharper.

Crop
Exclude part of an image. Cropping hides areas of an image without losing resolution quality.

Crop marks
Page notations where trimming will occur can be printed at the corners, center of each edge, or both.

Darken Only option
Replaces light pixels with darker pixels.

Default channels
The color channels automatically contained in a document.

Deselect
Command that causes the marquee to disappear from an area.

Diffuse filter
Makes layer contents look less focused.

Digimarc filter
Embeds a digital watermark that stores copyright information into an image.

Digital camera
Camera that captures images on electronic media (rather than film). Its images are in a standard digital format and can be downloaded for computer use.

Direct Selection Tool
Used to select and manipulate individual anchor points and segments to reshape a path.

Distance
Determines how far a shadow falls from the text. This setting is used by the Drop Shadow and Bevel and Emboss styles.

Distort filters
Used to create three-dimensional or other reshaping effects. Some of the types of distortions you can produce include Glass, Pinch, Ripple, Shear, Spherize, Twirl, Wave, and Zigzag.

Dithering
Occurs when a Web browser attempts to display colors that are not included in its native color palette.

Droplet
A stand-alone action in the form of an icon.

Drop Shadow
A style that adds what looks like a colored layer of identical text behind the selected type. The default shadow color is black.

Endpoints
Anchor points at each end of an open path.

Exposure property
Lightens or darkens the lighting effects ellipse.

Extract command
Used to isolate a foreground object from its background.

Extrude filters
Converts an image into pyramids or blocks.

Fade options
Brush settings that determine how and when brushes fade toward the end of their strokes.

Fastening point
An anchor within the marquee. When the marquee pointer reaches the initial fastening point, a small circle appears on the pointer, indicating that you have reached the starting point.

Feather
Method used to control the softness of a selection's edges by blurring the area between the selection and the surrounding pixels.

Filters

Alters the look of an image and gives it a special, customized appearance by applying special effects, such as distortions, changes in lighting, and blurring.

Flattening

Merges all visible layers into one layer, named the Background layer, and deletes all hidden layers, greatly reducing document size.

Font

Characters with a similar appearance.

Font family

Represents a complete set of characters, letters, and symbols for a particular typeface. Font families are generally divided into three categories: serif, sans serif, and symbol.

Foreground color

Used to paint, fill, and stroke selections. The default foreground color is black.

Frame delay

Length of time that each animation frame appears.

Freeform Pen Tool

Acts like a traditional pen or pencil, and automatically places *both* the anchor points and line segments wherever necessary to achieve the shape you want.

Fuzziness

Similar to tolerance, in that the lower the value, the closer the color pixels must be to be selected.

Gamut

The range of displayed colors in a color model.

Gloss Contour

Bevel and Emboss setting that determines the pattern with which light is reflected.

Gloss property

Controls the amount of surface reflectance on the lighted surfaces.

Gradient fill

A type of fill in which colors appear to blend into one another. A gradient's appearance is determined by its beginning and ending points. Photoshop contains 5 gradient fill styles.

Grayscale image

Can contain up to 256 shades of gray. Pixels can have brightness values from 0 (black) to white (255).

Grayscale mode

Uses up to 256 shades of gray, assigning a brightness value from 0 (black) to 255 (white) to each pixel.

Guides

Horizontal and vertical lines that you create to help you align objects. Guide lines appear in light blue.

Handles

Small boxes that appear along the perimeter of a selected object and are used to change the size of an image.

Highlight Mode

Bevel and Emboss setting that determines how pigments are combined.

Histogram

A graph displaying the frequency distribution of colors and is used to make adjustments in the input and output levels.

History palette

Contains a record of each action performed during a Photoshop session. Up to twenty levels of Undo are available through the History palette.

Hotspot

Area within an object that is assigned a URL.

Hue

The color reflected from/transmitted through an object and expressed as a degree (between 0° and 360°). Each hue is identified by a color name (such as red or green).

Image editing program

Lets you manipulate graphic images that can be reproduced by professional printers using full-color processes.

Image map

Composed of multiple hotspots and can be circular, rectangular, or a polygon.

Intellectual property

An image or idea that is owned and retained by legal control.

K

Kerning
Controlling the amount of space between two characters.

Keyboard shortcuts
Combinations of keys that can be used to work faster and more efficiently.

L

Landscape orientation
A document with the long edge of the paper at the top and bottom.

Layer
A section within an image on which objects can be stored. The advantage: individual effects can be isolated and manipulated without affecting the rest of the image. The disadvantage: layers can increase the size of your file.

Layer mask
Can cover an entire layer or specific areas within a layer. When a layer contains a mask, an additional thumbnail appears in the Layers palette.

Layers palette
Displays all the layers within an active document. You can use the Layers palette to create, delete, merge, copy, or reposition layers.

Layer set
An organizing tool you use to group layers on the Layers palette.

Layer thumbnail
Contains a miniature picture of the layer's content, and appears to the left of the layer name in the Layers palette.

Leading
The vertical amount of space between lines of type.

Libraries
Storage unit for brushes.

Lighten Only option
Replaces dark pixels with light pixels.

Lighting Effects filter
Applies lighting effects to an image.

Liquify feature
Applies distortions to layers using distinct tools in the Liquify dialog box.

Liquify session
From the time you open the Liquify dialog box to the time you close it.

List mode
The default display of actions in which all action detail can be viewed.

Logo
A distinctive image that you can create by combining symbols, shapes, colors, and text.

Lossless
A file compression format in which no data is discarded.

Lossy format
File format that discards data during the compression process.

Lossy GIF format
Compresses files while maintaining image quality.

Luminosity
The remaining light and dark values that result when a color image is converted to grayscale.

M

Magic Eraser Tool
Lets you erase areas in an image that have similar-colored pixels.

Magic Wand Tool
Lets you choose pixels that are similar to the ones where you first click in an image.

Marquee
A series of dotted lines indicating a selected area that can be edited or dragged into another document.

Mask
A feature that lets you protect or modify a particular area and is created using a marquee.

Material property
Controls parts of an image that reflect the light source color.

Menu bar
Contains menus from which you can choose Photoshop commands.

Merging layers
Process of combining multiple image layers into one layer.

Mesh

A series of horizontal and vertical gridlines that are superimposed in the preview window.

Modal control

Dialog boxes that are used in an action, and are indicated by an icon in the Actions palette.

Mode

Amount of color data that can be stored in a given file format, and determines the color model used to display and print a document.

Model

Determines how pigments combine to produce resulting colors, and is determined by the color mode.

Monitor calibration

Process that displays printed colors accurately on your monitor.

Monotype spacing

Spacing in which each character occupies the same amount of space.

Morph

Blending multiple images in the animation process. Short for metamorphosis.

Motion Blur filter

Adjusts the angle of the blur, as well as the distance the blur appears to travel.

Noise filters

Add or remove pixels with randomly distributed color levels.

None

Anti-aliasing setting that applies no anti-aliasing, resulting in jagged edges.

Normal blend mode

The default blending mode.

Opacity

Determines the percentage of transparency. A layer with 100% opacity will obstruct objects in the layers beneath it, while a layer with 1% opacity will appear nearly transparent.

Open path

Has two distinct endpoints, such as an individual line.

Optimized image

Reduces an image size without sacrificing image quality.

Orientation

Direction an image appears on the page: portrait or landscape.

Other filters

Allow you to create your own filters, modify masks, or make quick color adjustments.

Outline type

Type that is mathematically defined and can be scaled to any size without its edges losing their smooth appearance.

Out-of-gamut indicator

Indicates that the current color falls beyond the accurate print or display range.

Palettes

Floating windows that can be moved and are used to modify objects. Palettes contain name tabs which can be separated and moved to another group. Each palette contains a menu that can be viewed by clicking the list arrow in its upper-right corner.

Palette well

An area where you can assemble palettes for quick access.

Path

One or more straight or curved line segments connected by anchor points used to turn the area defined within an object into an individual object.

Path component

One or more anchor points joined by line segments.

Path Component Selection Tool

Used to select an entire path.

Paths Palette

Storage area for paths.

Pen Tool

Lets you draw a path by placing anchor points along the edge of another image or wherever you need them to draw a specific shape.

Picture package

Contains multiple sizes of a single document selected from 11 layouts.

Pixel

Each dot in a bitmapped image that represents a color or shade.

Pixelate filters

Used to sharply define a selection.

Plug-ins

Additional programs—created by Adobe and other developers—that expand Photoshop's functionality.

Points

Unit of measurement for font sizes. Traditionally, 1 inch is equivalent to 72.27 points. The default Photoshop type size is 12 points.

Portrait orientation

A document with the short edge of the paper at the top and bottom.

PostScript

A programming language created by Adobe that optimizes printed text and graphics.

Preferences

Used to control the Photoshop environment using your specifications.

Preset Manager

Allows you to manage libraries of preset brushes, swatches, gradients, styles, patterns, contours, and custom shapes.

Properties color swatch

Changes the ambient light around the lighting spotlight.

Proportional spacing

Each character may take up a different amount of space, depending on its width.

Radial Blur filter

Adjusts the amount of blur and the blur method (Spin or Zoom).

Rasterize

Converts a type layer to an image layer.

Rasterized shape

A shape that is converted into a bitmapped object. It cannot be moved or copied, and uses a much smaller file size.

Reference point

Center of the object from which distortions and transformations are measured.

Render filters

Transform three-dimensional shapes and simulated light reflections in an image.

Resolution

Number of pixels per inch.

Resulting color

The outcome of the blend color applied to the base color.

RGB image

Has three channels (one each for red, green, and blue).

Rollover

Changes an object's appearance when the pointer passes over (or the user clicks) a specific area of the image.

Rulers

Help you precisely measure and position an object, but are not shown by default. Rulers can be displayed using the View menu.

Sans serif fonts

Fonts that do not have tails or strokes at the end of some characters, and are commonly used in headlines.

Saturation

The strength or purity of the color, representing the amount of gray in proportion to hue (measured as a percentage from 0% [gray], to 100% [fully saturated]). Also known as croma.

Save As

Command that lets you create a copy of the open document using a new name.

Scanner

Electronic device that converts print material into an electronic file.

Screening back

An illusory effect in which type appears to fade into the imagery below it. Also known as screening.

Selection

An area in an image that is surrounded by a selection marquee.

Serif fonts
Fonts that have a tail, or stroke, at the end of some characters. These tails make it easier for the eye to recognize words; therefore, serif fonts are generally used in text passages.

Shading
Bevel and Emboss setting that determines lighting effects.

Shadow Mode
Bevel and Emboss setting that determines how pigments are combined.

Shape
A vector object that keeps its crisp appearance when it is resized and, like a path, can be edited.

Shape layer
A clipping path or shape that can occupy its own layer.

Sharp
Anti-aliasing setting that displays type with the best possible resolution.

Sharpen More filter
Increases the contrast of adjacent pixels, and can focus blurry images.

Size
Determines the clarity of a drop shadow.

Sketch filters
Apply a texture or create a hand-drawn effect.

Slices
Smaller sections of an image used to create unique effects. When a file is opened for

the first time in ImageReady, the entire document is contained in a single slice. When you create a slice, ImageReady automatically renumbers existing slices.

Smart Blur filter
Adjusts the quality, radius, and threshold of a blur.

Smooth
Anti-aliasing setting that gives type more rounded edges.

Snapshot
A temporary copy of an image that contains the history states made up to that point. You can create multiple snapshots in an image and you can switch between snapshots.

Splash screen
A window that displays information about software.

Spot color
A color that isn't easily re-created by a printer. This is used to make it easier for a printer to create a difficult or unique color.

Spread
Determines the width of drop shadow text.

State
An entry in the History palette, or the appearance of a rollover in the Rollover palette in ImageReady.

Status bar
The area located at the bottom of the program window (Win) or the document window (Mac) that displays information such

as the file size of the active window and a description of the active tool.

Step
Measurement of fade options that can be any value from 1–9999, and equivalent to one mark of the brush tip.

Stop
A command that interrupts playback, or includes an informative text message for the user, so that other operations can be performed.

Stroking the edges
The process of making a selection or layer stand out by surrounding it with a border.

Strong
Anti-aliasing setting that makes type appear heavier, much like the bold attribute.

Structure
Bevel and Emboss setting that determines the size and physical properties of the object.

Style
18 predesigned styles that can be applied to buttons.

Stylize filters
Produce a painted or impressionistic effect.

Subtractive colors
The result of cyan, magenta, and yellow absorbing all color and producing black.

Swatches palette
Contains available colors that can be selected for use as a foreground or background color. You can also add your own colors to the Swatches palette.

Symbol fonts
Used to display unique characters (such as $, ÷, or ™).

Texture filters
Give the appearance of depth or substance.

This Layer slider
Used to specify the range of pixels that will be blended on the active layer.

Threshold
The Normal mode when working with bitmapped images. The threshold is the starting point for applying other blending modes.

Thumbnail
Contains a miniature picture of the layer's content, appears to the left of the layer name, and can be turned on or off.

Title bar
Displays the program name and filename of the open document. The title bar also contains buttons for minimizing, maximizing, and closing the document.

Tolerance
The range of pixels that determines which pixels will be selected. The lower the tolerance, the closer the color is to the selection. The setting can have a value from 0–255.

Tonal values
Numeric values of an individual color that can be used to duplicate a color. Also called color levels.

Toolbox
Contains tools for frequently used commands. On the face of a tool is a graphic representation of its function. Place the pointer over each button to display a ScreenTip, which tells you the name or function of that button.

Tool options bar
Displays the settings for the currently active tool. The tool options bar is located directly under the menu bar, but can be moved anywhere in the workspace for easier access.

Tracking
The insertion of a uniform amount of space between characters.

Transform
Change the shape, size, perspective, or rotation of an object or objects on a layer.

Tweening
The process of selecting multiple frames, then inserting transitional frames between them. This effect makes frames appear to blend into one another and gives the animation a more fluid appearance.

Twirl filter
Applies a circular effect to a layer.

Type
A layer containing text. Each character is measured in points. In PostScript measurement, 1 inch is equivalent to 72 points. In traditional measurement, 1 inch is equivalent to 72.27 points.

Type spacing
Adjustments you can make to the space between characters and between lines of type.

Underlying Layer slider
Used to specify the range of pixels that will be blended on lower visible layers.

URL
Uniform Resource Locator, a Web address.

User-slice
A slice created by you in ImageReady. A user-slice has a solid line border.

Vector graphics
Made up of lines and curves defined by mathematical objects.

Vector mask
Makes a shape's edges appear neat and defined on a layer.

Video filters
Restricts colors to those acceptable for television reproduction and smooth video images.

Vignette
A feature in which the border of a picture or portrait fades into the surrounding color at its edges.

Vignette effect

Feature that uses feathering to fade a mar-quee shape.

Warping type

Feature that lets you create distortions that conform to a variety of shapes.

Web Image Gallery

Contains a thumbnail index page of all exported images, the actual JPEG images, and any included links.

Web-safe colors

216 colors that can be displayed on the Web without dithering.

Wind filter

Conveys the feeling of direction and motion on the layer to which it is applied.

Workspace

The entire window: from the menu bar at the top of the window, to the status bar at the bottom border of the program window.